REDIRECTING
THE GAZE

THE SUNY SERIES

CULTURAL STUDIES IN CINEMA/VIDEO

Wheeler Winston Dixon, editor

REDIRECTING THE GAZE

Gender, Theory, and Cinema in the Third World

Edited by

DIANA ROBIN
and
IRA JAFFE

STATE UNIVERSITY OF NEW YORK PRESS

Published by
State University of New York Press, Albany

© 1999 State University of New York

For information, address State University of New York Press,
State University Plaza, Albany, N.Y., 12246

Production by Marilyn P. Semerad
Marketing by Patrick Durocher

Library of Congress Cataloging-in-Publication Data

Redirecting the gaze : gender, theory, and cinema in the Third World
    edited by Diana Robin and Ira Jaffe.
        p.   cm. — (The SUNY series, cultural studies in cinema/video)
    Includes bibliographical references and index.
    ISBN 0-7914-3993-3 (hc : alk. paper). — ISBN 0-7914-3994-1 (pb :
alk. paper)
    1. Women in the motion picture industry—Developing countries.
    2. Women in motion pictures—Developing countries. I. Robin, Diana
Maury. II. Jaffe, Ira, date. III. Series.
PN1995.9.W6R45 1999
384'.8'082091724—dc 21   98-3355
                                                                  CIP

10 9 8 7 6 5 4 3 2 1

To the Memory of
María Luisa Bemberg
(1922–1995)

CONTENTS

ILLUSTRATIONS

ACKNOWLEDGMENTS

We would like to express our gratitude to friends, colleagues, and institutions whose support has made this book possible. Our principal thanks go to the chief readers of our anthology in its various stages, Julianne Burton-Carvajal and Zuzana Pick. A pilot version of this book appeared as a special volume of *Frontiers: A Journal of Women Studies* in 1994, and we take pleasure in thanking the editors of that special volume—Louise Lamphere, Jane Slaughter, Shane Phelan, and particularly the managing editor, Elizabeth Cahn—for their help in producing it. A grant from the University of New Mexico Research Allocations Committee covered expenses for the final stages of this book. Manthia Diawara made vital comments about two chapters early in the project. John Hazlett offered invaluable suggestions about style and content as the manuscript neared completion. Finally we thank Marlene Stutzman, our editorial assistant, without whose help this anthology would have had no hope of seeing the light.

INTRODUCTION

DIANA ROBIN and IRA JAFFE

The essays in this anthology treat the work of women filmmakers located outside the dominant industries in Hollywood and Europe. These women include independent Black American and Chicana directors in the United States as well as filmmakers and video artists from Argentina, Bolivia, China, Cuba, India, Mexico, Senegal, Tanzania, Venezuela, and other so-called Third World nations. Although the representatives of the nonaligned nations who met at Bandung in 1955 coined the term *Third World* to signify their independence from both the Soviet bloc and the members of NATO, the term came to connote both political and economic dependency. In the 1960s, some filmmakers in Latin America adopted the term *third cinema* as a declaration of their political and cultural independence from and resistance to the dominant cinemas of the West, including Hollywood-inspired *first cinema* and European auteur-centered *second cinema.* In the 1968 manifesto *Towards a Third Cinema: Notes and Experiences for the Development of a Cinema of Liberation in the Third World*, Argentine filmmakers Fernando Solanas and Octavio Getino called for the expansion of Third Cinema, which they defined as a militant, international Marxist cinema dedicated to ending injustice and inequality throughout the Third World and beyond.[1] Though its origins were Latin American, Solanas and Getino saw the aims of Third Cinema as international: it was to be a political program that would mobilize workers around the world in a struggle against imperialism, racism, and colonialism.[2] As Teshome H. Gabriel defined Third Cinema in 1982, its main characteristic was not so much where it was made as the ideology it espoused and the consciousness it displayed.[3]

1

More recently Zuzana Pick and B. Ruby Rich have argued that Third Cinema as an ideology no longer provides a viable prescription for, nor adequately describes, the current cinemas of resistance in Latin America, much less those elsewhere in the world.[4] What distinguishes contemporary filmmaking practices, especially those of women, is the diversity of aesthetic practices by which alternative models for resistance are proposed. The women filmmakers represented in this anthology have moved beyond the totalizing, gender-neutral and dehistoricized discourses of Third Cinema. Their works foreground the *interconnectedness of race, gender, and class* in the context of discourses on nation, postcoloniality, and globalization. They focus on local differences and alternative forms of solidarity rather than such abstractions as Third Cinema's "aesthetics of liberation."[5] Examples of this diversity of practice, this privileging of difference, can be found in each chapter in this anthology. The protagonists in the films discussed here do not work the parched earth, nor do they aspire to the militancy of Brazilian director Glauber Rocha's "aesthetic of hunger."[6] They nonetheless struggle to overcome a moral order that shrinks from and stifles passion, ideas, freedom, and difference.

The essays in this anthology concern above all the cinematic portrayals of *women by women* directors. While some women filmmakers featured in this volume have been acclaimed in their own countries, scarcely any are well known in the United States and Europe. Some films and videos discussed here, even ones by influential women filmmakers, are not yet available for distribution in the United States. We hope that one result of this volume will be to encourage distribution of such works to a wider audience. It is time now to move on to a description of the specific essays in this volume—essays on a complicated cinema whose core trait lies in its oppositionality.

In the preface to her chapter on Mexican filmmaker María Novaro's film *Lola*, film scholar Diane Sippl traces the history of women's filmmaking in Mexico City. Unlike the women artists in some countries represented in this volume, women in Mexico have had a history of achievement as filmmakers. They were actively engaged as writers, directors, and producers of film from the time of the industry's prerevolutionary inception onward. In the early days of Mexican cinema in the 1920s, the actress Mimi Derba wrote several feature films. The documentary filmmakers Dolores and Adriana Elhers produced and directed the newsreel series *Revista Elhers* (1922–1929). Between 1928 and 1939, Candida Beltrán Rendón and Adela Sequeyro each wrote, produced, and acted in a number of feature films; and the pseudonymous "Duquesa Olga" (Duchess Olga) was credited as the writer and producer of ten films. During the 1940s and 1950s, filmmaker Matilde Landeta wrote and directed three fiction films that problematized issues of race and gender: *Lola Casanova* (1948), *La Negra Angustias* (1949), and *Trotacalles* (*Streetwalker,* 1951). In 1950, Carmen Toscano compiled a powerful documentary history of Mexico, utilizing clips from five decades of footage from her father Salvador Toscano's personal archives.

In the 1970s and 1980s, Marcela Fernández Violante not only produced two feature films about the failure of the Revolution to solve the nation's social and economic woes; she also made the film *Misterio* (1980), a parodic critique of Televisa, Mexico's privately owned media monopoly, and *En el país de los pies ligeros* (1981), a film about a Mexico City boy who tries to live in an Indian community in the Tarahumara region. Sonia Fritz's film *Yalaltecas* (1981) treats the revolt of the women in an Indian community against their boss; and a documentary by Mari Carmen de Lara, *We're Not Asking for the Moon,* treats the struggle of Mexico City seamstresses to form an independent union after the devastating 1985 Mexico City earthquakes.

Most recently, filmmakers Marise Sistach (*I Know the Three of Them*), Dana Rotberg (*Intimacy,* 1989; *Angel de Fuego,* 1991), and María Novaro (*Lola,* 1989; *Danzón,* 1992; *El Jardín de Edén,* 1994) have made films that center on problems of sexuality, motherhood, work, and recreation in contemporary women's lives.

To sum up the situation in the industry, while a national cinema took root in Mexico early in the century, since the 1920s Hollywood imports have virtually monopolized Mexican screens, a circumstance that has only continued to worsen over time despite national subsidies and infusions of money from both private and public agencies. In the 1980s and 1990s, for example, United States studios and filmmakers simply invaded Mexican studios—and with the help and encouragement of the Mexican government. Despite all these hurdles, serious filmmaking in Mexico continues, some of it financed by universities, popular networks, European sponsors, and Mexican trade unions.

The second part of Sippl's chapter presents an analysis of María Novaro's film *Lola* and the 1980s "New Wave" movement in Mexico that Novaro's film exemplifies. Sippl argues that Novaro's work, like the Mexican film industry itself, cannot be understood outside the context of the country's economic problems—its soaring unemployment, its status as a haven for cheap labor for United States industry and the multinationals, and the invasion of Mexican markets by Euro-American commodities. Novaro began her career in *Cine Mujer,* a women's filmmaking collective. As an unmarried mother herself, her first work was a documentary on women and poverty in Mexico. Novaro's first two feature films, *Lola* and *Danzón,* tell the stories of women who are either unemployed or working at low-paid jobs. While the central characters in *Danzón* are a telephone operator and her working-class friends, Novaro's characters in *Lola* are the disenfranchised, marginalized, unemployed poor in the Mexico City of the 1990s. Far from the spare social realism of postwar Italian and other European cinema, Novaro's representation of her characters and their lives is full of vibrant color and lighting, and pulses with "fusion music," derived from blues, jazz, reggae, disco, salsa, and gospel sources.

In contrast to the dark vision of exploitation and oppression depicted in the recent films of Bolivia's Raquel Romero and Jorge San-jinés, or Africa's Safi Faye, Novaro's *Lola* presents a very different genre of Third Cinema filmmaking that is nonetheless highly oppositional. Taking as its departure point the spirit of French *nouvelle vague* (New Wave) cinema that rocked bourgeois audiences in Europe and the United States for the brief period of its ascendancy at the end of the 1950s and early in the 1960s, Mexican 1980s "New Wave" uses the "conspicuous emblems of mass culture, worn or performed as insignia" to represent a "flat, superficial toptext of failed consumer conformity." In Novaro's *Lola,* the stance and attitude toward Euroamerican cultural imperialism is ludic and parodic. Her characters, Lola and Ana, "talk back" to the "toptext" of the invasion of commodities—the rock music from London, the Banana Republic denim jackets designed in New York and sewn in the Philippines or Taiwan, the cornflakes, and the posters of the supernova of all commodified supernovas—Madonna. Interwoven here is another text, the text about unemployed and underemployed women in Mexico, who need work to support themselves and their children, but who are shunted off to the "informal sector," to do work that "doesn't count": either unpaid domestic work, that is, or paid work in the economies of sex and consumption—prostitution and shoplifting.

Sippl tells us that the practice of "80s New Wave" mainly involves filmic *bricolage,* which "emerges from any combination of audio/visual/narrative juxtapositions, disruptions, inversions, perversions, and appropriations of 'found . . . objects.'" In its appropriation of "New Wave" and *bricolage* techniques, Novaro's *Lola* is woman centered in the sense that women's internalization of mass culture might constitute, as Jean Franco has argued, new kinds of feminine subjects.[7] This *bricolage* mocking of the dominant culture can be seen, for example, in Lola and her five-year-old daughter's lip-synching, hip-gyrating miming of a male rock singer's performance in the opening of the film, in Lola's "lifting" of bras, panties, and a plastic jar of honey from a department store, or in her parody of an exotic hula. Her alienation from commodified TV images of motherhood can be seen in her swigging booze from a paper bag in the street, and in the bed that she and Ana sleep in, which is strewn with cornflakes and articles of clothing.

Lola is the defiant "New Wave" woman who refuses traditional, male-identified, commodified roles of femininity; she is not the mother but the child, not the employee but the rip-off artist, and not the wife or girlfriend but the free-floating, hula-dancing, guitar-stomping sister of her daughter.

Catherine Benamou's chapter, "Cuban Cinema: On the Threshold of Gender," presents a broad overview of the rise of the "women's wave" in Cuban cinema—the rise of women directors and producers in an industry barred to women prior to 1959 (the year of the revolution), with particular emphasis on the treatment by these new filmmakers of issues of difference along the lines of gender, race, class, and sexual preference. In this essay, Benamou discusses the emergence of a number of women in the filmmaking industry in Cuba in the context of the rise of a revolutionary national cinema since 1959. In contrast to other Latin American cinemas, women's filmmaking in Cuba developed within one of the most centralized cultural institutions in the modern world, the Cuban Film Institute (*Instituto Cubano del Arte e Indústria Cinematográficos*), and was supported, Benamou argues, "by a long-term effort at gender reform that permeated all social sectors."

For women, the situation in Cuban film—even after the revolution—was very different from what it was in Mexico. It was not until the 1980s in Cuba that the prerevolutionary prohibition of women in the media industries finally came to an end. The few early Cuban films that dealt with the issues of women and gender equality were Humberto Solás's films *Manuela* (1966) and *Lucía* (1968), Octavio Cortázar's documentary *Con las mujeres cubanas (With the Cuban Women,* 1975), Sara Gómez's *One Way or Another* (1974/1979), and Pastor Vega's *Portrait of Teresa* (1979). In these films, such themes as the problem of *machismo* in Cuban society, women's quest for entry into male-identified professions, men's resistance to sharing household chores, and the sexual double standard were foregrounded. Still, women were primarily constructed in these films as laboring subjects, whether that labor took place in the home or factory. Moreover, films that vaunted a sensitivity to the concerns of women, such as Tomás Gutiérrez Alea's *Memories of Underdevelopment* (1968), came nonetheless from the point of view of a white male consciousness, and depicted women as the usual stereotypes—wife, maid, mother, prostitute. Since then—even in the films of the 1980s—such character types persist, as in Solás's *Cecilia* (1982) and Juan Carlos Tabio's *¡Se Permuta!* (1984). Moreover, the leading actresses in these feature films have been predominantly white. Thus, the problematization of race has been suppressed in most Cuban films, as has, Benamou argues, the way in which women's oppression under patriarchy is differentially impacted by race.

Only in the films of the Afro-Cuban woman filmmaker Sara Gómez are the issues of race, class, and gender explicitly interconnected. With the exception of Gómez's work, the absence of attempts to interconnect issues of race and gender is a feature not only of works by other filmmakers described by Benamou, but also of the majority of the films analyzed elsewhere in this volume. In *De cierta manera (One Way or Another,* 1974–1977), after the shooting of which Gómez died of an asthma attack, and in her documentaries—*Iré a Santiago (I'll go to Santiago,* 1964), *Y tenemos sabor (We've Got Rhythm,* 1967), *Poder local, poder popular* (1970), and *Atención prenatal*—Gómez firmly locates in prerevolutionary, colonial society the roots of the *machismo* and the patriarchal structures she depicts as characteristic of Havana's "subproletariat," as Zuzana Pick categorizes the predominantly black and mulatto poor of Cuba's largest city.[8] Always inextricably enmeshed, neither gender nor race is ever privileged over the other in Gómez's films. *De cierta manera,* a love story between a middle-class teacher and a factory worker, reveals the persistence of "prerevolutionary forms of oppression"—racism and sexism, that is—in spite of institutional reforms.

Subsequent to Gómez, women's filmmaking emerged in the early 1980s at the Cuban Film Institute (ICAIC) almost wholly in the form of short documentaries. These important new documentary filmmakers include Rebeca Chávez, Miriam Talavera, and Mayra Vilásis. Though these and other women have been excluded from feature-length fiction filmmaking, their achievements as documentary cineastes have been considerable. In discussing Marisol Trujillo's documentary, *Mujer ante el espejo,* the story of a ballet dancer dealing with her own physical changes after pregnancy, Benamou makes the point that the protagonist's attitude is not one of combativeness *against* society but of "discovery on the threshold between public and private spheres." In these new documentaries, we are seeing a focusing on *process*—on the revolutionary female subject-in-the-making—rather than on the finished depiction of woman as either victim or hero. In other words, documentary theory as well as practice mandates a redistribution of power between filmmaker, subject (character), and audience.

Characterization in these new women filmmakers' films is facilitated in part through the emphasis on very private spaces: in Marisol Trujillo's *Paisaje breve* (1985), for instance, the camera lavishes attention on personal objects in a dishevelled room, while in Rebeca Chavez's documentaries, *Cuando una mujer no duerme* (1983), *Rigoberta* (1985), and *Una más entre ellos* (1989), the past is reconstructed from family albums and newspaper clippings that mingle personal memory with official history. There is no conflict between private and public issues, or between personal and societal goals, Benamou emphasizes, in these "Women's Wave" documentaries. Issues of revolution and socialism in Cuba are "givens" within the context of the need to "decolonize the screen."

The Cuban-American film theorist and scholar Coco Fusco notes that Cuban film practice is very different from Euroamerican feminist film in that women's films in Cuba are not seen as an oasis for personal expression. Benamou argues, however, that women cineastes in Cuba are operating within a centralized cultural institution where feminist discursive practices are already embedded in revolutionary discourse. Moreover, Cuban feminism is about the formation of a revolutionary female subjectivity that also involves a new notion of aesthetics. Production itself has a different method and aim from that of Hollywood cinema. At the Cuban Film Institute (ICAIC), the emphasis is away from the shaping hand of the individual director/genius and toward the collective structure where the members are—theoretically, at any rate—equals.

Transparent Woman (Mujer transparente, 1990), a series of five short features, each produced by a different team under the direction of Hector Veitía, Mayra Segura, Mayra Vilasís, Mario Crespo, and Ana Rodríguez, suggests that the equality of women mandated by the Family Code of the 1978 Cuban constitution (quoted in the opening credits of the film) is far from realization. As Zuzana Pick says, "the perspectives brought to *Transparent Woman . . .* might [nonetheless] be a first attempt to liberate the imaginative and creative power of women's desire in Cuban cinema."[9]

Although the present generation of Cuban filmmakers may not, as Benamou has suggested, have succeeded yet in a new figuration of, or commentary on, sexual desire, and while women may not yet have passed successfully into positions of full responsibility, nonetheless the collective working groups, the introduction of small format video, and the references to alternative forms of sexuality in the new "cine mumusa" ("gay cinema") produced by students at another school, the EICTV (*Escuela Internacional de Cine y Televisión*), should definitely have an impact on Cuban cinema.

In "Making History," Patricia Mellencamp discusses two films by the widely acclaimed black American filmmaker, Julie Dash. *Illusions* (1983) and *Daughters of the Dust* (1991) represent two different modes of the black experience in America. *Illusions* concerns the theme of "passing" and the erasure of black people as significant actors in American history. The film portrays the career of a black woman film executive in Hollywood in the early 1940s who can hold her job only by passing as white. *Daughters,* the first feature-length film by a black American woman to gain wide theatrical distribution in the United States, represents the recovery of the history of an independent, self-governing community of blacks living on an island off the coast of South Carolina, who were never brought to the mainland as slaves. Whereas the central female character in *Illusions* has reason not to advertise her blackness, Dash's camera in both films glories in the Africanness of her subjects, in their difference.

Mellencamp argues that in both films the filmmaker recasts herself as a revisionist historian, rewriting black history—and other history as well. In Hollywood's version of history, there were no black women studio executives in the 1940s; and in the received history of the antebellum South, there were few free blacks. In this chapter, Mellencamp traces Dash's vision of the remapping of the history of this country, including the history of film.

The black Hollywood executive in *Illusions,* Mignon Duprée, understands the sense in which film *is* history. "History is not what happens," she insists. "[People] will remember what they see on the screen. I want to be there, where history is being made." While Duprée notes that film determines what people remember, Mellencamp says of *Daughters of the Dust,* "The whole film is about memories." In the way that Teshome Gabriel has characterized Third Cinema as the "guardian of popular memory," Mellencamp sees *Daughters* as a film about the recovery of memory and the process of remembering for a new future. For Dash, history is reincarnated in the figure of Nana Peazant, the historian and great grandmother of *Daughters of the Dust,* "who keeps history alive." Moreover, the focus in *Daughters* is on process, on becoming, and on living speech rather than the printed word—on what happens in the spaces between experience and thought, sound and image, and between women. *Daughters* attempts to represent through the conversations among women of various generations an orally transmitted understanding of history that is both broader in scope and at the same time more personal than any official history. Dash's portrayal of black women as subjects in such conversations completely departs from the racially coded stereotypes familiar from Hollywood cinema. These conversations in *Daughters,* moreover, convey the kind of "emotional and expressive authenticity of popular memory" that *The Courage of the People* (Jorge Sanjinés, Bolivia, 1971) sought to capture in documentary reconstructions of past events that were pieced together from oral testimony.[10]

bell hooks' statement about history and history writing—"We black people see our history as counter-memory, and use it as a way to know the present and invent the future"[11]—well describes Dash's journey from the vision of history she presents in *Illusions* to that in *Daughters. Daughters* is a more affirmative film than *Illusions*: "it embodies hope, not despair," Mellencamp writes.[12]

Both bell hooks and filmmaker Toni Cade Bambara, Mellencamp notes, have seen *Daughters of the Dust* and *Illusions* as profoundly oppositional to Western film practice. For hooks, Dash's films "employ a deconstructive filmic practice to undermine existing grand cinematic narratives even as they retheorize subjectivity in the realm of the visual."[13] Both the content and processes of recording history in Dash's work differ decisively from those of other Western filmmakers. Central to memory and the processes of remembering in *Daughters* is a sense of collective identity and community that is Afrocentric rather than Western. Bambara also characterizes Dash's narrative technique as an "African-derived . . . nonlinear, multilayered unfolding," comparable to the storytelling traditions of African cinema.[14]

As these women—so central in her work—tell their stories, relate history, and manipulate time, they dominate the sound track as well as the screen. Like the women characters in *Sarraounia* (Med Hondo, Mauritania, 1987) as described by Manthia Diawara, Dash's characters, though they are not warrior queens like Hondo's protagonist, offer "aesthetic pleasure by showing [women] . . . taking the hero position . . . and becoming larger than life."[15] The unusual emphasis on black women's voices in Dash's films—their speech in *Daughters* and their singing voices in *Illusions,* in which off-screen black voices replace the weak voices of white female stars—sets both films apart from mainstream practice. The foregrounding of the female voice and the elevation of the status of sound which in standard film practice plays a role subsidiary to that of the image contributes, Mellencamp argues, to a strategy that assists and parallels the recovery of black women's subjectivities in Dash's films.

Mellencamp suggests that Dash's emphasis on black women's speech in *Daughters* reflects an important cultural fact, noted by bell hooks, that in the home black women were the ones who preached the sermons. Moreover, in a rare moment in which she foregrounds her own positionality, Mellencamp identifies with women for whom speech and spirituality are of extreme importance, for she places a similar value on such activities in her own life. Her reflections on these issues arise in relation to a major question for feminism that is also raised by N. Frank Ukadike in his essay in this volume—the (im)possibility of women, regardless of differences of color and culture, uniting around specific values and concerns. In quoting the dramatist August Wilson's comment, "Someone who does not share the specifics of a culture remains an outsider," Ukadike suggests limits to the chances for worldwide feminist unity, or even for feminist sharing. Mellencamp, on the other hand, disagrees with bell hooks' prediction that white spectators of *Daughters* will find it hard to relate to the (black) characters in the film. Conceding that "the blindspots of white feminists . . . regarding women of color have been glaring," Mellencamp argues that empathy and identification from a white woman spectator like herself are by no means unusual, and that the values in *Daughters* that move Mellencamp and align her with the film's characters involve not only speech and spirituality, but also family, rural life, nature, hard physical labor, the companionship of women, and, above all, the collective struggle to become the writers and enunciators of their own histories.

African film scholar N. Frank Ukadike contributes the only chapter in the volume that is devoted to images of women in African cinema. Ukadike discusses filmmakers who reposition black women as narrative agents, placing them at the center of films about African life. He observes that women have been marginalized not only in colonialist and Hollywood cinema, but in many films that address the oppression of black peoples in Africa and the black diaspora. African women have had to deal not only with various forms of colonial and postcolonial oppression, but also with the tendency of black men to redirect against women the exploitative mechanisms and attitudes that they themselves have endured. In order for the "rehumanization"—in Ukadike's formulation this term suggests the dehumanizing conditions under which many African women live and work—of black women to proceed, images of women must occupy the center of films by men as well as women. These films, he argues, should undertake a historical and materialist analysis of black identity in the black diaspora as well as in Africa. Such analysis and "rehumanization" are only likely to occur, he suggests, when black women and men control the cinematic apparatus, which includes economic as well as technical resources. Along with black African control of the industry will come opportunities for a more diverse representation of African and Diasporan subjectivities of both women and men.

Ukadike looks to the black diaspora as well as to Africa for new cinematic images of black women. In his view, black cultural workers both inside and outside continental Africa are linked by a common outrage against dehumanizing representations of Africans and the peoples of the diaspora. Much of this widespread ferment, says Ukadike, gains inspiration from the "invocation of Afrocentricity" as well as from a sense of shared origins and a common interest in more communal forms of working and living. Noting in passing the prominence of black diasporic women directors Julie Dash, Tracey Moffatt, Zeinabu Irene Davis, and Ngozi Onwurah, he also calls attention to the growing number of African-born women filmmakers, including Thérèsa Sita Bella (Cameroon), Anne G. Mungai (Kenya), Fanta Regina Nacro (Burkina Faso), Flore M'mbugu Shelling (Tanzania), and Efua Sutherland (Ghana), whose works have won international acclaim. The core of the essay is devoted to a discussion of the cinematic treatment of African women in the fiction films of four noted African filmmakers, one of them a woman—Ousmane Sembene, Med Hondo, Desiré Ecaré, and Sarah Maldoror—and the documentary films of the African women directors, Safi Faye and Salem Mekuria.

Ukadike presses the point that African filmmakers seeking to advance more positive images of women must oppose a range of colonialist and African conceptions that depict African women as ineffectual figures occupying the margins or the background of human activity. As Manthia Diawara notes in his recent book, *African Cinema*, African women are still being denied the right to speak and be heard. In Ukadike's view, African women are victims of both European attitudes and modern

African patriarchy, whose origins he and other African intellectuals—including the influential African feminist writers Ama Ata Aidou and 'Zulu Sofola—trace to the invasion and domination of African societies by Islamic/Arab and Christian/European religious and economic interests. In the depiction of precolonial African woman in *Ceddo* (Ousmane Sembene, Senegal, 1977), however, the central character is a regal figure who proudly protects her people from foreign domination.

Similarly, Med Hondo's *Sarraounia* (Mauritania, 1987), the next film discussed by Ukadike, tells the story of an African queen who was a brilliant military leader who mobilized her nation against the invading French army. A more contemporary drama forms the subject of Desiré Ecaré's *Faces of Women* (Ivory Coast, 1985), in which a woman finds a path to power and self-assertion through private enterprise. Bernadette, on whom numerous male relatives depend for their subsistence, owns a fish-smoking company and seeks a bank loan to expand the business. The male loan officer, however, threatens to link the granting of Bernadette's loan to his erotic interest in her two teenage daughters, for whom she strives to provide a role model of female economic independence. The final fiction film Ukadike discusses, *Sambizanga* (Angola, 1972), was directed by one of Africa's most prominent women filmmakers, Sarah Maldoror. The film depicts the courage and solidarity of African women who rally around Maria, who becomes a militant supporter of the Angolan patriots' struggle against the colonial Portuguese regime, when her husband is murdered by colonial agents.

Women directors have been active not only in producing fiction films, but also in making documentaries. Ukadike discusses the depiction of women's experiences of poverty, famine, and exile in two documentaries by women—Safi Faye's *Selbe: One Among Many* (Senegal, 1982) and Salem Mekuria's *Sidet: Forced Exile* (Ethiopia, 1991). *Selbe* examines, perhaps with more intensity than any of the other films Ukadike discusses, the plight of contemporary women in rural Africa. While Faye shows the women in this film struggling day and night to feed their children and their families, she depicts the men, as Ukadike comments, "as village parasites—totally indifferent toward familial bonds." Although he admires Faye's ability to convey powerful images of female subjectivity and the strong sense of community that is palpable among the women in Selbe's village, he is critical of Faye's failure to directly address Africa's larger societal problems—particularly in the areas of health, welfare, and education. Nonetheless, he admits, the posing of such issues as family planning, illiteracy, and the access to schooling not only for male but also for female children (who are less likely to be sent to school) is implicitly suggested in the structure of Faye's documentary.

In Salem Mekuria's documentary *Sidet,* the struggle for survival seems all but lost. Disease, famine, and exile from their homeland in Ethiopia afflict women who temporarily reside in a Sudanese settlement camp and dream of the opportunity to enter a relatively prosperous nation outside Africa such as Australia. The quest for renewal of black identity reaches a tragic pass, as survival requires removal to the black diaspora. The dubious reward of African independence and of the end to colonial rule appears to be the end of home and community. Yet the women in this documentary remain resilient, and find ways to morally and materially support their families and each other. In facing exile, they draw hope from improved prospects for the education and physical sustenance of their children.

The values and issues that stand out in Ukadike's discussion of images of women in films from Africa are the same ones that appear in other chapters in this anthology on Third World women filmmakers: in particular, the repositioning and reempowering of women both in front of the camera and behind it; the rediscovery and retrieval of women's histories and subjectivities; the role of women in promoting the ideals of community; and, last but not least, the assumption by women of a more oppositional stance toward colonial and patriarchal forces.

In her chapter "In the Shadow of Race: Forging Gender in Bolivian Film and Video," Elena Feder argues that in Bolivia, where two out of every three citizens are either Qhechwa- or Aymara-speaking Indians, and where a white-identified minority has oppressed and exploited the Indian-identified majority for five centuries, gender issues must be looked at within the related contexts of racism, colonialism, and imperialism. Moreover, the problem of gender and its treatment in Bolivian cinema cannot be understood apart from the official culture's reductive formulation of the nation's more than fifty distinct indigenous (not to mention other immigrant) ethnolinguistic groups in terms of the white/Indian dyad. So pervasive has been the connection between power and privilege, on the one hand, and ethnic identification, on the other, that the French social anthropologist, Danielle Demelas, has coined the term *pigmentocracy* to describe what Feder calls Bolivia's "intricate web of racially coded social relations."[16]

Thus, the interlocking themes of race and class oppression and colonialism have been central to Bolivian cinema since its inception in the

1920s. In this chapter, Feder explores the relation of these themes to those of gender in Bolivian films and videos by women directors, particularly in projects that involve the retrieval of women's histories—whether the repressed histories of poor women or those of women writers and artists of the dominant classes, whose work has often been better known in Europe and the United States than in Bolivia. While Feder describes the widespread use of video among women active in social reform, she also warns that women video- and filmmakers in Bolivia are still few in number and come almost solely from the urban middle and upper classes. Feder's discussions of recent Bolivian cinema by women filmmakers, such as Raquel Romero's *Ese sordo del alma (Deafness of the Soul)*, the first film to deal with domestic violence in a middle-class marriage, are as much about the social/sexual climate in Bolivia in the 1990s as they are about the films themselves.

Until 1979, the participation of women in the highly oppositional cinema of Bolivia, which acquired an international reputation disproportionate to its size, principally because of the films of Jorge Sanjinés, was almost nonexistent. Sanjinés' *The Courage of the People* (1971), a film that depicts the massacre by government troops of hundreds of men, women, and children at the Siglo XX tin mines, as they celebrated the feast of Saint John on the night of June 24, 1967, was an early exception to the general exclusion of women from the filmmaking industry in Bolivia. In this film, which has been considered one of the most important films in the New Latin American cinema, the political leader, Domitila Barrios de Chungara, together with other women and men who had survived the 1967 massacre, not only reenacted the roles of the miners and their families but also took part in writing the film's script and thus in the reconstruction of the massacre as *they themselves* remembered it.

More recently women film- and videomakers have been active in the recuperation of women's popular histories. In 1988, a group of middle-class women, who were the founders of the cinema collective Tahipamu (Taller de Historia y Participación de la Mujer), made the video *Siempreviva*, a fictional documentary that portrays the founding of the Bolivian Union of Florists in the social and political context of the anarchist movements of the 1920s and 1930s. In the same genre, French-born Danielle Caillet made the ground-breaking fictionalized documentary *Warmi* (1980), which tells the story of four women struggling to support their families— a peasant, a miner, a street vendor, and a textile worker. Another woman videomaker to focus on popular memory is the Bolivian social historian,

Silvia Rivera Cusicanqui, whose experimental video-poem *Remembrance of Things Future (Khumskuiw*, 1990) depicts the life story of a musician and composer in the context of the rise of the labor unions in Bolivia in the 1920s and 1930s. On the down side of women's videomaking projects, foreign (primarily United States) capital has been poured into projects aimed at fertility control—funding which has been decried by Jorge Sanjinés and other Bolivians as yet another neocolonializing strategy.

Because informed Bolivian cineastes have been more preoccupied with issues of race, class, imperialism, and colonialism than with those of gender, Raquel Romero's 1990 fiction film *Ese sordo del alma,* about a middle-class woman who is routinely beaten by her husband, created a sensation when it was first screened. The film opened to a standing-room-only house, and the debate that followed the screening revealed the extreme hostility of the audience to the film. Interestingly, Feder comments that although the physical abuse of Indian women's bodies has long been a central theme in Bolivian cinema, the struggles of women of the dominant classes in their own homes have had "the lineaments of a taboo."

Despite the complexity of Bolivia's social, economic, and cultural problems, in light of the outcome of the democratically held national elections of 1993, Feder sees reason to be hopeful about the new cinema in Bolivia and its role as an agent of change.

Karen Schwartzman's chapter deals with the work of one of the most highly acclaimed women filmmakers in Venezuela, Solveig Hoogesteijn. Schwartzman's is the only piece in the volume that enlists what has for two decades now been the dominant approach in feminist film criticism—post-Freudian, post-Lacanian psychoanalytic theory, influenced principally by the work of Kaja Silverman, Julia Kristeva, E. Ann Kaplan, Laura Mulvey, and Mary Ann Doane. The subject of her chapter, Hoogesteijn's historically grounded fiction film *Macu, the Policeman's Wife* (1987), begins like Sophocles' *Oedipus,* as a murder mystery. An investigation is called for when the bodies of three slain boys are found, one of them the adulterous lover of Macu, the wife of Ismael, a policeman. With its oedipal plot and relentless focus on triadic relations in each of its scenes—mother/father/child, daughter/mother/grandmother, mother/daughter/mother's lover, husband/wife/lover, the three murder victims—Macu clearly lends itself to a psychoanalytic approach, but with a different twist.

Schwartzman sees *Macu* as a powerful feminist statement in which—unlike the traditional Latin American melodrama about a wife's adultery and her husband's revenge—the maternal figure (Macu) emerges as the hero of the tale. Although this piece may be the most demanding chapter in the collection for readers unfamiliar with film theory, we feel that it brings a crucial perspective to the anthology in terms of both its psychoanalytic approach to the figuration of woman in film and its focus on the construction of an oppositional female subjectivity.

Schwartzman argues that *Macu* exemplifies recent theoretical reformulations of the New Latin American Cinema movement—such as those of Ana López and Zuzana Pick—that not only call for oppositional articulations of national identities and a deconstruction of aesthetics, but also problematize the erasure of marginalized subjectivities *within* the national cinemas of the Third World, be those subjectivities regional, racial, or sexual.[17] As Pick has argued, "the critical modernism of . . . the New Latin American cinema operates within a conscious awareness of yet untold and multiple narratives of cultural identity. This is the principle upon which Latin Americans have challenged fixed ideas of identity and imagined new utopias."[18] In foregrounding female subjectivity in a genre characterized by its *machismo*—the popular genre known in Venezuela as the "common crime" film—*Macu* subverts the codes of both the genre and the culture "by seducing the spectator into participating in the creation and legitimization of an alternate history." Thus, in *Macu,* the aesthetics of the genre (the "common crime" film) are revised, as are the political conventions of gender, *machismo*, and femininity that inform the genre; and thus the story of Macu, her husband, and her lover reconstructs itself as a feminist project.

Schwartzman uses post-Freudian and post-Lacanian theory—specifically, that of Julia Kristeva and Kaja Silverman—to illuminate the ways that this new female subjectivity is formed in *Macu.*[19] Kristeva emphasizes that this subjectivity is not simply formed at the time of the subject's entrance into language—the realm she terms, after Lacan, the "symbolic," rather, subjectivity has its earliest beginnings in the physiological exchanges that occur between mother and child in utero and that continue after birth. These preverbal exchanges, which prefigure the child's entrance into language, belong to the realm Kristeva terms the "semiotic." In Kristeva, these two modalities together, the semiotic and the symbolic, work to constitute the subjectivity of the child. The symbolic represents the construction of subjectivity in and through language, while the semiotic refers to the preverbal forming of the subject—to the drives and their manifestations as prelingual rhthyms, that is, to intonations, presyntactical, prelexical utterances and sounds of the subject.

Kristeva's unique contribution to psychoanalytic theory is her spa-tialization of the semiotic, preverbal stage of subjectivity in her notion of the *chora*. Kristeva's *chora* ("enclosed space," in Greek) is a figure for pre-oedipal oneness of, and seamless unity between, mother and child. According to Kristeva, after the subject acquires language and enters into the symbolic, the archaic mother—the archaic sense of oneness, that is, and the space of the *chora*—continue to live on within the subject. Thus, the *chora* assumes two guises, that which the infant experiences and that of the speaking subject. In *Macu,* the semiotic (that is, the *chora*) mani-fests itself as a group of formal strategies such as flashbacks and recurring sound effects such as drumbeats, flute tones, colors, creaking doors, flut-tering wings, metallic tinkling, and silences. There is in this film, as in life, a constant dialectic, Schwartzman points out, between the semiotic and the symbolic, and a constant irrupting of each of these modalities into the other, which results ultimately in the assumption by Macu of a new position within the symbolic—and, by implication, within the cul-ture.

But Silverman posits another road to female subjectivity, and one closely related to Kristeva's hypothesis of an enduring mother-child bond and its location in the *chora*: Freud's "negative Oedipus complex," in which the female child bonds affectively not with the father, but with the mother over against the father. While for Freud the "negative" Oedipus complex is only a precursor to the little girl's eventual "positive" Oedipal bonding to her father, Silverman stresses the crucial nature of the "nega-tive" Oedipus complex for the forming of a space for female subjectivity, as an "opening out" into, or desire to return to, an archaic unity with the mother. She also suggests that the Freudian/Lacanian "third term"—so necessary for the child's break with the mother and her entrance into the symbolic—does not have to be figured as male. The third term can also be a woman or the child the daughter desires to give to the mother.

Macu's journey to new female subjectivity involves her return to, as Schwartzman says, the "deep past" of childhood memory. When she dis-covers that Ismael is the murderer of her lover and his friends, she returns to her mother's apartment, where she finds herself inundated with mem-ories. She remembers and relives three traumas of her childhood: the wit-nessing of her mother's coming to orgasm with her live-in lover (the pri-mal scene, in Freudian terms); her mother's lover's communicating to Macu (the young child) the "fact" of her castration—registered in his act of offering her a piece of toilet paper in the bathroom—a "fact" which she rejects; and her rape/incest by her mother's lover (who turns out to be Ismael), and her mother's subsequent "selling" of her in marriage as a child to Ismael.

Schwartzman sees *Macu*—which was one of the biggest box office successes in Venezuelan film history—as a tale of female empowerment. Macu is empowered by her knowledge—her psychoanalysis, as it were. On her return to the house of her childhood, she is able to come to terms with the *choric* remnants of her past, to break with the old mother-daughter bond while reconstituting that bond in her relationship with her children, and to find a new place for herself in discourse, as the enunciator of her history. At the end of the film, Macu breaks through the barrier that separates her from us, and turns to confront us—the spectators—with a challenging gaze. Making explicit the "analogy between the narrative and the social predicament of the country," Schwartzman writes, this stare is the bold "challenge from a woman to . . . a society that sells (out) its children and, by implication, its future."

The four last chapters in the anthology consider a Chinese, a Chicana, an Indian, and an Argentinian woman filmmaker's representations of the status of women in the patriarchal family and nation. Also queried, implicitly if not always explicitly, is the applicability of Western feminisms and Western theory to the works of non-Western women filmmakers who define themselves as feminists or as woman centered. Echoing sentiments voiced repeatedly in this volume, Indian film scholar Sumita S. Chakravarty cautions that "cinemas are culture-specific and nation-specific, so that distinctive [national and cultural] modes of critique must evolve that directly address different systems of meaning and signification. A feminist reading of patriarchy that would view all versions of woman's signifier as one and the same is in danger of producing its own brand of essentialism and universalism."[20]

Similarly, Hu Ying, in her chapter "Beyond the Glow of the Red Lantern; Or, What Does It Mean to Talk about Women's Cinema in China?," follows the lead taken by Chinese film theorist Rey Chow in her recent book, *Primitive Passions*.[21] Hu Ying warns in her chapter against the naive use of Western feminist approaches, such as gaze theory, in analyzing Chinese films. At the same time, she also challenges the assertion of one of the foremost feminist critics in China, Dai Jinhua, who states that a "feminist" cinema is almost nonexistent in contemporary China.[22] Ying argues that a cinema that interrogates the status of women and moves women from the margins to the center of discourse does exist in China, but its relationship to Western feminisms and Western theoretical assumptions must be differently formulated.

Ying does just this in her comparative analysis of Chinese films by two directors, both of whom belong to the so-called Fifth Generation of filmmakers who graduated from Beijing Film Academy after the Cultural Revolution: the first is *Raise the Red Lantern,* by the internationally acclaimed male director Zhang Yimou; the second is *Bloody Morning,* by the less well-known woman director, Li Shaohong. Both films portray traditional marriages which end in tragedy. But this is where their similarity ends. Whereas Zhang's *Raise the Red Lantern* is set in the context of an unreal China—timeless, static, dehistoricized, and largely devoid of social, economic, and cultural hybridity, Li's *Bloody Morning* renders a more complex, less exoticized picture which pertains to the world well beyond China. Central to Ying's analysis of *Bloody Morning,* the plot of which was borrowed from a story by the Latin American writer García Márquez, are the film's cross-cultural implications. Li has transformed Márquez's work, *Chronicle of a Death Foretold*—a colorful Latin tale of *machismo,* a deflowered bride, and a groom's vendetta set in Colombia in the 1920s—into an austere drama set in rural China at the time of the New Economic Policy in the 1980s. In Li's version of the tale, the seducer is no smooth Don Juan but a schoolteacher and misfit in the village, and instead of the slow, sensuous undressing of the bride on her wedding night typical of Western-influenced Chinese cinema, Li's bride Xiuquin is shown struggling to take off numerous red sweaters while her groom looks on bored. Rituals are not lavishly displayed, as they are in *Raise the Red Lantern*; they are subverted, and underlying all traditions is the "overwhelming factor of economics." In place of Chen Kaige's beautiful young girl sumptuously veiled and dressed in red on her wedding day in *Yellow Earth,* Li's brides wear gray peasant clothing and cover their hair with dingy towels. Hollywood conventions are also subverted in Li's film; the male gaze is no longer dominant and the female body is not eroticized. The result, argues Ying, is that Li depicts women's marginalized position in society in such a way that both Hollywood film conventions and typical Fifth Generation culture films, such as *Raise the Red Lantern, Red Sorghum,* and *Yellow Earth*, are debunked in *Bloody Morning,* and their representations of gender demythologized. "If this not so-exotic China is 'adapted,'" Ying concludes, "from a 'foreign' text about another modern hybrid culture in flux, and if as such it resists interpretation as 'national allegory,' then its very 'inauthenticity' effectively stages the cross-cultural nature of Chinese, and more broadly non-Western, filmmaking."

In *National Identity in Indian Popular Cinema,* Sumita Chakravarty introduced the concept "imperso-nation" to put forward the case that the ubiquitous linkages in Bombay popular cinema after 1947 between the struggles of nation formation and those of emerging postcolonial identities—in terms of gender, ethnicity, and class—within the nation suggest a dynamic between the two that has been anything but simple. Among the typically marginalized characters in popular Indian melodrama, Chakravarty proposed the courtesan as a "masquerading and liminal figure, an impersonation writ large—culturally, individually, sexually . . . [yet who provided] a sense of continuity, a connection with the past . . . that [was] laced with pathos."[23]

Chakravarty's chapter in this volume, "Can the Subaltern Weep?" focuses on the figure of a similarly marginalized public woman—the professional mourner. Taking as her departure point Gayatri Spivak's influential critique of the Subaltern Studies historians' collective for denying voice and subjectivity to women, lower-caste members, tribal peoples, and untouchables,[24] Chakravarty argues that a sense of nationhood will not and cannot emerge until the voices of women and all of India's oppressed racial and tribal constituencies are heard. Women in Indian society have always played the mourners, never the mourned. The marginalization of women as mourners has been symptomatic of a larger malaise in India—that is, its inability to mourn its past and to articulate its grief and pain. But because women alone are the nation's mourners, only they—according to Eric Santner's mapping of loss and survival in his book *Stranded Objects*[25]—can speak with validity for the culture. Citing Santner, Chakravarty explains that to become a speaking subject one must already have "assumed one's fundamental vocation as survivor of the painful losses . . . that accompany one's entrance into the symbolic order. . . . In the writings of numerous poststructural theorists, historical suffering is believed to spring from a failure to tolerate the structural suffering—the always already shattered mirrors of the Imaginary—that scars one's being as a speaking subject."[26]

Theorizing the "subaltern as woman and woman as the being-in-pain," Chakravarty relates the film *Rudaali* (*The Crier,* 1992), directed by the Bombay woman filmmaker Kalpana Lajmi, to the story on which it is based by the Bengali woman author Mahasweta Devi, and to the history of Indian subaltern women since Independence. The forties and fifties saw the development of the traditions, identities, and popular understanding of Indianness and the construction of a national Imaginary. At this time women writers played an active role as writers and poets in mourning the past. The late sixties and seventies, however, marked new fissures in the culture. The new cinema in India, which attempted to end the devaluation of women performers in the earlier decades of popular Indian film, was largely ignored by serious scholars and literary critics, while the Subaltern historians seemed oblivious of the question of gender and the oppression of women before and after the Partition. More recently, recognizing that such omissions were casualties of the rise of "bourgeois nationalism" in the postcolonial state, the historian Partha Chatterjee has called for a radical reconsideration of women's representation and self-representation in "the interlocking fields of social and political history, cinematic modes and institutions and emergent state apparatus."[27]

Like Spivak, Chakravarty incorporates Marxist, poststructuralist, and feminist perspectives that enable her to explore the "politics of gender in third cinema and the interlocking dynamics of the signifiers of 'body' and 'voice.'" Woman in both Devi's story and Lajmi's film is represented as not merely the emotive/expressive enunciator of the culture but as its rational/verbal one, too, in her role as professional mourner. In her analysis of mourning as both practice and symbol, art and artifice, body and voice, Chakravarty's avowed intention is to "muddy" the conventional dichotomies: logos/pathos, mind/body, nature/culture, intellect/emotion, and subject/object.

In *Rudaali*, the professional mourner Sanichari does not weep as an involuntary emotional act. Instead, weeping becomes for her a calculated and subservient activity that inhibits personal expression and deprives her of a sense of agency and strength. But her voice also speaks words that empower her. In a film largely structured as a series of flashbacks, her voice seems to "dredge up from the depth of her experiences a flow of words that give her the control over her fate, even if retrospectively, that is vital to her self." The climax of the film comes at its melodramatic conclusion when the *rudaali*, who has been unable to weep even at her husband's death, is at last capable of weeping freely and openly over the death of Bhikni—the friend she later learns is her mother. Enhancing her sense of power and control, her voice has come to represent—as both intellect and feeling, mind and body—the reunified self.

Chakravarty notes that Devi's orginal story does not have the hopeful closure provided in Lajmi's *Rudaali* by Sanichari's genuine tears. Other such concessions to the Indian filmgoer include the addition in the film of a love affair between Sanichari and the young lord of the village as well as instrumental music, song, and dance, all essential ingredients in Indian melodrama. The possibility of reconceiving "the unity of the national Imaginary" in cinema so that it includes mourning and heterogeneity as integral parts of the whole seems consistent with the formal and thematic implications of *Rudaali,* a film that joins the traditions of popular melodrama and social realism in a narrative about the creation and production of the subaltern woman as an enunciating subject in control of her own body and voice. But if *Rudaali* suggests a new discourse for women and the nation in India and a new place for mourning within that discourse, it does so with the future-perfect proviso that the bodies of women will not mourn until they have been mourned.

It may be that no work in this anthology offers a more intimate portrait of the desires, memories, and fears that motivate a director to embark on a search for her roots—her relation to family, nation, and hence narration—than does Rosa Linda Fregoso's chapter on Chicana filmmaker Lourdes Portillo's melodocumystery, *The Devil Never Sleeps.* In *Chicanos and Film,* Chon A. Noriega cites Fregoso as one of a small group of influential film scholars who have virtually defined the field of Chicano/a film studies.[28] Making clear her own bicultural identification with the filmmaker and with her autobiographical narrative of her journey back to Mexico, Fregoso points out that while such an odyssey holds the promise of "a return to the self," for a clearing, for long hoped-for disclosures, it must also ultimately reveal a "fragile and uncertain terrain"—a tale filled with disguises, deceptions, and coverups. As Portillo proceeds to divulge the secrets her family has denied or papered over, she is seen as violating the "sanctity" of her family's privacy and threatening the fabric of the state. Her film interrogates the concept of the Mexican nation as an inviolate community based on the model of the family and vouchsafed by patriarchal discourse. Her film fits (though it is more complex than this) the category of *testimonio,* which Noriega defines as the "personal recollection of a communal experience."[29]

Portillo's journey home to her family begins when she learns by telephone of the death in Chihuahua of her favorite uncle, Tío Oscar, "under mysterious circumstances." Now either the victim of an assassin or a suicide, Tío Oscar had been a political leader and mayor of the city with strong ties to Mexico's ruling party. As Portillo investigates the case, she discovers her uncle's darker side, including his involvement in environmental pollution and his possible homosexuality. Confronted by her family's insistence that a "sanitized image" of both itself and Tío Oscar be preserved, Portillo is determined to act. She resolves to reveal the supposed "facts" about her family, recalling Third Cinema filmmaker Fernando Birri's call for a cinema of "economic, political, and cultural liberation and also the liberation of the image."[30]

The succession of challenges to authority and to official discourse posed by *The Devil Never Sleeps* includes its challenge to the status of documentary films as a privileged medium of truth and objectivity. Fregoso argues that Portillo conducts this interrogation by various means, not the least of which involves inserting herself into the documentary as the central protagonist and narrator with "multiple screen roles," including those of detective, documentarist, niece, and Catholic Chicana. Her melodocumystery reflects both her own multiple personae and those of her Mexican family more than it does any one "truth" or "reality." The documentarist thus engages in an inquiry into the nature of the documentary and of melodrama, its production of knowledge, identities, and its "truths," similar to the inquiry Trinh T. Minh-ha pursues in an essay in which she asks regarding the documentary form: "Which truth? Whose truth? How true?"[31]

Both Portillo and the other characters in *The Devil Never Sleeps* often narrate, without attempting to distinguish the "real" from the "not real," what Fregoso calls "culturally specific forms of knowledge," such as legends, gossip, and *telenovelas*, which Fregoso sees as existing beyond the boundaries of "official" documentary discourse. Tía Luz abruptly shifts, in the middle of her official interview with Portillo, from discussing Tío Oscar's wife, a topic directly related to solving the mystery of his life and death, to "a frivolous interpretation of plot details" from a Brazilian *telenovela* she has been watching during the interview. Rather than omit or marginalize Tía Luz's digression, Portillo makes it central: "the camera zooms in to the television set," observes Fregoso, and "the visual and narrative focus shifts away from the interview to the *telenovela*, effecting a slippage between two forms of discourse, the 'official' interview and the more properly 'popular' discourse of the *telenovela* . . . refusing to privilege one form over the other." Portillo's film rejects a single narrative path as well as a single discourse that would reach a single end, such as solving the mystery of Oscar's death. Put another way, the film rejects what Trinh T. Min-ha has described as "positivist thinking whose impetus is to supply answers at all costs, thereby limiting both theory and practice to a process of totalization."[32] Fregoso points out that in juxtaposing without priviileging different forms of knowledge, Portillo represents what Foucault called "differential knowledge incapable of unanimity"; her focus on differential knowledge is consistent with Chela Sandoval's commitment to "denying any one ideology as the final answer, while instead positing a *tactical subjectivity* with the capacity to recenter."[33]

Elsewhere Fregoso has characterized Chicana/o film as "a space where subjectivity is produced."[34] In negotiating diverse discourses and exposing the conflict and scandal that lie hidden behind the edifices of family and nation, which must be read as reflections of one another, *The Devil Never Sleeps* opens the door to a new Chicana space, position, and subjectivity. In her analysis of Portillo's journey, Fregoso draws on both Renato Rosaldo's imaging of the border as that which "directs our attention to the spaces within and between what were once sanctified as 'homogeneous communities'"[35] and Trinh T. Minh-ha's as the "space in between, the interval to which established rules of boundaries never quite apply."[36] As the character who occupies multiple roles within and outside of the family, the nation, and diverse discourses, writes Fregoso, Portillo offers the spectator a model for standing at "the crossroads of incompleteness," for making a break with the past, and for shaping new forms of cultural expression and cultural freedom.

The final selection offers the only extended personal statement in this volume by an artist about her own life and work. María Luisa Bemberg's observations on her privileged upbringing as daughter of one of Argentina's wealthiest families and her belated emergence as a filmmaker are accompanied by her commentaries on *Miss Mary* (1986), the most autobiographical of her six features. Neither an interview nor an essay, this piece is a "testimonial mosaic" compiled by Julianne Burton-Carvajal after the filmmaker's death in 1995 from hundreds of newspaper and magazine articles and interviews. The selections reproduced here have been chosen by the compiler from three subsections of "Opening Doors and Windows or, Destiny Defied," the final section of Burton-Carvajal's forthcoming book *Three Lives in Film*, a collection of life histories of pioneering Latin American women filmmakers.[37]

The innovative nature of this piece, and the painstaking labor of culling and reassembly that produced it, are a fitting tribute to the meticulous artistry of Latin America's most accomplished woman filmmaker, whose declaration to interviewer Beatriz Iacoviello (Buenos Aires, 1991) serves as epigraph to the compiler's preface to the Bemberg section of *Three Lives in Film.*

Editing means finding the best frames and putting them in just the right place. It means knowing exactly where to begin, where to end, what to avoid, what to abbreviate, what to eliminate. Everything has to work like some immense inner ear. It's passionately absorbing. I think I make movies in order to edit.

Bemberg also made movies in order to "open doors and windows for women," beginning to do so during the dark years of military dictatorship and the infamous "Dirty War" against internal "subversives," when she had to struggle against censorship. Her third feature, *Camila* (1984), began shooting on December 12, 1983, the day after Argentina officially returned to democracy with the inauguration of President Raúl Alfonsín, whose first official act was the abolition of all forms of censorship. Bemberg's version of the Camila O'Gorman story—a long-censored episode in Argentine history involving the pursuit, capture, and execution for treason of a pair of young lovers—was an unprecedented success in Argentina "because of the cathartic way that this period melodrama, the epic of a mis-formed nation, marked the repudiation of military-authoritarian modes of government and other forms of patriarchal control at the precise moment of Argentina's return to electoral democracy."[38]

As Burton-Carvajal observes in her general introduction to *Three Lives in Film*, each of María Luisa's three subsequent features addressed aspects of personal, national, and transnational identity in ambitious, engagingly varied ways. *Yo, la peor de todas / I, the Worst of All* (1990), based on the life of the seventeenth-century nun Sor Juana Inés de la Cruz, is one of the great feminist biographies in world film history—not only because of its "larger than life" subject, but also because of its audacious use of evocative and deliberately abstract—rather than conventionally realistic—studio sets and tableaus. Bemberg's sixth feature, *De eso no se habla / I Don't Want to Talk About It* (1993), set in provincial Argentina in the 1930s and starring Marcello Mastroianni as suitor and spouse to a talented dwarf, is a wistful parable about resistance to bigotry and intolerance. *Miss Mary* depicts the last, bittersweet days of Argentina's landed oligarchy and puts an original spin on the postcolonial condition, since here the colonization is voluntary and the colonizer (the governess, Miss Mary) is also a subordinate—not only among the Argentine oligarchy but also "at home" in London.

Like the rebellious women whom she portrays in her films, Bemberg fought in her own life to overcome a moral order that suppressed passion, ideas, freedom, and difference. In their direct and indirect challenges to patriarchal law, her films have little in common with the ethos and politics of the Third Cinema first theorized and put into practice in Argentina more than a decade earlier. Rather, they exemplify the shift toward greater subjectivity and interiority that accompanied—and, arguably, also occasioned—redemocratization movements in the "Southern Cone" countries of Brazil, Argentina, Uruguay, and Chile.[39]

While the generation of film and videomakers of which Bemberg was a member "evolved at the margins of traditional politics and outside the anti-imperialist rhetoric of the cultural nationalism of the 1960s," as Zuzana Pick writes, they nonetheless addressed through their films and videos "the relevance of the personal to relocate activism beyond the public space of partisan politics."[40] Viewing these developments similarly, B. Ruby Rich adds, "In this new environment, a cinema which turns inward and which begins to enable viewers to construct an alternative relationship— not only with their government but with an authentic sense of self—is an indispensable element in the evolution of a new sociopolitical environment."[41] Bemberg's *Camila* is not just the intimately told tale of the passion of a young girl and a priest but also a cautionary tale of the fate of citizens living under a military dictatorship. In *Camila*, writes Pick, love is "incompatible with state formation. Instead of being a founding principle that reinforces harmony, love serves to reveal the nation's violent origins. . . . The death sentence [imposed on Camila and her lover] exposes the antagonism between sexuality and the law within a patriarchal society."[42]

In statements about the making of *I, the Worst of All*, a film that portrays the life of the Mexican poet, scholar, and nun, Sor Juana Inés de la Cruz, Bemberg stresses her desire to achieve an "atemporal, universal tone . . . free of local references."[43] To Bemberg, Sor Juana, like Camila and the daughters in *Miss Mary*, is a victim of a totalitarian system that may arise anywhere and at any time. With this emphasis on what she called the "universal"—by which she clearly meant not to devalue local differences but to evoke alternative forms of solidarity for women and to foreground the significance of women's history—Bemberg maintains her focus on Sor Juana as "the thinking woman . . . who recognize[s] no boundaries." The dwarf Charlotte, the central character in *I Don't Want to Talk About It*, functions as a similarly collective figure. "I believe," said Bemberg shortly before her death in Buenos Aires in 1995, that Charlotte stands "for all minorities who suffer the repressive pressure of the majority who believes itself the owners not only of truth but also of social order."[44]

Considered together, the filmmakers represented in this anthology have produced a new aesthetics. All are bound together in the work of resisting, refusing, and opposing the conventions and stereotypes not only of Hollywood with its goal of commercial profit but also of Third Cinema with its adherence to a Marxist ideology that subsumes, and thus erases, the particularities of sexism and racism. And, though the body of work that is represented in this anthology is diverse, certain characteristics persist across this corpus—traits that can be called feminist or woman centered. The first and most obvious of these is that the figures of ordinary women—working women, lower-class women, and mothers, among others—have been moved from the margins of the discourse to the center. Secondly, the specificity of the cultures, nations, local discourses, and critiques, within which these women's lives are enmeshed, is valued and foregrounded. Thirdly, the problematization of motherhood and the maternal imaginary takes precedence in these filmmakers' works over the conventional heterosexual romance plot. Maternal figures in feature films such as *Lola* (María Novaro), *Rudaali* (Kapana Lajmi), and *Macu* (Solveig Hoogesteijn) are more likely to play sisters than mothers to their daughters, albeit in different ways in each film. Other mothers—notably in the documentary *Selbe* (Safi Faye) and the feature film *Faces of Women* (Désiré Ecaré)—are represented not only as caregivers but as the main breadwinners in their families and communities. And when the protagonists in these women's works are involved in a search for self, it is not through a lonely odyssey but via attachments to other women, which are often articulated as attempts (not always successful) to reconcile with their mothers. This quest for self tends to be represented as an ongoing process rather than a *telos*. These protagonists value the building of their familes, their communities, and the collective, not over against but *as integral to* the work of self-discovery. Above all, they and their filmmaker-creators seek a retrieval of a history in which women are repositioned in the center of things, as narrative agents of their own lives. It is with the perspective of such an aesthetics—an aesthetics that is, as we have shown, inseparable from the politics of the gaze—that all study and understanding of the films discussed in this anthology must begin.

NOTES

The authors wish especially to thank Julianne Burton-Carvajal and Zuzana Pick, whose many criticisms and suggestions have contributed substantially to this Introduction and to the rest of the anthology.

1. Solanas and Getino's article is available in translation by Julianne Burton-Carvajal and Michael Chanan in Chanan, ed., *Twenty Five Years of the New Latin American Cinema* (London: British Film Institute and Channel Four, 1983).

2. On the differences between United States, European, and Third Cinema see esp. Julianne Burton-Carvajal, ed., *Cinema and Social Change in Latin America: Conversations with Filmmakers* (Austin: University of Texas Press, 1986), xi; see also David A. Cook, *A History of Narrative Film*, 3d. ed. (New York: Norton, 1996), 877–78. On the convergence of international and national aims in Third Cinema, see "The Third Cinema Question: Notes and Reflections," in Pines and Willemen, eds., *Questions of Third Cinema* (London: British Film Institute, 1989), 1–30.

3. See Jim Pines and Paul Willemen, eds., *Questions of Third Cinema* (London: British Film Institute, 1989), vii.

4. Zuzana M. Pick, *The New Latin American Cinema: A Continental Project* (Austin: University of Texas Press, 1993), 35; and B. Ruby Rich, "An/Other View of New Latin American Cinema," in *Iris* 13 (1991): 5–28.

5. Cf. Third Cinema theorist Jim Pines, Preface, in Pines and Willemen, *Questions of Third Cinema*, pp. vii–x with feminist theorists B. Ruby Rich, "An/Other View," 5–28; Zuzana M. Pick, "Territories of Representation," in *Iris* 13 (1991): 53–62; and Karen S. Goldman, "A Third Feminism?" in *Iris* 13 (1991): 87–95.

6. Glauber Rocha, "An Aesthetic of Hunger," translated by Burnes Hollyman and Randal Johnson, in Chanan, ed., *Twenty-Five Years*, 15.

7. Jean Franco, "The Incorporation of Women: A Comparison of North American and Mexican Popular Narrative," *Studies in Entertainment: Critical Approaches to Mass Culture,* ed. Tania Modleski (Bloomington: Indiana University Press, 1986), 199–200.

8. Zuzana M. Pick, *The New Latin American Cinema: A Continental Project* (Austin: University of Texas Press, 1993), 130; on Gómez see also 131–37.

9. Pick, *New Latin American Cinema*, 82.

10. Pick, *New Latin American Cinema*, 121.

11. bell hooks, *Black Looks* (Boston: South End Press, 1992), 130.

12. Willemen, "The Third Cinema Question: Notes and Reflections," in Pines and Willemen, eds., *Questions of Third Cinema*, decries the portrayals in

popular cinema of the Third World as a utopic, preindustrial Eden (18–19), but it should be noted that *Daughters* has nothing to do with this genre.

13. bell hooks, 130.

14. Bambara, "Reading the Signs, Empowering the Eye: *Daughters of the Dust* and the Black Independent Cinema Movement," in *Black American Cinema*, ed. Manthia Diawara (New York: Routledge, 1993), 118–44.

15. Diawara, *African Cinema: Politics and Culture* (Bloomington: Indiana University Press, 1992), 154.

16. Demelas, *Nationalisme sans nation? La Bolivie aux XIXème et XXème siecles.* (Paris: Éditions du Centre National de Recherche Scientifique, 1980), 95.

17. On *Macu* as a revision of Solanas's and Getino's manifesto for a Third Cinema, see also Karen Goldman, "A Third Feminism," 87–95.

18. Pick, *New Latin American Cinema*, 11.

19. Kaja Silverman, *The Acoustic Mirror: The Female Voice in Psychoanalysis and Cinema* (Bloomington: Indiana University Press, 1988) and Julia Kristeva, *Desire in Language: A Semiotic Approach to Literature and Art,* translated by T. Gora (New York: Columbia University Press, 1980), are the key texts.

20. Sumita Chakravarty, *National Identity in Indian Popular Cinema 1947–1987* (Austin: University of Texas Press, 1993), 273.

21. See Rey Chow, *Primitive Passions. Visuality, Sexuality, Ethnography, and Contemporary Chinese Cinema* (New York: Columbia University Press, 1995), 55–67; see also Fredric Jameson, "Third World Literature in the Era of Multinational Capital," *Social Text* 15 (Fall 1986); see also Aijaz Ahmad reply to the latter, "Jameson's Rhetoric of Otherness and the 'National Allegory'" in *Social Text* 17 (Fall 1987): 3–25.

22. Dai Jinhua, "Invisible Women: Contemporary Chinese Cinema and Women's Film," in *Positions: East Asian Cultures Critique* 3/1 (1995): 269–70.

23. Chakravarty, *National Identity*, 288; 304.

24. Gayatri Chakravorty Spivak, "Subaltern Studies: Deconstructing Historiography," in *The Spivak Reader: Selected Works by Gayatri Chakravorty Spivak,* ed. Donna Landry and Gerald Maclean (New York: Routledge, 1996), 203–35 (previously published in Ranajit Guha, ed., *Subaltern Studies IV: Writings on South Asian History and Society* [New Delhi: Oxford University Press, 1985], 330–63).

25. Eric L. Santner, *Stranded Objects: Mourning, Memory, and Film in Postwar Germany* (Ithaca, N.Y.: Cornell University Press, 1990), 9–10.

26. Santner, *Stranded Objects*, 9–10.

27. See also Partha Chatterjee, *The Nation and Its Fragments: Colonial and Postcolonial Histories* (Princeton, N.J.: Princeton University Press, 1993), 154–57.

28. Chon A. Noriega, *Chicanos and Film: Representation and Resistance* (Minneapolis: University of Minnesota Press, 1992), xiii.

29. Noriega, *Chicanos and Film*, 159.

30. Fregoso, *The Bronze Screen*, xx. See also Fernando Birri, "For a Nationalist, Realist, Critical and Popular Cinema," *Screen* 26, nos. 3–4 (May–August 1985): 89–91, 90.

31. Trinh T. Minh-ha, *When the Moon Waxes Red: Representation, Gender and Cultural Politics* (New York: Routledge, 1991), 32.

32. Trinh T. Minh-ha, *When the Moon Waxes*, 31.

33. Fregoso, *The Bronze Screen*, 98. From Chela Sandoval, "U.S. Third World Feminism: The Theory and Method of Oppositional Consciousness in the Postmodern World," *Genders*, no. 10 (Spring 1991): 3.

34. Fregoso, *The Bronze Screen*, xix.

35. See Fregoso, *The Bronze Screen*, 65. From Renato Rosaldo, *Culture and Truth* (Boston: Beacon Press, 1989), 217.

36. See Fregoso, *The Bronze Screen*, 68. Original source not provided.

37. Julianne Burton-Carvajal, *Three Lives in Film: Illustrated Memoirs of Latin America's Foremost Women Filmmakers* (Austin: University of Texas Press, 1999).

38. Ibid.

39. On Third Cinema and the politics of feminism see Goldman, "A Third Feminism?" *Iris* 13 (Summer 1991): 87–96.

40. Pick, *New Latin American Cinema*, 35.

41. Rich, "An/Other View," 35.

42. Pick, *New Latin American Cinema*, 88.

43. Burton-Carvajal: 93-V-196. See Burton's list of interviews with María Luisa Bemberg.

44. Julianne Burton-Carvajal, *Three Lives in Film: Illustrated Memoirs of Latin America's Foremost Women Filmmakers* (Austin: University of Texas Press, 1999).

CHAPTER ONE

Al Cine de las Mexicanas: Lola *in the Limelight*

DIANE SIPPL

The reporters were there, too, the gringo newspapermen and photographers, with a new invention, the movie camera. Villa was already captivated. . . . He was well aware that the little machine could capture the ghost of his body if not the flesh of his soul— . . . his moving body . . . that, yes, could be captured and set free again in a dark-room, like a Lazarus risen not from the dead but from faraway times and spaces, in a black room on a white wall, anywhere in New York or Paris.

—Carlos Fuentes, *The Old Gringo*

I often hear it said that less than a handful of women have ever been able to make films in Mexico, and it does not surprise me that most North Americans believe this to be true. Since very little has appeared on United States screens by Mexicanas, it would seem that very little exists. But I have read about Mexican women's filmmaking, thanks largely to the correspondence and lectures and publications of Julianne Burton and other scholars. In the last decade Women Make Movies in New York has distributed some films by Mexican women, mostly documentaries (such as

Carmen de Lara's *We're Not Asking for the Moon*), and Hollywood entertainment networks have acquired United States commercial rights for
some dramatic features (such as María Novaro's *Danzón)*. Archives, muse-
ums, and community arts projects have organized tours including their
films, and international festivals have exhibited them, sometimes recognizing them with competitive awards. Certainly there is much to discover
in this rich and growing body of work, in particular the fact that it has
remained largely invisible to us (and I include myself, living in Hollywood, the "film capital of the world").

So it is that I set about the task of offering this capsule history—perhaps a hidden history for many of us—of women's filmmaking in Mexico. Here I can only hint at the variety of talent and tenacity of purpose
their work has demanded, but at least I can suggest that these women
have demonstrated the capacity to challenge the prevailing representations of gender, class, and race in their respective eras.

Women have participated in the production of Mexican cinema
from its pre-Revolutionary inception. In fact most of them wore more
than one hat, helping to develop the industry in multiple ways. As in
most countries, the cinema in Mexico began as an international enterprise. Once the Lumière brothers released their fascinating flickers on foreign shores, Mexican impresarios bought stock and equipment from
metropolitan suppliers and projected their magic lanterns in music halls
in Mexico City and in cafes and tents along the newly built railway lines
across the country. Occasionally banned for their "lascivious excess," the
moving pictures took over the capital by 1903. Picturesque land- and
seascapes, city architecture, and popular pageants caught the eye in their
new form. More important, by 1910, most production, distribution, and
exhibition was in the hands of Mexicans.[1] One of three partners who
founded Azteca Films in 1917, Mimi Derba was Mexico's first female
movie star. A comedienne who bridged the silent screen and the sound era
with *Santa* in 1931, she wrote several features, is said to have directed *La
Tigresa,* and was photographed as supervising editing.[2] Documentary
filmmakers Dolores and Adriana Elhers, two sisters who studied cinema
in the United States, launched the newsreel *Revista Elhers,* which ran from
1922 to 1929. Candida Beltran Rendon served as writer, director, lead
actress, producer, and set designer for *The Grandmother's Secret (El secreto
de la abuela)* in 1928.[3]

After the transition to talking pictures it was radio publicity that
brought fame to Adela Sequeyro as "Perlita," writer, actress, and producer

for *Beyond Death (Más allá de la muerte)* in 1935, who filled the same functions as well as directing for *Nobody's Woman (La mujer de nadie)* and *The Devils Next Door (Diablillos de arrabal)*, both in 1938. Mysterious Mexican producer and writer "Duquesa Olga" also achieved fame as Chilean pianist Eva Limiñana; she wrote films for the actor and director José ("Che") Bohr, a Chilean who associated himself with the tango fashion in Buenos Aires and thrived in Hollywood, but who gained more leverage in Mexico, where "the Duchess" earned credits for producer, original story, adaptation to the screen, and dialogue for ten films in which he acted in the 1930s. In 1942 she also directed, but without Bohr's company, and was later forgotten in his memoirs.[4]

Now let's consider the conditions under which these films were made. As early as 1911 there were already forty-six theaters (with a capacity of 25,000) programming cinema in Mexico City alone, but the new Mexican state, with all its extensive cultural programs under Vasconcelos's campaigns as Minister of Education (1920–1924), offered no funds for Mexican filmmaking or exhibition. At the same time it placed no quotas on Hollywood imports, which by 1925 filled 90 percent of Mexico's screens.[5] Even in 1938, when the film industry was the second largest in the country after oil, and fifty-seven films were produced within a year, Mexico's own product made up only 14.8 percent of the domestic market share (compared to the United States figure of 67.7 percent); Mexico's share rose only to 18.4 percent in 1949 when 107 films were made.[6] State money was provided for private producers, whose crews and actors were often trained in Hollywood. The Golden Age of Mexican cinema—the 1940s—generated original work with nationalistic themes and styles, but ultimately yielded to the cultural favoritism won by monopolistic producers, distributors, and exhibitors who increased their own profits through state investment. Closed-shop unions prohibited the development of talent, locking out new members for thirty years.[7]

While the state continued to subsidize mostly *churros* (formulaic "quicky" movies) and "Palmolive *tele-tamales*" produced by a cinema/TV mafia,[8] Matilde Landeta chose to work beside her brother, Eduardo Landeta. After years of up-through-the-ranks apprenticeship as "script girl" and assistant director, for example, she wrote and finally directed *Lola Casanova* (1948), tracing Mexican culture to its pre-Colombian roots through the desires of a white woman. Then she shifted her focus in *La Negra Angustias* (1949), her most important film, to a free-spirited *mulatta* colonel in the Mexican revolution who exerts power outside the confines of gender, only to face a color conflict with her male literacy teacher. In Landeta's next film, *La Trotacalles (Streetwalker)* (1951), she turned to the hallowed genre of prostitution melodrama and *cabaretera* film.[9] She was not to make another film in over three decades after that, but would eventually be saluted and brought back into public recognition by another woman to follow in her footsteps.

In the 1950s the cine club movement created a forum for film theory and a showcase for new talent. It was the seedbed for an "independent" cinema parallel or oppositional to the dominant film industry. The University Center for Cinematographic Studies (CUEC) was founded by the 1958 López Mateos regime, and advocates formed *Nuevo Cine*, which founded a journal debating Italian neorealism, French New Wave, and auteur theories, and proclaiming the need for independent cinema in Mexico. This brought pressure on the film union (STPC), which answered by launching an Experimental Film Contest in 1965 that inspired the longstanding commitment and support of Gabriel García Marquez, then working in Mexico as a screenwriter, to new directors—some forty in the next decade.[10]

An older cultural nationalism began to yield to a cosmopolitanism in filmmaking; this direction was boosted by a movement called *la onda*—a modernist grab-bag of United States rock music, beat poetry, novels, dress/hair/make-up fashions, and general linguistic playfulness, a dismembering of old codes by a 1960s youth culture that would be violently repressed. Beginning in July 1968 a growing student movement was met with bazooka raids by the governing PRI (Institutional Revolutionary Party). Regarded as "the most articulate and threatening outburst of public disaffection in modern Mexico," one in which "the students' courage and commitment had begun to inspire others," the youth movement gained force with the Olympic Games scheduled for October 12. But on October 2, 1968, when six thousand students and others congregated in one of Mexico City's central plazas (Tlatelolco), several hundred were massacred by the army and some two thousand were arrested.[11]

The subsequent regime, striving to accommodate the unrest, elicited a full range of reactions from filmmakers. Echeverría actively reached out to oppositional filmmakers in Mexico and elsewhere (Chilean Miguel Littín, for example) and actively courted a third-worldist film discourse. The new president's anti-imperialist rhetoric—upholding the autonomous development of Mexican film as a quality product on the world market—was backed by active programs and funding. His brother Roberto headed the leading national film agency. But there were those who saw Echeverría's politics as stifling both creative film language and an expression of class conflict within Mexico. The rhetoric was labeled by some as "leather-jacketed" populism that extravagantly endowed lush "political" film enterprises on the backs of Mexico's workers.[12]

In 1950 Carmen Toscano's compilation documentary of half a century of Mexican history was released. This film, along with the work of Matilde Landeta, became the subject of a biographical film by Marcela Fernández Violante. Violante herself graduated from and was appointed the director (1985) of CUEC, the film school of Mexico's national university. She made a thesis film on Frida Kahlo in 1971, long before the artist had been resurrected for international cultural attention. Violante wrote and directed two features regarding the failures of the Mexican revolution, one narrated through the eyes of a young girl, *Whatever You Do, It's No Good (De todos modos Juan te llamas)* in 1975, and *Cananea* in 1977, narrated through the eyes of a North American mine owner in northern Mexico, also based in history.[13] In 1980 she made the internationally esteemed *Mystery (Misterio)*, a parodic critique of Mexico's privately owned media monopoly, Televisa,[14] followed by *In the Land of the Light Feet (En el país de los pies ligeros)* in 1981, in which a Mexico City boy tries to adapt to Indian life in the Tarahumara region.[15]

Meanwhile some new topics—family codes, bourgeois conformity, machismo, heterosexuality, and Mexico's uneven socioeconomic development—were being interrogated in the Mexican cinema as never before. Youthful disillusionment and rebelliousness in the face of betrayed ideals of the Revolution were taken up via filmic strategies that were increasingly self-reflexive.

During the *sexenio* of López Portillo, the country suffered the loss of the *Cineteca* collection. Marcela Fernández Violante claims:

> Under the Echeverría regime, we spent $9 million to cover royalties for American films. Under López Portillo, we spent $60 million. . . . Margarita López Portillo did a lot to encourage these "aristocratic" airs. Her tenure as head of the film industry is the blackest chapter of Mexican film history. She literally let a time bomb explode. When the old nitrate prints stored "temporarily" in the basement of the *Nacional Cineteca* (film achive) caught fire, many lives were lost and the entire history of Mexican cinema went up in smoke. . . .

Mexico had already surrendered a huge share of the Latin American film market to U.S. interests, and I doubt that we will ever be able to win it back.[16]

Though President Miguel de la Madrid established the National Film Institute in 1983, only nine out of ninety-one films that year were made by the state.[17] The Mexican government financed half of John Huston's film *Under the Volcano*. The studios were invaded by foreign directors such as Carlos Saura (Spain) and Sergei Bondarchuk (USSR), who made their worst films at great cost—to their budgets and to Mexico. Dino de Laurentis leased Churubusco Studios for the production of *Dune*. Michael Douglas simply bought Alatriste studios. Foreign productions provide jobs for some crew members, but the important technicians are brought in from outside. This leaves Mexican directors, screenwriters, cinematographers, and composers unemployed beside their own country's studios.[18]

It is understandable that the decade of the 1980s produced several strong documentary filmmakers whose work is committed to social change. It is also encouraging that a growing number of these filmmakers are women. Sonia Fritz, interested in the indigenous population, made a short film, *Yalaltecas*, about real events in 1981 when the women in an Indian community overthrew their boss and formed their own union. Likewise in 1986 Mari Carmen de Lara documented the formation of the independent seamstresses' union in Mexico City in response to government inaction and incompetence after the devastating earthquake of the previous year. Her film was initially designed as an organizing tool, but it achieved a critique of contemporary Mexican politics at the same time by cross-cutting official and unofficial reactions to the earthquake: government statements and television commentaries in contrast to the social dislocation and despair voiced by the seamstresses and their families. *We're Not Asking for the Moon (No les pedimos un viaje a la luna)* addresses mass cooptation, resistance, and repression under the PRI party, in power in Mexico for over half a century. De Lara's current projects are a collectively produced film regarding environmental issues and a hybrid docu-drama on Mexican terrorism and political prisoners.[19]

Marise Sistach made *I Know the Three of Them (Conozco a las tres)*, a fiction film about three women struggling together to keep a sense of humor in male-dominated Mexico City.[20] And recently Dana Rotberg has made two feature films very different from each other—a bedroom comedy called *Intimacy (Intimidad)* in 1989, ridiculing a professor in midlife crisis, and a dark fable of incest and religious evangelism called *Angel of Fire (Angel de Fuego)* in 1991. During the same period María Novaro has won acclaim for her films *Lola* (1989) and *Danzón* (1992), both concerned with the needs and desires of mothers in Mexico City today. María Novaro, if not by education or choice of production sites then at least by training and style, demonstrates a transnational practice in her work. Studying filmmaking in Mexico and receiving development resources and technical assistance in both Cuba and the United States, she exemplifies Mexican independent filmmakers who are reaching for international exchanges through cultural institutions, festival circuits, and international television programming and distribution.

For nearly two decades the most serious filmmaking in Mexico—fictional as well as documentary—has been done by independents whose financing comes from universities, popular networks, European sponsors, and Mexican trade unions. These directors are seeking alternative distribution and exhibition outlets. While it lasted, *Lafra*, a Cuban-sponsored film exchange, was the most important alternative distribution network in Latin America, providing the possibility for filmmakers from both hemispheres to see each other's work when commercial outlets ignored and rejected it. Other international networks of communication are slowly becoming viable avenues for filmmakers from Mexico, and women are exploring these opportunities. And so it is becoming possible to see even those earlier images "risen . . . from faraway times and spaces, in a black room on a white wall . . . in New York or Paris . . ." but also on a movie-mall screen or a video monitor, even in Hollywood, where they have rarely been seen before.

TRAVERSING MEXICO'S FAULT LINES

> The challenge of modifying frontiers is also that of producing a situated, shifting, and contingent difference in which the only constant is the emphasis on the irresistible to-and-fro movement across (sexual and political) boundaries.
>
> —Trinh T. Minh-ha, *When the Moon Waxes Red*

"In 1985 a devastating earthquake shook Mexico City, and the country faced both negligence and incompetency on the part of the government

in the aftermath," explained María Novaro as she introduced her first feature film.[21] *Lola* (1989), shot amid the rubble that remained largely
untouched except for graffiti, derives from various kinds of fault lines in
Mexico today: deep rifts in the socioeconomic system that produce parallel but significantly stratified spheres of living; political failures that both
provoke blame and merit culpability; and short-circuit behaviors that
reroute emotional energy or flair up in the urban setting. These structural,
functional, and stylistic "fault lines" are expressed in Novaro's innovative
film language, which employs a ludic politics that evolved with what I will
label "Eighties New Wave" cinema. We shall discover how Novaro
"speaks" this playful language in *Lola*, her first feature—how she traces
the emotional sparks of female youth subculture in Mexico City that
allow an unusual perspective on Mexican women today.[22]

Since the beginning of the Salinas de Goitari regime in 1988, Mexico has experienced 20 percent unemployment and at least 40 percent
underemployment.[23] An outward reorientation of the Mexican economy—the so-called National Solidarity Program (dependency on
transnational capital and import-substitution industrialization)—has
driven a significant portion of the population to Mexico City and to "*el
norte.*" Those who remain in Mexico are facing dramatic ruptures of the
traditional patriarchal family system. A woman often strives to keep the
father of her children in the country, difficult as it may be to keep him in
the home (let alone functioning as an economic provider, reliable care-
taker, housekeeping partner, and loyal companion.) In fact much popular
literature in Mexico today, especially in the *libros semanales*, provides
working women with models for how to keep men in the family while
they themselves keep their "freedom" in the labor force.[24] Most Mexican
women need to work to support themselves and their children, and the
unavailability of jobs, coupled with recent cuts in welfare allotments, is a
severe problem. However, should a mother manage to obtain employment outside the home, another problem presents itself: the traditional
sources of servants (historically hired even by very modest families) have
dried up. Child-rearing and housework in Mexico, alongside other
economies such as street vending and industrial homework, comprise
"hidden" economies that are represented, if at all, without the imprimatur
of official data.[25]

The "informal sector." The "second economy." "Unofficial"
employment/work. These are sites of labor that "doesn't count" only
because it *doesn't get counted*—labor that threatens to upset favorable

statistics, class and gender relations, the status quo. Not only is there hidden labor in the midst of the market place—illegal, underpaid, sporadic, minimal labor without medical benefits, pensions, or day care for children—but there is also labor hidden in the home—reproduction, education, health care, socialization, food preparation, household maintenance. Today this labor is performed often enough by single mothers and grandmother caretakers, by unofficial networks of support in the face of the state's denial of such activity as labor. But there is also other work that *is* recognized by the state, work for which women are prosecuted, work within the economies of sex and consumption—casual prostitution and shoplifting.

LUDIC POLITICS FOR A MATERIAL WORLD

María Novaro structures *Lola* within all of these overlapping and competing economies. In so doing she shares with us not only scenes of exposure, in which she casts light on Mexico's political economy, but also spaces of performance, in which she spotlights the language of resisting subjects. It is this subcultural language that brings us to the concept of "Eighties New Wave" in conjunction with *Lola*. The Mexican experience of Eighties New Wave as a global mode of expression is more visible every day as national borders become more porous and boundaries between domestic and international arenas more blurred. Mexico City has become a cosmopolitan octopus with tentacles reaching out to every pocket of postmodern culture-product on the market. But Eighties New Wave cannot simply be reduced to postmodern mass culture any more than it can be neatly correlated with the ludic characteristic of Mexico's cultural traditions.[26]

The term *Eighties New Wave* is rooted in youth *sub*culture consisting of various components and exchanges of socioeconomic, ethnic, and sexual difference.[27] To the extent that constituents of subcultures resist their oppression (even when flagging and celebrating their marginalization), they may appropriate elements of mass culture, decontextualizing and transvaluing them as new forms of cultural expression. In the last decade inscriptions of race and gender accompanied by socioeconomic oppression have been transcribed as global markers of postcolonial dislocation, but Eighties New Wave is more specific than postmodern cultural disorientation or diffusion, in Mexico or any other country. Its language is a performance of subcultural identity that evades reappropriation by others.[28] Conspicuous emblems of mass culture, worn or performed as insignia by subcultural cohorts in everyday life, comprise a flat, superficial toptext of failed consumer conformity. *At a given moment in time,* this language serves as back-talk to a dominant culture, parody by defiant subjects who endow familiar cultural objects and behaviors with new meanings that emerge only from shared subcultural rituals. This process has been termed *bricolage,* and it comprises the language of Eighties New Wave.[29]

María Novaro has herself experienced the contradictions of the contemporary Mexican economy, the reconfigurations of the family, and subcultural identity in the face of mass culture. She (and also her screenwriting collaborator, her sister Beatrice) earned a degree in sociology at the National Autonomous University of Mexico. At the age of twenty-eight, as an unmarried and intermittently employed mother of two young children, María Novaro found a job researching a documentary film about impoverished women in Mexico City neighborhoods.[30] In the 1980s she joined *Cine Mujer* and entered the Center for Cinematographic Studies.[31] *Lola,* Novaro's debut feature, can be seen in some ways as a hybrid product of both Cuba and the United States as well as her own Mexico. Novaro developed her script for *Lola* at the Sundance Institute's lab for independent directors under the mentorship of Robert Redford.[32] Gabriel García Marquez has followed Novaro's work ever since she took that script to the film school of his new Latin American Film Foundation in San Antonio de los Banos, Cuba.[33]

María Novaro's work to date consists mainly of four fiction films: *An Island Surrounded by Water (Una Isla Rodeada de Agua),* 1985; *Lola,* 1989; *Danzón,* 1992; and *Garden of Eden (Fronteras),* shot in Tijuana in the spring of 1992 and not yet released. Novaro's lens in each of her films captures a female's journeys to the exotic, both real and fantasized, which in conventional postcolonial terms may be regarded as naive flights to the repressed Self at the expense of the Other, but in this filmmaker's pursuits become fruitful ventures into the discovery of "difference," differences both between and within Mexican women. Novaro proposes that, contrary to confronting difference simply as a threatening, exploiting, or appropriating enterprise on the part of colonizing persons, we may regard it as encounters among the colonized—that rather than recognizing difference only in its pejorative prospects, whether at the phobic or narcissistic ends of the same spectrum, we may discover difference as processes of enjoyable ambivalence, as encounters that *can be beginnings*, of *learning* and *changing* through *desire.*

Whereas in Novaro's other films the female sojourner enjoys the privileges of being a visitor and emerges as a *pro*active subject, Lola, a refugee from the exploitation and abuses of class and gender, is a *re*active subject. Her reaction, however, is to participate in an alternative world of subcultural affiliations and practices, of youthful fantasies in the face of disemployment within the world market economy. Novaro portrays Lola's self-exile in a youth subculture of loss and retrieval as an articulation of alienation, independence, and resistance.[34]

OPEN WIRES AND FLYING SPARKS:
EIGHTIES NEW WAVE CINEMA

Popular culture is a relation to everyday life that is not only ideological but sensuous or, more literally, "sensation-al"; for example, filmic color and sound—vibrations of light and air upon the eye and the ear—are physically pleasurable, but they satisfy demands for pleasure before they require understanding, and that pleasure may be bitter when joined by a developed consciousness.[35] Nevertheless, in good measure our relation to the world is through our affective investments. Though this relation is formed in fragments, it suggests the possibility of a totalized sense of reality.

Eighties New Wave cinema is a popular cross-cultural style of 1980s filmmaking rearticulating any of the genres of classical Hollywood cinema (westerns, melodramas, comedies) in response to 1960s culture clashes. While the 1960s gave rise to the cinema movements most widely recognized by the label—French *nouvelle vague*, Czech New Wave, New Latin American Cinema—since the beginning of the 1980s both the popular music and the everyday practices (dress, furnishings, habits, and pastimes) of youth subcultures have acquired the term *New Wave*, owing much to the work of British sociologists Stuart Hall, Dick Hebdige, and Angela McRobbie, for example.[36] Eighties New Wave expressions have survived into the 1990s in part because it took a decade of communication for the practice to be recognized and shared globally. Transcultural cinema has been one of the more prolific transmitters of this particular "Wave," which is also not to be confused with what has very recently been termed a "new wave" of *Mexican* filmmakers (including such female Eighties New

Wave proponents as María Novaro and Dana Rotberg), who have earned the label largely for their work as independent *auteurs* of "art cinema" bringing a long-awaited resurgence of creativity to Mexican film.[37]

Effacing divisions between "art cinema" and "popular cinema," theory and practice, Eighties New Wave films draw viewers into a plethora of identity possibilities that are enacted in other arenas of cultural practice. Filmic bricolage emerges from any combination of audio/visual/narrative juxtapositions, disruptions, inversions, perversions, and appropriations of "found" (for example, from the fashion and media industries) "objects" (both tangible products and programmed responses).[38]

In this sense there is a particular perceivable style at play in this body of cinema even if it escapes genre classification. For example, characters emerge in Eighties New Wave films as transients—visitors or immigrants, refugees or self-exiles—who realign viewers not only in their displacement but in their alterity. This character/spectator alterity is usually enhanced in the films through the use of artificially vibrant color and lighting, violations of continuity editing, deadpan humor, magic and/or caution as pseudonarrative elements, and most of all, fusion music (drawing from African-American rhythm and blues, Caribbean jazz, disco, salsa, and gospel sources). In the nether world of New Wave we discover doubling and overlapping identities often arrived at by disruptions of memory. Verbal language barriers and mute tongues paradoxically become modes of discourse that facilitate and empower intersubjectivities. Class and culture collisions enter a mobile theater of camp stereotyping and kitsch commodification. All of these elements of style support a politics that engages spectators in a dynamic process of what Dick Hebdige has called *noise*—"interference in the orderly sequence which leads from real events and phenomena to their representations in the media."[39]

In her investigation of the variety of uses of popular narratives today among United States and Mexican women, Jean Franco raises three challenging questions germane to this discussion of *Lola* as Eighties New Wave cinema. First, given that the pluralism of mass culture narratives (re)produces none of the social contradictions we would presume to be felt by women readers but rather "a process of constantly changing tactics and adaptations to circumstance," she asks whether we can claim that women's internalization (or, I would argue, "popular appropriation") of mass culture has constituted new kinds of feminine subjects that conflict with older national "femininities." Second, since we are dealing with transnational phenomena, she asks whether we shouldn't ignore national boundaries and locate mass culture products within the international division of labor. Third, she asks whether women are incorporated differently into the dominant order than are men.[40]

Considering these pertinent questions, let us now turn to *Lola* itself to discover the ways in which María Novaro plays with the possibilities of Eighties New Wave cinema to bring to light popular practices of Mexican women as we may not have recognized them before. In conjuring up *Lola*,[41] I would simply like to call to the mind's eye and ear a few moments of the film, to rehearse the *modes by which* sight and sound in time may speak a language of subculture, and to recite that language as lived by a Mexican woman.

PHANTOM DANCING AND THE AURAL FANTASY

> Music is a herald, for change is inscribed in noise faster than it transforms society.
>
> —Jacques Attali, *Noise*

> Music in film covertly directs the affective responses of viewers far more than they know.
>
> —Susan McClary, *Feminine Endings*

> The cynicism of these times
> Is better than the half-truths.
> A great violence cannot be kept down
> With just a little love between your legs.
>
> Love me, love me a little,
> And I'll love you, love you like crazy . . .
>
> —Omar, with the Fabulous Thunderbirds
> "La Marcha de Zacatecas," *Lola*

(during the song, c.u. LOLA, sober, quarter-profile facing left frame, eyes cast downward, then left, then upward . . . *Mater Dolorosa*. Then downward gaze, face turning slowly to quarter-profile facing right frame, eyes cast down . . . *Pietà*).

Lola opens with a performance; or rather, I should say, with a black screen. Before we even "open our eyes," we open our *ears*. The pulsing beat of a youthful guitar engulfs us in its rhythm. Then our diva bursts through the curtain, pulls a mike out of her guitar, flings her body into the music, and guns us down with direct address—*Bad luck can be quicker than the eye*—with a crash to the floor on the "appropriate" (consummate *macho* heavy metal) phrase—*The bullet can win out over life, So much it seems a waste . . .*

But wait. Our diva is no operatic prima donna, nor even a hip "girl musician"; she's a girl, *period*. And she hasn't even been singing. Her dimple-cheeked little face has been lip-syncing (and not very "accurately"), her pudgy child-body miming the "live" performance (mediated by an audiotape recording) of a male singer.[42] The spotlight struggles to follow the five-year-old's wanton movement, her mike flailing at arm's length from her lips while she "sings"! But on the *bold* phrase, . . . *to watch the pretty women on the street . . .* she pops in, voice and all, and belts it out: *Together we are united, A little because of you and a little because of us. And again it's said we're not all the same. Because as you well know, happiness doesn't come cheap.*

At this cue another performer mounts the "stage," grabs the mike, and joins in; the camera closes in on the swaying hips of an adult woman sewn into her jeans. A voyeuristic lens? She swings her body in closed-eye reverie, strumming away on the toy guitar hardly bigger than her hands, her voice joined by the girl-spectator's: *And here we are without you, Together with all the rest, We ask ourselves disbelieving, Where the hell this bus is taking us, And where each of us gets off.* On the first "where" the camera follows the woman away from the clothespinned blanket-curtain as her *spot*light becomes a *flash*light that she shines over the "props" of their dark apartment-"set," motivating our point of view in search of her daughter. The camera pans with the roving light over a portable tape deck (the diegetic source of the music) to a scenic paper mural "backdrop" of a beach upon which the flash becomes the sun over the water, floating freely from the painted palm trees to a shiny 3–D plastic Christmas tree and the girl's toys. Then the spot of light drops off the screen *but rises again* toward the ceiling (in the form of a transitional kleiglight), appearing as two alternate but overlapping illuminations, a white full moon in a black background and a red sun in an amber aura. This "cosmic" (Aztec) duo-universe evoked in a domestic space casts its light upon the livingroom disco as a sociopolitical arena as well when the male voice, now unaccompanied by female singing or lip syncing, continues, *The enemy is invisible here, No one worthy of pub-*

lic acclaim. Here the only crime is to be alive. Here the death we all know never shows signs of life . . . of life . . . of life . . .

The cruising light in the game*play* of a parent seeking a child becomes a police light in the game*plan* of seeking the enemy. Though the visual track discovers little Ana in hiding, the audio track retrieves the male singer, her father, Omar, when the scene is punctuated by the ring of a telephone: he won't be there for the planned Christmas party that the apartment lights now illuminate on the table. The two voices of the father—singing and speaking—are like sound bites flickering between mediated presence and structural absence (Omar is rarely at home).[43] Likewise the theater "set" of a wife and a daughter appropriating and celebrating the agency of a husband and a father alternates in our perceptions with the daily "setting" of a missing person (an absent man). In turn Lola's facial expression and tone of voice on the phone reveal an auto-surveillance of the hidden enemy within—the person who allows or even unconsciously facilitates her companion's negligence.[44] This is not to say that Novaro restricts her scope to either Lola's or Ana's internalization of the conflict, nor is it to say that the conflict stops at home. With one sad mother-daughter kiss on the lips, the two "girls" take to the street, and a neon night-walk through Mexico City—past a giant dazzling sign "Fénix"—becomes a backdrop for the film's initial credits.

Lola employs several parallel scenes of media self-reflexivity. Omar's small-time band rehearsal, set in a domestic space with children playing and women cooking, suggests that his music may still be a personal and shared subcultural expression, a grassroots outlet, that has not yet been co-opted as a marketable commodity. An echo of the overall persistent use of diegetic, as opposed to nondiegetic, music in *Lola*, it serves as a fundamental interrogation of mass media entertainment in its simultaneous power, inadequacy, and exploitation.[45]

Lola stages a number of interventions in mediated performance, be that performance theatrical or social or one and the same. Imagine Ana and her father tuned into their new color TV airing an old musical in Spanish with a Mexican actor in an Arabic costume singing a take-off on the Calypso "Banana Man"—praying to Allah because he is sentenced to die for his "sin" of *machismo*—joined not only by on-stage belly dancers but also by Ana and her dad, Omar, who mime their movements. In case we should insist on distinguishing between authenticity and representation anywhere along the continuum of this exercise in kitsch, the act to follow it affords just as little opportunity to do so at the other end of the spectrum. The real mother Lola returns home and has a real conversation with the real Omar at the refrigerator door while opening a beer: no, she's not angry about spending Christmas Eve "alone with the rug-rat." In the cross-cutting, Ana's eyes roll from ear to ear; Lola and Omar kiss; Ana lies back on the couch, knees in the air, legs spread in a specular position, unconsciously miming Lola—or is it parody? The next time we see Ana doing Arabic dancing it's on the street, flipping her skirt up to "show a little doggie some tail."

Exoticism and eroticism have much to do with the ways that New Wave film expresses itself as a movement. Skeptical of both representation and its concomitant ideological inscriptions, Eighties New Wave dodges the linguistic and mocks dominant cultures with a kaleidoscopic carnival of tricks and stunts, often those of magicians or circus players who invert or pervert the dominant order, thereby inviting participants to discover themselves in new forms but also *in new ways*. Lola and Ana practice these rituals a bit more euphemistically, through dance; in their intermittent acts they both savor and mimic their own seductive capacities. But more important, they achieve a mutual outlet for romance, escape to faraway deserts and islands of the imagination where their self-expression of emotional longing—albeit, through the silent soliloquies of pantomime—deliver them from their dystopian environment.

Both the mother-girl and the daughter-woman use dolls as extensions of their egos by animating them with their own voices. A spoof of gender and colonial puppetry is enacted by Lola when she plays the Gorilla begging a dance from Ana's Ballerina at the ball, suggesting that the coy dancer accept the jungle beast as a partner. "I don't play that way," grumbles Ana, but Lola shows her how fun it can be to change the rules. Is Lola fetishizing the racial Other, displacing his voice with her own?

In fact, as is not unusual in New Wave films, *Lola* includes a silent character, in this case "Muto," Lola's comrade-in-vending, virile, supportive, speechless. Eighties New Wave, having generated its own music as a primary subcultural expression, has often used film quite ingeniously and ironically to endow the deaf, the mute, and the silent with a cacophony of language. Lola's and Ana's performative muteness can be read in multiple ways (particularly against Omar's singing voice): as disenfranchisement, censorship, resistance, but also as masking their vital, visceral, co-communication and as rejoicing in their own pleasures and identifications, their travels in aural fantasy. In any context, these are transformative fantasies they share *with each other:* in reinforcing reciprocal exchange without fear and guilt, they foster and nourish mother-daughter, or better, sisterly bonds of solidarity. But furthermore, their joint retreats into reverie are rehearsals, experimental grounds for developing and nurturing these bonds with others, "different" as they may be within histories of colonization. A fluctuating movement *between* cultures and codes of meaning (including audio, visual, and verbal)—a celebratory "choreography" of new affiliations with women far and wide as well as those close at home—adds an edge to a politics of resistance.[46]

FLASHES IN TIME, WAVES IN WATER

So far we have discussed Novaro's strategies for presenting sound and image; these are generated by and reiterate her concept of time and her approach to narrative. As a fiction film, *Lola* never tells a "story," yet there is a certain integrity to be felt in its lyrical expression and an uncanny wisdom to be reckoned with in its ludic whole. These are pleasure-effects derived from the deployment of time itself as a mediator in the experience of "events." The principle that guides Novaro in creating her playful politics is the implosion of performance with multiple layers of representation contesting each other's validity, the elaboration and random collisions of flashes in a diary rather than the consequential events of a narrative. These are so many uncontained sparks, valuable only in their erratic, fragmentary energy and manifest most of all in the private expanse of self-reflection.

The diary structure of other films has been appreciated as facilitating "a descriptive, nonexplanatory mode of representation and a transitory limning of identity."[47] These filmic modalities are integrally related to Lola's subjective experience as a worker on the run, a street vendor of clothing in the unofficial sector of the Mexican economy. In at least three separate, pronounced moments, Novaro trips the fuses in *Lola* and intervenes in the flow of energy to steal it away to Lola's dark subconscious. These occasions have to do with clothes. The very "things" by which Lola strives to earn her living exploit her, but in terms of labor and social marginalization, not in terms of self-expression.

The first of these scenes expands time by evoking a ritual of previous off-screen domestic strife; at this stage Lola vents her feelings in actions rather than words. The players are Lola and Omar; Ana is positioned as the spectator-chorus, singing her girl's songs in wry commentary, the only human sound in this scene's unspoken exchange. Omar is packing his suitcase to depart for a one-year gig in Los Angeles. Lola nonchalantly and adroitly tosses the contents, piece by piece, from his suitcase out through the open window. In extreme slow motion they float dreamily through the sky, catching on the electricity lines like so much laundry drying in the breeze—or frying on the wires. This amid the surreal thunder of an earthquake.

The second example, again expanding time in a surreal relation to the setting, establishes Lola's detachment from the bourgeois notion of clothing as lucrative, either as a commodity to be sold or as an insignia of class standing to be worn. At the garment factory where she routinely obtains stock for her outdoor clothes rack, the manager spins out the usual sales talk: "They're exclusive models. You won't find them anywhere else." His ad-hype discourse fades into the lulling drone of the electric fan, blowing Lola's hair and psyche into an empty no-(wo)man's-land of paradoxical alienated reverie. Conceit melts from masculine vanity to feminine fantasy as the clack of women's sewing machines takes over the soundtrack, itself dissolving into the rhythmic scraping of another vendor's pocket knife: with a subsequent visual dissolve this aficionado carves Lola's name in the tin shingles of the building where he awaits her on the street.

Clothes serve two purposes for Lola, physical survival and personal expression. They help her feed Ana and they let her be herself. Her denim jacket is every bit as much—and more—an emblem for her as the fashion products of her "trade" may be for anyone else, but the "more" is precisely the point, not the look nor the meaning, but the excess, the sparkly bright sequins that make it a kitschy overstatement of the prescribed role of clothing for women in a capitalist, patriarchal society. It's within this context that we are positioned as celebrants in another of Lola's rituals: shoplifting.

The film's devaluation of commodities playfully subverts the social order when the whole principle of profitability from "surplus" production (i.e., surplus *labor*) is parodied in surplus consumption—that is, consumption enacted outside of market value, a value that is thereby reappropriated as use value.[48] Lola is a rip-off artist. But worse yet, so is her daughter, who teases her mom into buying the plastic honey bear instead of the jar because "it won't break" (when Lola throws another tantrum and flings it against the wall). Ana knows they can afford it because they'll "lift" it. But in a treacherously unending moment with multiple refrains, "boon" turns to "bust" (and back again). "Products" come out of hiding from Lola's shirt and Ana's pockets over the desk of surveillance—panties, bras, candies. Ana hides sheepishly behind Lola, who announces glibly, "Now we have nothing." To avoid a legal penalty Lola wages an illegal bargain, the next in the layers of "surplus labor" in the patriarchal economy. Ana returns home to devour a juicy telenovela and TV snacks in one fell swoop as Lola "satisfies" the invasive appetite of the supermarket manager with her trade-off for a jail sentence.

In the three moments I have recalled, time is exposed by contradictions of meaning. Lola's three transgressive actions in the face of three sources of dominance—a negligent husband, a capitalist middleman, and a hypocritical law enforcer—represent her battles of production and consumption in her daily life. To shed light on these battle zones Novaro subverts the artifice with which time is usually made invisible in the projection of separate frames of film.[49] Not simply through slow-motion footage but also through the extended, elaborated, personal narrative moment, Novaro invades time with subjective experience to impinge upon the social order, and it's worth noting that her subjectivity is a uniquely feminine one in its capacity for polyvalent bonding born of female alienation in 1980s Mexico City.[50]

It's easy to see this same invasion applied to space.[51] Most of Novaro's exterior shots of Mexico City indiscreetly reveal the damage done by the 1985 earthquake, left untouched by repair or rebuilding; these shots include the juxtaposition of a government billboard slogan, MEXICO IS STILL STANDING, with a children's mural capturing the emotional experience of the earthquake itself, painted in the genre of naive primitivism over the cracks of an inadequate but obstinate "wall left standing."

Novaro also plays with luminous color throughout her film. The hypercoloration and flattening of surfaces produced by casting magical flourescent hues of light upon otherwise dreary structures does more than create a scintillating ambience of immediate stimulation. It exposes the excesses of inscribing women with exchange value based on appearance; it exposes the hyperanxiety within women to "cash in" on the Hollywood-style fashions reproduced on Mexican screens, to enact gender performances that signify consent even as the objective property relations governing them vanish in these women's daily lives. Even as such women continue to live without the same superficial beauty, luxury, and youth in their world, they *also* live without men in their households who are economically capacitated or politically disposed to perform the other side of the gender contract.[52]

If sparks and short circuits are the metaphors Novaro uses to conduct color and light as energy diffusions, water is her mode for proposing recuperation and fluid identities. Lola's bath water offers her two escapes: to drown in her own tears or to emotionally come to terms with all that the water "washes up."[53] The erotic sounds of water motivate the camera in transporting Lola to the exotic imaginary of hula, a "place" where wishes are transmitted in talking hands and swishing grass skirts. Her departure comes, oddly enough, from a rehearsal of the art of writing the letter "O" as she takes over Ana's homework assignment when Ana is not performing "up to par" according to the judgment of her school teacher. The amplified sound of sensuously dripping water motivates the panning camera from the repeated Os on the page to the waves on the wallhanging to the water tower outside (via a seamless cut), and then the camera swerves down like a giant wave along the exposed plumbing of an urban building to the tune of a ukelele and follows the water pipes to the painted ocean backdrop of an outdoor stage where dozens of little girls barely past the age of toddling wiggle their hula hips in a community Mothers' Day pageant.

With the illusion of one big swirling sway of the camera, we are transported to "Hawaii." In a subsequent parallel scene on a sandheap outside their apartment, Lola mimes Ana miming the language of hula, already a Polynesian pantomime. Once again, the fallacy of representation gives way to the primacy of the signifier when the exotic is employed in a so-many-times-removed way to structure the erotic in an economy of deprivation. Desires and pleasures take on a short-circuit vitality in a new currency of the experiential.

Ocean water poses an alternative space for Lola and her peers and her daughter, an interior "island" devoid of dominance, a utopian spa where the Phoenix rises up from her ashes, an oasis where natural light emits the primary colors of children at play, children of any age. Ana claims it as her vehicle: "If you lie down on a cloud, will you fall off?" "I guess so," Lola tells her, "because clouds are pure water and you can fall right through." Perched on a cliff at the beach, looking out over a real ocean this time, they gaze at the shifting configurations in the sky with their magical rose illumination. "What if we *did* climb onto a cloud?" Ana persists. "Well, where would we go?" muses Lola. And Ana's offscreen voice giggles, "Wherever it takes us."

LIKE A SHOOTING STAR: ANNINA AND MADONNA

> He is like a god
> She is like a virgin
> And the gods showed them how to sin
> And in eternity the two united their souls
> To give life to this sad love song
>   to this sad love song.
>
> —"Triste Canción," *Lola*

We have already seen, very early in the film as Omar performs in a night club, a close-up on Lola that recontextualizes two imposing images in iconographic history, images moments apart from each other in religious mythology: Mary's gaze upward to Christ on the cross and her gaze downward upon his body lying in her embrace. Lola's sorrowful face slides from the first pose to the second with potent but inverted resonance as she *rejects* Omar's wounds as her own. Part of Omar's attraction is his painful alienation, but it's not Omar she's worried about losing. Unlike Mary, Lola mourns over neither a man nor a son. Her loss is embodied in Ana.

Beside her playground of the exotic and the erotic as enabling of female agency, Novaro articulates an adjacent arena of inversion and appropriation, one even more ambivalent—that ever-sliding turf between grownup and child, mother and daughter. Through a metaphoric tilt of the frame, a twist of the angle, Lola's lackadaisical housekeeping becomes a whimsical emblem of protest, but her perpetual brown-bag slugging of alcohol on the street carries sharper connotations vis-à-vis the conventional wisdom: "This is the kind of mother whose child, unattended, drops objects from city overpasses," the mainstream thinking goes, suggesting one of Ana's more pleasurable pastimes. But Ana is also beyond her years; it is she who asks her mother if she has to take her skates off or wash her hands as she sits down to the dinner table, the answer being, "As you wish." In general Ana prepares her own meals. She even finds her own illumination during a power outage when Lola leaves her home alone in the evening, and she falls asleep with a burning candle in her hand.

This particular conflict, mother-as-child, is the fulcrum point of the film's see-saw. A delicate balance rather than a center of gravity, it likewise evokes a song rather than developing a narrative. The thought that she has abandoned her child moves Lola to tears. The next sequence could be regarded as Novaro's interpretation of the New Wave filmic mode of the road movie and the traveling identity. The scene parallels an initial one in which Lola and Ana stalk the streets like two girl buddies. This time Lola has flung the sleeping Ana over her shoulder like one more duffle bag. In an extended traveling shot across a predawn Mexico City, Lola enacts a solitary, self-scourging Passion Play, trekking along the streets as the camera reveals not only the extent of the city's lasting devastation from the earthquake but the emotional dislocation of its inhabitants. In a long shot against a purple sky, three columns of sneakers hang from the telephone wires like so many sacrificed youths.[54] The only nondiegetic singing in the film, that of Vivaldi's *Stabat Mater*, frames Lola's subjectivity through the duration of this physical and spiritual journey.

> Stabat Mater dolorosa,   A sorrowing mother stood
> Juxta crucem lacrimosa,   weeping beside the cross
> Dum pendebat Filius . . .   while her son hung there . . .

It is significant that Novaro chooses for her film a performance of this *Stabat Mater* played on the instruments, but not sung by the voice for which it was composed, a (female) contralto. In *Lola* it is sung by a countertenor, which now replaces the castrato (physically "neutered") voice used in the Roman Catholic Church for more than three hundred years. By writing this solo explicitly for a girl (and one with a low voice), Vivaldi himself departed from the canon of falsettists singing alto parts and castratos singing soprano parts, which erased women from the practice of choral recital. He nurtured the recognition and audibility of what was idiomatic to the female voice, ambiguous as it tended to be among the prevailing "curtailed" male voices.[55] Even so, the performance of his girl choir was restricted to "tones" through the "accursed grills" of "barred-off galleries," depriving the singers of visibility.[56] Vivaldi was an early supporter of female agency through the female voice. Why would Novaro elect a male voice in its place to frame the subjectivity of her female heroine, particularly in singing a *Stabat Mater* as she grieves over her own daughter?

Its lyrics as old as the conquest of the "New" World, the *Stabat Mater* was revived at the end of Mexico's colonial era. In the film the song, written for girls, is sung by a countertenor, an adult male voice imitating a boy soprano's voice. Novaro thereby appropriates, reinscribes, and finally displaces gender roles within the context of centuries of colonization by the Catholic church. Vivaldi composed the music for this *Stabat Mater* for the all-girl choir at the *Ospedale della Pietà*, a Venetian orphanage designed to accommodate abandoned and indigent girls by training them in music. Intermittently dismissed from his thirty-five-year-long service at the Pieta for "unbecoming conduct" as a priest, Vivaldi succeeded there in enabling scores of female performers to find and use in music what their society denied them. His pupil, Anna Giraud, also known as "Annina della Pietà" throughout her twenty-five-year opera career, together with her sister who nursed Vivaldi, traveled (in)famously with him as his life companions.

Today the "authenticity" of this voice is a matter of "keen dispute" and irresolvable ambiguity.[57] This very ambivalence is implemented as a strategy by Novaro. The castrato is the male singer displacing the female voice and visibility, but also the male deprived of the maturation of his body and his own agency as a man. In using the contemporary match of this voice (the countertenor), Novaro highlights a historically patriarchal politics of gender. But also, through the ludic politics Novaro generates in her film, the "lyric"—in music and sound, space and time—is poignantly empowered with a rejection of binary gender divisions in the singular, crisp clarity of a voice "in-between," a plaintive, disembodied, non-genderable voice bearing the strongest emotive agency in the film, carrying the most empathy and sorrow at the film's crucial moment, the low point at which a crisis of identity (as a wife, as a mother, as a woman) is closest to begging a resolution. Neither contralto (female-as-female) nor castrato (male-as-oppressed) nor falsetto (the failure of representation) but countertenor—the clearest mismatch for Lola's image in a curious mettle of mirror-match possibilities for sound, but one that paradoxically carries with it a polyphony of historical voices—provides the most starkly ambivalent, and therefore the most potentially subversive, challenge. New Wave, that *movement between* subculture and dominant culture, now oscillates between genders, defying fixity, stasis, identity. "Like an open wire," it empowers resistance.[58]

Near the end of Novaro's film, an extreme close-up slowly pans from a tropical miniaquarium to stray corn chips on a bed to Lola's and Ana's sleeping bodies tangled together. In its frame the camera catches a late 1980s poster of Madonna, evoking the first time we saw this bed and this wall—the bed bearing Omar's suitcase being emptied out (through the window) by Lola and the wall bearing a poster of his band, the "Fabulous Thunderbirds." The image of Madonna, master of provocation through the contradictions she enacts regarding both gender and representation, here supplants Omar's icon. The pin-up of Madonna, supernova of popular youth subculture, coyly displaces the Thunderbird and recalls the neon *Fénix*.

In the film's final scene Lola and Ana have traveled to the beach and stroll hand in hand to the romantic lyrics of *Si tú te vás* (*If You Should Leave*). Conventionally evoking a male-female couple, the song has already been appropriated for the communal bonding of Lola and her cohorts when introduced in the film on a road trip to the beach immediately following the *Stabat Mater*. Then the song, celebrated in the alternative, antiurban ocean setting, symbolized suffering, cleansing, and renewal in Lola's life as a mother. Now *Si tú te vás* simultaneously culminates and reopens *Lola* as the song sets the stage for an alternative "couple." Two mother-daughter sisters, Lola and Ana, embark on a bright journey of their own.

LUMINOUS DOUBTS AND FATEFUL FANTASIES

Lola surely indulges in the culturally remote (whether in the film's actual settings or in Lola's imaginary escapes) as exotic and erotic. This so-called fetishizing aspect of colonization has taken up much theoretical space among culture critics, and the film confronts topical quandaries involving all the "isms." The polysemy of Eighties New Wave film goes beyond a mere implantation of the colonizer's racism, sexism, cultural chauvinism, and imperialism, so *Lola* should not be viewed as a self-representation of Mexico's own pre-, post-, and colonial phobias.

Novaro's presentation of cultural infatuation—or at least cultural fascination—with Arabic, Caribbean, and Hawaiian rituals parodies the exoticizing practice inherent in imperialism by showing us that an attraction to "difference" can be "the same" the world over. Thus Novaro also ignites in us an empathetic identification with the sociocultural "castaways" of Mexico as she resounds their rituals of resistance. Like a mermaid, Novaro seduces us away from ourselves as inscribed by others, inviting us to swim in fresh waters. A traveler at play in the world, she extends and elaborates her own cultural tradition through fantasy and reverie. And in these imaginary and symbolic journeys (through music, dance, lip-sync, mime, poster pin-ups, and wallhangings) she brings the ludic back home—the lyric *of* Mexico to play *with* Mexico, to bear *upon* Mexico.

María Novaro animates her characters' conflicts by means of lyrical performances, the "disappearing acts" of a mother-as-child, a girl-mother, an absent father, and a grandmother-as-mother that register as sad, imaginative, tragic, and resilient by turns. Stylistic indulgence in these scenes redirects our focus to the players, not just in their blinking *jouissance* but in all that circumscribes them. Inflated stereotypes burst in the hyper-representation of Novaro's film language, and her play positions us within the very gaps and excesses—superfluity, kitsch, and camp—in which Lola, Ana, and company live their heterotopian lives. Their existence, marginal because it is structured as dispensable in their society, is projected in spaces of performance that enable us to recast the lyrical glow of the film's toptext as back-talk. *Lola* is Novaro's critique of cultural imperialism through her own self-practicing exoticism in all its pleasurable and parodic potential.

As long as a New Wave film can sustain a tenet of "difference" it may survive uncooptible. In this sense *Lola* demonstrates that Eighties New Wave cinema is rather anarchic and amoebalike, however self-inscribing and self-circumscribing it may be. The demise of its characters is their perception of identity confusion as a frustration that must be resolved rather than as an anticipation and affirmation of infinite change. When anxiety regarding identity becomes the structuring conflict of a given film (and not simply one subcultural aspect among others), thereby begging a resolution, that work lends itself readily to reappropriation by a dominant cinema discourse. The temptation to "settle" the ambivalence of identity formation in New Wave films is one Novaro bypasses in *Lola*.[59]

In the beginning of this chapter I raised Jean Franco's claims that today's transnational mass culture constitutes new kinds of feminine subjects who are incorporated differently into dominant social orders than are men. I would now like to refine her observation by suggesting that Eighties New Wave cinema may (sparked by global economic and cultural dislocation) facilitate a subversion of older national (colonial and neo-colonial) gender formations. My consideration of Franco's premises is not to suggest that New Wave practices are simply exercises of global mass culture; we have already regarded them in terms of fluctuating subcultural practices that stem from specific asymmetrical, nonreciprocal social relations. But as fluid popular cultural expressions they always risk pollution by the mainstream and cooptation by the dominant circulation of power, every bit as much as they threaten the mainstream with contamination.

Acknowledging this aspect of Eighties New Wave, we may take note that it also generates what I would call "masculine" expressions—not essentially male-*made* products, but films that tend to construct gender within the vast residue of patriarchy. Yet as we continue to experience Eighties New Wave cinema (Alex Cox's *Highway Patrolman* [1992] and Dana Rotberg's *Angel of Fire* [1993] are other examples in Mexico), we must bear in mind that each film is a composite of diverse strategies that work not within "the text" but in the fields of play surrounding it. A certain obstinate proof is to be found of the nonessentializing character of New Wave films in their multifarious modes for expressing race, class, gender, and sexuality.[60]

What I propose is that in *Lola* María Novaro employs Eighties New Wave film practice as a vehicle for her own self-expression which, while manifesting many of the contradictions of cultural imperialism, manages to playfully, flagrantly thrust them back into the face of "Empire." By further adding a gender inflection to this already unique Third World contribution, she challenges Eighties New Wave cinema to respond in its utmost potential to the needs it voices.

NOTES

1. John King, *Magical Reels: A History of Cinema in Latin America* (New York: Verso, 1990), 15.

2. Paulo Antonio Paranagua, "Pioneers: Women Filmmakers in Latin America," *Framework* 37 (1989): 129–30.

3. Paranagua, "Pioneers," 130.

4. Paranagua, "Pioneers," 131–32.

5. King, *Magical Reels*, 33.

6. King, *Magical Reels*, 47.

7. Marcela Fernández Violante, "Inside the Mexican Film Industry: A Woman's Perspective," in Julianne Burton, ed., *Cinema and Social Change in Latin America: Conversations with Filmmakers* (Austin: University of Texas Press, 1988), 203.

8. King, *Magical Reels*, 130–31.

9. Paranagua, "Pioneers," 134.

10. Burton, *Cinema and Social Change*, 203.

11. King, *Magical Reels*, 135.

12. King, *Magical Reels*, 137.

13. Marcela Fernández Violante made her film, *Whatever You Do, It's No Good*, concerning a historical political event quite parallel to the one alluded to in Miguel Littin's *Letters from Marusia*. Both features were made in Mexico in 1975. Littin, a Chilean exile, made his as an international coproduction with Italian and Greek talent; it cost eighty times as much to make as *Whatever You Do, It's No Good*, according to John King, *Magical Reels*, 137.

14. According to Marcela Fernández Violante (Burton, *Cinema and Social Change*, 202), Televisa "makes it its business to strangle any attempts at independent production for television. They'll blacklist anyone who tries it. Yet they produce all sorts of films for theatrical release. And their films do well at the box office because they are widely promoted on television."

15. Burton, *Cinema and Social Change*, 203.

16. Burton, *Cinema and Social Change*, 205.

17. King, *Magical Reels*, 141.

18. King, *Magical Reels*, 204.

19. Liz Kotz, "Unofficial Stories: Documentaries by Latinas and Latin American Women," *The Independent* (May 1989): 21–27.

20. King, *Magical Reels*, 142.

21. Novaro made this statement in a roundtable discussion at the Mannheim-Heidelberg International Film Festival in Germany on October 15, 1990.

22. My phrase is inspired by Teresa L. Ebert's provocative and engaging article, "Ludic Feminism, the Body, Performance, and Labor: Bringing *Materialism* Back into Feminist Cultural Studies," *Cultural Critique* 23 (Winter 1992–93): 5–50. According to Ebert, "ludic" feminism is more discursive than materialist, and more interested in rhetoric than in social change. Ludic postmodernism is defined as cultural politics rather than transformative politics. It concerns itself with language-effects that change cultural representations, as opposed to collective practices that change social institutions through a "resistance" postmodernism. Ludic postmodernism displaces and discredits politics as emancipation from systems of exploitation such as patriarchy and capitalism; it substitutes *jouissance*, the body, desire, and performance for critiques of theories for change. According to Ebert, "Ludic postmodernists address reality as a the-

ater of 'simulation,' marked by the free-floating *play* (hence the term ludic) of disembodied signifiers and the heterogeneity of differences" (14). Ebert believes that a ludic concept of power substitutes a logic of social contingency for a logic of social necessity. Foucault, she says, regards power as a "multiplicity of force relations" engendering "local and unstable states . . . everywhere" that produce a "plurality of resistances." Jean Franco and Michele Mattelart (see subsequent notes) would probably agree with Foucault; Novaro may well agree with Ebert. I leave the matter to the spectator.

23. Ricardo Grinspun and Maxwell Cameron, "Mexico: The Wages of Trade," *Report on the Americas*, NACLA, XXVI:4 (Feb. 1993): 34.

24. Jean Franco, "The Incorporation of Women: A Comparison of North American and Mexican Popular Narrative," in Tania Modleski, ed., *Studies in Entertainment: Critical Approaches to Mass Culture* (Bloomington: Indiana University Press, 1986), 199–220. Franco discusses primarily Harlequin novels and *libros semanales* (comic book literature).

25. See, for example, the ethnography of urban women in the mid-1980s relating to new configurations of the patriarchal family due to the informal labor sector in Lourdes Beneria and Martha Roldan, *The Crossroads of Class and Gender: Industrial Homework, Sub-Contracting and Household Dynamics in Mexico City* (Chicago: University of Chicago Press, 1987).

26. The "ludic" as a characteristic of Mexican culture can be seen, for example, in the film and cultural criticism of Jorge Ayola Blanco.

27. Much fieldwork and theoretical formulation had already been presented by the mid-1980s. See Raymond A. Calluori, "The Kids Are Alright: New Wave Subcultural Theory," *Social Text: Theory/Culture/Ideology* (Fall 1985): 43–53.

28. For a discussion of the problems this presents for the critic-interpreter, see Lawrence Grossberg, "Teaching the Popular," in Cary Nelson, ed., *Theory in the Classroom* (Chicago: University of Illinois Press, 1986), 195. It is important to recognize that spectator-participants engage in New Wave films through broader collages of cultural rituals, so that to try to reduce any one film to a single, inner, readable text is beside the point. According to Stuart Hall, a cultural symbol gets its meaning in part from the social field into which it is incorporated and the practices with which it articulates and resonates. Cultural participants access New Wave films at levels *other than* the linguistic or the ideological (the signifying and the representational). See Stuart Hall, "Notes on Deconstructing 'the Popular,'" in Raphael Samuel, ed., *People's History and Socialist Theory* (London: Routledge and Kegan Paul, 1981), 235.

29. Dick Hebdige, *Subculture: The Meaning of Style* (New York: Methuen, 1987), 133.

30. Tim Golden, "*Danzón* Glides to a Soft Mexican Rhythm," *New York Times* (Oct. 11, 1992).

31. Coco Fusco, "Dance and Remembrance," *Village Voice* (Aug. 27, 1991): 72.

32. Kevin Thomas, "A New Generation of Filmmaker from Mexico Dances into the Scene," *Los Angeles Times* (Oct. 16, 1992): F10.

33. Golden, "*Danzón* Glides."

34. A subculture is an affective alliance that embodies the accumulated meanings and means of expression through which a group of people in a subordinate position negotiates or opposes a dominant meaning system. Through collective attempts to come to terms with the contradictions of their shared social situation, these members develop symbolic resources that they or others may draw from to make sense of their own situation and to construct a viable identity that can be achieved outside of one ascribed by class, education, or occupation. While subcultures may be regarded as forms of resistance to ruling ideologies, they generally offer only temporary solutions that are solved at the cultural and not the material level. Youth culture is not concerned with transitions from childhood to adulthood, leisure to work, and lack of responsibility to fullness of responsibility, but with youth as a social difference, pleasure as a celebration inscribed on the body, and postmodernity as an orientation toward the future that reflects uncertainty and anxiousness. With good reason it seems questionable to regard youths, women, or working-class people, for example, as comprising separate subcultures derived from any of these three categories *distinctly*. It makes more sense to note the ways that these groups play out their mutual (or conflicting) relations to mass cultural practices that may imply shared popular taste. See the work of Graham Murdock and Mike Brake as discussed in Calluori, "The Kids Are Alright," 44–45.

35. Michele Matellart, "Women and the Cultural Industries," *Media, Culture, and Society* 4 (1982): 141.

36. See, for example, Dick Hebdige, "Skinheads and the Search for White Working-Class Identity," *New Socialist* (Sept.–Oct. 1981): 38–41; and also Stuart Hall, *Resistance through Rituals* (London: Hutchinson, 1976), including such entries as Angela McRobbie and Jenny Garber, "Girls and Subculture: An Exploration."

37. The new trend in Mexican filmmaking has been labeled a "new wave" by William Grimes in "The Emerging *Feministas* of Mexican Cinema," *The New*

York Times (July 31, 1993): 13, and also by Leonardo Garcia Tsao in "New Mexican Tales," *Sight and Sound* 6, (1993): 30–33.

38. For a definition of bricolage in relation to subculture, see Hebdige, *Subculture: The Meaning of Style*, 126.

39. Hebdige, *Subculture*, 90. Compare this definition with Jacques Attali's discussion of music and noise in *Noise: The Political Economy of Music* (Minneapolis: University of Minnesota Press, 1992). "All music, any organization of sounds is then a tool for the creation or consolidation of a community, of a totality. It is what links a power center to its subjects, and thus, more generally, it is an attribute of power in all its forms. Therefore, any theory of power today must include a theory of the localization of noise and its endowment with form" (6). "If an excess of life is death, then noise is life, and the destruction of the old codes in the commodity is perhaps the necessary condition for real creativity. No longer having to say anything in a specific language is a necessary condition for slavery, but also of the emergence of cultural subversion. Today, every noise evokes an image of subversion" (122).

40. Franco, *The Incorporation of Women*, 199–200.

41. *Lola* is not yet in distribution on celluloid in the United States. A vhs tape may be purchased from the Latin American Video Archive, however.

42. For a discussion of lip syncing, live performances, and recorded music—of the ideological "need" for positing a centered subject and an event existing prior to its representation—see Steve Wurtzler, "She Sang Live, but the Microphone Was Turned off: The Live, the Recorded, and the *Subject* of Representation," Rick Altman, ed., *Sound Theory, Sound Practice* (New York: Routledge, 1992), 93–94. I believe lip syncing may evoke admiration for the "heard" singer, express "fan"dom and favor for the singer, demonstrate a shared social experience among those present, and celebrate spontaneity in performance.

43. In this case the film also plays upon structur*ed* absence—the conventional code of classical Hollywood cinema usually reserved for women who, as full and autonomous persons, pose a threat to men, so are therefore not granted the filmic authority to motivate the camera, dominate the frame, or sustain their narrative voices so as to convey (their own) "valid" and significant points of view or decisive actions. In other words, the female point of view and/or action becomes a structured absence on the screen. Novaro's film subverts these conventions by endowing Lola and Anna with audio and visual agency in the filmic language and within the narrative, and at the same time diminishing both the aural-visual screen time and the narrative presence/consequentiality of Omar.

44. Autosurveillance may imply a kind of passive replication of programs of discipline and control by the individual—"learning to do it to yourself." But

Fredric Jameson reminds us that "doing it *to* yourself" also implies knowing how to "do it *for* yourself," and that such a "technology" can be used for a "collective political project of emancipation," as explained in his foreword to Attali, *Noise*, xiii.

45. There is a widely held claim, especially among Third World filmmakers, of the manipulative nature of nondiegetic music (music emanating from outside of the setting, action, or story on the screen). Consider Ousmane Sembene's "cinema of silence," which relies upon diegetic sound for its meaning and feeling, as he explains in *Cineaste* VI:1 (1973): 29.

46. One of the best theorists of this kind of sociopolitical "dance" for Third World (diaspora) women is Trinh T. Minh-ha, who writes in *When the Moon Waxes Red* (New York: Routledge, 1991), 104–105, "where they remain constantly at odds on occupied territories women can only situate their social spaces precariously in the interstices of diverse systems of ownership. Their elsewhere is never a pure elsewhere but only a no-escape-elsewhere, an elsewhere-within-here that enters in at the same time as it breaks with the circle of omnispectatorship, in which women always incur the risk of remaining endlessly a spectator."

47. Ivone Margulies, "Delaying the Cut: The Space of Performance in *Lightning over Water*," *Screen* 34:1 (Spring 1993): 58.

48. For a compelling explanation of the "play between" use value, exchange value, and commodity fetishism in the context of Latin America, see Michael Taussig, *The Devil and Commodity Fetishism in South America* (Chapel Hill: University of North Carolina Press, 1988), 17, 26–27.

49. Stephen Heath, "Film performance, repetition time; Notes around 'Structuralist materialist film,'" *Questions of Cinema* (Bloomington: Indiana University Press, 1981), 114, cited by Margulies, "Delaying the Cut," 64.

50. Mattelart offers an interesting discussion of the challenge time presents for representing women in popular culture when "pleasure poses a problem," in "Women and the Cultural Industries," 141–48.

51. The kind of "invasion" I suggest here is analogous to elaborations of sound and image I have discussed earlier in this chapter. The Thirteenth Ohio University Annual Film Conference: *Sound in Cinema* (November 7–9, 1991), presented several excellent panels chaired by Chris Straayer, Robin Blaetz, Michele Sansone, and Diane Scheinman, for example, offering new insight into gender, sexuality, and race in relation to sound in cinema. However three of the four papers chosen from the conference for subsequent publication in *Wide Angle* 15:1 (Jan. 1993) do their best to extract considerations of sound from any social, historical, or cultural context. The most perplexing of these is Joseph D. Ander-

son's "Sound and Image Together: Cross-Modal Confirmation"; the most potentially useful of these is Claudia Gorbman's "Chion's *Audio-Vision*," in which she discusses five exemplary filmic strategies that Chion identifies based on the illusory nature of audio-visual redundancy: added value; the acousmatic and the *acousmetre*; anempathy; synchresis; and the audio-visual scene (extension, magnetization, and materializing sound indices).

52. See Jean Franco, *The Incorporation of Women*, 130–37.

53. Lola might make the kinds of feminine subliminal associations—familial and social—dreamed in Frida Kahlo's bathing self-portrait, *What the Water Gave Me* (1938), given the pictorial composition and the narrative position of this sequence and the ways that they allude to the painting.

54. "Shoes hanging from city wires" is a vivid illustration of New Wave polysemy. Rather than attempting to deconstruct the ritual to retrieve a particular meaning, I suggest entertaining ethnographic testimony, which varies according to class, race, age, and nationality, at least. What follows is a range of remarks: "Performing the feat of tossing someone else's shoes (Adidas, jogging shoes, hi-tops, sneakers) over city telephone wires is a contemporary cross-cultural urban practice. Performers subvert the original owner's access to the use value of the commodity by displacing it as a fetish of that power system; they thereby demarcate new, self-proclaimed boundaries for the 'circuit' of that 'power' and appropriate that power for reinscription by participating in the playful pleasure of not only posing threats to rivals but competing in skill contests among peers"; "As a practice of youth subculture, throwing shoes on the wires suggests more than street play among opposing affiliations but less than organized gang warfare"; "Tennis shoes are good to use—all you need is shoes with long strings. . . . It means anarchy. . . . Surfers like to tag their turf along the beach strips. . . . You fling your shoes up when they get old and worn, to locate yourselves 'at the top'—it means 'We have the power.' . . . it reminds people of the 'open wires.'" My personal response to the image in viewing *Lola* is a powerful emotional "memory" of youths slaughtered in protest in Mexico City in 1968 prior to the Olympic Games. But I think that the image itself is "an open wire."

55. Stanley Sadie, ed., *The New Grove Dictionary of Music and Musicians* (Washington: Macmillan, 1980) 20: 32. Biographical information about Vivaldi is also extracted from this entry, and information about the poem *Stabat Mater*, from 18: 36–37. References to the distinct voice ranges and overlaps are in Sadie, ed., *The Norton/Grove Concise Encyclopedia of Music*, (New York: W. W. Norton, 1991).

56. Christopher Hogwood, record notes, *Vivaldi* (London: Decca Record Company, 1976).

57. Sadie, *The New Grove Dictionary*, 179.

58. I take the "open wire" as a visible and audible emblem of Eighties New Wave culture—for example, as enacted by Sinead O' Connor in live concerts in which she "plays" with this form of "uncontrolled power" in a wire bouncing on the floor of the stage, as she herself "gets down" to make her raw, scraping sounds accompanying the sparks, or as she tears up a photograph of the Pope over her head on a TV talk show to protest strict indoctrination of children by organized religion. However she is not the only female "mediator" of this energy. I am perpetually fascinated by the full range of reactions Madonna provokes—from idolatry to contempt—in popular "fan"dom and criticism as well as in the academy. I direct the reader to the immense body of fascinating work relating to her career by such scholars as Susan McClary in *Feminine Endings: Music, Gender, and Sexuality* (Minneapolis: University of Minnesota Press, 1991), John Fiske in *Reading the Popular* (Boston: Unwin Hyman, 1989), E. Ann Kaplan in "Feminism/Oedipus/Postmodernism: The Case of MTV," *Postmodernism and Its Discontents: Theories, Practices* (New York: Verso, 1988), and Sarah Evans in "Madonna Wannabe," *cineACTION* 24/25 (1991). I would also like to say, regarding my approach to *Lola* as Eighties New Wave cinema, that neither am I proposing a categorical salute to New Wave practices nor am I regarding them as unproblematic in their power potential vis-a-vis dominant systems of control.

59. *Desperately Seeking Susan, I've Heard the Mermaids Singing,* and *White Room* all insist on the sorting out or resolving of mistaken and overlapping female identities, unlike *Truth or Dare* and *Lola,* which resist such a reading.

60. To "flesh out" the body of New Wave cinema, compare, for example, the gender codes in the east-coast, southern, and western American road movies—*Something Wild, Stranger than Paradise, Down by Law,* and *Thelma and Louise,* with their subversion in *Delusion* and *Highway Patrolman*—circular journeys through the Mojave Desert and the Mexican high plains. Contrast the traditional idealizing and problematizing of prostitution in *Blue Velvet* and *Mona Lisa* with its playfully pithy demystification in *Whore.* Recall the different contexts for same-sex bonding in *My Own Private Idaho* and *My Beautiful Launderette* vis-à-vis those in *I've Heard the Mermaids Singing* and *The Crying Game.* Look at the rebelliousness without resourcefulness of women characters in *Betty Blue, Little Vera,* and *Eskimo Woman Feels Cold* with respect to the ingeniously facilitating relations of female bonding in *Bagdad Cafe, Letter to Brezhnev, The Hearse,* and *Housekeeping.* Consider the naive and inadequate gender-role reversals in *Sex, Lies, and Videotape* and the lack of agency imposed on female characters in *She's Gotta Have It, La Femme Nikita, Jungle Fever,* and *Mississippi Masala* in contrast with the imaginative out-of-gender survival skills honed in *The Nasty Girl* and *Gas/Food/Lodging.* Compare the female cult performances of *Diva* with

those of *High Heels* and *Truth or Dare*. I mention the thirty films above to show that the political scope and range of strategies for gender inflection within Eighties New Wave cinema is matched by the cultural diversity of its filmmakers, which in this list spans North America and Europe ("East," "West," and "Central") as well as Mexico, the Caribbean, India, and Pakistan, but outside of this sample stretches across all continents. For example, Japan, Taiwan, Australia, South Africa, Algeria, Guinnea-Bissau, Brazil, and Nicaragua have produced New Wave films. Female diaspora characters abound on these screens. Mira Nair from India, Flora Gomes from Guinnea-Bissau, and Dana Rotberg and María Novaro from Mexico are examples of women from Third World countries who have taken up the task of Eighties New Wave filmmaking. I draw my sample in the text from at least eighty films made between 1980 and 1993, while still referring to "New Wave" as based in the 1980s.

CHAPTER TWO

Cuban Cinema:
On the Threshold of Gender

CATHERINE BENAMOU

In Cuban director Tomás Gutiérrez Alea's film *Memories of Underdevelopment* (1968) there is a brief scene in which a panel of male, erudite, and middle-class-looking Latin American writers are discussing the role of the intellectual in Latin American society, only to be interrupted by an "anonymous" member of the audience (North American playwright Jack Gelber). Why, he demands, if they are so revolutionary, do they not allow for a more active engagement on the part of the audience? Immediately preceding this intervention, Edmundo Desnoes, author of the novel on which the film is based, has expounded on the tendency of North Americans to view all Latin Americans as "blacks" while an Afro-Cuban waiter, positioned to the left of Desnoes in the same frame, silently pours glasses of water for the panel's light-skinned participants.

This scene anticipates, in a metaphoric nutshell, a dilemma recently facing postrevolutionary Cuban cinema: have issues of difference along lines of gender, race, and sexual preference (in addition to class) been adequately addressed *within* the established institutional channels, or is there a pressing need to create more *autonomous* spaces within which diverse subjectivities and identities can be represented "on their own terms"?[1] I will be addressing the specific directions taken by women's representation in postrevolutionary film, in the hope that this will contribute toward a cross-cultural dialogue.

In any social and artistic context, the struggle toward cinematic "self-representation" for individuals and collectivities on the margins involves an interrogation of hegemonic styles and themes, as well as of the mechanisms traditionally barring access to the means of production and distribution. For women in relation to Cuban cinema, this struggle has been inextricably tied to the presence of, and the direction taken by, the revolution. Not only were there few women technicians and *no* women film directors prior to 1959, but the possibility of altering public images of women—away from the passive, stereotypical constructions in the form of mother, seductress, domestic servant—had to await the emancipatory changes in status for the majority of women that accompanied large-scale, socioeconomic transformations in the postrevolutionary era.

Cuban researchers have noted a marked increase in women's activity and expression within the public sphere after 1959, underscored by their dramatic entry into the labor force in "non-traditional" as well as "traditional" occupations.[2] To some extent, this effort at integration, together with a general push toward cultural democratization, bore an impact in the areas of theater and dance, where women gained access to positions of creative control; and in radio and television, where, by the early sixties, the depiction of women's initiatives in building a new society was replacing their objectification in advertisements.[3] By the early eighties, many of the taboos surrounding women's mastery and control over communications technology had lifted, and in television production, significant numbers of women could be found in key technical and directorial categories of employment.[4]

In the cinema, however, women's representation has followed a particularly uneven course of development.

GUNS, BUT NOT CAMERAS

The first screen references to women's concerns were articulated by male directors in fictional epics and dramas, such as Humberto Solás's *Manuela* (1966) and *Lucía* (1968), and in documentaries, like *Con las mujeres cubanas /With the Cuban Women* (1975) by Octavio Cortázar, well after women had fought as combatants in the revolutionary struggle. [Figure 2.1] At the time of their release, these films both reflected and helped to frame intense debates

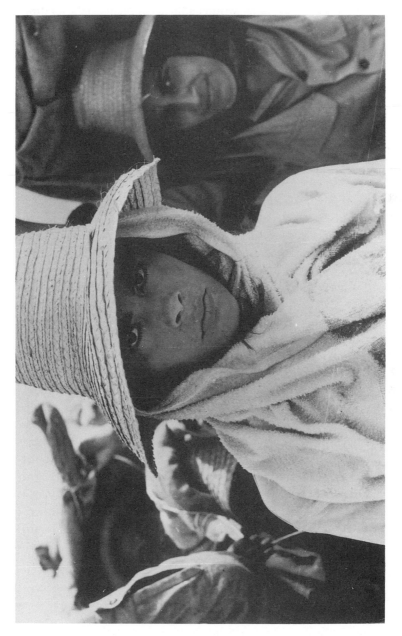

FIGURE 2.1. Actress Adela Legrá as Lucía in *Lucía*, Part III (Humberto Solás, 1968). Courtesy of Center for Cuban Studies, New York, N.Y.

over women's equal participation in the labor force, involving the social and legal definition of what constitutes "women's work" (brought to the forefront of national attention by the Federation of Cuban Women in the sixties and seventies); and, concomitantly, responsibility for housework and child care (the latter being formally given to fathers as well as mothers in the Cuban Family Code of 1975).[5] The portrayal of tensions in the domestic sphere, always shown to be linked to broader socioeconomic transformations, was especially instrumental in foregrounding the social undesirability of *machismo*, along with other "subjective" barriers to women's employment (as delineated in "Thesis Three" of the First Congress of the Cuban Communist Party).[6] Themes ranged, accordingly, from historical perspectives on women's access to the "man's world" of armed struggle, literacy, and politics (*Manuela, Lucía,* and Juan Padrón's animated feature *Elpidio Valdéz,* 1979), to men's resistance to household chores and women's activities outside the home (*Portrait of Teresa,* directed by Pastor Vega, 1979). The old romantic theme of marital infidelity was also reworked to reveal the ways in which the double standard reinforced masculine power and control inside and outside the domestic sphere (*Portrait of Teresa,* and Tomás Gutiérrez Alea's *Hasta cierto punto/Up to a Point,* 1983).

An early example of the extent to which the narratives in these films took their cue from the changes in women's lives brought by the revolution can be found in the "mirroring" of actress Adela Legrá's personal trajectory by her screen personae (*Manuela, Lucía*). Without any formal training in film or theater, she was "discovered" by director Humberto Solás while working with the Federation of Cuban Women in Baracoa in the mid-sixties; she had taught herself to read and write, much like her character "Lucía" in *Lucía's* third segment; and, prior to acting in *Lucía,* she had joined a woman's agricultural brigade.[7] At the peak of their development, these films also coincided with a surge in international recognition for Cuban cinema, and it has mainly been through films such as *Lucía* and *Portrait of Teresa* that North American and European audiences have come to associate women's quest for equal status with the larger project of the Cuban revolution.

UP TO A POINT

Notwithstanding their effectiveness in promoting women as active protagonists both within the narrative and on the stage of social change, many of these films (like much of the political discourse of the period) tended to construct women as preeminently laboring subjects at the expense of their other attributes and their intimate selves. The immediate context for change was often the nuclear family as a productive/reproductive unit (even when the change implied divorce), while the ultimate referent and protagonist for change was the national collectivity. Surprisingly, female characters were rarely depicted in positions of public decision making, and were often shown being counseled at times of crisis by sympathetic men (*Lucía*, Part III, *Portrait of Teresa*), even though the mid-seventies were characterized by the expansion of women's political leadership through the Federation of Cuban Women (in existence since 1960) and the more recently formed popular power (*poder popular*) organizations.

Alternately, films that did explore the persistence of "subjective" obstacles to gender equality in the realm of leisure, as well as work, tended to emphasize the white male consciousness as the key locus for inner struggle and revelation. Frequently this emphasis would be subtended by the formal privileging of the male protagonist's viewpoint, imprinted by means of camera placement and movement, along with his vocal presence on the soundtrack. The consequences of such a bias are illustrated in the film *Memories of Underdevelopment*. Here, the central character Sergio's confrontation with his habitual treatment of women forms an integral part of his process as a bourgeois individual within the larger dialectic of the revolution, while the display of women as sexual objects in banned North American films and in Sergio's own capers is introduced as a cinematic sign of prerevolutionary decadence.

Yet the experiences of the women who have left their mark on Sergio's life (his maid, his former wife, an "aspiring actress," his mother, a motherly prostitute, his European-born "first love") are revealed to us either in a series of reveries "authored" by Sergio, in which the sound of his voice-over narration is disjunct from silent images of his imagined or remembered interaction with them, or in sequences shot and recorded mainly from his perceptual and psychological viewpoint—and synchronized—in the narrative present. The possibility that these fragments might be assembled by way of an oppositional reading into parallel "dialectics" belonging to separately evolving feminine selves is precluded by their detainment in the audiovisual documentation of Sergio's conscious and preconscious experience (i.e., their narrative presence is contingent upon and conditioned by their ability to figure and satisfy his needs, fears, and desires); and by the fact that, tucked away into spatio-temporally separate episodes, they never phenomenally meet each other (nor are they "made to meet" through formal manipulation). The only possible exception to this rule—the masquerade that results from the donning of Laura's (Sergio's ex-wife's) cast-off dresses by his teenage lover Elena—works to underscore Laura's and Elena's differences in social class and age, rather than unite them.

With no particular agency of their own, these women-images begin to blur into an uneven, refractory surface against which *we* can detect Sergio's social background and *he* can redefine himself as a male. Even the marital rupture initiated by Laura is filtered through his grotesque (if desperate) parodying of her femininity and "clandestine" tape recordings he made of their conversations. [Figure 2.2] Meanwhile, Laura's characterization as a materialistic *señora* seeking comfort in exile dampens our expectations of her personal and political growth once she boards the plane for Miami and exits the primary narrative. Elena's ideological critique of Sergio: "I think you're neither revolutionary nor counterrevolutionary . . . you're nothing,"[8] also fails to produce a meaningful narrative or psychic rupture, and is neutralized by her apparent opportunism and willingness to buy into the moral codes and behaviors prescribed by traditional patriarchy. As a result, we are encouraged to attribute the lucidity of this remark to Elena's adolescent irreverence, rather than read it as a sign of a maturing political consciousness.[9]

The only women in *Memories of Underdevelopment* who do seem capable of articulating an emergent revolutionary discourse incorporating subaltern or feminist concerns are "off limits" for Sergio—and by extension, for the spectator—by virtue of the social and textual spaces they occupy. I am referring to the Afro-Cuban woman whose mixed expression of fear and surprise is caught in a candid freeze-frame during the film's opening title sequence, and to the woman soldier who defiantly recounts in newsreel footage the beating she received at the hands of male counterrevolutionaries during the Bay of Pigs invasion. These women are even more spatiotemporally segregated than their fictional counterparts, in that the first appears as part of a heterodiegetic prolepsis (a violent *rumba* gathering shot in hand-held, documentary style which Sergio encounters later in the film), and the second is an actual witness in court hearings held after the invasion, a heterodiegetic analepsis used in the film to illustrate an article Sergio reads in a newspaper.[10] Since they are not "essential" to Sergio's process, the women remain nameless and somewhat ambigu-

FIGURE 2.2. Sergio Corrieri in the role of Sergio parodies his wife Laura's femininity in *Memories of Underdevelopment* (Tomás Gutiérrez Alea, 1968). Courtesy of Center for Cuban Studies, New York, N.Y.

ous as signifiers of gender identity in relation to broader revolutionary change. Paradoxically, the very aspects that lend the film its potency as a form of political commentary—the fact that *none* of the characters are able to ideologically transcend their sociohistorical positioning in the early years of the revolution; that the audience is asked to identify with a bourgeois male protagonist whose personal cowardice, slovenly domestic demeanor, and political fence sitting make him progressively unlikeable; that Elena's alienated ambitions at becoming a movie star spark a demystificatory critique of an alienating type of cinema—detract from its possibilities of delivering a thoroughgoing critique of machismo focalized by its women protagonists.

Even when woman's improved status is putatively established as an ultimate "stake" within men's films such as *Lucía* (Parts II and III) and *Portrait of Teresa*, her activity is circumscribed at the level of textual construction and characterization. In some cases, a reversion may even be made to her figuration as a source of sexual/political debility or "lack," to be developed or "assisted" in accordance with the prerequisites of a male-driven, and occasionally, male-focused narrative agenda (Elena in *Memories of Underdevelopment*; *Lucía*, Part III; *Manuela*; the faith healer in *Los días del agua/Days of Water*, Manuel Octavio Gómez, 1971).

These "men's films about women" were also temporally circumscribed in their transformative potential, for, as filmmaker Mayra Vilásis has aptly observed, one finds marked discontinuities in the focalization of gender relations—even in works by the same directors—when comparing feature films from the seventies with those of the eighties.[11] More recent films have tended either to become even more lax in their critiques of patriarchy (*Hasta cierto punto* and *Lejanía*, directed by Jesús Díaz, 1985), or have replaced more complex characterizations and narrative tensions with the mystificatory and reductionist portrayals of women mandated by generic convention, such as are found in melodrama or situation comedy (*Cecilia*, Humberto Solás, 1982; *Se Permuta!*, Juan Carlos Tabío, 1984, respectively). [Figure 2.3] This refuge in the patriarchal imaginary may enter into contradiction with the combativeness (on or off screen) of the principal women actresses, and it has been complemented by the predominant absence of transgressive articulations of film form in relation to gender themes, even though such innovation may be evident at other levels of the text.

Finally, throughout the wave of "men's films about women"—from woman as emancipatory social symbol to woman as enigma or foil—the

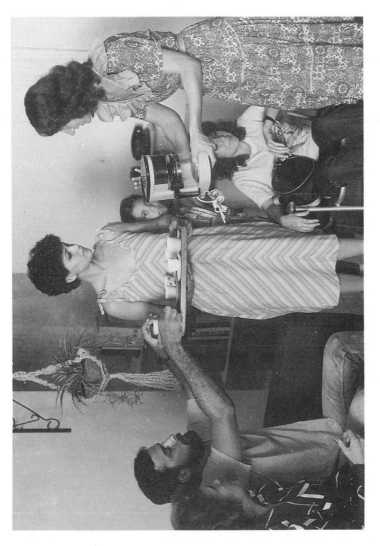

FIGURE 2.3. Beatriz Valdés as the dutiful wife serving coffee in Jesús Díaz's *Lejanía* (1985). This domestic ritual figures as a trope of patriarchy in *Mujer transparente* (segments directed by Mayra Segura and Hector Veitía, 1990). Courtesy of Center for Cuban Studies, New York, N.Y.

casting of prominent female protagonists echoes that of the male characters in that regardless of class or level of revolutionary/feminist consciousness they are predominantly white, ranging at most to light mulattoes in phenotype. Since these are the men and women who have been chosen to struggle on the screen, the issue of race as a codeterminant of women's self-perception and social treatment is significantly elided. The only explicit exceptions may be found in the work of Humberto Solás (*Lucía*, Part I; *Cecilia*) and Sergio Giral (*The Other Francisco*, 1975; *María Antonia*, 1990), all of which focus on life in Cuba prior to the revolution. Meanwhile, the fact that *all* women spectators, regardless of race or ethnic background, are rhetorically exhorted—through a primary symbolic identification with "nation" (from which that of "woman" is indissociable)—to identify with such characters mitigates against their recognition of how race has differentially affected their oppression by patriarchy, and consequently, of how they might avail themselves of alternative sources of empowerment.

SUBALTERN EXPRESSIONS

Until the early eighties, the solitary exception to the trend of films by men was the work of Sara Gómez, who, in her early documentaries, and then with her first and only feature film *De cierta manera* (*One Way or Another*, 1974–1977), penetrated beneath the surface of the uniformly national and into the realm of the subcultural. In Gómez' first documentary, *Iré a Santiago /I'll Go to Santiago* (1964), a freely roving camera strays away from colonial monuments into urban spaces intimately inhabited by the local black population. There, it pauses respectfully on doorsteps to be greeted by warm faces and proud silhouettes. By recognizing the city as much for its human resilience and hospitality as for its economic, political, or architectural legacy, Gómez makes a claim for Santiago as a vibrant point of origin where (especially Afro-)Cubans can recover their ties to a neglected cultural heritage.

More crucially, in this and in another early documentary, *Y tenemos sabor (We've Got Rhythm*, 1967), a treatise on Afro-Cuban music and its instruments, featuring seasoned practitioners, Sara inscribes herself as a black woman participant-observer in the cultural phenomena she documents. Her physical presence as a narrator and interlocutor on the soundtrack and occasionally in the frame helps convey a tone of informality, which elicits a casual, even complicitous response on the part of her film subjects, while inviting the uninitiated viewer to partake of otherwise recondite or parochial realms of experience. Gómez thus places communication at the forefront of her cinematic concerns, forging a close, seemingly unmediated bond between filmmaker, subject, and spectator that ensures the survival and evolution of subcultural practices long after they have left the screen. As Gutiérrez Alea later commented, "Sara would have liked to make films without cameras or microphones, directly."[12]

Gómez' attentions later turned to women's concerns in documentaries (*Poder local, poder popular/Local Power, Popular Power*, 1970; and *Atención prenatal/Pre-Natal Care*, 1972) and in *De cierta manera*, which, aside from being the first feature film to be directed by a woman in Cuba, was also one of very few to locate the ideological roots of machismo in the Cuban colonial and patriarchal past. Unlike many of her male counterparts, however, Gómez did not thematize gender at the expense of race and cultural identity, but instead sought to demonstrate how historically they have been intertwined.

In *De cierta manera*, Gómez once again creates an open, "readerly" text, this time through an interplay of documentary and fictional strategies that are used, on the one hand, to follow the twists and turns of romance for a socially and racially mixed couple (Yolanda is light-skinned and middle-class; Mario is *jabao*, or a light-skinned mulatto, who hails from a Havana slum); and on the other, to expose residual areas of "marginality" in Cuban society at large. [Figure 2.4] Potentially a pejorative label used by the urban middle class to designate social "undesirables" from the urban "underclass," marginality is resignified in the film to refer both to the ensemble of physical and psychosocial conditions that have prevented blacks, women, and the very poor from fully participating in *any* national power structure; and to the surviving manifestations of machismo in men's attitudes toward women and *toward each other*. By positing marginality as a form of subjectification harking back to the colonial master-slave relationship, and eradicated—along with the slums of Las Yaguas in Havana, where it has taken root—only through hard "voluntary labor" in the present, Gómez is able to show how prerevolutionary forms of behavior, expectations, and oppression can coexist with institutional, "objective" opportunities for change and an increasingly revolutionary collective "superego."

Further, by placing the couple at the nexus of a struggle with ever-widening social implications, Gómez carefully avoids placing the burden

FIGURE 2.4. Mario Balmaseda (as Mario) and Yolanda Cuellar (as Yolanda) come to grips with their own social stigmas and their differences as a couple within the larger process of the Cuban revolution in Sara Gómez's *De cierta manera* (1974–77). Courtesy of Center for Cuban Studies, New York, N.Y.

of "reform" on the socially disadvantaged, while guarding the romantic narrative against the conventional tendency toward "closure" in both characterization and narrative resolution. Various "crisis points" in the narrative—up to the end of the film—are used to reveal how men *and* women, alone *and* together, must confront prejudices and stigmas *across* class, racial, and gender lines. [Figure 2.5]

Finally, no single viewpoint can be said to dominate in this film, and, given the integral relation established between form and thematic content, this provides an additional step toward cultural and ideological "openness." The dialectical interplay of perspectives belonging to a range of characters (Mario, Yolanda, their peers, community members, "anonymous" observers in the archival segments), combined with the structural interdependence of the "documentary" and "fictional" sequences come to symbolize the cinema's special capacity for registering the dynamics of inner consciousness as well as "external" action. Even though Gómez never goes so far as to represent the personal preconscious or imaginary realms of experience, these dynamics are narratively conveyed in candid exchanges of words and gestures by the characters, inscribed within what might be termed a "micropolitics of location": perched on a hill overlooking Havana's neighborhoods in transition, Mario and Yolanda confide their prerevolutionary past selves; unwilling to date a man of a lower class (with a gold tooth to boot), Yolanda's friend Migdalia lags behind her more openminded companions on the street, then drops physically out of the frame, so that her social and physical isolation can be emphasized with a freeze-frame in another shot; after denouncing his buddy Humberto's dishonesty to the other workers, Mario does not stay in the assembly hall, but seeks the natural solitude of the street to mull over his divided loyalties to Humberto *versus* the collectivity, which has embraced new values and behaviors.

This double capacity, Gómez seems to insist, is essential for the medium to serve in any context as an effective vehicle toward self-knowledge and collective empowerment. The latter is achieved in *De cierta manera* as the spectator, continually urged to reposition him/herself with respect to the people and events on the screen, becomes caught between what Walter Benjamin would call states of "contemplation" and "distraction."[13] Film, for Benjamin, is the art form that is most likely to induce "distraction" as a mode of reception for the viewer—and, concomitantly, alienation as a condition of labor for the performing actor—not only due to the positioning of the viewer within a mass audience (even when the

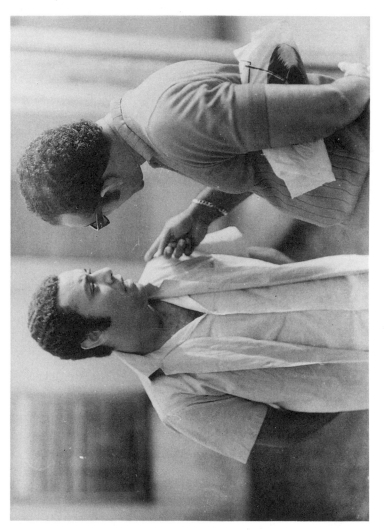

FIGURE 2.5. Mario Limonta (Humberto) challenges Mario Balmaseda (Mario) to act as his confidant in defiance of the working group ethic in *De cierta manera*. Courtesy of Center for Cuban Studies, New York, N.Y.

theater is empty), and of the performer before the refractory "mirror" of the camera, which then transmits the replicated image to unknown masses; but as a result of the intervention of the camera-editing-projection *machine,* which causes the audience to identify with the same camera (recording the image at twenty-four frames per second) that has stripped the actor of his/her "aura," and irreparably fragmented that actor's performance *prior* to its transmission.[14]

This process is disrupted—symbolically, if not mechanically—by the textual juxtaposition of professional and nonprofessional performers in the "documentary" and "fictional" sequences of the film.

Professional actors must test their social reflexes in scenes where documentary spontaneity is called for, given the direct contact they have with an intratextual audience of nonprofessionals who authentically go about their tasks. Conversely, by witnessing the "integral performance" of the trained actors in the scripted portions of the film, participating community members obtain the distance necessary from their habitual performance to gain a critical perspective on their experience of marginality. In turn, the resulting personal testimonies by the mothers of Yolanda's students, along with group debate among Mario's fellow factory workers, encourage a kind of contemplation on the part of the viewer through identification with alternatingly familiar and subaltern subject positions, while the syntactical joining together of fictional and documentary sequences encourages distraction once again, peaking at points where we see the metaphoric image of a wrecking ball swinging against slum walls.[15]

Benjamin also states that the appreciation of the aura of an art work harks back to its ritualistic use, whether religious or secular; whereas "the technique of reproduction detaches the reproduced object from the domain of tradition."[16] Again, while the narrative structure of *De cierta manera* charts the passage of the Miraflores community from ritual practice (*Abakuá:* religious contemplative mode) to socialist society (democratization of production and consumption: distractive mode) as the primary framework for the formation of gendered and social identity, the ritual forms (*Abakuá, santería,* street dancing) are reinscribed and, in a sense, preserved by their display in documentary images of life in marginal Cuba. [Figure 2.6] Thus, together with the shots of the wrecking ball, the ritual images allude to a "double movement" within Gómez' twist on the historical materialist dialectic to accommodate gender and racial concerns: modernity is beneficial insofar as it eradicates the oppression inherent in archaic social relations, but it should not occur at the

82

FIGURE 2.6. An *Abakuá* ritual, originally practiced in the area now known as the African Congo, is celebrated by Cuban men in one of the "documentary" segments of *De cierta manera*. Courtesy of Center for Cuban Studies, New York, N.Y.

expense of forms of expression that play a crucial role in the ability of Afro-Cubans (and other subaltern groups) to affirm their cultural identity. Indeed, such an affirmation is essential to the equitable representation of such groups within the new social order.[17]

The degree of innovation suggested by these two instances of contemplation-distraction found woven into the film's mode of construction comes into relief when compared with similar scenes in Cuban men's films that treat gender relations: together with the narration and *guaguancó* music, the images of street dancing develop much further the kind of extradiegetic commentary (violence stemming from masculine competition and staking of territory) that is only alluded to in the opening "murder at the *rumba*" scene in *Memories of Underdevelopment;* while the workers' debates around Humberto's truant behavior anticipate the public, largely male debate over Teresa and Ramon's dispute at the end of *Portrait of Teresa*—without impinging on the agency and participation of the feminine protagonist. More importantly, the textual openness and shifts in spectator response in *De cierta manera* work to incorporate gender and race into a problematic that has remained at the heart of revolutionary filmmaking in Latin America, and has only adequately been addressed in Cuba (without the gender component) by Julio García Espinosa's *The Adventures of Juan Quin Quin:* that of stimulating a self-reflexive critique while providing effective modes of popular identification for the audience.[18]

It was not until the early eighties, nearly a decade after the initiation of this project and Sara's death,[19] that women's filmmaking reemerged at the ICAIC (Instituto Cubano del Arte e Indústria Cinematográficos), almost wholly in the form of short documentaries. With the exception of Marisol Trujillo, who worked as a scriptwriter prior to breaking into production with two documentaries in the late seventies, the women who made these works belong to what filmmaker Rebeca Chávez has referred to as a "third generation" of documentary makers, who were given the "director's chair" as part of an attempt to bring new creative blood into ICAIC under the administration of Julio García Espinosa.[20] The time gap in women's production, as well as the form taken by the resurgence, can be attributed mainly to the hierarchical process of training and initiation within ICAIC, which remained in force throughout the eighties. After learning skills "hands on" as apprentices under established directors, aspiring cineastes would eventually go on to direct short films—usually documentaries—and, in a few select cases, would be admitted into the prized realm of feature-length fiction.

Although the importance of documentary should not be underestimated in the Cuban context, given its historical effectiveness as a form of popular education, coupled with its early primacy as a vehicle for aesthetic and thematic experimentation, this system has had a "funnelling" effect (*la ley del embudo*) where the gendered division of labor is concerned. Compared to men, women have not only had more difficulty in obtaining the backing to direct longer fictional works, but have continued to occupy the more traditionally "female" positions as editors, screenwriters, and continuity people.[21] The screen credits of the eighties are punctuated with the names of Gladys Cambre, Natasha Tola, and Miriam Talavera in the role of editor; and of Mayra Vilásis and Miriam Talavera as screenwriters under the names of male directors. Finally, the most feminized area of production—that of documentary—has increasingly played "second fiddle" to fictional works, receiving smaller and tighter budgets, along with less promotion and critical attention than the latter, at home and abroad.[22] This has had the overall effect of curtailing the visibility, as well as the institutional power, of feminine talent.

Other factors delaying the accession of women to the field of film production include the absence, for many years, of opportunities for formal film study outside ICAIC in Cuba, along with the need for a costly technical infrastructure and proximity to laboratory and distribution facilities, which have contributed to the concentration of production in centralized state institutions (with varying degrees of autonomy) located in the nation's capital.

The new harvest of women's documentaries in the eighties brought the exploration of personal, subjective experience to new prominence, without abandoning references to the relationship (whether harmonious or tension riddled) of the individual to the broader collectivity. The great majority of these films take the lives of distinguished Cuban women in politics and the arts as their central subject, as if to emphasize the role of film in unearthing what has been taken for granted or left "invisible" within the historical record: they involve a filtering of *cine rescate* (cinema of historical retrieval, to use Michael Chanan's term)[23] through the lens of gender. Here, gender is treated as both a controversial "issue" (the context provided by the filmmaker) and one register of identity interacting among others (the responses of the film subject).

Echoing Gómez' example, the strategies used by these films to reveal the constraints and emancipatory strength surrounding the femininity of each woman recall three of the precepts delineated by Julio García

Espinosa in his proposal for an "imperfect cinema."[24] Two of these—the choice of protagonists who "struggle" and the narrative engagement of the spectator in the "process" whereby a problem (collective, as well as personal) is exposed and confronted, as opposed to the recounting of an "analysis" and solution that have been elaborated a priori by the filmmakers[25]— are exemplified in the depiction of *performance* as a means whereby women can remake their own images, not by cinematic sleight of hand but through the hard work of a de/reconstruction of roles and inner self-questioning. In *Mujer ante el espejo/Woman Facing the Mirror* (Marisol Trujillo, 1983), we see classical ballet dancer Charín grappling with the changes her body undergoes during and after pregnancy, accepting her absence from the stage, and revising her own idealized images of herself in performance once she returns. In *Yo soy Juana Bacallao/I Am Juana Bacallao* (Miriam Talavera, 1989), skillful cross cutting shows the varied personae of the singer/performer both alone at a beauty parlor and before a public audience. In contrast to the characterization of lead actress Daisy Granados in *Portrait of Teresa*, the posture in these films is not one of resolution and steady combativeness in society at large, but of hesitation and discovery on the threshold between public and private spheres of interaction.

Upon being represented on the screen, this very notion of "process," of a revolutionary artist/subject in-the-making, works to extinguish the conventional boundaries between the proscenium and the flow of the "nonperformative" quotidian so that the links between challenges faced by the performer experienced in both spheres become visible (and comprehensible) to spectators in the society at large.[26] At this point, the "process" comes to intersect with a third precept of imperfect cinema: that of an active exchange and redistribution of power in the triangular relation obtaining between filmmaker, subject or character, and audience (or interlocutor).[27]

In these films, one sees an expansion inward from the *cine testimonio* (a variant of documentary cinema, based on the testimonial genre in revolutionary literature), in which both camera and sound recorder are used to elicit and bear active witness to the character's narrative, delivered in their own words; to what could be termed *cine retrato* (cinema of portraiture), in which a feminine subjectivity becomes doubly inscribed through the positioning of woman as "speaking observer" in relation to woman in the more traditional role of "specular object."

This positioning may take the form of a dialogue between filmmaker and subject, with the filmmaker visibly present within the frame (reiterating Gómez' procedure in her documentaries), as in Marisol Trujillo's *Motivaciones /Motivations* (1988) and Rebeca Chávez' *Castillos en el aire/Castles in the Air* (1986). One also finds a repeated reliance on personal modes of address on the soundtrack—even when filmmaker and subject do not actually share the same space-time—as exemplified in the use of the second-person singular in voice-over commentaries to address Marilyn Monroe in *Oración/Prayer* (Marisol Trujillo, 1983) and Winnie Mandela in *Con luz propia/In Her Own Light* (Mayra Vilásis, 1988).

An aura of intimacy with the film subject is further cultivated on the visual track with the probing of the camera into very private spaces: Juana Bacallao is shown in extreme close-up in an unglamorous face mask; Charín is shown doing her laundry; and in *Paisaje breve/Brief Landscape* (Marisol Trujillo, 1985), the portrait of the artist includes the roaming of the camera around a disheveled room to pause on items of apparently incidental significance, such as a pet cat. In Rebeca Chávez' films, history is reconstructed with found materials (family photos, archival footage, and newspaper headlines) that chart personal as well as public remembrances (*Cuando una mujer no duerme/When a Woman Doesn't Sleep*, 1983; *Rigoberta*, 1985; *Una más entre ellos/One More amongst Them*, 1989).

The syntactical links between shots and scenes in these films— whether their material content is derived from homo- or heterogeneous sources—mark a departure from the principle of poetic collision and resonance advanced by documentarist Santiago Alvarez in his moving word-image collages. Instead, editing seems to be based on a principle of interweaving, emphasizing contiguity between spaces and actions. In Trujillo's and Talavera's portraits of artists, domestic and social spaces are welded together into a spatial continuum through the sustained use of music or the artists' own voices on the soundtrack, underscoring the equal weight these spheres have in shaping their growth and self-affirmation. In the "political" portraits by Chávez and Vilásis (of Rigoberta Menchú, Tamara Bunke, and Winnie Mandela, respectively), the contrapuntal use of the female voice, archival images, and music drawn from different spatiotemporal contexts emphasizes the historical connection between the protagonists' evolving sense of identity and their national arenas of struggle, without losing sight of the affective influences on their inner-developing consciousness.

Together, these strategies promote both a Brechtian distancing of the spectator from the screen subject and the formation of a free-floating, identificatory (or, at least empathetic) bond. Thus, a feminine line of communication is set up, while the conventional mechanisms favoring the idolization or fetishization of the performer/protagonist and the disempowerment of the female spectator are avoided. Finally, since the inscription of the filmmaker always occurs in the context of a dialogue, it does not lead—as in many of the male-derived narratives—to the imposition of an authoritative voice: the spectator is left to ponder the protagonist's choices, explore the nuances in their representation, and arrive at his/her own conclusions.

THE DIALECTICS OF MACRO- AND MICROPOLITICS

Should one dismiss these women's representations as a complementary "ying" to the masculine "yang" of Cuban films about women, positing their focus on the experience of historical individuals as addressing one "half" of the official dichotomy (set up by the FMC) between "objective" and "subjective" influences on women's status in Cuba? No matter how centered around "intimacy" as a chosen space for women's communication and growth, one can hardly conclude that fundamental conflict exists between the gender politics of the "women's wave" and a prior commitment (on the part of woman filmmaker and subject) to broader social concerns. In most films, one finds the larger context of the revolution figuring as a "given," regardless of whether one finds that context explicitly referenced as it is in the "men's films." Off screen, moreover, this area of film practice tends to be defended as a "front" to be fought within a larger struggle to decolonize the screen, taking its cue from the organized political efforts to improve the status of women, rather than an oasis of personalized, politically noncommittal expression.[28]

This extra- (if not intra-)textual tendency to broaden the political agenda might be traced to an identification with Cuba's shared plight as a Third World country, in which, to use Mayra Vilásis' words,

> confronted with a systematic attempt to sterilize and defamiliarize the richness, diversity and authenticity of Latin American culture, the search for, and strengthening of, our national and continental identity becomes our only mode of existence and subsistence, combat and labor.[29]

It might also help to explain the absence of a pointedly "feminist agenda," when considered with respect to women's film practice in the

United States, as Coco Fusco has noted.[30] Any such comparison, how-ever, must take into account the very different institutional contexts in which the two bodies of filmmaking emerged. Women's films in the United States have tended to be independently produced (there is still a dearth of women directors in Hollywood), and their survival has depended partly on the extent to which the director can assert herself as an "author" in the alternative marketplace; whereas in Cuba, as I men-tioned earlier, women's filmmaking has historically developed within one of the most centralized cultural institutions, and has been sustained, where possible, by a long-term effort at gender reform that has perme-ated all social sectors.[31]

At the same time, the discourse around gender in these films cannot simply be attributed to, or subsumed within, any official state policy, just as the mementoes and intimate spaces represented in them do not have a "place" outside the experience of the individual subject portrayed. When closely compared to the "men's films," the films in the "women's wave" appear as a truly emergent form of discourse around not just gender, but the formation of a new revolutionary identity on the one hand, and of a new film aesthetics, on the other.

Occupying a central position within the national spheres of both production and reception, the feature-length films by men in the late six-ties and seventies filtered the terms of then-hot debates over gender equal-ity (indeed, how could they not?) into plots that integrated women as his-torical protagonists into a "master narrative" of the revolution. Through the development of women characters that, whether socially regressive or progressive, projected unambiguous role models as national cultural "types" (e.g., woman as *sister-combatant*), the gender problematic—at least for women—thus came to be reinscribed within the realm of the national and ideological.

By contrast, the short documentaries by women, coming on the heels of major legislation and the center-stage debates, and elaborated at the margins of the film institution, were able to loosen and even break the "necessary" synecdoche character-collectivity/woman-nation, and offer in place of the resulting typage a more particularistic vision of the challenges facing women, which, paradoxically, allowed for a broader definition of social identity to include signs of racial and ethnic difference (Rigoberta Menchú's *Quiché*; the Yoruba ritual in *Yo soy Juana Bacallao*; the refer-ences to *Abakuá* in *De cierta manera* and *Buscando a Chano Pozo/Looking for Chano Pozo*, by Rebeca Chávez, 1988). Instead of a ready-made ideology, the references in the space-time of the films to "imperfection" and "hesitation" (in some cases used to demystify female public figures) have called attention to the contradictory forces at work in the process of subjectification. For instead of focusing on the conflict within an individual *self* (as mainstream versions of feminist ideology would have it), they worked to expose how the woman subject is variously "produced," while giving her—protagonist *and* viewer—the agency to produce *her*self in alignment with or against dominant models of gender behavior.

What is at stake, then, is not only the articulation of personal and public expression as distinct "fronts of action" in the search for gender equality, but a qualitatively different notion of subjectivity itself, one that acknowledges, as in Félix Guattari's definition, that it is "essentially social, and assumed and lived by individuals in their particular modes of existence," while containing the possibility for a process of "singularization" to take shape—"a way of rejecting all pre-established forms of codification" through the reappropriation by the individual of the different registers on which their subjectivity has come to be experienced.[32] As these films show us, this reappropriation may take many different forms, and, given their emphasis on process, the tensions it creates between the social superego and the deviant vectors of desire and identification in the individual subject may never be resolved. This is so as much for a character like Mario in *De cierta manera*, who is trying to abandon old, machismo-based codes of social conduct to pave the way for an egalitarian love relationship and active participation in a workers' society, as it is for his buddy Humberto, a "socially regressive type," who relies on the code of male honor to protect his freedom to philander while bolstering his possibilities of loafing on the job.

The priority given to subjectification over ideology also leads to the violation of certain boundaries concerning "realism" as the chosen aesthetic for political narratives. Paradoxically, we do not find these boundaries violated as forcefully in many of the men's fiction films about women. The need to experiment has led, in the work of Marisol Trujillo and others, to the adoption of fictional techniques within the documentary framework, "asking the person giving the testimony to internalize his/her memory—which is an unconscious form of acting."[33] In turn, the exploration of the feminine imaginary, together with the documentary framework, has permitted the manipulation of emergent forms of identity through *personae*, avoiding the fixity of characters or the public constructions of historic individuals.

CHANGING THE RULES OF THE GAME

Two developments since the mid-eighties may have alleviated the above-mentioned infrastructural obstacles to women's productions in Cuba, notwithstanding the extreme economic pressures on the nation as a whole. First, with the founding in 1986 of the Escuela Internacional de Cine y Televisión (EICTV) in San Antonio de los Baños under the initial directorship of veteran Argentine documentary maker Fernando Birri, a space was provided outside Havana where young Cubans could study film production alongside students from other Third World countries. Even though the school was created less in response to the need of Cubans for diversified training in film than as part of a broader effort to stimulate the growth of autochthonous, independent, socially critical filmmaking ("New Latin American Cinema") on a continental scale, the school provided a context in which students, regardless of nationality or gender, could gain direct access to all aspects of fiction filmmaking, while having the opportunity to sharpen scriptwriting skills in a laboratory setting.[34]

Second, the restructuring of production at ICAIC away from the hierarchical "clusters" beneath individual directors and toward more heterogeneous, collectively run working groups has been working in the nineties to remove the structural distinctions and power differential between old and new generations—and to a lesser degree, between directors of different generic persuasions—that have promoted inequality across gender lines. Although these groups have remained identified in the aggregate with the work of more seasoned *auteurs* such as Gutiérrez Alea and Solás, the latter have had to submit their ideas at various stages of production to group criticism, while, conversely, newer film workers at ICAIC have had unprecedented input in creative decision making and in the setting of production agendas.[35] Like the effort to promote new directors in the early eighties, this reorganization was carried out under the leadership of Julio García Espinosa at ICAIC.

Some of the fruits of the foundations laid by these initiatives, as well as of the innovations in viewpoint, film portraiture, mode of address, and political discourse around gender exhibited in the "women's wave," are found crystallized in the anthology of fictional shorts by both men and women directors and screenwriters titled *Mujer transparente/Transparent Woman* (1990).[36] In its portrayal of the trajectory of women's struggle for equality and self-realization, the film oscillates between a kind of "memories of underdevelopment" focused on mature, women protagonists

("Adriana," written and directed by Mayra Segura, about an elderly woman whose lonely moments in later years are filled only with fantasies of marriage and servitude to men; and "Laura," written by Osvaldo Sánchez and Carlos Celdrán and directed by Ana Rodríguez, a bittersweet recollection of a middle-class woman's youth and life choices in the Cuba of the sixties, which even "quotes" the same documentary footage of Cubans leaving the airport for Miami used in Gutiérrez Alea's *Memories of Underdevelopment*); and the elaboration of emergent feminine identities that come into direct conflict with the gender—and by extension, the social—status quo ("Isabel," written by Tina León and directed by Hector Veitía, about a disgruntled middle-aged wife and mother, who finds little recognition at home for her achievements as department head in a government agency; "Julia," written and directed by Mayra Vilásis, about marital infidelity and a woman's decisions about when and when not to satisfy sexual desire; and "Zoe," written by Osvaldo Sánchez and Carlos Celdrán and directed by Mario Crespo, depicting a young school dropout who has chosen painting as a way of achieving autonomy and "singularization" for herself as a woman).[37]

Linking these five episodes is the use of voice-over narration to "transparently" enunciate the female protagonists' inner desires, memories, and reflections over images depicting the protagonists' actions, which are frequently more ambiguous and always in a disjunctive relationship to the narration. Not only does this work to shatter any sense of spatio-temporal unity, so that the portrait of femininity is symbolically dephased between lived and imaginary, regressive and emancipatory registers throughout, but it splits the viewpoint along a syntagmatic axis between aural-"subjective" and visual-"objective" spheres of observation, allowing the viewer, again, to participate in a complex process of confronting problems that are never sealed by narrative closure in any of the episodes. Further, the lighting style throughout the film is predominantly that of chiaroscuro, drawing us into the contemplative, meditative mood of each protagonist (we strain to discern objects and physical features that are lost in shadow). On the one hand, this effect contradicts the "transparency" of the narration; on the other, it is symbolically ruptured at two points (the endings of the "Julia" and "Zoe" episodes) by the sudden, deliberate overexposure of the entire frame ("distraction" for the spectator, "demystification" for the protagonist). Finally, as one of many devices impeding the self-containment of the five episodes—and by extension, narrative closure and the reinforcement of individual authorship—the repeated reference to the "habitual performance" of serving coffee to one's husband/master ("Isabel" and "Adriana") not only calls attention to the structuring of gender relations in the national culture of everyday life, but serves as a "gauge" against which the emancipation of the protagonists can be measured.

While it does not problematize the intersecting (and, from a sociological perspective, inseparable) issues of class and race along with that of gender, this episodic feature film clearly could not have been produced outside of a collaborative framework in which the more subtle forms of women's oppression and dissident expression could be explored, along with new modes of representation (building on the work of women cineastes previously mentioned).

Mujer transparente stands as a testament to the fact that, even though the "men's" and "women's" films have been referred to in this chapter as constituting historically and aesthetically distinct bodies of work, one cannot account for their differences solely on the basis of the gender (or other essential, identifying marker) of their makers. The documentaries by men of the "third generation" (such as *Mamá se va a la guerra/Mama Goes to War*, by Guillermo Centeno, 1984, and *Campeonas/Champions*, by Oscar Valdés, 1988), that focus on women's postrevolutionary experience while sharing some of the formal characteristics (if not ideological thrust) of the women's wave, only reinforce this assertion.

Instead, one must look to the point where access to the medium and aesthetic innovation have intersected—at the implications of documentary production, located at and beyond the margins of the institution, and produced by first-time directors, students, and aficionados with scant time and resources—for the horizon of debate and change. If the singularization of these filmmakers—black, white, and mulatto men and women—working within various institutional constraints has rarely led to the open representation of and appeal to sexual desire, even in the sheltered space-time of the marginal screen imaginary; and if their textual politics has not led to women's full passage into positions of cinematic responsibility, one is encouraged to await the cumulative effect of the restructuring of production at ICAIC into collective working groups, of the introduction of small format video, and of the references to alternative forms of sexuality in the new *cine mumusa*[38] produced by students at the Escuela Internacional de Cine y Televisión (EICTV). Such new strategies and approaches may not only enable the thematization of subjects once taboo in Cuban film and video, as in the explicit references to homosexual desire in Alea and Tabío's *Strawberry and Chocolate* and Niurka Pérez's video portrait of artist Zaida del Rio (*Zaida*, 1993). Such practices may also prompt a reevaluation of the work of prominent men and women directors whose sexual positionality, never explicit in the past, might now be seen, by way of queer theory and other critical lenses, as unmistakably informing their preoccupation with and figuration of gender relations on film.

NOTES

Briefer versions of this chapter have appeared under the title "Women's Interventions in Cuban Documentary Film," in the exhibition catalogue *Cuba: A View from Inside: Short Films by and about Cuban Women* (New York: Center for Cuban Studies, 1992), 7–11; and under the same title in *Trasimagen* (Otoño-Invierno, 1993), 93–97.

1. Postrevolutionary film history has witnessed the emergence of at least three Afro-Cuban directors—Sara Gómez (d. 1974), Sergio Giral (now living in exile), and Gloria Rolando—as well as film editors Nelson Rodríguez and Miriam Talavera (also a director of shorts). Sexual preference is the theme of Tomás Gutiérrez Alea's *Chocolate o Fresas* (1994); while ICAIC filmworkers Ivan Arocha and David Hernández collaborated with videomaker Kelly Anderson on *Looking for a Space/Buscando un Espacio* (1994), a documentary on the same subject. For an interesting characterization of the national politics surrounding sexual orientation in Cuba, see Anderson's chronicle of the collaboration in *Felix* 2 (Spring 1992): 66–69, 127.

2. In 1953, 86 percent of all Cuban women worked *inside* the home, whereas by 1979, 36.7 percent of married women and 24.8 percent of women in "free unions" were engaged in labor *outside* the home. (Although not located, the percentage for single or divorced women is probably much larger.) These figures are based respectively on the 1953 Cuban census and on systematic studies conducted at the national level, both of which are cited in Josefina Zayas and Isabel Larguía, "La Mujer: Realidad e Imagen," in *La Mujer en los Medios Audiovisuales: Memoria del VIII Festival Internacional del Nuevo Cine Latinoamericano* (Mexico, D.F.: Coordinación de Difusión Cultural, Universidad Nacional Autónoma de México, 1987), 62 and 77.

3. For women's participation in the other arts, see Margaret Randall, *Women in Cuba: Twenty Years Later* (New York: Smyrna Press, 1981), 107–21; for changes in radio and television programming, see Zayas and Larguía, "La Mujer," 68–69, 72.

4. See the table in Zayas and Larguía, "La Mujer," 90, which indicates that by 1981, 39 percent of producers, 32 percent of scriptwriters, 76 percent of editors, and 13 percent of directors in Cuban national television were women.

5. The legislation and political problematization of these issues are discussed in detail in Randall, chapters 1 and 6, and appendix 1. See also Marjorie King, "Cuba's Attack on Women's Second Shift, 1974–1976," in *Women in Latin America* (Riverside: Latin American Perspectives, 1979), 118–31.

6. The full title of this thesis was "On the Full Exercise of Woman's Equality"—*Sobre el Pleno Ejercicio de la Igualdad de la Mujer* (Havana: Departamento de Orientación Revolucionaria del Comité Central del Partido Comunista de Cuba, 1976)—and it incorporated the findings of the Second Congress of the Federation of Cuban Women in 1974.

7. Teresa González Abreu, "Monólogo de Manuela," interview with Adela Legrá in *Cine Cubano* 109 (1984): 69–71. The FMC-ANAP (National Association of Small Farmers) Mutual Aid Brigades were established in 1966 to help rural women become active outside the home, while increasing the rural labor force at critical moments in the agricultural cycle. These brigades became extremely instrumental in the drive to increase the sugar harvest by 1970. See Randall, 58–59.

8. The original dialogue in Spanish is "*Creo que no eres revolucionario ni gusano; nada, no eres nada.*" Elena is the most tangibly real of the female characters in that she forms part of Sergio's narrative present (i.e., the primary narrative) and actually responds, albeit hesitatingly, to his advances.

9. This is not to underestimate the degree to which, as Brazilian filmmaker Ana Carolina has suggested, this kind of adolescent energy in a female protagonist can act as a catalytic force for change with regard to the patriarchal order.

10. According to Shlomith Rimmon-Kenan, who builds on the terminology developed by narratologist Gérard Genette, a "heterodiegetic prolepsis" is a "narration of a story-event at a point before earlier events have been mentioned" that refers to "another character, event, or story-line"; whereas a "heterodiegetic analepsis" is a textual segment that "provide[s] past information . . . about another character, event, or story-line." See Shlomith Rimmon-Kenan, *Narrative Fiction: Contemporary Poetics* (London: Methuen, 1983), 46–47, 49. Since these women's paths never cross phenomenally with Sergio's (he does not *notice* the Afro-Cuban woman when this scene is repeated later in the film, and he was not physically present at the Bay of Pigs hearings), they also occupy an extradiegetic space in relation to the primary narrative, although the ideological potential of this positioning is never fully explored by Alea.

11. See Mayra Vilásis, "La mujer y el cine: apuntes para algunas reflexiones Latinoamericanas," in *La mujer en los medios audiovisuales*, 56.

12. Tomás Gutiérrez Alea, quoted in "Tribute to Sara Gómez," in *Cuba: A View from Inside: Short Films by and about Cuban Women*, 20. The importance to Sara's shooting techniques of proximity to the subject and immersion in the world being filmed have also been commented on by Cuban photographer Marucha Hernández, *Cuba: A View from Inside*, 18.

13. Benjamin uses these terms to refer to the fundamentally different modes of reception, or consumption, corresponding to two historically distinct phases in the production and circulation of art: one in which individual viewers contemplate, or allow themselves to be "absorbed" by individual works, which, if they do not constitute "original" creations in and of themselves, at least bear a traceable relationship to an original, thereby emitting an aura of authenticity; and one in which the aura is lost due to the creation of the work through a process of mechanical reproduction and its intended diffusion to a mass audience: the viewer can only absorb the work in a distracted state. See Walter Benjamin, "The Work of Art in the Age of Mechanical Reproduction," in Walter Benjamin, *Illuminations*, ed. Hannah Arendt (New York: Schocken Books, 1969), 220–23, 238–40.

14. See Benjamin, "The Work of Art," 228–31.

15. "The distracting element of [film] is . . . primarily tactile, being based on changes of place and focus which periodically assail the spectator." Benjamin, "The Work of Art." 238. *De cierta manera* thus embodies and elicits at the level of the text's *narrative construction* responses that Benjamin linked only to the "external" or mechanical characteristics of the medium, without referring to the possible impact of variations in narrative structure, formal properties, or content.

16. Benjamin, "The Work of Art," 223–24 and 221, respectively.

17. I take strong exception here to those who have read the denunciation of machismo in association with the *Abakuá* male "secret societies" in the film's archival segments as a Manichaeistic condemnation of Afro-Cuban religious practices as counterrevolutionary. There are many other types of denunciation in the film (some are directed even at the state apparatus), as well as sympathetic treatments of Afro-Cuban culture, for example, in the scene where community dwellers are shown worshiping Yoruba deities (*santería*), and in the symbolic, contrapuntal use of "feeling" and *guaguancó* music on the soundtrack. See Osvaldo Sánchez Crespo's comments on the latter in "The Perspective of the Present: Cuban History, Cuban Filmmaking" (*One Way or Another* by Sara Gómez), in *Reviewing Histories: Selections from New Latin American Cinema*, ed. Coco Fusco (Buffalo: Hallwalls Contemporary Arts Center, 1987), 204.

18. Refining Benjamin's notion of "mass art" along sociopolitical lines, Julio García Espinosa in his essay, "For an Imperfect Cinema," distinguishes between "popular art," in which the barriers between those who produce and consume, and between art and other activities, are eradicated; and "mass art," in which the few produce—and decide—for the many, and in which art is produced and circulated as a segregated arena of activity. Only the former can help develop the characteristic taste and identity of a given people. See Espinosa in Fusco, ed., *Reviewing Histories*, 170–71. Clearly, *De cierta manera* exhibits a recognition of the notion that only through popular art can issues around race and gender identity within the national sphere be fully addressed.

19. Sara Gómez did not live to see the completion of *De cierta manera*, the editing of which was completed under the supervision of Tomás Gutiérrez Alea, Julio García Espinosa, and assistant director R. López. For some critics, this has thrown the authorship of the film into question, even though Gómez left explicit instructions as to how she envisioned the completed text.

20. The new directors include Rebeca Chávez, Miriam Talavera, and Mayra Vilásis. García Espinosa, himself a filmmaker and film theorist, advocated mechanisms permitting both the revamping of the power structure and the kinds of films produced at ICAIC throughout his administration as executive director, from 1982 to 1991. See Dennis West, "Reconciling Entertainment and Thought: An Interview with Julio García Espinosa," *Cineaste* XVI:1–2 (1987–88): 20–26, 89. This new generation of men, as well as women, arrived after the technical and aesthetic foundations had been laid by Santiago Alvarez in the sixties, then elaborated upon by those who made the ICAIC Latin American newsreel in the seventies, as well as by soon-to-be directors Jesús Díaz and Orlando Rojas. See Mercedes Santos Moray, "Aparte con Rebeca Chávez," *Cine Cubano* 122 (1988): 25–26. For a fuller discussion of documentary production in the postrevolutionary era, see Michael Chanan, *The Cuban Image* (Bloomington: Indiana University Press, 1985), 148–202.

21. Although women occupied 55 percent of the technical and professional category in Cuba in 1986, around the same time, there were no women at all in the more technically specialized positions of cinematographer, assistant cinematographer, lighting technician, or sound recordist at the national film studios; from Zayas and Larguía, "La Mujer," 88, 91.

22. See Chávez in Santos Moray, "Aparte," 27–28; see also interview with Miriam Talavera in *Cuba: A View from Inside*, 38.

23. See Chanan, *The Cuban Image*, 165.

24. As it was formulated in his 1969 essay, the term *imperfect cinema* was less a reference to standards of technical perfection in the cinema of the Third

World than to the attempt to develop a more popular, engaged (as opposed to "high art" or "mass") cinema which, in addition to the strategies mentioned above in note 16 and in the text below, would exhibit an eclectic freedom with respect to genre; increased involvement of the spectator (following Brecht); self-reflexivity; and an "open," rather than "closed" narrative structure. See García Espinosa, "For an Imperfect Cinema," in *Reviewing Histories,* 166–77. These concepts found their first paradigmatic practical expression in the film *The Adventures of Juan Quin Quin.*

25. See García Espinosa, "For an Imperfect," 174–76.

26. See for example, the analysis Milagros González makes of Trujillo's portrait of Charín in "La Luz del Hecho Cotidiano: Mujer Ante el Espejo," *Cine Cubano* 109 (1984): 84.

27. See García Espinosa, "For an Imperfect," 171, 173–75.

28. See, for example, Mayra Vilásis, "La mujer y el cine: apuntes para algunas reflexiones latinoamericanas," in *La mujer en los medios audiovisuales* (Mexico, D.F.: Dirección de Actividades Cinematográficas, Coordinación de Difusión Cultural, Universidad Nacional Autónoma de México, 1987), 52 and 57.

29. Vilásis, "La mujer y el cine," 51; my translation from the Spanish.

30. See Fusco, "Films by Cuban Women: A Feminist Context?" in *Cuba: A View from Inside: Short Films by and about Cuban Women,* ed. Sandra Levinson (New York: Center for Cuban Studies, 1992), 11–12.

31. In spite of the very definite historical and ideological differences between them, there are shared characteristics where documentary is concerned, as suggested by critic/practitioner Julia Lesage's characterization of United States feminist documentaries in the early seventies: "biography, simplicity, trust between woman filmmaker and woman subject, a linear narrative structure . . . ;" Lesage, "The Political Aesthetics of the Feminist Documentary Film," *Quarterly Review of Film Studies* 4 (Fall 1978), 508.

32. Félix Guattari and Suely Rolnik, *Micropolítica: Cartografias do Desejo* (Petrópolis, Brazil: Editora Vozes, 1986), 33 and 17, respectively; my translation from the Portuguese.

33. Wilfredo Cancio Isla, "Marisol Trujillo ante el espejo." *Trabajadores,* 10 November 1984.

34. One of the more prominent early instructors in this area was Nobel laureate novelist Gabriel García Marquez.

35. Indeed, one of Gutiérrez Alea's scripts submitted in the early stages of this initiative was rejected by the collective with which he was affiliated. Conversation with Rebeca Chávez, April 28, 1990, New York City.

36. All of the directors featured in this anthology, screened at the "Festival Latino" in New York City, August 1991, are members of a new generation of filmmakers. Meanwhile, Rebeca Chávez has been elaborating her first fiction film.

37. As Felix Guattari has pointed out, in both advanced capitalist and "bureaucratic-socialist" countries, "revolutionary microprocesses need not take the form of social relations . . . the relationship of an individual with music or painting can unleash an entirely new process of perception and sensibility"; in Guattari and Rolnik, *Micropolítica,* 47; my translation from the Portuguese.

38. "Mumusa" is defined in an article on the subject as "slang for homosexual" in Panama and an "affectionate term of endearment in the gay community"; see Francisco Gonzalez, "Cine Mumusa/Queer Havana," *Latino Collaborative Newsletter* (July–August 1992), 1.

CHAPTER THREE

Making History:
Julie Dash

PATRICIA MELLENCAMP

If history is a way of *counting* time, of *measuring* change, then feminists, whether white, black, brown, or red, are operating another temporality, questioning the timing of history. In an essay about Claire Johnston,[1] Meaghan Morris argues that because feminism is both "skeptical" (of history) and "constructive," it is "untimely" for most historians. "To act (as I believe feminism does) to bring about concrete social changes while *at the same time* contesting the very bases of modern thinking about what constitutes 'change' is to induce intense strain."[2]

Feminism is untimely history that is ongoing, never over, or over there, but here and now. For women, history is not something to be recorded or even accepted, but something to be used, something to be changed. But first, history must be remembered. As bell hooks so poignantly said, "As red and black people decolonize our minds we cease to place value solely on the written document. We give ourselves back memory. We acknowledge that the ancestors speak to us in a place beyond written history."[3]

Julie Dash calls her history *what if,* "speculative fiction," what Laleen Jayamanne, a Sri-Lankan/Australian filmmaker, would call "virtual history."[4] *Cultural difference more than sexual difference provides the context.* (As hooks and many critics have pointed out, the concept of "sexual difference" at the base of feminist film theory is "racialized.")[5] The local (differences of appearance, custom, law, culture) illuminates the global (our commonalities of family, fiction, thought, feeling). The local, women's history, becomes the ground of the global, feminist theory. Thus, we learn about differences *and* experience the recognition of sameness. We feel history, as presence, passed on from grandmother to daughters and sons, a living history that is nourishing, not diminishing. The result is cultural appreciation, not cultural appropriation, to paraphrase hooks's distinction.

Although much history is not recorded in print or film, it cannot be erased. Like age, we carry our history, our forebears, on our faces, their spirits indelibly imprinted in our memories. For Dash, history can be reincarnated, recollected, its spirit given new life as living memory. Nana Peazant is the historian, the great grandmother of *Daughters of the Dust* who keeps history alive. "We carry these memories inside us. They didn't keep good records of slavery. . . . We had to hold records in our head."

Dash balances the experimental and the experiential, making *affective* history, a history of collective presence both material and spiritual. What I call empirical feminism—archival and activist—invokes history and acts to alter the course of time.

By locating issues of race and gender within specific contexts that are simultaneously historical *and* experiential, Dash's films expand the contours of female subjectivity—both onscreen and in the audience—to include women of all ages and appearances, complex emotion, and collective identification.[6] When the enunciation shifts into women's minds and into history (which includes our experience and memory), we cease thinking like victims and become empowered, *no matter what happens* in the narrative. As Collette Lafonte (a woman of color) asks in Sally Potter's *Thriller* (1979), "Would I have wanted to be the hero?" Like Potter (a British independent filmmaker/performance/theorist involved with *Screen* culture of the 1970s/early 1980s) who has a successful feature commercial film in 1993 release, *Orlando,* Dash's films resolutely answer YES! without hesitation, knowing that "being the hero" is a state of mind as well as action, a condition of self-regard and fearlessness. Being the hero is, precisely, *not* being the victim.

ILLUSIONS

Mignon Dupree becomes such a hero. This light-skinned African-American passing for white in Julie Dash's *Illusions* is an executive assistant at

National Studio, a movie studio. The film makes it clear that Mignon has status and influence at the studio—which she is willing to risk. She is given the difficult task of salvaging a musical that has lost sync in the production numbers. A young black singer, Esther Jeeter, is brought in to dub the voice-over for the blonde, white star, Leila Grant. Esther recognizes Mignon's heritage; they become friends and speak freely to each other. Mignon negotiates a fair deal for the singer's work. Meanwhile, Mignon is surrounded by racist comments from the white bit players. She is also being pursued by the studio boss's son, a lecherous soldier on leave who hangs around the office making passes. After finding a photograph of Mignon's black boyfriend, Julius, he confronts Mignon with his knowledge of her secret. Rather than back off, Mignon fearlessly acknowledges that she is passing. She speaks passionately against the industry that has erased her participation. The point of view *and* the voice-over narration, which frames the film, both belong to this beautiful and powerful character.[7]

The setting of this 1983 short film is a Hollywood movie studio in the 1940s, during World War II. The historical recreation of the time period is remarkable for such a low budget film. Historically, Mignon, a sophisticated and stylish African-American woman, resembles Lela Simone, a sound editor with the Arthur Freed Unit at MGM until the early 1950s. This gorgeous, fashionable white woman, who also served as executive assistant to Freed, was reportedly one of the best editors in the business. She was given the arduous task of synching music with the production numbers of the MGM musicals. In exasperation with being asked to do the impossible, she finally walked off the team, and out of film history, during the postproduction of *Gigi*. Unlike Simone, Dupree determines to remain in the industry and change things.

However, like so many women in Hollywood, what she really wants she is unable to get—film projects of her own. She wants the studio to make important films about history, including the contribution of Navajos during the war—their language could not be deciphered by the Japanese code breakers. Like Dash, Dupree is impassioned about the importance of film: "History is not what happens. They will remember what they see on screen. I want to be here, where history is being made."

Although *Illusions* has no illusions, no happily ever after of romance, whether marriage or the climb to stardom for Esther Jeeter or a promotion to producer for Mignon Dupree, the star of *Illusions* is a black woman who is powerful, ambitious, intelligent, and supports another black woman. This is a film about women's work and thought. Mignon's goal is to be a filmmaker and to change history. Unlike women in 95 percent or more of Hollywood movies, she is not defined by romance or flattered by male desire; neither is she bullied by, or affected by, the white male gaze.

Illusions revises Hollywood studio history, which erased African-American women from representation and history by synching their off-screen voices to on-screen white women. Women of color were heard, but not seen or recognized. When women of color were there, on the sound-track or passing on screen, they were not remembered or not recognized. *Illusions* inscribes the point of view missing from United States film history, African-American women (both on-screen and in the audience), granting visibility *and audibility* by synching image to off-screen voice. *Illusions* also charges Hollywood, and the nation, with hypocrisy and racism—by not making films about people of color even during World War II.

Illusions is a substantial revision of *Singin' in the Rain* (a 1952 MGM/Arthur Freed musical that mythologizes the coming of sound in 1927 to Hollywood, turning economics into romance). While both films concern the problem of synched sound, *Singin'* gives us fiction *as* history; Dash reveals history *as* fiction. She remakes history and changes it. She reveals what is repressed by the "cinematic apparatus"—and it is actual, not imaginary; in reality, not in the unconscious.[8] Synchronization—the dilemma of holding sound and image together in a continuous flow, of giving voice to face, of uniting the acoustic and the visual—is not just a technique, and not just played for laughs as it is in *Singin'*. Sound editing and synchronization are *strategies*[9] that conceal the politics of racism.

Illusions corrects absences in film theory. The disavowal of *Singin'* (that some of Debbie Reynold's songs were dubbed by another singer) becomes the repression of race in *Illusions*. Like the seamless continuity style that conceals its work (e.g., editing, processing, discontinuity), Hollywood cinema has concealed or erased (and prohibited) the work of people of color, on and off screen. Thus, the psychoanalytic mechanism of the spectator—disavowal, denial, and repudiation[10]—at the base of film theory, and the key to the feminist model of sexual difference, is revised and complicated by this film.[11]

Rather than the white male star, Don Lockwood/Gene Kelly who dominates *Singin'* in center frame, closeups, and voice-over, along with performance numbers and the story, this film stars a black woman as a studio executive. She is given the voice-over, center frame, closeups, and the story. While the dilemma of the 1952 musical was love at [first?] sight and romance—celebrating the coupling of the proper white woman (the good girl) to the [white?] male star—this film concerns women's professional work and thoughts. Mignon Dupree's power does not come from sexuality, but from talent, ability, high purpose, and self-confidence. Unlike Cathy Selden, she makes it on her own, not through the intervention of men.

Singin' divided women against each other—Cathy Selden versus Lina Lamont—and humiliated Lamont in public—while *Illusions* unites black women. Men pursuing women is sexual harassment in *Illusions* while in *Singin'* it is romance. The problem in *Singin'* was synching the proper white female voice with the white female face, staged as backstage film history. *Illusions* says this momentary repression is only the tip of the iceberg, which *Singin'* conceals through its partial revelation. *Illusions* declares that behind white faces were black voices—the source of pleasure and profit. Black performers were in history but they were not remembered, there *and* simultaneously erased. The studios profiteered on this presence/absence, this lack of stardom and publicity.

On the theoretical level, just as the work of the sound track has historically been subservient to the image track, so were women of color subordinate to white women. And in the rare instances when actresses of color were on screen, they could only fill stereotypical roles: lustful temptresses, servants, or mammies, off to the side, marginal to the star's center frame and hence barely noticed. Often, masquerade would make them white Anglo—as happens in *Singin'* to Rita Moreno who plays Zelda, the starlet. Being beautiful meant looking white—young, thin, smooth.

The dubbing sequence in *Illusions* is thus a very powerful revision of this white aesthetic: with Mignon looking on, and reflected on the glass wall of the sound recording booth, *Illusions* intercuts the blonde actress with shots of the black singer dubbing in her song. Jeeter is given glamour shots and the last, lingering close-up while the white no-talent actress is only a bit part. Without voice, she has no substance. Dash reverses the blonde standard of the star system that defined conventions of female beauty within a regimented, standardized uniformity.

For Gilles Deleuze and Félix Guattari "The first deviances are racial." "Racism operates by the determination of degrees of deviance in relation to the White-Man face." Racism has nothing to do with the other, only with "waves of sameness." "The Face" represents "White Man himself"; "the face is Christ."[12] (I think of the messianic ending of D. W. Griffith's *Birth of a Nation* with the superimposition of the white Jesus Christ hovering over the happily-ever-after couples and indeed the entire nation. It is only recently that these conventions of representing race are beginning to be regularly challenged.)[13] While speaking of difference, film theory has perpetuated sameness—whiteness (and heterosexuality). However, film theory, if not film history, is richer than its application. The theoretical base can also reveal blindspots. Thus, the baby need not be thrown out with the bathwater.

Along with film (and national) history and the work of sound, the "illusion" of the title is the practice of "passing": Mignon Dupree is a black woman "passing" as white.[14] *Illusions* complicates the relation between sight and knowledge, giving us a process of double vision, double knowledge, a revision of the concepts of masquerade, camouflage, and mimicry. The film provides an inversion of John Berger's 1972 distinction (in *Ways of Seeing*) of women seeing themselves being seen. Mignon watches herself being seen incorrectly. In effect, she is being seen but not always recognized. The story plays off misrecognition. She is not merely the object of sight but also the witness, the seer more than the seen.

Mignon is "seen" in double vision—white characters see her one way, African-Americans another. At one moment, her concealment is in jeopardy. Dupree looks apprehensive that Jeeter's remarks will give her away to the other women in the office. But she is immediately reassured by Jeeter who says: "Do you pretend when you're with them? Don't worry, they can't tell like we can." For the spectator, who "they" and "we" are becomes a question. When Mignon is talking to her mother on the telephone, she says: "I am still the same person . . . they didn't ask and I didn't tell. I was hoping that after the war things would change . . . and I wanted to be part of that change. If they don't change in this industry, then they won't change at all." The truth is, of course, that she *is* the same person in spite of what *they* think.

In his "Seminar on the Purloined Letter," Jacques Lacan describes the connections between seeing and knowing, a system that extends looks in time. The gaze in cinema has many permutations and options.[15] To Laura Mulvey's triad of the looks of the camera, character, and audience, must be added seeing (and not seeing); interpreting (and misinterpreting); and knowing (and not knowing). To the representation and the audience (film spectators) can be added gender (men at men, men at women, women at men, women at women), age, sexual preference, race, cultural history, and class (although in the United States, this can be amorphous). Seeing depends on knowing; scopophilia (the sexual pleasure of sight) is linked to epistemophilia (the sexual pleasure of knowing).

Passing has to do with sight, interpretation, and knowledge—with seeing (or not) what is visible (or not), there to be known (or not). Near the end of the film, Mignon says: "Now I'm an illusion, just like the films. They see me but they can't recognize me." Passing depends on whites not seeing, misinterpreting, and not knowing. This ignorance says something about the reason for the practice of passing—institutional and legal racism.

Passing is hiding, out in the open. Rather than being buried beneath the surface, the secret is immediately visible but not seen. As Edgar Allan Poe and neocolonial subjects so well knew, the surface can be the best hiding place. In "The Purloined Letter," Dupin, the detective, discovered that the letter was hidden in plain view, among other letters. "Because it was right out in the open, right in front of everyone's eyes, the letter was not noticed." The "principle of concealment," to paraphrase Poe, is the "excessively obvious"—which escapes observation. The "intellect . . . passes unnoticed considerations too obtrusive, too self-evident." Sometimes the most "sagacious expedient" is *not* concealing something. However, after someone shows us what is there, its existence becomes obvious. We can see only what we know, until someone shows us something else.

When the white soldier sexually bothering Mignon throughout the film discovers the photograph of Julius, her black boyfriend, his ardor cools. His scopophilia depended on his lack of knowledge. Thus, breaking the linkage between scopophilia and epistemophilia has great possibilities for feminism. Rather than intimidating Dupree, the revelation empowers her, concluding the film on a courageous and optimistic note—although bell hooks would disagree with this interpretation. When questioned by the GI, Mignon replies: "Why didn't I tell you I wasn't a white woman? I never once saw my boys fighting. . . . You have eliminated my participation in the history of this country. We are defending a democracy overseas that doesn't exist in this country." Perhaps when it comes to white men, history, the military, and power, "we" could include white women.[16]

Showing us Esther Jeeter, the black female voice behind the white female image, is one revelation of the repressed of history. This tactic reverses Poe's second strategy: the contents of the incriminating letter are never revealed within the story or to the reader. (This is akin to *Singin'*: Debbie Reynolds does not sing all of her songs in the film.) Thus, the film issues a challenge to film history as well as theory. Whiteness is not neutral, natural, or real—but a system, a "racialized" convention of the continuity style of Hollywood cinema. In fact, race, its absence and its presence as stereotype, might be a main attribute, along with heterosexual romance, of the continuity narrative and style. Race is prominent in the Motion Picture Production Code of 1933. This was the film industry's self-imposed, self-regulated code, which governed film content for many years; under "Particular Applications, Item II.6," it reads: "Miscegenation (sex relationship between the white and black races) is forbidden." Segregation has been the legal or operative rule for exhibition throughout this century—with either segregated theaters or separate spaces within theaters.

Dash enriches feminist film theory through her model of double vision/double knowledge, which she complicates by address—which unsettles any easy assumptions about spectatorship, race, and gender. Like Sally Potter's *Thriller* (which also starred a woman of color) and its key role in the formulation of feminist narrative theory, *Illusions* provides an advanced modeling of representation and reception—critically revising theories of vision through knowledge and sound.

Illusions makes intellectual arguments through the soundtrack, including pronouns that define and address subjectivity. The white female secretary says to Mignon: "You certainly are good to them. I never know how to speak to them." Mignon replies: "Just speak to them as you would to me." Who is "we" and who is "them" depends on what one can see and understand, and on history, which includes race. In this film, African-American women are together, united, and stars; white women are blonde bit players, either big-boobed bimbos, vapid stars, or prejudiced secretaries, subservient to, and accomplices of white men—unlike the intelligent black stars who know more than the white men.

Illusions concludes with a prophecy, in voice-over: "We would meet again, Jeeter and I. To take action without fearing. I want to use the power of the motion picture . . . there are many stories to be told and many battles to begin." Mignon Dupree is a film ancestor of Julie Dash. And indeed, they soon meet again.

AFTERTHOUGHTS

Other critics, although fewer than one would imagine, have written about this short film, with interpretations different from mine. Manthia

Diawara, however, recommended an essay with which, to my chagrin, I was not familiar.[17] (I am grateful to Diawara for his suggestions, to a degree made with the presumption that the author knew little of film theory—he recommended critics who have written about feminist film theory and race.[18] He suggested that I cut out a section on Eisenstein/Deleuze on film affect.)

For S. V. Hartman and Farah Jasmine Griffin, *Illusions'* critical flaw is the use of Hollywood conventions of narrative representation to critique dominant cinema. "Unless the form as well as the content of the passing tale is challenged, [its oppositional] possibilities remain severely limited."[19] This critique is predicated on the belief in the radicality of artistic form, the notion that aesthetics can change the world.

Like many scholars who were influenced by Soviet film theorists, Brecht, and Godard, and who participated in 1960s activism and 1970s theory/organizing, I advocated this position, as did Laura Mulvey in "Visual Pleasure and Narrative Cinema." In fact, my belief in the radicality of form was the reason I did not write about this film years ago. Many of us—for example, Peter Wollen, Peter Gidal, and Stephen Heath—believed that revelation of the apparatus, of the concealed work of cinema, would result in political change, which has hardly been the case. Thus, like many activists/critics writing about popular culture, my position has changed and become more inclusive. I now see radicality of form as one, not the only, option.

Yes, *Illusions* does imitate, does aspire to be, to replace, what it is critiquing, Hollywood film. (And, for example, it doesn't have the production budget to pull this off, particularly on the soundtrack where editing is doubly denied, very intricate, and highly expensive, or in the visual editing, which is off just enough seconds to make it awkward. I would love to see Dash add more research and make a big budget feature from this version.) But *Illusions* also wants to change things. And there are many tactics to bring about change. One of the most effective is to tell the story in a familiar style but switch the point of view and enunciation. Many viewers will not notice that the political ground has shifted.

But this is only the first of my differences with Hartman and Griffin. They see the synching sequence as emblematic of the film's disavowal, its central flaw: the voices of Mignon and Esther "become unanchored from their black bodies and are harbored within white female bodies . . . their work requires the decorporealization of the black female voice . . . to render docile, the threat of the black body."[20] On the contrary, I would suggest that this is true of Hollywood film, not this film. This scene has double vision. By inscribing the presence of black women, the lie of absence is revealed. It is the white body that is unanchored, particularly from the star system.

Black women are given center screen, the narrative, and voice. White women are banal and boring, particularly Leila Grant. She cannot sing or dance. Unlike Esther, she is not star material. While black women are given great dialogue, white women make only vapid or racist remarks. Black women are beautiful, intelligent, and various. White women are stupid and bland carbon copies.

The authors have serious reservations about the "passing tale" because "blacks occupy subordinate and supplemental positions." "The traditional mulatta is a character for white audiences, created to bring whites to an understanding of the effects of racism . . . the passing tale calls for agency on the part of the white viewer." The tale "foreclos[es] a discussion of black lives" and presents "an essential idea of blackness," defined as "a natural body." The essay does concede that "Dash successfully challenges the conventions of the traditional mulatta melodramas. . . . Dash's passing heroine realizes the possibilities of some of her desires . . . nor does she cease to aspire toward power and authority in the white man's world."[21]

Although Dash "attempts to make Mignon a figure with whom black viewers identify," "Mignon facilitates Esther's consumption by the cinematic apparatus. . . . Esther's own agency seems confined to witnessing and pretending." The authors conclude that "To identify with Mignon would be to accept our position as subordinate to her, to engage in an act of self-hatred. Though Dash attempts to establish a relationship of equality between Esther and Mignon, between the black woman viewer and Mignon, that relationship is a farce. Mignon occupies a space of privilege denied black women. Our only healthy response to her is ultimately one of rejection."[22]

This analysis caused me great consternation. Could this be true? Was I so far off? Was my identification with Mignon's courage and compassion, and with the sisterly bond between the two women, the proof of the film's disavowal of black women? Did the film ultimately address white women, like the tragic mulatta tale? Was there a "white" response and a "black" response?[23] But then I remembered that bell hooks and I were in agreement. The next day, Diawara's newly published anthology, *Black American Cinema,* arrived at the bookstore. Toni Cade Bambara seconded the positive response. She argues that Mignon's goal was not to "advance a self-interested career. . . . Mignon stands in solidarity with Esther. Unlike the other executives who see the Black woman as an instrument, a machine, a solution to a problem, Mignon acknowledges her personhood and their sisterhood."[24]

Coming across this essay almost two years after I wrote about the film, I was pleased to find other commonalities: "The genre that Dash subverts in her indictment of the industry . . . is the Hollywood story musical." Regarding the humiliation of Jean Hagen [Lina Lamont, in several scenes], particularly the film's conclusion, she asks "Does the Reynolds character stand in solidarity with the humiliated woman? Hell no, it's her big career break. *Singin'* provides Dash with a cinematic trope. . . . The validation of Black women is a major factor in the emancipatory project of independent cinema."[25] What she does not mention is the strange displacement in *Singin'*: Rita Moreno, Lina's friend, passing as Anglo.

Like Bambara, bell hooks argues that the "bond between Mignon and . . . Jeeter is affirmed by caring gestures of affirmation . . . the direct unmediated gaze of recognition." Mignon's "power is affirmed by her contact with the younger Black woman whom she nurtures and protects. It is this process of mirrored recognition that enables both Black women to define their reality . . . the shared gaze of the two women reinforces their solidarity." She calls the film "radical," opening up a space for the assertion of a critical, Black, female spectatorship . . . new transgressive possibilities for the formulation of identity."[26]

("Subversion" is the flip side of the belief in radical action through aesthetics. However, "subversion/transgression" is linked to popular rather than avant-garde forms; it is derived from cultural studies, not the art world. Of course, art and popular culture are no longer separate turfs—if they ever were. And like radical aesthetics in "art," I think "subversion" overstates the effects of watching TV or seeing a movie, particularly one that accepts and admires the Hollywood "mode of production." We can think, we can change, but "subvert"?)

Like many proponents of black independent cinema (in ways, recapitulating white critics' 1970s embrace of avant-garde cinema), hooks claims subversion for this film: a "filmic narrative wherein the Black female protagonist subversively claims that space." Dash's representations "challenge stereotypical notions placing us outside . . . filmic discursive practices." The film calls into question the "White male's capacity to gaze, define, and know." *Illusions* "problematizes the issue of race and specta-torship. White people in the film are unable to 'see' that race informs their looking relations."[27] But *after* the film, this is what we all would under-stand (or "see"), if we were listening.

DAUGHTERS OF THE DUST

> All the distributors turned it down. I was told over and over again that there was no market for the film. . . . I was hearing mostly white men telling me, an African American woman, what my people wanted to see . . . deciding what we should be allowed to see.[28]

In spite of delays and difficulties with financing and distribution, Dash took the film on the festival circuit, beginning with Sundance in Utah, in 1991. (After seeing an earlier trailer at a PBS "weekend retreat at Sun-dance," American Playhouse, and then the Corporation for Public Broad-casting funded it to the tiny tune of $800,000.)[29] In the past two years, this commercial release by a woman has attracted substantial audiences and acclaim. *Daughters of the Dust* has made film history.

Unlike the contemporary features by African-American men, this tale is told from the multiple, intersecting points of view of women of all ages—historical women, modern women—including the spirits of the unborn. *Daughters* is about love, respect, acceptance, and beauty rather than fear, hatred, and neglect. It embodies hope, not despair. It celebrates harmony and life rather than disaster and death. No wonder the distrib-utors had trouble! From *Grand Canyon* (which I hated) to *Boyz N the Hood* (which I loved), contemporary United States cinema, like television news, hawks male fear and high anxiety.

History is the setting of *Daughters*—the Sea Island Gullahs off the coast of South Carolina at the turn of the century. Dash calls this the "Ellis Island for the Africans," the "main dropping off point for Africans brought to North America as slaves." Due to its isolation, Africans main-tained a distinct culture that is recreated, recalled, recollected. A voice-over, of Nana Peazant, the old woman, the powerful head of the family-clan, speaking through the ages, says: "I am the first and last, I am the whore and the holy one . . . many are my daughters. I am the silence you cannot understand. I am the utterances of my name." After invoking the ancestors through speech, the spirits of the unborn, we go to Ibo Landing, the Sea Islands of the South, in 1902. The landscape is paradise, a splendid tranquility composed of pastels, the pale blue sky, the golden beach, the azure ocean, sounds of water. The scene is a family celebration, a beautiful, bountiful feast for this extended, rural community.

Yellow Mary, the prodigal daughter, is arriving, returning home from the mainland. With her is Trula, her female friend/lover wearing yellow; Mary's Christian sister in grey, Viola Peazant; and a male photographer, Mr. Snead. The Peazant family—gloriously dressed in pure, dazzling white—awaits her on the beach. Some revile Yellow Mary as a prostitute; most accept and love her, particularly Eula, the young mother of the unborn child. Mary accepts them all, and her life. Hers is the tolerance of experience seasoned with wisdom. This is a celebration not of her homecoming but of the extended family's departure from this island for the mainland. Coming and going, their paths cross.

A young girl's voice sets up the drama in voice-over: "My story begins before I was born. My great-great grandmother . . . saw her family coming apart." The girl continues as the storyteller: "The old souls guided me into the new world," as the camera pans the house. Thus, the tale is of the past, of history, a story of memory, or remembering, what Toni Cade Bambara calls "cultural continuity." It is an ending and also a beginning—like life itself. There are no dualities in this film. Things end only to begin anew. Like their ancestors from Africa, this family is beginning a journey to a new land.

The film—poised at the moment of the move from agrarian life to the migration to the city—"reminds us that there was some richness to that agrarian life." hooks refers to the sense of loss that came with the migration, what she calls a "psychohistory," which for her is emblematized by St. Julian Last Child, the Native American in *Daughters,* who stays behind with his African-American bride. This is a recovery of the history of intermarriage between African-Americans and Native Americans. "That intermarrying has never been depicted on the screen, a Native American and an African American mating, bonding, creating a life together that wasn't just built upon some lust of the moment." Dash later asks "Where have you ever seen a Native American win in the end and ride off in glory. When have you ever seen an African American woman riding off into the sunset for love." For Dash, film history exists in this film—"I was drawing on what I had experienced watching films by Spencer Williams, films from the 1930s, like *The Blood of Jesus* and *Go Down Death.*"[30]

Nana Peazant, the great grandmother, is the historian, the guardian of legend and the spirits. History comes from oral tradition, from experience. This is remembered history that lives through stories and through spirits. For Nana, age is wisdom, age is strength, age is to be respected: "We carry these memories inside us. We don't know where our recollections came from." But there is a tragic reason for recollection: "They didn't keep good records of slavery. . . . We had to hold records in our head. The old souls could recollect birth, death, sale. Those 18th century Africans, they watch us, they keep us, those four generations of Africans. When they landed, they saw things we cannot see." This is the history of survival, not defeat.

The spectrum of women spans several generations—they wear white; Nana wears dark blue as did her ancestors, slaves who worked planting the cotton, dying the cloth, staining their fingers dark navy. That past of slavery haunts the present, in scenes of dark blue intercut into the pastel tranquility of the family celebration. Although Dash's historical advisor on the film, Dr. Margaret Washington Creel, told her that the indigo stain would not have remained on their hands, "I was using this as a symbol of slavery, to create a new kind of icon around slavery rather than the traditional showing of the whip marks or the chains." For hooks, this is a tactic of "defamiliarization."[31]

Nana Peazant believes in the spirit more than the body. "Respect your ancestors, call on your ancestors, let them guide you." Power doesn't end "with the dead." Nana responds to her grandson's anger about his wife's rape: "Ya can't get back what you never owned." Nana's attempt to fortify the family for their journey, to give them their heritage, is also the film's gift to the audience and to African-American history. "I'm trying to learn ya how to touch your own spirit . . . to give you something to take north with ya. . . . Call on those old Africans. Let the old souls come into your heart . . . let them feed you with wisdom." Nana calls upon the spirits, carried by the wind. We glimpse the young girl, as yet unborn, running. Then we see this spirit enter her mother's body. The spirits can be felt, experienced.

An aesthetics of history is inscribed on bodies that dance, stroll, gesture, talk, and listen—a choreography of grace-filled movement, poetic voices and words, one group leading to another, then shifting the players. The beauty is a remarkable achievement in twenty-eight days of "principal photography shot with only natural sunlight," and 170,000 feet of film edited in Dash's living room. The film is lush with group shots and closeups of beautiful African-American women, talking, listening, laughing. "I saw Africa in her face," says Nana. The film caresses these faces of many styles and ages, taking time to let us see them, to cherish their presence and experience what they might be thinking. They are so different yet connected, "unity in diversity." For hooks, the film "breaks new ground in its portrayal of darker-skinned black people."[32] Dash: "We used Agfa-Geveart film, instead of Kodak because Black people look better on Agfa."[33]

The actresses in the film represent another history. "I really tried to use the actresses who had worked . . . in Black independent films." Dash mentions Cora Lee Day (Nana Peazant) in Haile Gerima's *Bush Mama*, Kaycee Moore (Haagar Peazant) in *Killer of Sheep*, Barbara O (Yellow Mary) in *Diary of an African Nun*, Alva Rogers (Eula) in *School Daze*. "These people worked months on films for little or no pay at all; so, now that I was finally able to pay them . . . why look somewhere else?"[34]

Dash understands the affective quality of photography—of composition and the close-up. She uses still photography as an emblem of turn-of-the-century technology coincident with the historical setting of her film in 1901. A series of photos by James Van Der Zee of "black women at the turn of the century" fascinated her. "The images and ideas combined and grew."[35] The young photographer, Mr. Snead, has come to record the auspicious event; this is modern history, abetted by photography, not memory; by images, not spirits or words. For Dash, Mr. Snead had "a secret mission. He has another agenda" in which the people are "primitive." "For me, he also represents the viewing audience." This feature film is a series of striking portraits, the faces of beautiful African-American women of all ages. Dash rewinds the camera to 1901 and begins another film history, from another beginning. This is history as a becoming, where the photographs are brought to life, made to speak, and surrounded by context.

Still photographs lead to sound and to story, and comprise an affective logic. For John Berger, like Bazin, photographs are relics, traces of what happened. To become part of the past, part of making history, they "require a living context." This memory "would encompass an image of the past, however tragic . . . within its own continuity." Photography then becomes "the prophecy of a human memory yet to be socially and politically achieved." The hint of the story to come "replaces the photograph in time—not its own original time for that is impossible—but in narrative time. Narrated time becomes historic time" that "respects memory."[36]

The film begins from something remembered—as Freud says, "every affect is only a reminiscence of an event"—and then begins to construct what Berger calls "a radial system" around the photograph in "terms which are simultaneously personal, political, economic, dramatic, everyday, and historic." In an interview with Zeinabu Irene Davis, a wonderful filmmaker, Dash says: "The whole film is about memories, and the scraps of memories, that these women carry around in tin cans and little private boxes. . . . African Americans don't have a solid lineage that they can trace. All they have are scraps of memories remaining from the past." Dash thought about "what it would be like to have a child . . . taken away, sold away in slavery. I mean, exactly how would that feel? . . . How do you maintain after that kind of personal tragedy? What happens to you?"[37]

This film sketches what Deleuze calls a "geography of relations." This "geography" can recall what has been ignored, or gone unrecorded, fashioning a "logic of the non-preexistent." "Future and past don't have much meaning, what counts is the present-becoming." Nana Peazant is living history. The Self—of the maker, of the audience, and of ancestors—is invoked in a spirit of cultural continuity rather than rupture. The focus is on *becoming*, on *relations*, what happens *between* experience and thought, between "sensations and ideas," between sound and image, between cultures, between women. This is a logic of "and," of connections, of actions. Becomings "are acts which can only be contained in a life and expressed in a style."[38]

What I have described in another essay as the empirical avant-garde destabilizes history by the experimental, granting women the authority of the experiential (which includes knowledge and memory).[39] Embodying the mutuality of art and life, the empirical avant-garde connects fiction and history in a manner comparable to Walter Benjamin's distinction between the story and the novel. For Benjamin, the story comes from "oral tradition" and shared experience. Storytellers speak of the "circumstances" they have directly learned or they "simply pass it off as their own experience." Thus, the listener has a stake in hearing and in remembering the story that exists in "the realm of living speech," of shared "companionship."[40] This living speech, forged in mutual experience and placed within history is intriguing for feminism—a hearing as much as a seeing, a fiction as much as a fact, a life as much as a history.

These films exist in the intersections between sound and image, history and experience, Art and Life. Affect and intellect emerge from the relations between women. Rather than ontology or duality, the logic is what Deleuze calls the "Anomalous,"[41] and Laleen Jayamanne calls hybrid, a tactic of assimilation, not, however, from the point of view of the colonizer.[42] As bell hooks reminds us, "white cultural . . . appropriation of black culture maintains white supremacy," which occurs with the "commodification of blackness."[43] Which, of course, relates to politics—these are films by women of color.

The past, a question of memory *and* history (which is intimate and emotive), haunts the present like a primal scene. I am not thinking of Freud but of something he could never understand—the mutual struggle of women for independence, of mothers and daughters to love *and* to let go, to be together and separate, to be alike *and* different. This lifelong journey, away from and with the mother, is taken into history.

The film asks that we listen, carefully—there is much to hear on the soundtrack. The screenplay, written by Dash, is brilliant, poetic, instructive. Listening to these words, spoken from the heart, is inspiring. The music is haunting, rich, composed by Butch Morris to "incorporate South Carolina field cries and calls."[44] The film respects its oral traditions, it talks poetically, it speaks historically. hooks writes that "talking back" meant "speaking as an equal." In "the home . . . it was black women who preached. There, black women spoke in a language so rich, so poetic, that it felt to me like being shut off from life . . . if one was not allowed to participate. It was in that world of woman talk . . . that was born in me the craving to speak, to have a voice . . . belonging to me. . . . It was in this world of woman speech . . . that I made speech my birthright . . . a privilege I would not be denied. It was in that world and because of it that I came to dream of writing, to write. Writing was a way to capture speech."[45]

History is carried in the conversations that tell the story of our lives. Mary talks about the "raping of colored women . . . as common as the fish of the sea." The voice-over spirit says she needed to convince her father "I was his child." The men recall the slave ships. Mary tells the story about her baby, born dead, so she nursed another baby. Nana—shown in close detail, often apart from the group, old, wiry, tough, a survivor—cannot understand how the family can leave.

The family is divided, momentarily, historically, over spirituality versus Christianity. Nana's daughter-in-law says "I am educated. I'm tired of those old stories . . . they pray to the sun, the moon, they ain't got no religion. I don't want my daughter to hear about that stuff." The voice of the spirit girl: "We were the children of those who chose to survive." Shots of clothes drying are intercut. "I was traveling on a spiritual mission, but sometimes I would be distracted. . . . I remember the call from my great, great grandmother. I remember and I recall. I remember my journey home."

For many viewers, the film feels like "a journey home." The film comes to understand that "we are part of each other . . . we are all good women. We are the Daughters of the Dust." Although the family separates, four generations of women remain together. Yellow Mary became active in anti-lynching. The spirit's voice-over concludes this extraordinary film: "My mommy and daddy stayed behind, with Yellow Mary. We remain behind, growing older, wiser, stronger."

Bambara calls the film "oppositional cinema"—due to "dual narration" and "multiple point of view camerawork." The style is a "nonlinear, multilayered unfolding" comparable to the "storytelling traditions" of "African cinema." Dash compares the film's structure to an African griot, "The story would just unravel . . . through a series of vignettes . . . the story would come out and come in and go out and come in . . . go off on a tangent . . . and back again. Like a rhizome."[46] For Bambara, *Daughters* is "Africentric." In another essay, she says the "storytelling mode is African-derived, in a call-and-response circle." "The spaciousness in DD is closer to African cinema than to European and Euro-American cinema. People's circumstances are the focus in African cinema, rather than individual psychology."[47]

"I wanted the look of the film to come from a rich African base." The production design and set "were done by artists [e.g., Kerry Marshall, Michael Kelly Williams, Martha Jackson Jarvis, and David Hammond]. . . . All . . . are nationally known African American artists." The costumes (the way the scarves are tied meaning different things) and gestures (turning the head "slightly to the left when listening to an elder") all derive from West African culture. "The men have these hand signals [that] were derived from secret societies in West Africa." "I wanted to have a connection to the past. . . . Afrocentrism . . . is that your actions are derived from West African culture rather than from . . . Europe."[48] For hooks, the film is an interrogation of "Eurocentric biases that have informed our understanding of the African American experience."

Bambara's analysis of the use of space is akin to that of Bazin on Orson Welles—reaching very different conclusions. This is "shared space (wide-angled, deep focus)" rather than "dominated space," space which portrays conflicts that are "systemic," not merely "psychological." Bazin contrasted what can be called "spatial realism" with "psychological realism," the conventions of Hollywood continuity style. "Spatial realism" consists of shots in depth, of long duration, and the use of the moving camera. Thus, the spectator has the freedom to look around. In addition, cuts are not motivated according to the same cause-effect logic of continuity style—psychological character motivation is not the main logic of cutting; neither is point of view from, usually, a male perspective. Often, as with the films of Jean Renoir, this is called the cinema of mise-en-scène, which resembles what Bambara calls "shared space," without, however, her political connotations. What is significant, however, is the way this "technique" shifts when women tell the story *and* are the protagonists. Dash's shared space and Bazin's "spatial realism" are, paradoxically, worlds apart. What women and men are doing in that space is one measure of aesthetic difference. This debate over the politics of aesthetics is productive and important.

Daughters revises the history of photography and film, creating a moving picture that shows what could have been, what might have been, and now, what *is* on record. But this is not the same old story. This story focuses on mothers and daughters. Their centrality remembers the past and changes history. hooks writes "To bear the burden of memory one must willingly journey to places long uninhabited, searching for traces of the unforgettable, all knowledge of which has been suppressed." "Reconstructing an archaeology of memory makes return possible." This is "history written in the hearts of our people, who then feel for history."[49]

Dash was addressing "black women first, the black community second, white women third," a hierarchy that is reflected in her empathetic portrayal of black men in the film. As hooks argues, "to de-center the white patriarchal gaze, we have to focus on someone else for a change. . . . The film takes up that group that is truly on the bottom of this society's race-sex hierarchy. Black women tend not to be seen. . . . *Daughters* de-centers the usual subject—and that includes white women." hooks also suggests that "people will place *Daughters* in a world not only of black independent filmmakers, but also in the larger world of filmmakers."[50] I agree. I did not feel at all marginalized by the film. A much stronger experience than "being white" drew me in—that of being part of a large, rural family, of being an older sister, a mother and a daughter, with a wiry, thin, powerful 102-year-old grandmother who resembles Nana Peazant. Rose Sedlacek's hands were gnarled from heavy work in a house without electricity. She still rules the family roost, although her eldest daughter, my mother Mary Margaret, is now seventy-eight. I see this independent, strong woman every day—she is my support.

On the level of memory and affect, I felt kinship with the community of this diverse family, the pain of separation, the wisdom of aging, and the nourishing, loving companionship of strong women. My mother's parents were first-generation poor dairy farmers in Northern Wisconsin who raised ten children during the depression. All their work was God's work. Hard, physical labor in the fields and in the house was the source of happiness. They raised and preserved all their food and made their clothing. Prayers were at 4:00 A.M., milking by hand began at 5:00 A.M., and bedtime came after evening prayers, with darkness.

There was so much joy and faith and talk that I never noticed there was no money. I recalled summer feasts on the farm during community harvesting (called thrashing); I remembered staying in a house with straw mattresses and an outhouse. I recollected the differences, including smell, taste, and touch, between rural life and the city. At night, light came from only the stars. Night was an enveloping blackness. Sunday on the farm was different from every other day. On Sunday, we got dressed up, went to church, and did no work other than visiting, talking all the day long with "family." Everyone in Drywood was related by blood or marriage. My memory of Sunday is like hooks's—"Girlfriend, growing up as a Southern black woman, in the 1960s, my family felt that you should not work on a Sunday . . . we could not wear pants, for a long time . . . it was a day of rest."[51]

hooks argues "that viewers who are not black females find it hard to empathize with the central characters. . . . They are adrift without a white presence in the film." While my response is surely different, I didn't need, nor want, a white presence. On the contrary. I have much to learn about cultural difference from women of color. And I agree with hooks that it is wrong to assume "that strength in unity can only exist if difference is suppressed and shared experience is highlighted."[52] However, experience shared can lead to differences understood. "I see" also means "I understand." As hooks so wisely says, there is a difference between "cultural appropriation" and "cultural appreciation."

hooks wonders why "white women" are not starved for these images, as she is. I, too, am starved for portrayals of strong, interesting women of all colors, of women who love and identify with other women, of women who are intelligent, powerful. White women have few memories of these experiences in films. For me, *Daughters* has much to teach women of all colors. Like hooks's analysis of "contemporary black women," the "struggle to become a subject" is also linked to my "emotional and spiritual well being." I, too, come from a family of fast-talking, hard-working women; I, too, believe that self-love is revolutionary, for white women as well as women of color. Maybe we have more in common regarding mothers and daughters than we have imagined. Perhaps more than anything else, I, too, have a strong spiritual life, rarely acknowledged in film and scholarly writing.

When hooks asks, "Why is it that feminist film criticism . . . remains aggressively silent on the subject of blackness . . . disallows . . . black women's voices. It is difficult to talk when you feel no one is listening,"[53] I sadly concur. The blindspots of white feminists, including me, regarding women of color have been glaring. That is changing, as Doane and Gaines and others have demonstrated. But most importantly, we now have films to show us the way and books to point us in the right directions.

In their conversation, hooks and Dash recall the "ritual of dealing with hair grooming," the pleasure of "sitting in"—"It was a joy." Different West African hairstyles mean things, for example, "married, single, menopausal." The family "hairbraider" would braid "the map of the journey north in the hair design."[54] Nana Peazant's most powerful gris-gris was a lock of her mother's hair—often the only thing children had of the mothers during slavery. I didn't know this. I loved the learning. In fact, learning has always been my greatest pleasure. Now, as I look at a lock of Grandmother Rose's red hair, which still reaches to the small of her back, as it did when she was a girl on a farm in Northern Wisconsin, I understand much more. With understanding, comes acceptance and love—and these are the gifts *Daughters of the Dust* ultimately gives to us.

I wrote about this film after seeing it in February 1992, in New York, with my daughter, Dae. It came at a turning point in our relationship—to let go *and* to come together. The film addressed us on many levels. In the last few months, several insightful analyses have appeared. Although my interpretation has changed little since my first wondrous encounter with the film, an experience that included the audience's love, respect, and gratitude for the film, these important critics deserve mention.

In the introduction to his superb anthology, *Black American Cinema,* Diawara posits two types of Black American Cinema, one based on a model of time (linear, not simultaneous), the other on space. "Spatial narration" reveals and links "black spaces that have been . . . suppressed by White times," and validates "black culture." "Spatial narration" is "cultural restoration, a way for Black filmmakers to reconstruct Black history." In contrast, the "time-based narratives" are "performances of Black people against racism, and genocide," linking the "progress of time to Black characters." This structure is linear, the other is circular, *Boyz n the Hood* compared to *Daughters of the Dust.*[55]

This distinction resembles that advocated (for different political reasons, and predicated on different philosophical and aesthetic principles) by André Bazin between the continuity style and spatial realism. It also shares an attitude with Deleuze's distinction between time/movement and space/movement. However, Diawara disputes my tendency to interrelate disparate thinkers: "Is this not a way of effacing? The universal, being like Deleuze/Bazin, obliterates the local, the originality of Dash's films?" and, one could add, hooks's or Diawara's writing. I hear what he means. For me, however, it's not a question of either/or, with women granted the local and male theorists the global. The global also belongs to women. For me, hooks is of the same magnitude as Deleuze. This is what comparing them means, for me.

Diawara emphasizes what he calls the film's "religious system," which he states is African, leading to "a Black structure of feeling." He links what I call the film's spirituality (which is African and resembles Hindu, Buddhist, Muslim, and what I practice, Kasmir Shaivism), a mode of self and historical empowerment, to Cornel West's recent call for a politics of conversion, of feeling, which Dash's system of "ancestor worship" resembles.[56] For me the spiritual basis of the film is unifying—providing another way to think and feel and change history. Spirituality, the character of the unborn child, the wind, the soundtrack of noises, music, voice-overs, enables an identification with forces within each individual that are greater than the material world, powers that are indestructible and eternal. The spirit within each human being outruns the limits and prejudices of Western rationality and history.

In "Reading the Signs, Empowering the Eye: *Daughters of the Dust* and the Black Independent Cinema Movement," Toni Cade Bambara's brilliant analysis of this film posits three qualities of Dash's work: women's perspective and women's validation of women; shared space rather than dominated space (like hooks, she sees Mignon "in solidarity with" Esther Jeeter); and "glamour/attention to female iconography."[57]

For Bambara, the island setting is complex: "Occupying the same geographical terrain are both the ghetto, where we are penned up in concentration-camp horror, and the community, wherein we enact daily rituals of group validation in a liberated zone—a global condition throughout the African diaspora, the view informs African cinema."[58] For her, the beach is not "a nostalgic community in a pastoral setting. They are an imperiled group. The high tide of bloodletting has ebbed for a time, thanks to the activism of Ida B. Wells."

"The Peazants are self-defining people. Unlike the static portraits of reactionary cinema" (where characters never change but remain their stereotypical essence), "the Peazants have a belief in their own ability to change and in their ability to transform . . . social relations."[59] Bambara concludes by arguing that the next stage will be "pluralistic, transcultural, and international," with an "amplified and indelible presence of women."

These are exemplary analyses, particularly the emphasis on space, time, history, memory, and activism. "Looking and looking back, Black women involve ourselves in a process whereby we see our history as counter-memory, and use it as a way to know the present and invent the future."[60] However, in addition to these critics' visual analysis, I would also emphasize sound—the issues of enunciation/address, music, voice, and authority. In *Illusions*, Mignon possesses authority. She speaks up, fearlessly. Her voice-over claims history and a place in it. For me, Mignon/Dash outruns theoretical models predicated solely on vision. Her films enable all of us to move forward.

NOTES

1. Johnston was a British feminist film theorist and critic, considered by many to be a founder of feminist film theory. She committed suicide in the 1980s.

2. Meaghan Morris, unpublished talk/manuscript on Claire Johnston. Morris takes Gilles Deleuze's model of the "minor," derived from Franz Kafka's work, as a strategy of/for feminism.

3. bell hooks, *Black Looks: Race and Representation* (Boston: South End Press, 1992), 193.

4. Gilles Deleuze and Claire Parnet, *Dialogues* (New York: Columbia University Press, 1987). Australian intellectuals have been influenced by Deleuze for a long time, unlike the United States, where many scholars are just beginning to take note. For my analysis of Jayamanne's film theory, see *Fugitive Images from Photography to Video*, ed. Patrice Petro (Bloomington: Indiana University Press, 1995).

5. hooks, 122.

6. Freud posits three modes of identification—having, being, and group. It is the third instance so applicable to the public exhibition of film that is paradoxically ignored in film theory.

7. S. V. Hartman and Farah Jasmine Griffin, "Are You as Colored as That Negro? The Politics of Being Seen in Julie Dash's *Illusions*," *Black American Literature Forum* 25: 2 (Summer 1991): 361–75. Here is their description of the story:

> The film's narrative, set in the 1940s, focuses on Mignon [Dupree], a beautiful, fair-skinned movie executive who is passing for white. Mignon has come to Hollywood to "make the world of moving shadows work for" her. However, she winds up developing escapist entertainment fare. In the course of her duties at National Studio, she befriends a dark-skinned singer, Esther Geeter [the name is spelled Jeeter by others, including me], who has been hired to dub the voice of white film star Leila Grant and thereby save the studio's Christmas blockbuster. Esther's presence makes Mignon realize that she has become "an illusion just like the stories here." . . . After [her race is discovered by the boss's son, home on leave], Mignon confirms her desire . . . to tell real stories about real Negroes, and use the power of the film industry to present honest representations. (363–64)

8. I am referring to the influential essays by Jean-Louis Baudry and Jean-Louis Comolli on the apparatus—theoretical models that came to the United States in the late 1970s.

9. I am referring to Michel de Certeau's distinction between strategies and tactics, with strategies being institutional, dominant practices.

10. Disavowal, the maintenance of contradictory beliefs, is usually the only mechanism in film theory. But this notion may be complicated to include denial and repudiation. For more on this see my book *High Anxiety*. Repudiation explains how black voice/white face would work. We know something to be true, in reality, but block it out.

11. Homi Bhabha applied the theory of fetishistic disavowal to colonial subjectivity, without however, noting women. For another critique of Bhabha, see Manthia Diawara, "The Nature of Mother in *Dreaming Rivers*," *Black American Literature Forum* 25: 2 (Summer 1991): 283–98.

12. Gilles Deleuze and Felix Guattari, "Year Zero: Faciality," *A Thousand Plateaus: Capitalism and Schizophrenia* (Minneapolis: University of Minnesota Press, 1987), 167–91.

13. In "The Re-Birth of the Aesthetic in Cinema," Clyde Taylor discusses how aesthetics (often argued as "excess") were a cover-up for the film's "evil" racism. "It is this mystifying aura orchestrated by the art-culture system that has deterred the recognition of *The Birth of a Nation* as one of the most accomplished articulations of fascism, of twentieth century evil" (28). He notes, but doesn't emphasize, the film's linkage between rape and racism, the way the white woman becomes the pawn for lynching. (He even refers to Griffith's obsessiveness for young white girls in jeopardy.) In the film's prologue, Africans are the problem. In the film's epilogue, Africans have gone, replaced by white Christianity and couples. *Wide Angle* 13: 3/4 (July–Oct. 1991): 12–31.

14. Unlike Jeanne Crane, a white actress and 1950s star impersonating a black woman in *Pinky*, a feature film about "passing," Mignon is played by a black actress.

15. Jacques Lacan, "Seminar on the Purloined Letter," in *French Freud*, ed. Jeffrey Mehlman, *Yale French Studies* 48 (New Haven, Conn.: Yale University, 1972).

16. Like the film, pronouns are revealing, difficult. I can't fully claim "we" or "us" if I have not had the experience.

17. S. V. Hartman and Farah Jasmine Griffin, "Are You as Colored as that Negro? The Politics of Being Seen in Julie Dash's *Illusions*," in *Black American Literature Forum* 25: 2 (Summer 1991): 361–75.

18. Diawara recommended Mark Reid, Jacquie Jones, and Jacqueline Bobo. He also recommended that I read essays by Mary Ann Doane and Jane Gaines. Both women have been friends for years.
Mark Reid's book, *Redefining Black Film*, has a chapter on "Black Feminism and the Independent Film," previously published as an essay. Reid takes his cue from literary criticism, specifically Alice Walker, and distinguishes feminist films from black womanist films, a concept that "refers to . . . reading strategies whose narrative and receptive processes permit polyvalent female subjectivity" (110). Reid endorses Alile Sharon Larkin's analysis of triple oppression (economic, racial, sexual) for black women, unlike white feminists. "I cannot pick and

choose a single area of struggle. . . . Feminists . . . do not have to deal with the totality of oppression. . . . Feminism succumbs to racism when it segregates Black women from Black men and dismisses our histories" (118–19). "Black womanist films" include *Illusions* (with only a paragraph analysis) and *Nice Colored Girls* by Tracey Moffatt (without mentioning her name). *Daughters of the Dust* "dramatizes womanism . . . in a female-centered narrative with a pan-African sentiment" (120). Troubling, however, is that a black womanist viewing position "acknowledges that the goal of black feminist theory is a revision of gender relations and an open-ended sexuality." What, exactly, is "open-ended sexuality"? *Redefining Black Film* (Berkeley: University of California Press, 1993), 109–24. This chapter was published as "Dialogic Modes of Representing Africa(s) in *Black American Literature Forum*, 25: 2 (Summer 1991): 375–88. This was a special Black Film Issue, edited by Valerie Smith, Camille Billops, and Ada Griffin.

Jacquie Jones, the editor of *Black Film Review,* has a short and terrific review of *Daughters* in *African American Review,* 27: 1 (1993): 19–21. "African American life is freed from the urban, from the cotton picking . . . the complexity and shaded histories of Black women's lives take center stage. There are no whores or maids . . . no acquiescent slaves. No white people. . . . The film does have a certain preoccupation with beauty" (19).

19. Hartman and Griffin, 371.

20. Ibid., 368.

21. Ibid., 370–71.

22. Ibid., 371–72.

23. Ultimately, of course, the authors and I are both wrong—essentially speaking. There is no such thing as a unified "Black female subject" or a singular white female subject with built-in responses.

24. Toni Cade Bambara, "Reading the Signs, Empowering the Eye: *Daughters of the Dust* and the Black Independent Cinema Movement," *Black American Cinema*, ed. Manthia Diawara (New York: Routledge, 1993), 118–44.

25. Ibid., 141.

26. bell hooks, "The Oppositional Gaze: Black Female Spectators," in *Black Looks,* from which I quoted earlier, reprinted in *Black American Cinema,* ed. Manthia Diawara, 288–302.

27. Ibid. hooks, like Diawara, also quotes from Mary Ann Doane, but few other theorists involved in feminist film theory. I am thinking of Teresa de Lauretis, on narrative (in *Alice Doesn't*), and Kaja Silverman on sound (in *Re-Visions: Essays in Feminist Film Criticism,* ed. Doane, Mellencamp, and Linda Williams).

28. Julie Dash, *Daughters of the Dust* (New York: New Press, 1992), 25.

29. Zeinabu Irene Davis, "An Interview with Julie Dash," *Wide Angle*, 13: 3/4: 110–19.

30. Dash, 42, 42, 47, 28, 28.

31. Ibid., 31.

32. Ibid., 10, 13, 54.

33. Davis, 115.

34. Ibid., 113, 114.

35. Dash, 4

36. John Berger, "Uses of Photography," *On Looking* (New York: Pantheon, 1980), 56–63. The essay is subtitled, "For Susan Sontag."

37. Davis, 112.

38. Deleuze and Parnet, *Dialogues*, 56.

39. See "An Empirical Avant-Garde: Laleen Jayamanne and Tracey Moffatt," in *Fugitive Images from Photography to Video*, ed. Patrice Petro (Bloomington: Indiana University Press, 1995).

40. Walter Benjamin, "The Storyteller: Reflections on the Works of Nikolai Neskov," *Illuminations* (New York: Schocken Books, 1969), 83–110.

41. For Deleuze, the Anomalous is "always at the frontier," the "Outsider," *Dialogues*, 42.

42. See Manthia Diawara on hybridization/creolization, "The Nature of Mother in *Dreaming Rivers*," 293–94.

43. hooks, *Black Looks*, 32–33.

44. Davis, 114.

45. bell hooks, "Talking Back," *Discourse* 8 (Fall–Winter 1986–87): 124. When reading this, I identified. My experience with my mother, her five sisters (and four brothers), and their mother was constant talk, never silence.

46. Dash, 39.

47. Bambara, xiii, 124, 136.

48. Davis, 114, 116.

49. hooks, *Black Looks,* 172, 173, 183.

50. Ibid., 40, 65.

51. Ibid., 43.

52. Ibid., 130, 51.

53. Ibid., 124–25.

54. Ibid., 53

55. Manthia Diawara, "Black American Cinema: The New Realism," *Black American Cinema,* (New York: Routledge, 1993), 3–25. The essays are divided into "Black Aesthetics" and "Black Spectatorship."

56. Diawara, *Black American Cinema,* 18–19.

57. Bambara, "Reading the Signs," 120–21.

58. Ibid., 121.

59. Ibid., 123, 143.

60. hooks, *Black Looks,* 302.

CHAPTER FOUR

Reclaiming Images of Women in Films from Africa and the Black Diaspora

N. FRANK UKADIKE

Female subjectivity in Africa as elsewhere has often been defined by men rather than by women. Black women have fallen victim to a tendency to "de-womanize black womanhood"—to paraphrase Nigerian playwright ´Zulu Sofola.[1] Consequently, films made by African women and men are attempting to rehumanize portrayals of women and to reassert their identities. Furthermore, African women filmmakers are facing the challenge of regaining for women the power of self-definition and self-representation. Toward the accomplishment of such goals, new social and political currents in Africa and the Black Diaspora involve new levels of critical awareness and new challenges to Western intellectual hierarchies.

The hegemony of colonialist ideologies and Hollywood domination cannot be excluded from an historical investigation that seeks to provide a nuanced portrait of complex ethnic and cultural questions. For a long time questions of cultural difference have been neglected by the dominant cinema and by dominant media practices, thus discouraging the articulation of an accurate and wholesome black identity. Given the heritage of distorted images, some critics understandably regard the docile ancillary African woman seen in much international cinema today as a media creation.[2] Partly for this reason the calling into question of the "native informant," in Gayatri Spivak's term, is the sine qua non of the black woman's film project. As Maureen Blackwood and Martina Attille have noted, black women "must be the ones who define the areas of importance in [their] lives: work toward the breakdown of 'mainstream' conventions and popular assumptions perpetuated by existing forms of cinema and television."[3] Because of the ways black subjectivity has been constantly abused in films, a new sensitivity to black women's concerns indicates a concerted effort to move questions of the "other" toward the center. This stance also represents a movement toward thoroughgoing cinematic decolonization; in other words, the need for a "theory that takes into account the economic history of [black] (mis)representation and ensuing stereotyping, as well as the interaction between social realities (whole lives) and cinematic fictions (fragmentation), and . . . black women need to give that theory [and practice] its direction."[4] Hence black women must take the lead in a revisionist dialogue, an alternative discourse that requires culture-based interpretation around questions of ethnic identity and representation. In support of such efforts, I will examine alternative film practices of male as well as female filmmakers who seek to redefine and reclaim black/African female subjectivity from a history of filmic (mis)representation.

THE DIASPORIC EXPERIENCE: SOME SHARED FEATURES

Traditionally denied access to the medium of film, black women throughout the world have been taking more control of the camera and the cinematic apparatus in recent years. Seeking to advance the process of looking at themselves from within, these women filmmakers, including Julie Dash in the United States, Tracey Moffatt in Australia, and Sarah Maldoror, Safi Faye, and Salem Mekuria in Africa, have been exploring cultural directions and innovative strategies that challenge Eurocentric assumptions and readings of black female subjectivity in films and in other areas of culture. A number of black male filmmakers, including the Africans Ousmane Sembene, Desiré Ecaré, and Med Hondo, have been contributing to this challenge. This paper will focus primarily on the changing inscription of female identity and subjectivity in African films made by both men and women, but will first briefly consider aspects of the diasporic context in which African cinema has been evolving.

The efforts of black cultural producers to forge a distinct identity and to implement a positive representation of black people has been a struggle almost as fierce as the battles waged by the various African liberation movements to gain their independence. Throughout the history of film, filmmakers have relentlessly attempted to force a psychic transformation of Afrocentric mores, traditions, and values, into roles exemplified by Western definitions of culture.[5] Just recently, the veteran dramatist August Wilson, reflecting on decades of Hollywood's persistent caricature of black people, demanded a black director for the film version of his Pulitzer Prize winning play "Fences."[6] The playwright's position echoes the women's position suggested above, which seeks no negotiated "detente with Hollywood," to paraphrase the critic Kalamu Ya Salaam, and reflects the growing anger of members of the black community who support black control over black culture and its products. This demand for self-representation requires diversification of the production process. For Wilson, therefore, the time is now ripe for the black media to emerge as an uncompromising entity whose prerogative is to address the specifics of "black culture and its products." In this vein, black consciousness as a signifier of counterhegemonic representation is reflected in Wilson's declamation: "Someone who does not share the specifics of a culture remains an outsider, no matter how astute a student or how well-meaning their intentions."[7]

Wilson's statement has been widely discussed, criticized, and digested. Some, irked by it, call it racist. Some see it as rejuvenating because it mirrors the concerns of the disgruntled. If, as claimed by Wilson's critics, this proposal is a self-centered overture that does not affirm the sanctity of a multicultural federation, it is also clear that Hollywood has not attempted in good faith "to create a universal theater" that honestly reflects culture/gender specifics related to race, color, age, nationality, language, customs, and habits.[8]

Western exclusionist ideologies relegate black film practice to marginal status. Hollywood's monopoly of processes of production and exhibition, for example, have stifled black-directed films. In Britain, as in the United States, economic deprivation has fostered the death of early, sporadic black productions. Africa's late entry as film producer, accurately dubbed by film scholar Clyde Taylor the "last cinema,"[9] is a sad case. It was not until the middle of the 1960s, when African countries started freeing themselves from the yoke of colonialism, that indigenous African film practice emerged. Only recently has black film practice begun to expand in the United States, with women joining their male counterparts in constructing authentic images of black people. Here we remember Kathleen Collins for her film *Losing Ground*

(1982), which was never theatrically released but is on record as the first independent feature film by an African-American woman director. Julie Dash's *Daughters of the Dust* (1992) is the first feature film by an African-American female filmmaker to gain wide theatrical release. (Africa's first feature by a woman, *Kaddu Beykat,* was made in Senegal by Safi Faye in 1975.) The struggle by black people everywhere has diasporic significance since they all share and articulate protests against colonialist exploitation and deculturation. In terms of cultural production, black filmmakers aspire to portray the truth about their lives partly by producing works which exemplify a communal sensibility. Significant to this sensibility is the invocation of Afrocentricity as a profound cultural hermeneutic.

Daughters of the Dust, a tapestry of cultural history, is influenced aesthetically by African cinema more than by any other tradition. The film eschews the conventions of dominant Western practices, and instead deploys Afrocentric visual conventions, cultural symbolism, and codes that privilege black people. This African mode of address, as the author/director has stated in the Presskit and in various newspaper interviews, originates particularly in Igbo cultural symbols and traditions of eastern Nigeria.[10] Zeinabu Irene Davis's films, like Dash's, suggest meditations about the historical truths of black women's lives. *Cycles* (1989), for example, which illustrates moments of waiting for a woman's menstrual period to begin, is a simple story, but the multilayered cultural motifs and symbolism employed render it complex. Moreover, these motifs exemplify the filmmaker's "growing knowledge of spirituality" and, as she puts it, "connections with my Yoruba ancestors and with Yoruba-derived new-world religions such as Santeria (Spanish-speaking America), Vodun (Haiti and southern United States), and Candomble (Brazil)."[11] As in *Daughters of the Dust, Cycles'* elevation of woman's position is part of a filmic process that derives empowerment from decoding and recoding. Cinema here becomes a contested terrain, where conventional representations are challenged, and the black woman's subjectivity reclaimed.

It is from Australia that Tracey Moffatt's *Nice Colored Girls* (1987) emerges, presenting us with a distinctive view of black women under the yoke of colonialism—the exploitation of aboriginal women by white men. Moffatt's film links the violent colonial past to intolerable urban encounters in the present. The slave ship functions as an obtrusive reminder of the persistent truths of racial inequality.

In a similar fashion, Ngozi Onwurah's *Coffee-Colored Children* (1988) becomes a self-reflexive autobiographical essay on internalized

British racism. The film presents us with the depths of sociological conflict and trauma through the experiences and memories of children of a
mixed marriage of a white mother to an absent Nigerian father as the children grow up in a predominantly white British community.

All of the above films succeed in deconstructing or at least challenging
the traditional norms of filmmaking and film viewing experience. It is not
necessarily their innovative stylistic strategies alone that make them regener-
ative, however; rather, it is the full variety of ways in which they seek to
counter the subliminal racist and negative images that continue to define the
black image in dominant practice. Such challenges to dominant practice
throughout the Black Diaspora are strongly linked to the counterhegemonic
impulses within African film practice to which we now turn. I will examine
the construction of black female subjectivity in four African fiction films.
The first three are directed by men; the last one by a woman. These films are
Ceddo (Ousmane Sembene, Senegal, 1977), *Faces of Women* (Visages de
femme, Desiré Ecaré, Côte d'Ivoire, 1985), *Sarraounia* (Med Hondo, Mauritania, 1987), and *Sambizanga* (Sarah Maldoror, Angola, 1972). Then I will
discuss two African documentaries by women—Safi Faye's *Selbe: One among
Many* (1982) and Salem Mekuria's *Sidet: Forced Exile* (1991).

WOMEN IN AFRICAN FILMS

A cursory look at the image of black women in American films proves, as
critics have indicated, that "movies have not been a humanistic medium
for black women."[12] In these films the important contributions made by
all black people are downplayed or relegated to the sidelines. Often
women in particular appear ineffectual, and incapable of standing on
their own. Of course, such depiction of women would be as misleading
in African films as it is in American. As Senegal's Ousmane Sembene has
noted, "Africa can't develop [and has never developed] without the participation of women."[13] The grand prize of the PanAfrican Festival of Film
and Television (FESPACO), awarded every other year to the best competing film at the festival, is the bronze statuette of Princess Yennenga, an
African warrior riding a stallion and brandishing a sword. Hopefully this
figure will bear witness to the recognition of more African/black women
in the expanding history of African experience.

Africa's eminent novelist, Ama Ata Aidou, comments as follows on
the unfortunate European view of African female subjectivity:

This is a sorry pass the daughters of the continent have come to—
especially when we remember that they are descended from some of
the bravest, most independent and innovative women this world has
ever known. . . . The Lady Try of Nubia (ca. 1415–1340 B.C.E.), the
wife of Amenhotep III and the mother of Akhenatou and
Tutankhamen, . . . is credited with, among other achievements,
leading the women of her court to discover make-up and other
beauty-enhancing processes. Her daughter-in-law was the incompa-
rable Nefertiti, a black beauty whose complexion was nowhere near
the alabaster she is now willfully painted with. Again from the pha-
ronic era, we evoke Cleopatra, about whom—[quoting John Hen-
rik Clarke whose work Aidou says stems from "the impatience of
painstaking scholarship"] more nonsense has been written . . . than
about any African queen . . . mainly because of many writers' desire
to paint her white. She was not a white woman. She was not a
Greek.[14]

In many African countries, women remain, at best, sexual objects
enveloped in a culture of chauvinism; and, in the words of Ousmane
Sembene, they are "still refused the right of speech." Some African
films, especially those by Sembene, suggest that the problem in colonial times was compounded by Islamic/Arab and Christian/European
imperialism, which created hierarchical divisions that favored men at
the expense of women.[15] 'Zulu Sofola contends that the "de-woman-
ization of African womanhood" has been a direct result of colonial
brainwashing: "She [African woman] has been most viciously attacked
through the cosmology of the alien cultures of the European and Arab
that has left her stripped bare of all that made her existence worthwhile
in the traditional African system of socio-political order of gover-
nance."[16]

Sembene's *Ceddo* (1976), a film highly critical of colonizing religions, depicts the Ceddo resistance to Islamic patriarchy. An Arab-look-
ing imam embarks on neutralizing the African resistance by conquering
the men and forcing them to declare allegiance to Islam. This forced conversion makes it easier for the imam to marry Princess Dior. The king
(Dior's father) dies a mysterious death, probably murdered by the imam.
The village men then debate the authority of the princess. They refuse to
recognize her as a legitimate heir to the throne since her sexuality automatically signifies ineffectiveness and the inability to lead.

The film suggests that before the direct assault on African traditions by alien cultures most African societies were matrilineages lasting millenia, from the prepharonic period all the way down to the micronation like the Akans of Ghana. What changed the pattern in some areas were, first, Islam and, later, Christianity, since both religions were obviously patriarchal in orientation.[17]

As the representative of such a patriarchal tradition, the imam underestimates Princess Dior and never suspects that she is capable of killing him. He is wrong, of course, and dies. This woman brings dignity and pride to her people at a crucial moment when the men have been subdued and enslaved, and have renounced their traditional ways of worship. As an articulation of national struggle, a model social change is hereby constructed for Africa. Princess Dior not only rekindles her people's spirit and commitment to self-determination, but also projects a sense of direction in which capable and trustworthy women are leaders. The image of Princess Dior after her triumph is mythic; the camera privileges her, making her a prominent figure whose image is indeed larger than life. The final frame is emblematic of this assertion: she stands freeze-framed like a warrior, her eyes permanently fixed on her people.

Other African male directors besides Sembene have forcefully delineated woman's image in terms of her involvement with the independence movement and the resistance to colonial aggression. Med Hondo in *Sarraounia* vividly constructs a positive image of an African queen (Sarraounia), a warrior who successfully mobilized her forces and waged a stiff resistance to the invading French colonial army of occupation. Like *Ceddo,* this film dispels the myth, often propagated by traditionalist as well as colonialist assumptions, that women are not born to rule, or that they are simply sexual objects or exotic cliches. The queen, Sarraounia, is elegant; her imposing figure, magnificent. However, she becomes heroic not by using her beautiful body to seduce and kill, as might occur in Western movies, but by her tactical maneuvering to substantiate her role as commander in chief. When we see her in war attire addressing her subjects, we identify her not as a woman but as a warrior, a liberator. None of her soldiers are diverted by her sexuality. The preparatory war sequences are inundated by panegyric voices of community—a griot sings to her and to everyone about her people's loyalty, citing the common ground that upholds their movement toward national unity and transformation. Sarraounia's example perhaps supports the contention that "women have got a capacity which men have got to learn,"[18] or, the slogan might as well read, "what a man can do a woman can do better." It is interesting, though, that Sofola relates the latter slogan to African women of intellect, while her nonliterate counterpart would say, "what a woman can do, a man cannot do"[19]— suggesting that militant feminism is even stronger among the peasants, a thesis reminiscent of Frantz Fanon's and Amilcar Cabral's emphasis on the peasantry and on cultural emancipation.

Desiré Ecaré's *Faces of Women* suggests a feminist ethic that the contemporary African might well embrace.[20] Questioning Africa's cultural patrimony and the strategies of patriarchal subordination of women, the film suggests paths women can follow to liberate themselves from men. The film constructs a revolutionary ideology with a central focus that addresses feminine perspectives. The main emphases involve the refusal of women to succumb to the machinations of male domination and women's efforts to share control in the new market economies.

The central female character in the second of two parallel stories is Bernadette (Eugene Cissé Roland), a middle-aged industrialist who owns a fish-smoking business. Bernadette is deprived of a bank loan to expand her business by a male manager who later flirts with her daughters when they come to intervene on their mother's behalf. When he meets with the girls, the manager becomes very accommodating, apparently dazzled by their good looks. Although he does not approve the loan at first, his broad smiles and the manner in which he asks for a date with any of the girls ("when you are passing by") suggests that it is possible to bend the rules. Through Bernadette's assertiveness and articulation of Senegal's socioeconomic decadence, she demonstrates an intense understanding of African women. In a conversation with her daughter, Bernadette, still fuming about the bank's refusal to grant her a loan, lambastes the system, claiming that if everyone tried to own a business Senegal would be relieved of unemployment. Although this might seem a simplistic solution to Africa's complex economic quagmire, her actions demonstrate a motivation that is not evident in any of the parasites around her—the men in her family who depend on her for subsistence. Her strong desire to end male repression of progressive ideals and to install formidable and progressive change provokes her to counsel her daughter to go to the military academy after her high school examination to train and get tough like men.

Bernadette's position is diametrically opposed to her daughter T'Cheley's acerbic proclamation that as a beautiful woman she is well equipped to confront the problematics of social transformation:

Our bank is in our thighs, our breasts and our ass; with these we have got all the power; with my backside, mother, I can get the government toppled tomorrow if I want. I can get a new Ambassador appointed to Paris, to Peking and even to the Vatican. The Pope won't twig, God and women always see eye to eye. For that you've got to be twenty and good looking.

This statement, of course, reflects T'Cheley's youthful exuberance and her myopic view of contemporary life, which her mother shrugs off in disbelief as she continues to emphasize her progressive agenda. Yes, female sexual power exists in Africa as in other countries; however, the above picture of T'Cheley cannot be dismissed as a stereotypical image of African woman. Rather, Ecaré is reflecting on elements of social realities, and blends fiction with satire, sometimes metaphorically, to criticize contemporary inefficiencies and decadence. These problems are symptomatic of African society's effort to grapple with the changes wrought in chaos and conflicting ideologies. Moreover, *Faces'* narrative points to the potential of future sociocultural revolution, and challenges the viewer to reflect upon black sexuality. It contains what has been described as Africa's steamiest erotica, a controversial love-making sequence, which, arguably, is a manifestation of Western influence. Showered with favorable reviews in the West, the film is proscribed in Cote d'Ivoire. From a traditionalist/Africanist perspective, it is understandable that the film is considered lurid, since nudity and indecent exposure are generally taboo. Yet this controversial sequence has a positive aspect, in that sexual intimacy between African people is seldom depicted in Hollywood films.[21]

Thus, *Faces of Women* also enables us to use African aesthetics to repostulate the notions of feminism and feminist film theory exemplified by Laura Mulvey's seminal article, "Visual Pleasure and Narrative Cinema." In this regard, I have argued elsewhere that

it is possible to interpret the nude sequence as a feminist squeal or a phallocentric construction in which the woman's body no longer "holds the look" nor "plays to and signifies male desire" since the social and cultural implications bounce against the two characters. [Kouassi's and Affoue's bodies as shown in the nude sequence can be read as] sexual objects coded for erotic spectacle and the gaze of both male and female spectators—she for her body and he for his penis.[22]

The black body in this nude sequence is beautifully shot, provoking a series of harmonious images.

Sarah Maldoror's celebrated film *Sambizanga* (1972) gives female subjectivity special attention as it pertains to revolutionary struggles. Here, the colonizer/colonized syndrome is poignantly depicted as tension between exploiters and the exploited through a deliberately didactic revolutionary aesthetic. *Sambizanga* was shot in the People's Republic of Congo, and depicts the armed struggle by the militant freedom fighters of PAIG (African Party for the Independence of Guinea and the Cape Verde Islands) and MPLA (the Popular Movement for the Liberation of Angola). The film is not necessarily about the war, but it delineates the spirit of solidarity existing among individuals pursuing the same goals. While the camera follows Maria (Elisa de Andrade), who frantically searches for Domingo, her husband (who was abducted and tortured to death by the agents of the Portuguese colonialists), the feminist aspect of the film's structure becomes apparent. As in *Sarraounia,* it is aimed at giving credibility to woman's active participation and involvement in the dangerous business of revolutionary struggle. The character of Maria is exemplary, and suggests the spirit of solidarity existing between the women. When Maria learns that her husband has been murdered, the women, in the typical African gesture of communality, rally around her. They share the sadness of her loss, the joy of caring for an aggrieved neighbor, the comfort in wearing the traditional black mourning clothes and in taking care of her infant, who accompanied her all the while she confronted the intransigent colonial officers. This sense of collectivity and femininity is acutely captured with a lingering camera that pans almost endlessly on the women's emotion-laden faces. In challenging the traditional role of women, *Sambizanga*'s structure is markedly different from any of the above-mentioned films in two respects. First, its text, language, and form derive specifically from a woman's emotional experience. Second, it demonstrates distinctly economical as well as intelligent choices concerning profilmic elements—using what is available in terms of light, existing colors, and so forth.

Cultural critics contend that it is almost impossible to understand the concern in black film practice with the social construction of reality and of women without recognizing the influence of former styles of realism that black film practice rejects. Referring specifically to black British practice, though her remarks are relevant to the broad diasporan connection emphasized here as well, critic Kobena Mercer opines that the desire to rehumanize the distorted black image, reclaiming and revealing it vividly "like it is—should be understood as the prevailing mode in which counter-discourse . . . [is being] constructed against the dominant versions of reality."[23] This statement indicates the rebellious stance of feminist aesthetics—challenging norms of representation and established traditions of filmmaking, both dominant and (at times) oppositional. If "the focus is activism within the socio-political power game of contemporary world order," as Sofola argues, "there is no doubt that today's international feminist militancy could not have by-passed Africa."[24]

TWO AFRICAN FEMINIST-ORIENTED FILMS

It has been my intention to use the above discussion to reinforce the argument I want to present in the rest of this chapter. I am arguing here that while African film practice in general is alternative and counterhegemonic, within this structure African women's films can be read as constructing a paradigm. First and foremost, this paradigm consists of speaking from within, and attempting to compose a rich and varied portrait of the African woman via canonical modification and revisionism—something that male-dominated narratives have not completely grasped. From this perspective, two documentary films by women filmmakers are extremely significant: *Selbe: One Among Many* (Senegal, 1982), by Safi Faye, and *Sidet: Forced Exile* (Ethiopia, 1991), by Salem Mekuria. Both are significant for their examination of female characters with regard to the social and cultural parameters that define the spaces they occupy or seek to inhabit. Also significant are the ways in which the critical emphasis on reimaging and revisioning the African woman permeates the films' structure, thus rendering it far more than a mere appendage to male-oriented narrative.

As already stated, African film practice to this day is male dominated. Since 1963, a number of African women have ventured into the profession, including Cameroon journalist Thérèsa Sita Bella (*Tam Tam à Paris*, 1963), Ghana's Efua Sutherland (*Araba: The Village Story*, 1967), Tanzania's Flora M'mbugu Shelling (*Sun Sunup*, 1985) and Kenya's Anne G. Mungai (*Productive Farmlands*, 1990; *Wakesa at Crossroads*, 1986; and *Saikati*, 1992).[25] Others include Burkina Faso's Fanta Regina Nacro, whose film *Un certain matin* (1992) was the winner of the 1992 Carthage film festival gold medal award for short films, and Kenya's Wanjiru

Kinyanjui, a bright and promising young student in Berlin who has made two critically acclaimed shorts, *Black in the Western World* (1992) and *The Sick Bird* (1991). There are also a host of other women professionals working in television across Africa. However, Safi Faye remains the dominant figure in film production, and just recently, with the release of *Sidet*, Ethiopia's Salem Mekuria has been gaining visibility.

Selbe is a thirty-minute documentary that portrays the lives of women in a contemporary Senegalese village. As the men leave temporarily for the urban centers in search of jobs, the women bear the economic and social burden of caring for their families. Safi Faye reflects on the personal struggle of one woman whose story has collective significance. The film's structure is marked by an ethnographic perspective as well as African sensibility. Faye was trained as an ethnologist and as a filmmaker. In this film she works both to delineate the sociopolitical and economic problems of Senegal and to lend support to the oppressed Serer peasantry.

In all Faye's films, the characters participate in the filmmaking process itself—doing their everyday chores and expressing themselves as though oblivious to the camera's presence. The conversation between Selbe and the filmmaker is intimate at times, as there is no omniscient voice pushing or directing what the woman is saying or what the viewer should see, a technique which we might well trace to the heyday of *cinéma vérité*. I must point out, however, that in the American print there is an irritating and often distracting voice-over narration. Subtitles would have worked best for me, as extra narration was not necessary to convey action that was quite explicit. (The most powerfully indoctrinating sequences in the film, arguably, are the ones in which there is silence.) From the visuals, the viewer is provided with specific insights into the villagers; the historical, cultural, and sociopolitical milieu; and the culturally bound male/female relationships. Thus, when we see the women potters in action we also know why the men are absent: it is the dry season when there is no work for them to do at home. What is left are the familiar everyday chores—cooking, caring for the children, and providing food for the family. The film criticizes the village men who will eat without asking where the ingredients come from or how much they cost, and who do not help the women who are working ceaselessly. The men are portrayed as parasites, and as Selbe puts it, "scroungers." Providing the family with everyday nourishment in most cases has traditionally been the burden of women. At one point, Selbe, with a baby strapped to her back, has three other kids pester her as she draws water from the well, while the men sit idle—one smoking a cigarette—without providing any help. In another sequence in which the camera plays a discerning role, an ox-driven cart loaded with firewood arrives carrying Mamadou's wife, with her infant sitting on her lap. The cart stops in front of their house, and the woman is seen struggling to hold her kid as she manages to alight from the cart, after which she starts to unload the firewood. A slow pan to the left reveals Mamadou, her husband, sitting, completely nonchalant. When his wife asks for help he responds with impudence, saying, "I helped you yesterday." His indifference to the reality confronting him only reminds the viewer of the deprivation and indignation expressed earlier in the film when Selbe stated, "the strength of my arm is all I can rely on." When she is not cooking, she is collecting mussels to sell, the proceeds from which she uses to buy fish and rice to feed her family.

Selbe depicts the men as village parasites—totally indifferent toward familial bonds. There is no question of who is in charge here in the filmic process; this is a woman's story told with utmost realism. The development of female subjectivity here echoes the central characters in certain black literary works that explore the self. As Alexis De Veaux writes, "It's the self in relationships with an intimate other, with the community, the nation and the world. Self is universal in this context because it has an understanding of the one as the beginning one and then moves beyond that."[26] As Faye's title indicates, the film focuses on one woman's life (Selbe's), but as the subtitle "One Among Many" implies, there are many other Selbes—African women straddling the same pedestal trying to change their lives. The filmic mode employed, which juxtaposes fictional and documentary elements, draws attention to the national dimensions of the individual problems posed here. The film privileges women—people restricted by the community and by immense social, political, and economic forces. The legacy of monoculturism imposed by colonialism, and the neglect of rural life due to the entrenched economic impotence of Senegal and of virtually all African states, are shown to be sources of the contemporary quagmire.

However, *Selbe* deviates from traditional constraints by reversing the syncretic (Islamic/African) code of conduct forced on women by Islamic patriarchy. The filmmaker herself is a devout Muslim, and under a strict Islamic code would not, as a woman, interact publicly with men or put forward a representative and communal vision, as is foregrounded in this film. *Selbe's* narrative and documentary codes in the control of women criticize and revise traditional criteria of filmic content and conventions.

(Regarding traditional filmic criteria, I am comparing *Selbe* with earlier films that deal with women and Islam, such as *Xala* and *Ceddo,* which depict women as symbols of tradition—as taciturn figures whom critics have dubbed "silent revolutionaries.")[27]

Faye's narratives have a tendency to foreground communal concerns, and to invite spectator identification with these concerns. Faye states that her films "are not primarily focusing on women,"[28] since she is concerned with the plight of all Senegalese peasants, men as well as women. An examination of her narrative strategy, however, suggests that it is through female eyes, either hers or those of female characters, that this collective dimension emerges. Nonetheless, the quest for identity, community, and history as a collective enterprise does strongly emerge. Although *Selbe* foregrounds individuality, it uses individuality as a metaphor for the people. Moreover, national problems take on continental dimensions in this film, as visual evidence suggests the Pan-African nature of Selbe's experience.

The strength of the film lies in the powerful images that convey female subjectivity from the point of view of the filmmaker as she directs the viewer to witness the African woman's situation as a relentless struggle for survival. However, it is also from the details in these images that the viewer familiar with Africa's contemporary socioeconomic affairs begins to notice the obfuscation of important societal problems, which the film alludes to but does not address. For example, at the beginning of the film we are told that Selbe is thirty-nine years old and that she has lost one child and now has eight. Although one would admit that *Selbe* is not a United Nations' or Planned Parenthood commercial, one still wonders why in the face of the abject poverty afflicting all African countries there is such a tolerant attitude toward overproduction of children. In another scene, the film presents the case of a mother whose husband left the village to seek a job in the city only two days before his child died. It is worth noting that infant mortality is a perennial problem in Africa. Perhaps this is the reason Selbe is so industrious. Her children look healthy, but does the need for all this toil by Selbe reflect a lack of vision or courage on the part of the leadership in the contemporary period? "Leadership in this context," as Ama Ata Aidou puts it, "does not refer to the political leadership exclusively."[29] There was not any real enforcement of family planning in Africa until the late 1980s when the continent's economic stagnation, in conjunction with IMF's Structural Adjustment Programs, imposed inhumane austerity measures and hyperinflation on the people. These are topics that Safi Faye does not expand upon, but they are there in the film's structure—despite the brevity of the film, just thirty minutes, it still manages to acknowledge their existence. The most pathetic issue of the villagers' plight is elicited when, toward the end, a little girl asks her mother why she has not been sent to school. The mother's reply is that she has to stay home to help with domestic work. Again, one of the causes of Africa's illiteracy problems is identified, but not elaborated upon or presented as an issue that demands urgent attention. What seems to be the film's central theme is woman's aspirations for family cohesiveness with a husband who is constantly present, but completely irresponsible. In addition, by using a female character to hint at the problem of illiteracy, Faye indicates that in African societies women are less likely to be educated than men. Her narrative mirrors her antiestablishment stance and her critique of female marginalization. *Selbe* ends on an optimistic, albeit ironic, note with the women asking for God's help to provide food and a better life for the children. But how—since God cannot descend, feed, clothe, and educate the teeming African population?

Optimism is also a theme in *Sidet*, which takes place amid dreams of faraway Australia, the possible future home of Ethiopian refugees fleeing the ravages of war and destruction. *Sidet* documents the life stories of three Ethiopian women refugees driven from their homes to exile in the Sudan. The film highlights their miserable living conditions in exile and the women's efforts to cope with their families. The life stories of the three women inform the film's narrative, and it is from their point of view that the viewer understands the drama of their daily lives, their struggle for subsistence, and the collective mobilization that keeps the life of the refugees resilient. Camp life is submerged in scarcity; even as the women struggle to create life in exile, water is not free. It is also from the women that we learn about the international relief operations that have failed to meet the needs of the refugees. Equally pathetic are the diminishing health care resources resulting from budget cuts, and the consequent drastic decline in children's health care and nutrition.

The most prevalent cause of death for women and children in the camp is shown to be malnutrition. One sequence replays images of the famine victims of Ethiopia in the 1980s. As the screen is filled with skeletons in human skin, the narrator tells the audience that malnutrition is the greatest problem for children, and that 150 out of 1,000 die before they are five years old. Worse still, 55 out of 1,000 mothers die when giving birth. The film clearly blames Ethiopia's civil strife and the annexation of Eritrea, which institutionalized some of the most blatant human rights abuses in modern history.

Mekuria's camera captures with utmost intensity the refugees' difficulties under arbitrarily imposed conditions, and their struggle to survive while maintaining a strong commitment to their traditions. Thus, in the camp, a woman sustains her family by making and selling *injera,* a staple for most Ethiopians; others sell an illegal, locally brewed Ethiopian alcoholic drink, which must be hidden from Islamic Sudan's law enforcement agencies. The most painful moments are sequences dealing with refugees' reminiscences about their loved ones. Significantly emotional and especially haunting is the scene that dramatizes the pain of separation between Abeba Tsegaye and one of her little sons who has been left behind in Ethiopia. After a separation of five years, mother and child are aurally and spiritually reconnected through the replay of a recorded message that speaks of memory and longing. As Abeba listens, the little boy's voice sings, telling his mother how he would want to liberate his people from abject poverty through education. And this quest for knowledge is strongly reinforced following the emotionally charged poem he has written and sung to Abeba:

> To be strong and expand your mind
> There is no way except education.
> To develop our land, to find solutions to unlock
> the wealth of our earth it is not by miracle,
> but through education.
> To reclaim our countries' wealth to benefit ourselves and to
> help others it is through education.

Let us mention in passing that this liberationist and progressive message echoes the yearning of the little girl in *Selbe* who wants to be educated but is deprived of the opportunity. Similarly, the women in *Sidet* are continuously looking for the opportunity to break away from exile and, in some cases, to resume their education and normal life in Ethiopia when the fighting ends.

It is from the perspective of the women's struggle in *Selbe* that the ending, which involves the wait for manna from heaven, seems problematic. Such a solution is unsatisfying because hard-working Selbe and the other women require not a miracle but the assistance that an informed and capable government should provide to improve the living conditions of its people. One wishes the women would call pragmatically for basic improvements related to economic infrastructure, for example, and to a safe and ample water supply. Nevertheless, Selbe's self-motivation during most of the film epitomizes a major aspect of African feminism, which, in Filomina Chioma's terms, is "an abnegation of male protection and a determination to be resourceful and self-reliant."[30] Selbe addresses the issue of equality poignantly, unafraid to question the gender restrictions imposed upon women in her society. Following the little boy's thought-provoking message in *Sidet* is a sequence that projects the question of survival—an abiding concern of the majority of marginalized people in continental Africa. Particularly disturbing is the scene in which Abeba meets with representatives of the United Nations High Commission for Refugees, who help to arrange for the permanent emigration of Ethiopians to Western countries that will accept them. Isn't this the worst form of degradation and denigration of African and Third World peoples, who, after the euphoria of independence, find that the neocolonial structure has created such unprecedented poverty that they now aspire to get out to any place other than Africa? As Abeba learns that her visa to Australia is approved, she laughs, and initially a look of total relief and satisfaction can be seen on her face. Although she is delighted, she laughs reservedly, knowing that Australia is only a temporary refuge because her spirit will never leave her motherland, Ethiopia. If, as Sofola contends, "the world view of the African is rooted in the philosophy of holistic harmony and communalism rather than in the individualistic isolationism of Europe,"[31] Abeba's asylum in Australia negates the "principle of relatedness" that is indispensable to the African sociocultural fabric; as O. Ehusani states, "relatedness characterizes the African experience of the living person [and] if one is cut off from his/her community, one is considered dead."[32]

In appreciating her new status, Abeba talks about giving her little boy a good education. But it is also clear that she and her little boy are joining millions of other "lost" Africans driven into exile by Africa's menacing economic problems. They are in the United States, Australia, Europe, the Middle East, and Asia—wherever they can lead "normal" lives. But the "lands of milk and honey" they aspire to reach are also "deterritorialized," where blacks as "niggers" are constantly reminded that they should go back to Africa. For me, as someone in temporary exile living in the United States, Mekuria's film is symbolic as an exilic text that can be used to formulate a discourse of exile. This sweet/sour feeling is echoed in Hamid Naficy's notion of "exile as liminality": "This compound sense of pain and paralysis is not due solely to the displacing conditions one finds in exile, but also often it is related to the dire circumstances one has left behind. Tragedy at home, which often drives people out of their countries, looms larger, even larger in exile."[33]

It is interesting that *Sidet*'s message is so pointed and yet the women depicted cannot be said to be simply illustrating a point but rather initiating a dialogue in a process of mutual exploration that includes the filmmaker, the filmed, and the audience. The propriety and naturalness of this exploration are supported by the subtle cinematography, including the long takes and unobtrusive camera, and by culturally specific signifiers such as the lyrics and the music of stringed instruments. One can hardly ignore the emotional resonances of the song from the opening sequence:

> I'm thirsty, my sister
> I'm hungry, my mother.
> Who can I tell this to?
> I'm in exile
> Oh me, oh my . . .
> In silence all seasons
> I have nothing at all
> except old age and poverty
> I am crying about poverty
> give me injera
> I will eat it standing
> Since there is no respect for one in exile.
> Exiles don't raise their heads to look straight
> People in trouble never have enough.
> Poor people don't give injera to other people.

The woman who sings this song appears melancholic. Her mood and her song reflect the vast cultural and political problem the film attacks. The song is "infectious," because the structure of the film enables the lyrics to keep reverberating in the viewer's mind, serving not only as a voice of female experience, but as one that invites the audience to share that experience. As the song instructs us, "In silence all seasons," parallels the experience of many African women, and it is indeed rejuvenating to see, once again, this doubly marginalized group—African women filmmakers— taking control in an exceptional manner, eloquently confronting the "silence" that has eclipsed their lives.

Mekuria and Faye can also be seen as having developed methods of externalizing this silence—through their inquiring lenses and other devices related to the masterful integration of cinematic and cultural codes. Like *Selbe, Sidet* is deliberate in its dramatic rendering of feminine encounters. These perspectives, like diasporic black feminist discourse, are conveyed vividly and are devoid of fetishization and stereotype. Judicious use of the film medium and careful character delineation work toward a counterhegemonic conclusion. Both films speak for diverse audiences and marginal groups, but this captivating power is very specific in terms of choice of images, composition, camera movement, lighting, editing, and the overall narrative rhythm. Coupled with these features is a natural portrayal of mannerisms. Together, these characteristics signify Africanness, autonomy, and noncompliance, which tend to be deconstructive in terms of ideology and style.

African cinema has done considerable work in privileging women's issues, particularly the re-creation of female subjectivity. However, there obviously is much still to be done. On a global level, women filmmakers in the diaspora are "fixed on the same pedestal"—in Fanonian terms, trying to confront the hegemony inherent in mainstream production and distribution practices. In the films *Sidet* and *Selbe,* and in many other films made by women, it is clear that thematic and aesthetic prerogatives are determined by specific social, political, and gender objectives rather than by conventional spectacle and commercial success. In sum, the tension between the manifold identities of Third World and other marginalized peoples, on the one hand, and the pressures of colonialism and imperialism, on the other, marks the point of convergence for "alternative" cinema, which, understandably, female film practice embraces.

NOTES

1. 'Zulu Sofola is a professor of performing arts as well as a Nigerian playwright whose work is well known in the United States and elsewhere. Her paper, "Feminism and the Psyche of African Womanhood," delivered at the first international conference on "Women in Africa and the African Diaspora: Bridges across Activism and the Academy" at the University of Nigeria, Nsukka, June 1992, is invaluable to the advancement of the dialogue presented in this paper.

2. See, for example, Ama Ata Aidou, "The African Woman Today," *Dissent* 39 (Summer 1992): 320.

3. Martina Attile and Maureen Blackwood, "Black Women and Representation," in Charlotte Brunsdon, ed., *Films for Women* (London: British Film Institute, 1986), 203.

4. Martina Attile and Maureen Blackwood, "Black Women," 204.

5. I am referring to the hegemonic definition of races—in this case when nonwhite people arbitrarily connote "primitivity," "underdevelopment," "Third World," even "twelfth World"—in a word, the "other" in contradistinction to whiteness, which automatically translates to "First World," "advanced," "developed," "industrialized."

6. See August Wilson, "I Want a Black Director," *New York Times,* 26 Sept. 1990, A25.

7. August Wilson, "I Want a Black Director," A25.

8. For readers' responses to August Wilson's article, see *New York Times,* 12 Oct. 1990, A34.

9. Clyde Taylor, "Africa, The Last Cinema," in Renee Tajima, ed., *Journey across Three Continents: Film and Lecture Series* (New York: Third World Newsreel, 1985), 50–58.

10. *Daughters of the Dust* is distributed by Kino International Corporation, New York. Production kit and press releases may be available on request.

11. Zeinabu Irene Davis, "Woman with a Mission: Zeinabu Irene Davis on Filmmaking," *Voices of the African Diaspora* (University of Michigan's Center for Afroamerican and African Studies Research Review) VII: 3 (Fall 1991): 38.

12. Gladstone L. Yearwood, ed., *Black Cinema Aesthetics: Issues in Independent Black Filmmaking* (Athens: Ohio University Center for Black Studies, 1982). See Pearl Bowser's "Sexual Imagery and the Black Woman in American Cinema," 41–51.

13. Ousmane Sembene has conveyed this important fact on several occasions to his audience. It has also been cited in François Pfaff's *The Cinema of Ousmane Sembene* (Westport, Conn.: Greenwood Press, 1984), and in Ulrich Gregor's interview with Sembene, *Framework* (Spring 1978): 35–37.

14. Ama Ata Aidou, "African Women," 319. See also note 2 of her article.

15. Some African women have made progress in recent years. There are instances since 1975 of women becoming university leaders, government ministers, and members of parliament. In Mozambique, a country almost obliterated by Russian and American ammunition during its protracted civil war, women

account for 16 percent of the representatives of the House of Parliament (a higher percentage than in comparable institutions in Britain, the United States, or France). Sylviane Diouf Kamara's comparative analysis "Changing Roles? African Women at the Turn of the Century," *West Africa* 3837, 18–24, (March 1991): 403, is a stimulating commentary on women in African society and development.

16. 'Zulu Sofola, "Feminism and the Psyche," 2. (See n. 1 above.)

17. Ama Ata Aidou, "African Women," 321.

18. C. L. R. James, "Toward the Seventh: The Pan-African Congress— Past, Present, and Future," *At the Rendezvous of Victory* (London: Allison and Busby, 1984), 250.

19. 'Zulu Sofola, "Feminism and the Psyche," 24.

20. The film supports women's empowerment. However, African viewers find the portrayal of women misleading, at best, and downright false and compromising at other times. For example, an African woman would not call her husband stupid in public, while N'Guessan does.

21. This "rereading" of the lovemaking sequence stems from the discussion of the film in my "Cultural Issues in Cinema" class when one of my African-American female students made reference to this interesting analogy.

22. See my book, *Black African Cinema* (Berkeley and Los Angeles: University of California Press, 1994).

23. Kobena Mercer, "Recoding Narratives of Race and Nation," in *Black Film British Cinema* (London: British Film Institute: ICA Documents 7, 1988), 9.

24. 'Zulu Sofola, "Feminism and the Psyche," 1.

25. *Saikati* was shown at the 1993 FESPACO of Ouagadougou. With this film, Ann G. Mungai demonstrates her talent as a creative artist. The film deals with the subject of arranged marriage and the collision of African culture with Western influence, the theme of many other African films. It focuses on a young village girl's defiance of family pressures to give up her education to marry the chief's son. "Saikati flees the village to go to town with her cousin Monica who promises to find her a job." But her cousin Monica earns her living from prostitution. Saikati is not prepared to sell her body. She decides to go back to the village, escorted by Monica's tourist boyfriend. However, they make a mistake in reading the map and get lost in the Masaai Mara, where they are threatened by wild animals. It is in this rescue scene that the director loses her creative exuberance demon-

strated in the beginning of the film. The camera wallows in the menacing wildlife without knowing when to stop. Having watched Bryant Gumble's "Today Show in Africa" (which glorified African animals at the expense of African people) a few weeks before I left for Burkina Faso to attend the thirteenth PanAfrican Festival of Film and Television (FESPACO), I wondered whether this film was packaged for the promotion of the Kenyan Tourist Industry, given the sponsors of the film: African Tours and Hotels, Carnivore, Maria River Camp, and Serena Lodges and Hotels, to mention a few. To give the film true African sensitivity, some of the animal sequence—at least twenty minutes of it—ought to be eliminated.

26. Claudia Tate, *Black Women Writers at Work* (New York: Continuum, 1988), 54. As quoted in Gloria J. Gibson-Hudson's article, "African American Literary Criticism as a Model for the Analysis of Films by African American Women," *Wide Angle* 13: 3&4: 44–54.

27. See David Uru Iyam, "The Silent Revolutionaries: Ousmane Sembene's *Emitai, Xala,* and *Ceddo,*" *African Studies Review* 29: 4 (December 1986): 79–87.

28. This statement was made at the 1982 ASA conference, and is cited in Françoise Pfaff's *Twenty-Five Black African Filmmakers* (Westport, Conn.: Greenwood Press, 1988), 118.

29. Ama Ata Aidou, "The African Woman," 320.

30. *The Black Woman Cross Culturally* (Cambridge, Mass.: Schenkman, 1991), 35.

31. 'Zulu Sofola, "Feminism and the Psyche," 8.

32. O. Ehusani, *An Afro-Christian Vision "Ozovehe"* (New York: University Press of America, 1991), 86.

33. Hamid Naficy, "Exile Discourse and Television Fetishization," *Quarterly Review of Film and Video* 13:1–3: 85.

CHAPTER FIVE

In the Shadow of Race: Forging Gender in Bolivian Film and Video

ELENA FEDER

If Indians and *Cholos* are to intervene at all in the progressive evolution of Bolivian society, it will necessarily be through the passive route of a more or less rapid disintegration: as by-products of secretions spilled in and around the organic cavities of the social body or as residues scattered inside the deep recesses of the economy, so that from there they will no longer interfere with the complete purification and caucasian unification of the national race.

—Gabriel René Moreno[1]

> *Huayruro,* don't shoot
> on the bridge, be the bridge ...
>
> —José María Arguedas, *Deep Rivers*

From its inception, Bolivian film has attempted to come to terms with an extremely complex national set of social, economic, cultural, ethnic, and

149

racial formations. These have evolved over the course of five centuries of both armed and passive resistance to the colonial enterprise, including the unresolved wars of liberation leading to independence from Spanish rule in 1825, as well as the ongoing struggles between the ruling white-identified oligarchy and the Indian-identified national majority before, during and after the liberal-oligarchical period (1880–1930s), up to the revolution of 1952 and beyond.[2] From José María Velasco Maidana's foundational epic *Warawara* (1929) to the acclaimed *Vuelve Sebastiana* (Jorge Ruiz, 1953), and *La nación clandestina* (Jorge Sanjinés, 1989), issues of racial figuration have been central to the development of a cinematic idiom for this pluricultural and multilingual nation. So ingrained, in fact, with racial determinants have been both the ruling minority's military, economic, political, and cultural oppression and the indigenous majority's resistance to this oppression that we cannot look at gender issues in Bolivian cinema outside the socioeconomic and discursive mutations of what I will call here the white-Indian dyad, by which I do not mean either "real" or biologically determined racial entities but rather discursively defined, relational subject position(ing)s, the product of Imaginary and Symbolic processes of identity formation sedimented over time. In Bolivia, these have been as indelibly marked by racially coded power imbalances as laced with connotations stemming not only from economic practices traceable to colonial times, like the *encomienda* and *pongueaje*, but—as in the case of Gabriel René Moreno, whom I quote in the epigraph—by nineteenth-century positivist philosophies and subsequent eugenist policies as well.[3]

Today, after the long-awaited results of the elections of 1993, this scenario has taken a dramatically new turn. While Bolivia, like many of its neighbors, is benefitting from a return to democracy while struggling to keep down the devastating social costs of a free market economy imposed from above by transnational concerns, the recent elections are much more than a simple reflection of this high-priced oxymoronic logic. In the throes of a quiet revolution of their own, the Bolivian people have elected Harvard-educated Gonzalo Sánchez de Lozada and the Aymara Indian leader Victor Hugo Cárdenas as president and vice president of the country, effectively putting the *Movimiento Nacionalista Revolucionario* (MNR), the party that came to power in 1952 by first integrating and then betraying the mass peasant and worker revolts, back at the helm. This time, however, with the explicit mandate of making good their renewed promises of fair land reforms, equitable distribution of the national wealth, a reliable justice system, and an end to racial and gender discrimination. The task of upending the deeply ingrained and multi-faceted racism and sexism that have plagued Bolivia is nothing short of daunting. These democratically held elections represent not only the culmination of almost five decades of bloody popular struggles for self-determination but also a definitive blow to the military factions who ruled the country by massacre and intimidation until overthrown by the mass uprisings of November 1982, but did not in effect lose their power until the 1993 elections. Popular support for the MNR was mostly due to the party's unprecedented decision to include an Indian representative of vice president Cárdenas's prominence as a sign of its intention to participate in the reversal of centuries of racial discrimination and apartheidlike white minority rule. Where constitutional entrenchment of native rights is concerned, these elections have put Bolivia—the country with the largest conglomerate of Indian peoples in the Americas, though they enjoyed few civil rights, having been banned de jure from urban areas until the Revolution of 1952 and de facto from public places such as movie theaters long thereafter—in the forefront of American nations.

What follows is a glance cast back from this historical turning point at the epistemological interlacing of gender and the white-Indian dyad in the formation of national consciousness, as represented in Bolivian film and video up to 1993. This mapping of the visual representation of changing social and cultural configurations of the white-Indian dyad over time and the impact of these changes on equally changing parameters of gender, and vice versa, investigates a particular instance of what Homi Bhaba has described as the "multi-accentual …, Janus-faced discourse of the nation," a specific response to his suggestive invitation to "turn [. . .] the familiar two-faced god into a figure of prodigious doubling that investigates the nation-space in the process of articulation of its elements; where meanings may be partial because they are in medias res; and history may be half-made because it is in the process of being made; and the image of cultural authority may be ambivalent because it is caught in the act of 'composing' its powerful image."[4] The changes that follow the quiet revolution of 1993 need be the subject of a separate study.

IMAGING PIGMENTOCRACY

The French social anthropologist Danielle Demelas has aptly termed Bolivia's intricate web of racially coded social relations "pigmentocratic."[5]

Because, as lived experience, the white-Indian dyad has persistently colored the discursive practices of both Bolivia's white-identified oligarchy and the Indian-identified majority's resistant adaptation to it, practically all Bolivian cultural practices, from the cinema to literature to radio to older popular art forms like the carnival, have had to confront the symbolic power of this binary opposition governing the pigmentocracy since the Conquest.[6]

In order to understand the specific contribution of film and videomakers to the wider national discourse on gender, we need to have some sense of the complex framings and reframings of the racial parameters of the dyad since first contact. While Indian-identified Bolivians chart its most important constitutive moments along the two main axes of the Conquest and the Revolution of 1952—interpreted as the long and short horizons of national memory by the videomaker and social historian Silvia Rivera Cusicanqui[7]—the fact is that the finer aspects of the white-Indian dyad's adequations to the epistemic mutations of the last five centuries are just beginning to be mapped out, bringing us marginally closer to understanding the profound implications of the move from colonialism to neocolonialism, initiated in the nineteenth century via a nationalism cast in the mould of inherently racist ideologies of progress, well suited to capitalist expansion, and currently expressed by way of "thirdworldism," development theory, and the ever-spreading proselytism of the Protestant churches.[8]

The complexity of Bolivia's ethnic and linguistic figurations should come as no surprise in a country where over 50 percent of the population are illiterate (the majority women), where two out of every three citizens are primarily Qhechwa and Aymara speakers, and where Spanish, the official language, is not understood by over one-third of the country's inhabitants. Based on the1976 census, Javier Albó estimated that nearly 23 percent of the population spoke only Qhechwa, Aymara, or some other native tongue, while 41 percent were bilingual, with Spanish as their second language.[9] Comparing the results of the 1950 and 1976 censuses, he concluded that the number of habitual Qhechwa and Aymara speakers had in fact diminished, while the number of bilingual speakers with Spanish as the habitual language had increased, with a growing number of bilingual speakers (speaking both Aymara and Qhechwa or either language and Spanish) having become trilingual.[10] This trend toward hispanization (castellanización), largely due to a dramatic increase in the pace of demographic shifts since1952, is also becoming evident in previously inaccessible eastern regions. Besides the Aymara and Qhechwa, who live mostly along the Andean range, of the fifty other ethnic groups who live in the plateaus and jungles around the Amazon and La Plata basins, a 1985 study estimated that many speak both their own language and that of a dominating group in the region: either Aymara (like the Urus), or Guaraní (like the Chanés).[11] In addition, the current estimate of a total of thirty-two national ethnolinguistic groups does not account for the waves of immigration that followed some of the major upheavals of this century. Turkish, German, Jewish, Arab, Korean, Japanese, and other immigrants settled mostly in the cities, and their cultural integration has yet to be postulated, let alone accomplished.

Such ethnolinguistic variety is likely due to the fact that the Bolivian State never undertook a massive educational campaign to integrate the nation, similar to postrevolutioary Cuba's or to the one directed by minister of education José Vasconcelos after Mexico's 1910 revolution. Such a project would have had to be supported by an adequately planned and funded infrastructure, with roads, schools, school books, and teachers properly trained to deal with the linguistic and cultural challenges of the multiplicity of essentially oral cultures. Even after the revolution of 1952, the country's extreme poverty, together with the lack of political will on the part of those controlling the national wealth, caused plans for educational reforms to remain on the drawing board. Ironically, the result was to tip the scales in favor of the preservation of many of Bolivia's oral cultures whose language, rituals, and traditions have not only survived, with the inevitable adaptations, to this day but, as the growing Qhechwa- and Aymara-ization of Bolivian Spanish itself attests, have had a powerful impact on the West-identified culture of the dominant minority as well.

The crucial role of language in shaping national identity has been increasingly at the forefront of cultural debates. In 1993, when vice president Cárdenas delivered his acceptance speech in Aymara, Qhechwa, Guaraní, and Spanish, the public space he was linguistically bridging had already been a wind chest of inspiration for Bolivian artists and intellectuals for some time. In the immensely successful *Yawar Mallku*, the original Qhechwa title of *Blood of the Condor* (1969), for example, Jorge Sanjinés acutely portrayed the pigmentocratic character of language in defining class and gender alliances. [Figure 5.1] The wealthy doctor's *criollo* wife, who is strongly identified with Euro-American values and culture, speaks a heavily accented English to her children while Paulina (Benedicta Huanca), wife of Ignacio (Marcelino Yanahuaya), the *Mallku* or community leader over whose bleeding body the story unfolds, is

154

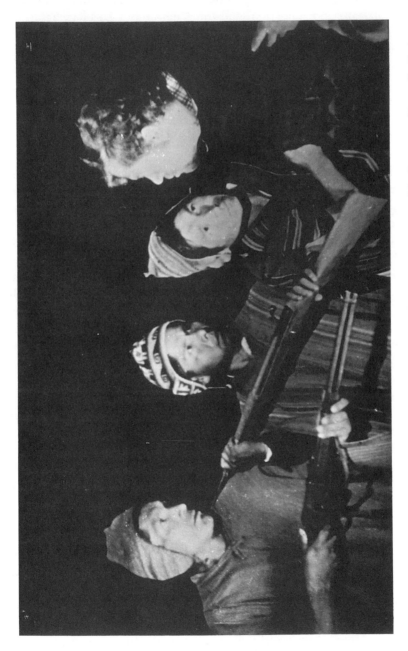

FIGURE 5.1. Four figures in *Yawar Mallku* (*Blood of the Condor*, Jorge Sanjinés, 1969). Courtesy of Jorge Sanjinés.

infantilized and unable to communicate with the Spanish-speaking *mestizo* intern at the dilapidated General Hospital because she lacks the language skills of either the bilingual child lying on a nearby bed or her assimilated brother-in-law, Sixto (Vicente Verneros).[12]

A look at axes of identity other than language, moreover, reveals that not only are assignations such as "Indian" and "white" marked by shifting historical, social, and psychological determinants. Class markers such as "peasant" and "worker" are also subject to multiple slippages and no less reductive, especially when used to supplement racial and gender ones. Silvia Rivera points out, for instance, that the designation "peasant," a term officially adopted after the revolution of 1952, tends to "mask contents developed over many years of struggle by the predominantly Indian rural population (Qhechwa, Aymara, Guaraní, etc.)"; and, as testimonials of miner and peasant women attest, such masking takes on different dimensions when gender comes into the picture.[13]

Since the Revolution of 1952 the dream of homogeneity has been consistently exposed as a hindrance to the articulation of a viable national project both by peasant and worker movements and by urban-based cultural workers, be they filmmakers or social and political theorists. René Zavaleta Mercado, the renowned Bolivian political theorist, aptly described Bolivia in Levi-Straussian terms as a "*bricolage* formation," by which he meant an irregular spatiotemporal patchwork made up of

> an heterogenous aggregate of peoples . . . where each group dresses, sings, eats, and produces in particular ways, speaks different languages with different accents without any of them even remotely qualifying as everyone's universal language. [Here,] true temporal densities coexist in the most variegated ways not just next to one another but touched by the particularism of every other region as well—because here each valley is a motherland.[14]

Zavaleta's spatiotemporal model opened new ways to think about the formation of Bolivian national identity that departed irreversibly from previous attempts to elide the stark reality of vast regional, linguistic, and cultural differences in the name of an unrealistic ideal of homogeneity—regardless of how fundamental homogeneity may be for the quantification (of time, space, labor, etc.) that is the condition of possibility for the capitalist mode of production to which the country has been trying unsuccessfully to adapt since Independence.

The singularity of the Bolivian experience of national identity has led scholars to consider it a "limit case," a challenge to the theoretical assumptions of their particular discipline. While cultural critics, such as Javier Sanjinés, argue that "only with the formation, stabilization, and consolidation of a nation-state will it be possible to speak of a national culture," others, like anthropologist Danielle Demelas, formulated her 1980 thesis on the formation of Bolivia's national identity as a question; her book is entitled *Nationalism without a Nation?*[15] The history of Bolivian cinema can be read as a long critical inquiry into this singularity.

SILENT FILM, A "MONSTROUS" BEGINNING

From the time of its arrival in Bolivia in 1897 film became an active participant in the formation of national identity, albeit not an innocent one. An imported technology, it heralded the advent of modernity and utopia with the promise to connect an essentially feudal country, with 90 percent illiteracy and hardly any roads, to the rest of the world. The sense of universality conveyed by this new wonder of science was supported by the presumably universal, if reifying, meaning of the human-interest stories it told about war, sex, and race. In 1904, the earliest known program of what a journalist termed the *Kinetoscopio Monstruo* brought Bolivian audiences closer to the war betwen Russia and Japan. The program of the 1905 Paris Biograph included the French *Novela de Amor* ("An instructive tragedy in eight scenes, reenacted for over one hundred consecutive nights in the theaters of Europe and America"), a musical interlude (Verdi's *Aida*), and a few comic strips. The program closed with, of all things, *Indian Revenge or Indian Cow Boys* [*sic*] ("the beautiful Mexican historical drama in seven scenes").[16] How this introduction to another culture's ways of othering Indians might have resonated with the select public who attended the plush *Teatro Municipal* (out of bounds to live Indians) can only be speculated, for no other record of the performance remains. What does remain, however, is the first film produced in Bolivia, *Portrait of Historical and Contemporary Personalities* (many of whom were undoubtedly members of that audience), a 1904 documentary which set the tone for the historicizing impulse that has characterized Bolivian film production since.

Until the advent of sound, which put a halt to what can best be described as sporadic but intense production flourishes, titles such as Italian-born Pedro Sambarino's *Corazón Aymara* (*Aymara Heart*), one of two feature-length fictional films released in Bolivia in 1925, and *La Gloria de la Raza* (1926), a documentary about the ruins of Tiahuanaku by Viennese explorer, anthropologist, and entrepreneur Arturo Posnasky, are rare but indicative of the first cinematic moves toward the kind of exoticization of Bolivia's internal Other that characterizes *indianista* fiction as a whole, and that was the hallmark of the country's cinema until 1953.[17]

The other feature-length film released in 1925 was the controversial *La profecía del lago*, by the most prominent filmmaker and producer of the period, José María Velasco Maidana. The obscure circumstances surrounding the film's eventual disappearance serves to illustrate the gender parameters within which the white-Indian dyad was permitted to operate at the time. Although no less exoticist than those of its contemporaries, *La profecía del lago* seems to have shocked the authorities to the point of becoming the subject of the worst case of film censorship in the country's history, with the municipal government going as far as to order its incineration. Hardly any record of the events surrounding this inquisitorial gesture is to be found in the press of the period, and much of what is known about the circumstances surrounding this film relies on word of mouth. Significantly, witnesses have attributed the public's outrage to the film's layered insinuation of a rarely portrayed love affair between a millionaire's wife and an Indian *peón* (scandalously played by Emmo Reyes, the Bolivian "Valentino") who worked at the couple's hacienda by Lake Titicaca, mythic site of origin of the Inca empire.[18] Velasco Maidana went on to make two more fictional films on the subject, the short fictionalized documentary *Amanecer Indio* (*Indian Dawn*, 1928), and the groundbreaking feature-length epic about the fall of the Inca empire *Warawara* (1929), loosely based on a novel by writer Antonio Díaz Villamil who, together with other equally prominent artists of the day, participated actively in the production.

Warawara (Qhechwa for "star") tells the story of an Inca princess who, to the chagrin and rage of her people, falls in love with a captured "good" and noble young Spanish *hidalgo* soon after becoming the sole survivor of her royal family after the huge and bloody battle that followed the infamous murder of Atahuallpa. *Warawara* took two years to film and was, in the words of Alfonso Gumucio Dragón, "the first homemade 'superproduction' of Bolivian cinema."[19] It was also the first film to use a language other than Spanish for the title (changed from the more pessimistic *The Decline of the Land of the Sun*). Velasco Maidana's return to the interracial theme that had given him so much trouble earlier was this time triumphant. Over and above its artisanal sophistication—which reportedly included technical feats like colorization *avant la lèttre*—*Warawara's* popularity (a one-week run) may have been due to the fact that the film circumvented the issue both by projecting it to a remote past and by inverting the sex roles of its protagonists. The result was a narrative that fit the more classic projections of gender since the Conquest which, like the Mexican Malinche story, put the blame on an American Eve for the loss of the Conquistador's dream of El Dorado.

Before the Chaco war (1933–36) and the advent of sound all but silenced Bolivian screens for over a decade, the racial theme was taken up once more in *Hacia la gloria* (*Towards Glory*, 1933). Directed by Mario Camacho, who began his career as Velasco Maidana's cameraman, this controversial tragedy of errors told the unlikely story of a child born out of wedlock to high-society parents who abandon him to die. Rescued and raised in the country by an Indian woman, he returns to the city as a young man to fall in love with a high-society girl who is beyond his reach because of his Indian blood. Brokenhearted, he enlists in the air force and is wounded when his airplane is shot down. Nurtured back to health by a nun who turns out to be his biological mother, the wounded hero learns from his mother's mouth that he and his beloved are both children of the same father, the Minister of War. The racial taboo thus displaced onto the purportedly insurmountable taboo of incest, the story ends with the hero's departure by train into the horizon, destination unknown.

Negative press and, as if predicted by the title, the arrival of *Sombras de Gloria* (*The Shadow of Glory*, 1930), Hollywood's first sound film shot entirely in Spanish, combined to relegate *Hacia la Gloria* to the dustbins of history. Nonetheless, by including in his gaze airplanes, trains, and the early rupture of social and racial conventions, Mario Camacho left to posterity the imprint of a country determinedly on the way to modernity. In its depiction of the private and public wars waged by its citizens, *Hacia la Gloria* registered both the closing of one chapter and the opening of another in Bolivia's national consciousness, albeit with its social and familial boundaries left practically untouched. The Chaco war dealt a final blow to the semifeudalism of the Bolivian state, leaving the way open for the consolidation of Marxist and anarchist doctrines and the revolutionary nationalism which fed the events that led up to the revolution of 1952.[20]

When, half a century later, the theme of interracial incest is again picked up by Paolo Agazzi in *Los hermanos Cartagena* (1985), a free and unsuccessful adaptation of Gaby Vallejo de Bolivar's novel *Hijo de Opa* (1977), it will be transformed into the underpinning of the foundational narrative of the State of '52 (narrative time beginning in those turbulent days and ending with the 1971 military coup), with the biblical drama played out instead over two generations (before and after the revolution) by two brothers, sons of the same landowner father but with one of the mothers as the legally wedded wife and the other as a mentally impaired Indian servant who the father repeatedly raped at his hacienda. Social mores in 1933 would, of course, not have permitted such explicit (and exploitative) treatment.

FILM AND THE REVOLUTION OF 1952

The Revolution of 1952 was a failure in the sense that the centralized party (MNR) ultimately appropriated the power of the popular militia and the peasant unions responsible for its success. From the Indian point of view, the event nonetheless marked a clear epistemological break with the past.[21] Because it was fought by peasants and workers, and because it embodied their demands—namely the nationalization of the mines, agrarian reform, and universal suffrage—it demonstrated the power of the masses to bring about change.

The years that followed the revolution not only reactivated what Silvia Rivera succinctly describes as the "subtle reconstitution of oligarchic-colonial forms of discrimination and domination," they also brought to the surface the cultural and political differences between Indians themselves. These differences were momentarily bridged by the burgeoning Indian movement that interpellated both peasants and workers by resorting to the appropriation of *Indio* as an all-inclusive positive term of reference, although the word was resisted for a long time by the vast majority for its colonial and racist history. Within a generation, the Indian movement transformed the fabric of society in such radical ways that any account of the participation of film and video in the formation of Bolivian national consciousness must reckon with the contents of the Indian struggle or remain incomplete.

In brief, different experiences of the short historical horizon of '52 affected the degree of radicalization not only of the Qhechwa and Aymara, but, most significantly, among the Aymara themselves. The Aymara who had participated in the political process—particularly those who were unionized and utilized their unions to articulate and negotiate their demands—considered themselves citizens and were more inclined to identify with the revolution and to call themselves peasants.[22] Those who migrated from the country and were exposed, often for the first time, to the racism of the cities, were more inclined to refer to the long horizon of historical memory, base their claims on precolonial and millenial forms of social organization and culture, and call themselves *Indios*.[23] Tracing their lineage to Tupaj Katari, the eighteenth-century fighter for independence from colonial rule, the *kataristas* prepared for armed struggle and founded revolutionary parties like the MITKA (*Movimiento Indio Tupak Katari*) and, under the leadership of now Vice President Cárdenas, the more radical MRTKL (*Movimiento Revolucionario Tupak Katari de Liberación*).

Twenty years after the revolution, the *kataristas* declared themselves to be "tired of being . . . strangers in our own land," and began to come to terms with the contradictions inherent in the reconciliation of ancient traditions and beliefs with the Bolivian version of the culture of modernity. In their 1973 manifesto they proclaimed, somewhat idealistically : "We have to technify and modernize our past, but under no circumstances are we to break with it. Every attempt to europeanize or 'yanquify,' as was attempted through education and politics, will only mean a new defeat. . . . Indians are noble and just, proud, worthy of respect, hard working, and profoundly religious."[24] Five years later, in a radical move, the national peasant union finally integrated the core beliefs of the *kataristas* into their "Political Theses of 1978" where, referring to the horizon of long memory, they publicly acknowledged the deeply rooted racism they continued to contend with: "Since 1492, we have been degraded to the condition of colonized, under the generic term *Indio*. . . . Our history is not only one of humiliation, but also of a struggle to transform this unjust creole society inherited from colonial times."[25] The movement finally took off in full force when peasant- and worker-unions joined forces in 1979, following the dissolution of the military-peasant pact (a delaying tactic of the state that ended in 1974, after the infamous peasant massacres of Tolata, Epizana, and Melga). From then on it was only a matter of time before the demise of the liberal-oligarchic state became a reality. In a matter of forty years, though at an enormous cost, the Indian movement managed to create the conditions of visibility that would guarantee the ethnopluralism of the Bolivian State of '93.

Whether directly or indirectly, all Bolivian cinema bespeaks some aspect of the dialectic between the culture's denial of, and insistence on, the memory of genocide during its long colonial and short revolutionary pasts. Because of their role as bearers of the political and cultural discourse of the nation, Bolivian film- and videomakers since 1952 have had to increasingly confront the atavistic interconnectedness of linguistic and cultural differences with class- and racially coded abuses and exploitation. This challenge has not been easy. It is indeed a tall order to ask white-identified creole or mestizo intellectuals who have been trained in Western-style educational institutions in the cities or abroad, to create new models of intersubjectivity that will not only honor the past by being both transformative and meaningful to historical agents on both sides of the white-Indian dyad, but also transgressive enough to desire and promote the removal of class and pigmentocratic privileges that had shaped their very being. In dealing with the threat of the potential disappearance of their sense of identity, in the mirror of an Other always already poised at the limits of the Self, Bolivian artists and intellectuals have had to confront behaviors that did not always coincide with their ideals.[26] Typical, for instance, are heated debates with accusations of reverse racism directed by the left at other urban intellectuals for adopting the term *Indio* as a banner for self-determination, accusations countered in turn by accusing the accusers for what social historian-cum-videomaker Silvia Rivera would call their "complete unwillingness to recognize the Otherness of Indian culture."[27] While such issues are far from settled, it can safely be said that the distinguishing trait of the Bolivian cultural project since 1952 has been an increasing tolerance of the profound differences as well as a growing acceptance of the similarities that both separate and unite indigenous and implanted cultures. People on all sides have slowly been learning to see themselves as their Other's other Other, an improvement in the formation of racial consciousness that, at least as expressed in film and video, has yet to be equaled when it comes to gender.

THE BOLIVIAN INSTITUTE OF CINEMATOGRAPHY

On March 20, 1953, scarcely one year after the revolution, the newly formed MNR government founded the *Instituto Cinematográfico Boliviano* to replace the Cinematography Department of the Ministry of News and Propaganda created in July 1952, three months after the revolution. The ICB was a state-supported institution designed to function as the propaganda arm of the Nationalist Revolutionary party, a mandate it never quite fulfilled. Instead, it served as a meeting place and springboard for practically everyone involved in the trade, going on to become, in the words of film historian and TV newscaster Carlos Mesa Gisbert, "the true point of departure of the new Bolivian cinema."[28] The ICB's first production was a ten-minute documentary on the revolution, *Bolivia se libera*, shot by Juan Carlos Levaggi and Nicolás Smolij, two young Argentinian cameramen hired to record the historical event by Waldo Cerruto, president Paz Estenssoro's brother-in-law and, technically, the official director of the ICB until 1956.[29]

During this period, the ICB was mostly engaged in the production of newsreels (purportedly some 150 between 1953 and 1956 alone), which remain the most telling documentation of this period. They not only introduced urban viewers to remote regions and unfamiliar customs, but inspired as well proto-*indigenista* shorts such as *Amanecer Indio, La leyenda de la kantuta,* and *Illimani,* shot by Levaggi and Smolij as early as 1953, with the intense collaboration of Bolivian artists, musicians, and scriptwriters. Gumucio Dragón calls these early hybrid fictions "musical documentaries," a genre that has endured as perhaps the most characteristically Bolivian.[30] A recent example is *El antruejo de los Andes (Carnival before Lent in the Andes,* Alfonso Seligman, 1986), a video essay on the consitutive role of music in syncretic Andean Christianity, beautifully shot by videoartist Néstor Agramont, one of the founders of the umbrella organization, Movimiento del Nuevo Cine y Video Boliviano.

In 1956, a change in government brought about the nomination of veteran filmmaker Jorge Ruiz (1924–) as technical director of the ICB. His enormously influential, thirty-one-minute ethnographic documentary *Vuelve Sebastiana,* winner of the 1956 SODRE Festival in Uruguay, had established Ruiz as the most prominent filmmaker in the country, and forerunner of the New Latin Cinema here and abroad.[31] An agronomist by profession (though he never practiced), Ruiz learned to speak Aymara while growing up on his family's hacienda in Luribay, an experience that would mark him for life. There, he shot his first film in 8–mm, *Frutas en el mercado (Fruit in the Market,* 1942), which he submitted unsuccessfully to a competition at the municipality of La Paz. Although the defeat of this rare short on rural life to *Barriga llena (A Full Belly),* Augusto Roca's story about three adventurous young city men, demonstrates the priorities of the jury, it did nothing to deter the eighteen-year-old filmmaker from his calling. Except for the two years he spent in remote rural areas with the army (1944–46)—an experience he believes added yet more fuel to his early identification with Indian culture—Ruiz has devoted himself entirely to film.[32]

In 1947, with the active support of U.S.-born Kenneth Wasson, Ruiz and Roca founded the production company Bolivia Films, later joined by the man who is now Bolivia's president, Sánchez de Lozada. Among its credits are *Virgen India* (1948), Bolivia's first sound film, *Donde nació un imperio* (*Where an Empire Was Born,* 1949), the first production in color about the Incas, and *Bolivia busca la verdad* (*Bolivia Seeks the Truth,* 1950) which, based on the national census, is the only film in the country ever to be distributed in three different languages (Spanish, Qhechwa, and Aymara), including as well the first scene shot with sychronous sound.[33] While the *indigenista* emphasis of these films is obvious from their titles, as Gumucio Dragón points out, they largely ignore the momentous events that were shaking the country, not least the countrywide Civil War which erupted in 1949.[34]

Filmed one year after the revolution, *Vuelve Sebastiana* marks a departure from Ruiz's earlier films. Also financed by Bolivia Films, under the auspices of the Instituto Indigenista de Bolivia, it was, according to Ruiz, "one of only four or so films I made out of my own free will in my whole career as a filmmaker; the rest were just commissions."[35] A fictionalized social documentary, in color, with indigenous actors as protagonists and shot by a crew of two plus a driver who lived with the Chipaya (with all the implied lessons and hardships) until sufficient familiarity and trust was developed to begin shooting, it established him as the pioneer of direct cinema, and went on to become a point of reference for all subsequent cinema in the country.[36] In showing two sides of the Indian struggle for survival, one Chipaya and the other Aymara, and in underscoring the complex relations of domination and resistance that can develop between two colonized peoples subservient in turn to the powerful interests of a (conspicuously absent) third, Ruiz in effect splintered the monism inherent in the term *Indio*, introducing urban viewers to a culture and a set of issues hitherto unacknowledged and, for all intents and purposes, unresolved to this day.[37]

The centuries-long antagonism and fatefully intertwined lives of the dominant Aymara and the slowly disappearing Chipaya, whose grasslands had been appropriated by the former in the film, are played out in the friendship that develops between two shepherd children, one Chipaya (Sebastiana Kespi, the "protagonist" who plays herself), and the other Aymara. When the boy introduces Sebastiana to the "fearsome" Aymaras and invites her into their world, her grandfather rescues her from the acculturating fascination, leads her back to her community, and before dying on the way, entrusts her with the continuity of their oral tradition and cultural identity. Thus Sebastiana, film historian Carlos Mesa tells us with a touch of nostalgia encouraged by the structure of the film, "returns to the origins of her own race."[38] That Ruiz does not develop any further the handing over of power from an aging patriarch to a young girl, not an unusual practice in Andean culture, is a fact that has gone, by contrast, virtually unnoticed by the critics.

While *Vuelve Sebastiana*'s peculiar twist to the Romeo and Juliet story transcends diegetically the bounds of ethnographical representation, the narrative is structured along traditional documentary lines. For example, for all their unprecedented degree of agency further strengthened by their fictionalization, the voices of native informants do not come close to undermining the authority of the voice-over narration that, in traditional documentary form, both contains and exceeds them.[39] It should also be remembered that, although the film lays a claim to greater objectivity both on the grounds of Ruiz's knowledge of Aymara and on the crew's familiarity with the Chipaya community, purportedly achieved about three weeks after their arrival, it was meant to correct and supplement the foreign gaze of French anthropologist Jehan Vellard, who had collaborated with the filmmaker in the making of the ethnographic study *Los Urus* (1951), the predecessor to *Vuelve Sebastiana*.[40] In the final analysis, the later film becomes a cautionary tale addressing specifically white-identified urban viewers, warning them against the dangers of Chipaya extinction and the potential loss of a whole culture at the hands of the Aymara, paradoxically, at a time when the state was embarked, at least on paper, on a nationalist program of assimilation and citizenship for all its subjects. Notwithstanding, in both its shortcomings and its contributions, *Vuelve Sebastiana* suggestively bespeaks a political and artistic agenda nearer to the spirit of the revolution of 1952 than to its letter. Its spark would be reignited by Jorge Sanjinés with the short *Revolución* in 1963, the year before he took over the post of technical director of the ICB left vacant by Ruiz.

JORGE SANJINÉS

Revolución received the Joris Ivens prize at the Leipzig Film Festival in 1964, the same year the bloody military coup of General René Barrientos set the tone for the culture of terror that soon spread to the rest of the continent. Because of the apparent influence of Eisenstein's narrative and compositional style, Gumucio Dragón has called this militant and poetically evocative film "his *Potemkin,*" although Sanjinés claims not to have seen this film until later.[41] Armed with the tools of historical materialist analysis and with a penchant for experimentation, Sanjinés tuned into the Indian-identified impulse in Bolivian cinema and began focusing his attention on the rapid mutations of the Indian-white dyad that had been taking place since the revolution. His films have developed dialectically, both functioning like the cultural barometer of the country and transforming as well as being transformed by the national discourse on race and, more tangentially, on gender.

I have already noted *Yawar Mallku*'s sensitivity to the issue of language. Sanjinés began using Qhechwa titles in his first fictional short *¡Aysa!* (*Landslide!,* 1964) (the title is also the only word uttered in the film) about the miserable lives of a miner and his family. After he became technical director of the ICB in 1965, he continued this practice with *Ukamau* (*That's the Way It Is,* 1966), his first incursion into peasant life, whose overwhelming success led to the establishment of the collective of the same name, and with *Yawar Mallku* three years later.[42] *Lloksy Kaymata* (*¡Fuera de aquí!, Out of Here!,* 1977), an Ecuadorean-Venezuelan coproduction Sanjinés made while in exile, was his last film with a Qhechwa title. The use of Spanish for the titles of his last two films, *La Nación Clandestina* (*The Clandestine Nation,* 1989) and *Para recibir el canto de los pájaros* (*To Receive the Chanting of Birds,* 1995), reflects the national trend towards "hispanization." [Figure 5.2]

In tandem with the New Latin American cinema movement, until the eighties the films of Sanjinés have both understood and aimed to address the needs of peasants and workers largely in terms of class, helping to elucidate the root causes of economic and political oppression and offering to provide the tools for their transformation. Until the internationally renowned *Blood of the Condor,* cultural and religious issues were mostly misunderstood and either relegated to the margins or ignored altogether (as in the testimonial reconstruction *El Coraje del Pueblo,* 1971), functioning generally as markers of national otherness within the unifying mosaic of a new "our America" in the making. However, while on the one hand, *Blood of the Condor*'s aim was to denounce the now well-documented Peace Corps eugenist policies of sterilization of Indian women, and was primarily structured to demonstrate how ethnocidal practices of

166

FIGURE 5.2. Three figures in *Para recibir el canto de los pájaros* (*To Receive the Chanting of Birds*, Jorge Sanjinés, 1995). Courtesy of Jorge Sanjinés.

this kind are condoned by a state willing to act as power broker for racially motivated neocolonial interests,[43] on the other, it goes beyond what Sanjinés described earlier as to merely "document the poverty and misery of certain strata of the population . . . , to remind the bourgeois audience that another class of people existed."[44] The film was the first to bring out in the open the self-serving blindness of the white- and U.S.-identified native bourgeoisie to the cultural and religious practices of Indian communities surviving for centuries by the skin of their teeth almost next door, and exposed their indifference as a crime equal to or greater than those of the imperial masters they more or less unconsciously serve.

But while the outrage *Blood of the Condor* provoked led eventually to the Peace Corps's expulsion from the country during the shortlived presidency of General Juan José Torres and the Popular Democratic Front (UDP), filmmaker and crew were criticized for some blindness of their own to the potential consequences of their own intervention in the life of the remote community they filmed, an experience which left its members even more vulnerable after the crew's departure to the kind of local abuses they so vehemently denounced.[45] The film itself reflects this kind of myopia as well. Although it is textured with early insights into the otherness of Qhechwa customs and beliefs, it too reinforces "the mythical fatalism attributed to indigenous cultures" that Zuzana Pick has rightly criticized in *Ukamau*,[46] also encouraging the kind of structurally induced separatism that, even though historically contingent, perpetuates the kind of power imbalances it had wished to undo. Moreover, not only does *Blood of the Condor* largely dehumanize its subjects by turning them almost exclusively into historical representatives of a particular class— worker, peasant, lumpen, middle, upper. It also pays absolutely no attention to the effect of sterilization on the lives and psyche of the women themselves, dwelling instead unrelentingly on the victimization of innocent people who, idealized as sacrificial victims, can purportedly do no wrong. Ultimately, they become undistinguishable from one another and, in the face of insurmountable obstacles, end up having little recourse but to be sacrificed to the struggle or to retreat into themselves, their language, their culture, and their hieraticism if they want to survive. In the end, and for the next twenty years of Sanjinés's filmmaking, the white-Indian divide would remain as impenetrable as the hermetic ruins of ancient Tiahuanaku.

La nación clandestina (1989), a stunning allegory of the transformation of Indian identity since 1952, represents by contrast an epistemological break with the classic historical materialist approach of Sanjinés's previous films. [Figure 5.3] Released after twelve years of virtual silence, the film's narrative is constructed so that, rather than trying to fit Indian-identified subjects within a prescripted analytical framework, it plants the subject of the enunciation firmly in the soil of Aymara culture, history, and cosmogony. As if from the other side of the mirror, *La nación clandestina* reconstructs the vicissitudes of the Indian-white dyad since the Revolution entirely through the Aymara Imaginary and in accordance with Andean Symbolic logic, addressing its viewers from the perspective of an Indian-identified filmmaker who speaks both to and from an Aymara worldview, with the rest of the nation invited to watch and learn the process. It is an exercise at the limits of intersubjectivity, whose aim is to achieve the kind of discursive equilibrium between language and speech (*langue* and *parole,* in structural linguistic terminology) that was posited as a goal two decades earlier in *Teoría y práctica de un cine junto al pueblo,* albeit in different terms. [Figure 5.4] In this 1979 text, Sanjinés and the Ukamau collective articulated the desire to create a cinematic language not only appropriate to an anticolonial model of national consciousness but also cast in the mold of Indian cosmogony and philosophy:

> Peruvian peasants, Arahuacans from the snowy peaks of Colombia, Mexican Tarahumaras, Bolivian Aymaras, Chibulean workers in Ecuador, and Qhechwas from Tarabuco, do not represent [the great American culture] because they belong to the Indian race, nor because they share a common past. They represent it because they think differently. . . .
>
> The acquisition of a new, freed and freeing language can only be born from the penetration and investigation of, as well as integration into, a living and dynamic popular culture. Revolutionary processes neither exist nor are realized outside the practice of the dynamic activation of a people. The same should be true for the cinema.[47]

La nación clandestina performs this "dynamic activation" in both structure and content through the perspective of Sebastián Mamani (Reynaldo Yujra), an acculturated Aymara who, like his namesake in Jorge Ruiz's classic *Vuelve Sebastiana,* and like Sixto at the end of *Yawar Mallku,* turns home to his roots. However, unlike Sebastiana's, who has little choice and no agency, and unlike Sixto's (whose raised-armed arm was

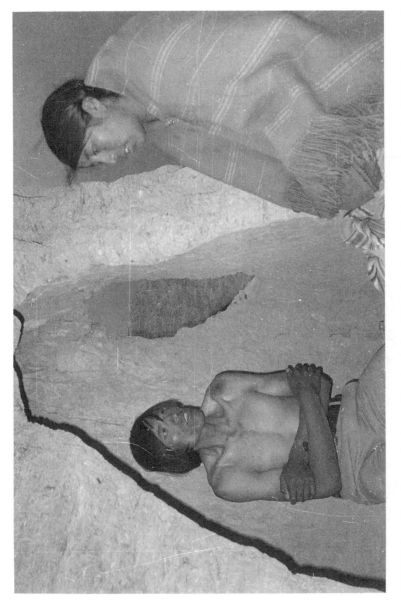

FIGURE 5.3. Two figures in *La nación clandestina* (*The Clandestine Nation*, Jorge Sanjinés, 1989). Courtesy of Jorge Sanjinés.

FIGURE 5.4. Filming *La nación clandestina*. Courtesy of Jorge Sanjinés.

joined by hundreds to become an icon of revolutionary struggle for the new Latin American cinema), Sebastián's journey in space also becomes one in time and inner consciousness. The consciousness of the white-identified left, by contrast, is dispensed with midway into the film, though not before it is unmasked as false consciousness in a dispassionately shot scene where a young middle-class Spanish-speaking intellectual calls the people whose cause he presumably had made his own "shitty Indians," as he is hunted down and shot by paramilitary forces during the bloody García Meza 1980 coup, the narrative's present.

When the film begins, Sebastián, a maskmaker living in the city, is in the midst of preparing his return. Having decided that his time has come to die, he builds for himself the mask used since ancient times for a death dance he remembers from childhood, and begins the journey home. Every step back is a test of courage and humility. By means of a very complex narrative ordering of memory and history, the film reconstructs Sebastián's journey both to and away from home, "reading" on the surface of the mountains and valleys that he crosses the "inscriptions" of his end foretold. Sebastián's life is pieced together by means of intricately woven flashbacks and flashforwards, which show him wrestling with his demons as he prepares to face the community whose survival he once endangered with his betrayal, for which he was consequently expelled. Now aware that the worst enemy is the enemy within, Sebastián confronts his internalized racism, refuses further complicity with his own victimization, reaches an understanding of the enormity of his shame, and comes to terms with the loss of self that resulted from his alienation from the values of his community, his return to his cultural roots symbolized by the burning of his city clothes.

Whereas in *Yawar Mallku* Sixto's disillusion and return to consciousness (also signalled by a change of clothes) was triggered by his brother's death, Sebastián's is prompted by the realization of his own spiritual death to alcohol, loneliness, and a city life devoid of meaning. Instead of pointing a finger (or a gun) elsewhere, he holds a mirror squarely before his eyes to learn the most devastating lesson of all: that by severing himself from his community, he had given up the only chance he ever had of the kind of (self-)empowerment that only comes from knowing where one fits in the larger scheme of things. He also realizes that not only has he castrated himself but, both by negating the values of his people and by removing himself violently from its fold, he has taken, so to speak, the wind out of his community as well. While, as artist and

maskmaker, he knows that subjectivity is a fiction that can be both constructed and shed, it is in the enactment of this shedding that he arrives
home to rediscover himself as both smaller than a speck of dust and larger
than life.

In this sense, *La nación clandestina* departs from *Yawar Mallku* not
only in the mode of analysis of the mechanisms of oppression but also in
the solutions it offers. Instead of what Zuzana Pick calls "resistance in the
context of insurrection,"[48] stressed by the celebrated closing shot of raised
guns in the earlier film, we have here resistance in the context of psychological awareness, crowned by community (self-)recognition and
(self-)acceptance. Whereas, earlier, Sebastián would have functioned
solely as an historical agent at the mercy of infra- and superstructures
that both enclosed and exceeded him, his character is here endowed with
a degree of introspection and self-consciousness rarely found in *indigenista* fiction. Constructed in nonlinear sequence, akin to the workings
of memory (another theme of the film), the narrative blurs the boundaries between reality and dream, memory and the present, time and
space, to produce a Proustian experience taken to an entirely new dimension: one where, among other things, death has a meaning beyond the
finality of the flesh. At the end of the film, Sebastián dances on the
screen after his death, a "surprising ending," which, as film critic Pedro
Susz has remarked, "proposes a message of renewed confidence in the
strength of Aymara identity."[49] Sebastián has earned the gift of being
remembered not only for his good and bad deeds but also for his gifts.
Because the "Danzanti" mask he returned with had been forgotten by
everyone but a couple of elders in the community, his gift to his community has become in fact the gift of memory, sorely needed by a culture increasingly impoverished by assimilation.

While, at one level, the message of *The Clandestine Nation* appears
to be that surrendering to the reality of death—self-betrayal being itself a
kind of death—is both the necessary condition for self-consciousness and
a function of the spiritual rebirth of the community as a whole, at a
deeper level, the film is an historical allegory that articulates the formation of Aymara consciousness, bringing it out of the clandestine status to
which it had been relegated in the official imaginary. More importantly
still, the film puts both history and myth in proper perspective since, in
gathering together the pieces of Sebastián's life to restore to it meaning so
that he can die with dignity and purpose, he does not simply enable his
community to recover a sense of wholeness that was lost—in the quasi-

organic sense of the reattachment of a limb to an amputated body—with his expulsion; he also reenacts the messianic myth of eternal return which lies at the core of Andean and *katarista* millenialism. The reawakening of Aymara nationhood fulfills Tupaj Katari's prophecy, uttered according to legend as his quartered body was scattered over the land two hundred years earlier, that he would return "converted in thousand thousands."[50]

As might be expected, such a major overhaul of subjectivity cannot but include a redefinition of gender and gender relations. Although not nearly as developed in the film as the understanding of race and cultural determinants, gender does play an important, if tangential, role in *La nación clandestina*. For example, it is Sebastián's wife's (Delfina Mamani) exemplary decision not to follow him to the city—and suffer the consequences of actions she clearly disapproved of, as she might have been expected to do in a different context—which gives her husband's betrayal its true measure. Her vision is in harmony with that of the community, and the community's laws are grounded in the pan-Andean concept of *Pachamama*, literally "Earthmother"—a complex metaphysical term which also encompasses the spatiotemporal synchronic and diachronic operations animistically believed to sustain Andean life since time immemorial. Although marginalized in the film, it is precisely Sanjinés's understated gendering of cultural difference that best reflects both the shift in and limitations of his understanding of the semiotic operations of this radically Other, paradigmatically distinct, culture which he has devoted his life to learn.

La nación clandestina's nonlinear, circular narrative, its lush use of color, the pictorial texture of its arid, mountainous landscapes, gradually revealed, as if by the painterly brush of a constantly moving camera, and the long silences punctuated by whiffs of memory and wind, are all intended to support the intensity of the slow, almost meditative longshots which Sanjinés has long believed to be narratively integral "to the internal rhythms of our people [and] their profound conception of reality. . . . The substantial difference lay in the way in which the Qhechwa-Aymara people conceive of themselves collectively, in the nonindividualistic form of their culture."[51] Pedro Susz describes the film as "the visual translation both of the Aymara conception of time as circular and of the indestructible ties between individuals from that culture with the natural and social surroundings."[52] Elements such as these help structure the film in terms of the Andean logologic of complementarity, thus implicitly rejecting the Western logologic of supplementarity that is at the heart of classical narrative.[53] Deconstructed by Jacques Derrida, and exposed as phallologo-centric by feminist philosopher Luce Irigaray, at its most abstract the logic of supplementarity is motivated by dialectic operations which, in the process of sublation (or sublimated production of a third term), end up covering up both the terms of the dialectical opposition and the relations between them.[54] The Andean logologic of complementarity, on the other hand, accounts for both terms of the dialectic as always reciprocally different and even opposite, simultaneously present, symmetrically related, and inevitably complementary. The untranslatable Qhechwa word *yanatin*, for example, denotes pairs of this kind, such as eyes, ears, hands, gloves, or man and woman.[55]

By choosing to speak from the side of the Andean logologic of complementarity, Sanjinés is in fact both rejecting the kind of subjectivity posited by liberal individualism since the Enlightenment—where the increasingly uprooted, isolated, and upwardly mobile individual is expected to pull together a community by his or her bootstraps while straying lost in a social void—and indirectly inviting his own white middle-class community of origin to examine the human costs of colonialism and acculturation, to reconsider how they themselves are implicated in the process. Read as such a pair, *Yawar Mallku* and *La nación clandestina* can be said to capture the flavor of that resilient yet resistant white-Indian double mirror of colonialism (Bhaba's Janus-faced monster) where, as Tristan Platt has noted, "a conflictive dynamic of interests [is] played out in a minutely intricate interlocking of mistrust, fear, obstinacy, opportunism, deceit, and passionate combativity."[56]

IMAGING WOMEN AND RESISTANCE IN FILM

The contribution of women to the resistance of the Indian-identified national majority to the colonialization and acculturation efforts of the white-identified minority is rarely portrayed in Bolivian film. An exception is Sanjinés's *The Courage of the People* (1971), which begins with the reenactment of the 1942 Catavi massacre of miners that followed the rebellion led by Maria Barzola, played out in the film on the plain named after her, and goes on to reconstruct the 1967 massacre at the Siglo XX mines. It also records the participation of Domitila Barrios de Chungara, whose now-famous testimonial, *Let Me Speak!* was published after her release from jail (where we see her being taken prisoner at the end of the film).[57] The introductory voice-over sequence chronicles "the courage of the people" by listing the numerous massacres perpetrated against both the peasant and working classes since the early 1940s by an army acting as the repressive apparatus of an essentially racist state. General Banzer's military coup, which ended the short period of democratic freedom enjoyed by the country during the failed experiment of the Popular Democratic Front, took place while Sanjinés was involved in post-production work in Italy. Sanjinés, Ricardo Rada, and *The Courage of the People* did not return from exile until after the fall of Banzer in 1979.[58]

The film presents Domitila as cofounder and spokesperson of the "Housewives' Committee" founded in 1961 by a group of women whose families had lived in misery for generations at Siglo XX, the company town named after what once was one of the richest tin-producing mines in the world. This group was instrumental in the rebellion of both men and women against outrageous government abuses in the mines, including orchestrated hunger. The main focus of the film is the rebellion that ended with the infamous 1967 St. John's Night massacre. Catapulted into international and, eight years later, national fame when the film was finally shown in Bolivia in 1979, the indomitable Domitila was also among the women who in December of 1977 started the nationwide hunger strike that brought down the military dictatorship of Banzer.[59]

Only in *The Courage of the People* does Sanjinés convey some measure of the important contribution of women to the historical struggle against oppression. Though their visibility as social subjects is largely the effect of the biographic nature of the genre of testimonials—where the focus is on the agency of the subject(s) rather than on the creativity of the filmmaker—the film does more than represent what Zuzana Pick describes as "the resisting function of collective address that characterizes the orally transmitted narratives of Andean cultures."[60] Beyond stressing the inseparability of the individual from the collectivity, the film also illustrates how the precolonial concept of active complementarity that is understood to exist between men and women is put into daily practice—a far cry, as Domitila would later point out in her testimonial, from the Western feminist concept of equal rights, which stresses competition over cooperation.

With few exceptions, issues of class, race, and culture have generally ended up taking precedence over issues of gender in Bolivian film. While in the mines, fields, and urban centers, women have always played an active role as leaders and imaginative solution seekers to long-term community problems, the powerful symbolism of gender-specific behavior—as both leaders and victims—has been used largely as a signifier of community cohesion and of strength in numbers against a minority government's brutality. Bolivia's de facto apartheid practices have required not only undaunted heroism and self-sacrifice from individuals in the name of collective survival but also a profound sense of solidarity between women and men in that struggle. Statements by peasant women leaders, such as "In the same ways that Bartolina Sisa fought [as an equal] at the side of Tupaj Katari, today's peasant women have to fight at the side of their husbands,"[61] are not uncommon and need to be understood in terms of the Andean concept of complementarity to which I referred earlier. For, by stressing the gendered dimensions of complementarity, and by introducing gender both into the class struggle and *katarista* ideology, such statements in effect take the Indian project of recovery of historical memory to its logical conclusions.

On the other hand, the symbolic emasculation of Indian men within a white-identified culture has made it difficult for Indian-identified women to address problems such as domestic violence and alcoholism other than as effects of poverty and exploitation. In *Let Me Speak!* for example, Domitila insists that "miners are douby exploited. . . . For by paying them such a small salary [the bosses cause] women [to] have to work harder at home. And, in effect, this means we give our labor for free to the bosses, doesn't it?"[62] Although hers might be a classic Marxist analysis of the sexual division of labor, it should be noted that while Domitila repeatedly stresses her identification with the plight of miners as a class, she never loses sight of the singularity of women's oppression or of their specific forms of adaptation and resistance.

The language of resistance of Domitila and other women miners has inspired not only the Bartolinas, as peasant women are called, to form a nationwide union but also urban, white- and Mestizo-identified middle-class women and men to become involved in national popular movements. For example, the legendary twenty-three-day nationwide hunger strike that began on December 31, 1977, initiated by four women from the mines, garnered such widespread support from people of all sectors of society that it finally toppled General Hugo Banzer's repressive government, restoring democracy, however short-lived, to the country; a momentous historical moment recorded by French filmmaker Alain Labrousse in his Super 8 documentary *La huelga de hambre* (*The Hunger Strike*).[63] Yet despite the intensive participation of Indian women in the struggle against colonial and neocolonial oppression, a film has yet to be made from the perspective of *their* resistance.[64] Indian-identified women have yet to step outside the roles of powerless and defenseless victims assigned to them in the great majority of Bolivian fiction films; they have yet to gain access to the cinematic apparatus to record their own version of history and reality.

WOMEN MOVE BEHIND THE CAMERA

The groundbreaking film *Warmi* (Qhechwa for "woman," 1980), a fictionalized documentary of the lives of poor Indian-identified women, is the work of French-born filmmaker Danielle Caillet, who immigrated to Bolivia to join her husband, cinematographer and director Antonio Eguino, cofounder with Jorge Sanjinés of the Grupo Ukamau. In this outstanding film, four women—a peasant, a miner (*palliri*), a textile worker, and a street vendor—typify the appalling living conditions of women of their class and the children they are usually left to raise alone. [Figure 5.5] In the short span of twenty minutes, Caillet provides a cultural, historical, and economic context for the personal accounts of her subjects. First, by underscoring the extreme contrast between the two fundamental national cults to Pachamama and the Virgin Mary and the dismal conditions of women's everyday lives; second, highlighting questions of education, health, aging, and the double or triple shift, all in their complex class contexts (the street vendor, a lumpen in the underground economy, is also a factory worker during the day as well as a mother); and, third, by the culminating voice-over narration of the long history of struggle by Bolivian women from different backgrounds, reminding viewers of their heroic resistance and inviting us to follow their example. The voice-over is accompanied by images representing the heroic figures to whom the text refers, some of them monumental sculptures in city parks, shot from extremely low angles in rapid succession so as to enhance their monumentality.

The strengths and weaknesses of Caillet's *Warmi* are those of its analytical tools: late-1970s socialist feminism and development theory. The film's central thesis is that Bolivia's progress will be hampered until women's education, health, and basic human rights become a national priority. Ignoring issues of cultural differences, ethnicity, or race, *Warmi* chooses instead to articulate its message in terms of class and gender, refer-

FIGURE 5.5. Woman with rock in *Warmi* (Danielle Caillet, 1980). Courtesy of Danielle Caillet.

ring to women as precious human capital gone to waste, and insisting that the country will not get out from underdevelopment and dependency until their loss as productive capital is recognized as such by all.[Figure 5.6]

In her next work, the 1989–90 series of made-for-television videos *Nosotras* (*Us*), Caillet's gaze takes a 180 degree turn to focus instead on the achievements of a select group of white-identified Bolivian women, including the internationally recognized painter Maria Luisa Pacheco, the sculptor Francine Secretan, the theater director Maritza Wilde, the poet and composer Matilde Casazola, and the talented young painter, Guiomar Mesa. Although all these women come from the dominant classes, they have been chosen by Caillet because their vision and artistic sensibilities are profoundly marked by their identification with the Andean landscape, the culture, and the people who *Warmi* had portrayed at arm's length. Each segment, ranging from ten to twenty-two minutes in length, is visually constructed to harmonize with the aesthetic grain of a particular artist, mimetically representing the rhythms, colors, sounds, and shapes that characterize their work. In the segment portraying the abstract expressionist painter Guiomar Mesa, for instance, the colors are stark, camera angles sharp and punctuated, and her fragmented and con-structionist aesthetics, as well as her thematics of sterility and the uncanny, are often replicated in the editing.

One of the shortcomings of Caillet's highly influential work is that, despite having explored the conditions of women on both sides of the Indian-white divide, it stops short of investigating the race and class-spe-cific relations that exist *between* them. In her work, as well as in the work of most other Bolivian film- and videomakers, we have yet to see, for example, how the lives of women of different class and ethnic identity come together in the practice of daily life; how the intertwining of their lives can be a source of resistance or friendship or, for that matter, enmity or contempt; and what are the shortcomings and potential of such crossovers. While it may well be that, as Caillet believes, documentaries by men and women differ in that the latter are "more a testimony impreg-nated with complicity than a cold didactic document; more than a cinema about women, a cinema *with* women,"[65] in *Warmi,* white-identified women remain, like Caillet herself, on this side of the camera, sympathetic absent presences in their Other's existence. In her later work, moreover, where a sense of Otherness is precisely what fuels the work of the women artists she has chosen to portray, that complicity has been transformed into a shared, though unstated, source of resistance. Every segment of the series

FIGURE 5.6. Woman with handle in *Warmi*. Courtesy of Danielle Caillet.

seems to suggest that the experience of being Other, specifically in a Bolivian context, grounds *all* women's identity elsewhere than the white-identified patriarchal culture with which they all have to contend. The difference between women on both sides of the race/class divide is perceived as one of degree rather than kind. "Professional women," Caillet stated in an interview, "do not suffer the same discrimination as women from the lower classes due to education, free time, and freedom of movement. However, while they may not be victims of frequent physical violence, they still have to endure unrelenting psychological violence."[66]

Caillet has called for what she has termed "cine POTENCIAL-MUJER," a complement to third cinema, whose "fundamental purpose would be to break with the blueprint of our patriarchal society by enforcing new perceptions of women's social roles." This cinema, moreover, would not only function as "an instrument to breach the shamefully abysmal gap that separates Bolivia from other countries." It would also address specifically Bolivian class and ethno-linguistic determinants of gender differences by "adapting our cinematographic language to the intellectual demands of each cultural group." For Aymara peasant women, for example, this might entail a "syntax of juxtaposition," slowly paced camera movement, long shots rather than a series of fragmented close ups, and a "'geometrifying' style" to imitate the expressions of native art. The more "westernized" women workers, on the other hand, might require a more direct, conventional style, with a thematic rather than stylistic focus.[67]

While the validity of such theories of the stylistics of culture remains to be demonstrated, it is nonetheless worth remarking that the ultimate goal of Caillet's cinematic theory is to reach a point of conciousness raising and training where the "transfer [of] the power of the technology"[68] to less privileged people can be readily accomplished, making others like herself redundant. As it stands, Caillet's groundbreaking contribution to the national debate on gender remains not only, as she herself commented ten years after completing *Warmi*, "'the alter ego' of Bolivian women," but also a spur to the nation's consciousness.[69]

"EL VIDEO ONG": (MIS)APPROPRIATING IMAGES OF THE INDIAN FEMALE BODY

The use of video has become widespread among both women and men involved in social movements, not always with positive results. In a country where the recording of history has been framed exclusively by the interests of the dominant classes and where historians are as rare as apple pie, the new technology is being used widely to record the present in the process of happening. With few exceptions, videos are generally used for the recovery of women's histories and experience, a practice just as frequently fraught with problems. Nongovernmental organizations (NGOs) such as the Gregoria Apasa Center for the Advancement of Peasant Women, for instance, have produced several educational videos covering topics such as the human reproductive system (like *Nuestras Vidas: Aprendiendo a Ser Mujer, Our Lives: Learning to Be a Woman*, Elizabeth Peredo and Lizzy Ernst 1985), badly designed to teach birth control methods to poor and illiterate women who have culturally distinct sexual mores and different ways of understanding the body that do not coincide with those presented to them by the video. Many such videos lacking awareness of the problematic nature of culture-blind mappings—be they of the body or other aspects of private life—have been produced in Bolivia by nongovernmental agencies in addition to the Gregoria Apasa Center, all entirely financed by foreign capital, giving rise to a new genre popularly known as "el video ONG" or NGO videos. As Carlos Mesa has commented about the films financed by U.S. capital between 1957 and 1963, with the full cooperation of the Bolivian Film Institute (ICB): "Such forced insertions [of money] point to the true meaning of paternalistic and exhibitionist intentions to cooperate, which are completely beyond understanding, let alone having knowledge, of the society where such cooperations take place."[70] Similarly, even though the explicit intention of the videos of the Gregoria Apasa Center and other such NGOs is to help disadvantaged Indian women attain control over their bodies and lives, these organizations often end up participating unwittingly in a wider neocolonial and racist project that includes curbing population growth in a largely underpopulated country. Given the high rate of infant mortality, it is not difficult to see such videos as still contributing (twenty-five years after *Yawar Mallku*'s exposé of the U.S. Peace Corps sterilization of Indian women) to a genocidal neocolonial strategy.

The Gregoria Apasa Center again went beyond its mandate when it sponsored the making of two videos by Eva Urquidi about two early twentieth-century feminist organizations, *Ateneo femenino* in La Paz, and the *Círculo Artístico e Intelectual de Señoritas* in Oruro, both of which were founded by and for the benefit of women of the dominant classes. Urquidi's first video is called *Dos mujeres en la historia* (*Two Women in*

History, 1987); her second, *Un largo camino* (*A Long Road*, 1988), includes a token interview with Lucila Mejía de Morales, executive secretary of the Bartolina Sisa National Federation of Peasant Women. No attempt is made in this video to describe, for instance, the vital contribution of the Bartolinas to the peasant movement as a whole or to make known the fact that it was they who insisted on forging the historical alliance between peasants and workers—unprecedented in Latin America—that was formed in 1979 when the peasant union publicly supported the general strike called by the Central Obrera Boliviana (COB) and incorporated themselves into this national workers union.[71]

The worldwide feminist tenet of consciousness raising has long been a centerpiece not only of the Peasant and Miner women's movements but of every one of the NGOs that focus on women's issues in Bolivia, out of the total of more than three hundred nationwide.[72] Feminist social activists from Europe and the United States have long channeled funds and other resources to support Bolivian NGOs whose work is geared specifically to empowering disenfranchised women by any means, including the facilitation of techniques and a language for private and public expression through consciousness-raising videos, radio soap operas, and *cuadernos* or educational booklets with a primarily visual message. The feminist conviction that for women to become aware of the more subtle, often repressed, elements of oppression it is necessary to first validate their experience, led NGO activists to use the more accessible video technology in an effort to recover lost chapters of the history of women's struggles in Bolivia.

The result has been, for the most part, a peculiar aberration of this world-historical phenomenon. As if fatally bound to a legacy of atavistic colonial habits, imported practices of consciousness raising and historical recuperation have generally done little but feed into Bolivian society's continued dependence on largely conditional "first world" handouts, masked as charity, which deepen the disempowerment of the recipients and reinforce the cycle of dependency in the long run. "The blame," as Rosario León, director of CERES, one of the largest women-focused NGO's, has self-critically stated, "lies with us, with the women who work for other women rather than working *as* women."[73]

One of the few notable exceptions to this rule is the video *Siempreviva* (*Immortelle* or *Everlasting Flower*, 1988), a moving fictionalized documentary that relates the history of the Bolivian Union of Florists, one of the many such unions of craftspeople, artists, and workers organized during the heyday of anarchist movements in the 1920s and 1930s.[74] *Siempreviva* was produced with the active help of three generations of florists whose participation was essential to the filmic process. It was coproduced by Nicobis, the umbrella organization of the Movimiento del Nuevo Cine y Video, and Tahipamu (Taller de Historia y Participación de la Mujer), an NGO largely devoted to the recovery of women's popular histories. Of the four organizers of Tahipamu, Bolivian-born Elizabeth Peredo and Ana Cecilia Wadsworth come from upper middle-class families and were educated abroad. The other two women, Ineke Dibbits from Holland, and Ruth Volger from northern Italy, are professional educators who have chosen to settle permanently in Bolivia.

The massive participation of white-identified, middle-class professional women in the numerous foreign financed NGOs that fund such videos has created new patterns of cross-class, racially coded relations and new tensions, the nature and effects of which have yet to be studied. Although NGOs have been criticized for designing self-serving development projects primarily geared to preserving white-collar jobs and perpetuating their own institutions, this is not always the case. Nonetheless, the blindness of the majority of NGO-sponsored projects to the radical Otherness of Indian culture is as much due to the assumptions of the white- and Mestiza-identified culture as it is to the crippling effects of foreign aid. A hard look at the accomplishments as well as at the failures of these projects is urgently needed. It is to be expected that as foreign contributions decrease, and as the competition for scarcer resources becomes more fierce, the performance of these women will be measured more by their accomplishments than by their avowed intentions. In the meantime, and to their credit, they will at least have left Bolivia with a legacy of visual documentation unparalleled in the country's history, second only to that of the ICB film newsreels of the earlier generation.

IMAGING THE (DIS)ENFRANCHISED
WHITE FEMALE BODY

When we think of the contribution of women to Bolivian film and video, it is important to keep two things in mind: first, that we are speaking of a small number of privileged women from a specific class and ethnicity; and second, that although these women may have had more privileged access to education and technology than the disenfranchised women and

men whom they set out to help, their participation in the culture industry continues to be hampered not only by an incipient self-consciousness
about their role in a society deeply divided along racial lines, but also by
deeply ingrained gender/power tensions with both men and women of
their own class.

The tentativeness of the intraclass gender debate in Bolivia was evident in the extensive newsprint coverage that followed the 1990 release of
Raquel Romero's fiction film *Ese sordo del alma* (*Deafness of the Soul*).[75]
Sponsored by UNICEF, the film was produced collectively by the
women's wing of the Movimiento del Nuevo Cine y Video Boliviano, the
umbrella organization founded in 1984 in order to protect film and video
production locally and promote it abroad. Beatriz Palacios, long-time
producer and codirector with Jorge Sanjinés (*Las Banderas del Amanecer,
The Flags of Dawn*, 1985), was one of the four founding executive officers
of this organization. Romero, one of the most active and talented women
film- and videomakers in Bolivia, was elected to the board in 1986. Her
script for *Ese sordo del alma* was chosen by a consensus of all the women
members of the M.N.C.V.B.—Liliana de la Quintana, Cecilia Quiroga,
Leni Ballón, Susana Cabezas, Elizabeth Machicao, and María Eugenia
Muñoz—each of whom participated in the making of the film in one
capacity or another.

Breaking with local tradition, Romero's script does not specifically
foreground the conditions of women of lower social strata. Instead, she
focuses on the trials of an urban middle-class woman, Jenny (Remy
Varela), who works as a secretary in an office where she is harassed, and
who is increasingly dissatisfied with her husband Rolando's (Willy Pérez)
stereotypical insensitivity to her as well as to their daughter's needs.
Although the film chronicles the current transition to less oppressive gender relations, it also underscores the iron grip of age-old (self-) destructive
patterns, expectations, and desires. Jenny's troubles with her husband cul-
minate in his brutal beating of her after a night out drinking with the
boys—the enduring Latin American custom of the *noche de soltero*, bach-
elor's night out. His excuse for the beating, this time around, is not finding her home on his return.

The film concludes with a close shot of Jenny crying, her sobs
drowned out by a voice-off replaying of the chilling sounds of her and her
husband's screams during their violent encounter. Alone, badly bruised,
and unable to count on the support of her own mother (Norma Merlo),
who is portrayed as more concerned with keeping up social appearances

than with her daughter's emotional or physical well-being, Jenny decides to pack her suitcases and leave. With few options and as if paralyzed by the lack of support from either family or friends, Jenny stops herself in the midst of packing, finally yielding to the pressure of her daughter's innocent questions. The film's ambiguous ending is designed to show the entrapments of the enduring small-town mentality of the Bolivian capital, which did not mushroom into Third-World-style modernity until the 1970s.

If public outrage is any measure of the "scandalous" nature of a film, *Ese sordo del alma* got more than its fair share. The projection hall at the Goethe Institute in La Paz, where the debate took place after the showing I attended, was filled to capacity. Latecomers stood lining the length of the walls. "Everyone is here," a friend whispered in my ear. Curiously, not a single question addressed the construction, aesthetics, or even the emotional subtleties of the film. Despite the video's painful probing into how an oppressive legacy can be handed over generationally from mothers to daughters, it was primarily criticized for being superficial, for feeding on stereotypes, and for creating "unnecessary antagonisms" between men and women. With the women in the audience remaining silent for the most part, questions about "truth" and intentionality dominated the debate.

In the end, the tenor of the debate reflected the reaction of the press. One reporter, who succinctly described *Ese sordo del alma* as "una mexicanada feminista" (feminism Mexican style), summarized one side of the split response by criticizing the video for its lack of critical distance, feminist pamphleteering and caricaturesque characters ("The bestial macho and the sacrificial woman, equivalent to the 'fascist pig' and the 'revolutionary martyr'") and attributed its political (in)correctness to "the dawning of revolutionary fervor in Bolivia. Our intellectual petit bourgeoisie has found in feminism and ecology its dogmas." Women reporters, on the other hand, rushed to the video's defense on account of its realistic portrayal of the issues, declaring the alleged shortcomings irrelevant in light of its courageous exposure of a nasty public secret. Bringing the debate to a close with a humorous touch, a letter to the following week's *TV Guide*, signed by five men and four women, proclaimed "the creation of the Bolivian Machista Movement, to take precautions against the established order and confront the outbreak of *hembrismo marimachista*" (roughly translated as dyke-ish female machismo).[76]

It is a reminder of the ideological power of narrative film to frame discourse by its omissions that, although rape and physical abuse of

Indian women's bodies have furnished the dramatic ground of Bolivian cinema,[77] this was the first time in its history that urban middle-class domestic violence was being represented on the screen. Romero's film is also an exception in its inclusion of the white-Indian dyad in a narrative that focuses on middle-class issues, even if the dyad is relegated matter-of-factly to the background. There are references to the combination of frustration and compassion in Jenny's relation, as lady of the house, to her eager-to-please though stereotypically clumsy Indian housekeeper (she trips and falls while serving lunch to Jenny's husband's taunting male friends). There is also some suggestion of cross-class identification between the two women around the issue of male violence since Jenny comes to her servant's defense when the men mock and scold her.

Although the consensus between most of the women I spoke with was that the film was simply stating the obvious (not to mention being "light years behind" in its portrayal of similar issues pertaining to gender and family relations when compared to films by "first world" and other "third world" women), it evidently touched a nerve still raw in urban Bolivia. Despite increasing involvement on the part of white- and mestiza-identified women in the public sphere, in programs designed to help the poor, for example, the struggles of urban and upper middle-class women in their own homes have been shrouded in silence. Until *Ese sordo del alma* came along, the topic of non-Indian-identified "male deafness of soul" had in fact the lineaments of taboo. Romero's video seems to have awakened ancient and angry gods from a deep slumber—hardly a bad thing in this case.

SILVIA RIVERA: BOLIVIAN VIDEO COMING OF AGE

After four decades of struggling with scant resources and little recognition, both at home and abroad, Bolivia's film and video community is slowly coming of age. Having struggled in the shadow of such internationally renowned figures as Jorge Ruiz, Jorge Sanjinés, and Antonio Eguino, a new generation of women and men has begun to demand long-overdue recognition. Currently under way, for example, is a concerted effort by the media community to enforce legislation recently passed in parliament that will guarantee basic rights to filmmakers and videomakers, starting with copyright protection. Despite economic hardship and frustrations associated with, for example, the lack of such basic legal protection as copyright, the vibrancy in the intellectual and artistic community is definitely papable. Debates take place constantly, including discussions concerning the search for cinematic alternatives, in both form and content, which would represent more adequately the *bricolage* character of Bolivian society.

A case in point is the debate that followed a jury's unprecedented decision in 1990 to declare null and void the "Amalia Gallardo" prize, named after film critic and promoter of Bolivian film who proposed its implementation, given in competition to first-time video artists. Sponsored by the municipality of La Paz (in support of efforts by the Nuevo Movimiento to enlist government support for Bolivian filmmakers and videomakers), the prize's stated aim is to promote local talent. Among the three finalists was the social historian Silvia Rivera Cusicanqui for her video *Khunuskiw, Recuerdos del porvenir* (*Khunuskiw, Remembrance of Things Future*, 1990). *Khunuskiw* chronicles in part the rise of the anarchist labor movement in Bolivia during the two decades that followed World War I, with a particular focus on the Chaco War with Paraguay (1932–35), and is based on Rivera's pathbreaking study of the period, *Los Artesanos libertarios y la ética del trabajo* (1988).[78]

In *Khunuskiw*, Rivera tells the story of the famous composer Lieutenant Colonel Adrián Patiño Carpio (José Aramayo), who, though a member of the oligarchy, was strongly identified with the cause of peasants and workers, spending most of his creative life as director of a Bolivian army band. "The thing about Patiño that I always wondered about," Rivera stated in a recent interview, "is a paradox. While, in the mestizo vein of his music, he expressed a grieved, pathetic Bolivia, joy and the explosion of energy come through in his indigenous tunes instead. This is exactly the reverse of the stereotype establishing that Creole music is happy and Indian music sad." For Rivera, Patiño represents the working-class "bridge between the particular, the idiosyncratic folklore of a group and the projection of that folklore onto a universal language."[79]

As a counterpoint to the history of the bloody Chaco War, and further framing Patiño's reflections on music and society, *Khunuskiw* also explores the relationships between permanence and flux, and between different conceptions of time and space, memory and oblivion, history and myth, through interspersed images of decaying precolonial and colonial stone structures, recent incidents of government repression, and the performance of Andean ritual. Rivera's nonlinear narrative moves between her reflections on the meaning and value of replacing ancient stone structures with new, badly built, modern buildings and her meditations on the relationship between construction and deconstruction in music and history, personal as well as collective. Celebratory and evocative of pathos, the video's rhythm—slow-tracking long takes, punctured dialogue, long silences, haunting and dislocated sounds—plays on perceptions and expectations set up by traditional narrative structures in ways reminiscent of Marguerite Duras's *India Song*, a similarly paced meditation on French colonialism from the point of view of women from both sides of the colonizer/colonized dyad. Although such focus on women's perspectives is absent from Rivera's video, *Khunuskiw* shares with *India Song* an emphasis on formal experimentation, in particular with relation to sound. Both explore the capacity of music and language not only to break through the narrative encasements of space and time, and subtly (de)construct mimetically assumed meanings and contents transmitted by the image, but also to access and reactivate memories and experiences stored elsewhere than in the conscious mind.

Khunuskiw, Rivera has insisted, is an experimental video. "It is not built as a historical narrative or conventional drama, but rather as the construction of a [temporal and physical] landscape and ambiance (*clima*) . . . , a narrative proposition, a *mise en scène*, a choreography."[80] The counterclaim voiced by the jury was that none of the works submitted was "good enough," that all showed "a lack of analytical will," and that "experimental does not mean that things are left hanging in the air." Ironically, Rodrigo Quiroga, the only member of the jury present at the debate and a well-known filmmaker in his own right,[81] articulated his critique in terms reminiscent of Pasolini's call for a cinema of poetry.[82] "The video poem, or poetic video, is a misunderstood form," Rodrigo said, adding that the jury, with whom he concurred, had criticized Rivera's video for its reliance on "subjective camera shots, " too much repetition of a "recurrent theme," and its "lack of clarity"—in short, for its ambiguous referentiality, paradoxically singling out among its shortcomings elements characteristic of poetry. Disregarding its experimental nature, the jury considered *Khunuskiw* unworthy of the prize on the basis of the insubstantial nature of the referent. In ironic defense of her work, Rivera acknowledged that it might have been a mistake "to think big" and that her faith in herself might have been "excessive," but insisted that in declaring the competition without a winner, the jury had not only "underestimated the public" but missed the point that her video was "trying to propose something altogether different."

But the jury missed more than just the referent in *Khunuskiw*. Blinded, among other things, by the privileging of vision over sound in traditional film criticism, Rivera's critics also missed the uniqueness of her way of exploring the important role music plays in Bolivian society as well as the theoretical underpinnings of her experimentation with asynchronous image and sound and cinematic structure. "My whole video is constructed in accordance with the structure [of Patiño's music], following an [emotive] contrapuntal system which ranges from gray to joyous. The video culminates in a kind of indigenous joy, the song 'It is Snowing'—*khunuskiw* in Aymara—and with the idea that what penetrates the soul and the hopes of the character Patiño is precisely this Indian tune, allowing him to perceive a more beautiful and harmonious country . . . a belonging to his landscape."[83] Ranging from Andean to pop and rock, music is used in *Khunuskiw* as a (dislocating) pointer of geographical (rural, urban, and foreign) and historically determined class and ethnic differences. Precisely because of its capacity to reinforce the primacy of the sign over the referent, music is also used deconstructively as a contaminating device, as a force that breaks through those categories of difference, exposing them as heuristic, hence nonessential.

From the bilingual title to its complex narrativization of time and space—with historical and mythical time endowing space with multiple layers of meaning which come alive again and again as memory changes space into place, nature into landscape—*Khunuskiw, Recuerdos del porvenir* is based on the Andean concept of *ñaupaj mapuni,* which translates as "looking into the past and the future at one and the same time." By deconstructing classical narrative time and space in this particular way, Rivera joins Jorge Sanjinés in *La nación clandestina* in inviting viewers to participate in an alternative structure of thought that is specifically Andean, albeit tapping into an altogether different point of entry for viewer identification. Though also a man and an artist, the hero of *Khunuskiw* is not an Indian-identified representative of a particular class or ethnia who returns to his cultural roots, but rather an historical character whom Rivera has rescued from oblivion because of his model capacity to slip in and out of categories of class and ethnic difference with his music.

As with Danielle Caillet's video about the poet and composer *Matilde Casazola*, Rivera's *Khunuskiw* features an artist whose work, like her own, explores in a nonessentializing manner the capacity of an art form such as music to simultaneously preserve and transcend cultural specificities, its capacity to be, in other words, a positive agent of transculturation. In the work of both musicians reverberate the words of another transculturated artist from the Andean region, José María Arguedas, who like Ernesto, his narrator in *Deep Rivers*, believed that "From the beginning the men of Peru have composed music on hearing it and seeing it wing accross space, beneath the mountain and the clouds, which in no other part of world are so extreme." For them as for him, music is, like Pachamama it(her)self, "surely the stuff of which I am made, that nebulous region from which I was torn to be cast among men. . . ." For them as for him, music, like blood and water—which in their unstoppable malleable flow "can filter through" even the"hard-as-steel Cordillerra"—has the unrestrainable capacity to break open the encasements of memory, to bore holes in the apparently seamless narrative space/time of dominant history.[84]

Music transports us, as Paul Gilroy has written with respect to the resistant adaptation of Black Atlantic culture, expressed in the particular form of the jubilee, to "a liberatory, aesthetic moment which is emphatically anti- or even pre-discursive"—to a preoedipal moment that is—which "has the upper hand over the pursuit of utopia by rational means."[85] Philosopher Tommy Lott's conclusion about Gilroy's theory of cultural retentions and reconstructions as expressed through music, namely that "there is no static African tradition frozen in time because remembrance of a preslave past is actively practiced in black music as recurring acts of identity operating through the call and response mechanisms produced in the interaction of performer and audience,"[86] could refer *mutatis mutandis* to Rivera's presentation in *Khunuskiw* of the role of music in the Andean region. If nothing else, the video and the ensuing controversy opened new avenues of debate in a country currently in search of new forms of self-definition as it negotiates the terms of its singularity in the new world order, into which it is being pulled so vertiginously.

TOWARD THE FUTURE

The 1993 elections will no doubt bring positive changes both to Bolivian filmmaking and videomaking and to the social and political milieus that inform those media. Not only is Vice President Víctor Hugo Cárdenas the first Indian to hold office in Bolivia, but President Gonzalo Sánchez de Losada has been interested in the film industry for years—having produced the (rather forgettable) adventure film *Behind the Andes (Mina*

Alaska, 1952) with the veteran Jorge Ruiz, and participated in the merging of Bolivian Films and Telecine, the conglomerate that led to the creation of the Bolivian Film Institute (ICB) in 1953.

Through democratic elections the country has put back in power the party that embodied (and progressively betrayed) the mass Indian-identified peasant and miner movements in the Revolution of 1952. Today, with the state self-consciously participating in the formation of a national identity ideally free of atavistic race and gender relations while it lays out the blueprint for a truly participatory democracy in the near future, the Indian majority finally has the potential (yet to be realized) to fulfill what Rivera has described as "a longing, frustrated to date, to form part of a national-popular project with truly democratic and pluralistic roots . . . , [where] they will be able to maintain their own identity . . . sustained by Indian cultural autonomy." Theirs has been, in Rivera's words, "a project of liberation" that has put the country on a path which "cannot be other than a process of profound and radical decolonization."[87] The challenge is to remember, as Homi Bhabha points out, that the "The marginal or 'minority'," which in Bolivia represents a vast majority with a rich and profoundly influential cultural history of its own, "is not the space of a celebratory, or utopian, self-marginalization. It is a much more substantial intervention into those justifications of modernity—progress, homogeneity, cultural organicism, the deep nation, the long past—that rationalize the authoritarian, 'normalizing' tendencies within cultures in the name of the national interest or ethnic prerogative."[88] So far, and perhaps not surprisingly, the association of Cárdenas and Sánchez de Losada has been conceptualized metaphorically as a *yunta*, an ancient type of plough pulled by two oxen, still used widely in indigenous small-scale agriculture, in order to symbolize the complementarity of what I have here called the white-Indian oppositional dyad. After all, "intersubjectivity," as Zavaleta noted, "exists before its (presupposed) material premises."[89]

Under the impetus of such radical social and political changes, it is to be hoped that issues not only of national identity and ethnicity but also of gender will be framed differently by Bolivian cinema and video in the future.

NOTES

1. Quoted by Silvia Rivera Cusicanqui, *Oprimidos pero no vencidos: Luchas del campesinado Aymara y Qhechwa de Bolivia, 1900–1980* (Geneva: United Nations Research Institute for Social Development, UNRISD, 1982) 11.

Gabriel René Moreno (1834–1908), positivist thinker, essayist, political affi-cionado, and literary and social historian, belonged to a prominent oligarchical family. He continues to be an important, if controversial, figure in Bolivian his-toriography. See President Lydia Gueiler Tejada's speech, *Centenario de la Uni-versidad Gabriel René Moreno: discurso de la Presidenta Interina de la República.* La Paz: Secretaría de Informaciones, December 15, 1979, and the collection of essays recently published in honor of the 150th anniversary of his birth, *Estudios sobre Gabriel René Moreno.* Santa Cruz de la Sierra: Editorial Casa de la Cultura, 1986. This author's derogatory reference to the indigenous population as *la indi-ada y la cholada* is untranslatable. Unless otherwise specified, all translations from the Spanish are my own.

2. Unresolved from the perspective of unofficial oral history. In the polit-ical theses approved by consensus in June, 1983, by the Second National Peas-ant Congress (*Confederación sindical única de trabajadores del campo de Bolivia,* C.S.U.T.C.B.), neither Simón Bolivar nor José Antonio de Sucre, national heroes of Independence, figure as liberators from Spain. Nor do their dates for liberation (officially 1805 for La Paz and 1825 for Bolivia as a whole) or, for that matter, geographical boundaries, coincide with those of official history. Instead, we read: "The great libertarian movements of 1780–81 shook the foundations of colonial domination, proving that the colonial power was not invincible. That is why we believe that the true liberators from colonial domination were Tomás, Dámaso and Nicolás Katari in the region of Potosí, Tupak Amaru and Micacla Bastidas in the Cuzco region [Peru], Andrés Tupak Amaru and Gregoria Apasa in the northern valleys of La Paz, and Tupak Katari and Bartolina Sisa in the Altiplano. The seed of liberation of the Katarista struggle descended from the Cordillera in Apolobamba and spread all the way to the eastern plateaus." Reprinted in *Oprimidos pero no vencidos,* p. 202. A more typical historiography is reported by James Dunkerley in his incisive analyis of the years of unrelenting political struggle in Bolivia. After the newly established liberal-oligarchs savagely crushed the 1899 rebellion of Zarate 'El Temible' Willka, where a large number of White and Mestizo people were also massacred, "The incumbent president, the mestizo Bautista Saavedra, . . . when acting as a defence lawyer for Willka twenty years earlier, had referred to the Aymara as 'blood thirsty orangutans,' stressing 'the profound perversion of Aymara moral sensibilities,' of the 'morally atrophied race, degenerating into dehumanisation' . . ." *Rebellion in the Veins* (The Thetfrod Press: Norfolk, 1984), 24.

3. Although there is no mention of Bolivia in Nancy Leys Stepan's ground-breaking study *"The Hour of Eugenics." Race, Gender, and Nation in Latin Amer-ica* (Ithaca, N.Y.: Cornell University Press, 1991), the mimetic mutations of the European eugenist movement in Bolivia merit a study of their own. *Encomienda* and *pongueaje* were colonial institutions enforced by Spain throughout the con-

tinent via the Viceroyalties. Indians were assigned in *encomiendas* to a Spanish colonizer (*encomendero*) as part of the land. The responsibility of the *encomendero* included their catechization. *Pongueaje* represented obligatory services rendered by Indians to church and civil authorities. With Independence, it became an institutionalized form of servile relations whereby access to small plots of land were permitted in exchange for labor in the *latifundios*.

For a site-specific analysis of changing patterns of land ownership in Bolivia, see Silvia Rivera and Tristan Platt, "El impacto colonial sobre un pueblo Pakaxa," in *Avances*, No. 1, La Paz, 1978.

4. *Nation and Narration* (New York: Routledge, 1990) 3.

5. *Nationalisme sans nation? La Bolivie aux XIXème et XXème siècles* (Paris: Editions du Centre National de Recherche Scientifique, 1980) see especially 95 and 191.

6. The colonial roots of the oligarchy are evident in the composition of the Bolivian state until recently, described by René Zavaleta Mercado ten years ago as being in the hands of "mining exporters (who combine the influence of medium range mining and that of the State, which they control), the Santa Cruz oligarchy, and in decreasing order, the other oligarchies, the army, and the Church in complex ways." "Las masas en noviembre," *Bolivia, Hoy* (México: Siglo XXI, 1983), 14, note 7. The Santa Cruz oligarchy, a newcomer to the club, is generally associated with the drug cartel.

7. *Oprimidos pero no vencidos,* passim.

8. For an analysis and critique of the postwar division of the planet into first, second, and third worlds, see Peter Worsley, *The Three Worlds: Culture and World Development* (Chicago: University of Chicago Press, 1984). For a study of the growing involvement of Protestant Churches—such as the Church of Latter Day Saints, which has seven buildings in La Paz alone—and the complex operations of a messianic message, which finds echoes in Andean thought, and vice versa, see Juliana Ströbe-Gregor, *Indios de piel blanca* (La Paz: HISBOL, 1989). Brazilian director Hector Babenco's *Playing on the Fields of the Lord* (Brazil-U.S. 1991) addresses, albeit problematically, the world-historical implications of the Protestant Church's massive takeover of Indian social and religious life throughout the continent.

9. *Lengua y sociedad en Bolivia.* La Paz: Instituto Nacional de Estadísticas. Proyecto INE-Naciones Unidas, 1976. See also his *Los mil rostros del Quechua.* Lima: Instituto de Estudios Peruanos, 1974.

10. *¿Bodas de plata o réquiem para una reforma agraria?* (CIPCA: La Paz, 1979) 23–24.

11. Pedro Plaza Martínez and Juan Carvajal Carvajal, *Etnias y Lenguas de Bolivia* (La Paz: Instituto Boliviano de Cultura, 1985), 13. While Javier Albó insists that the acculturating trend toward widespread bilingualism, both in urban and rural areas, does not mean that native languages are being abandoned in favor of Spanish. By 1978, however, the Bolivian peasant union saw in this trend a reason for concern: " The diverse peoples who inhabit this land, even though we speak different languages, have different systems of organization, conceptions of the world, and historical traditions, are connected in brotherhood through continuous and permanent struggles. . . . Many rural and urban workers have lost their own cultural roots through assimilation (*mestizaje*), hispanization (*castellanización*), and acculturation. They are victims of the dominant colonial mentality. Because we are all oppressed, we have a common cause of liberation." "Theses of the Bolivian Peasant Union, Aproved during the VII National Peasant Congress," March, 1978. Reprinted in *Oprimidos pero no vencidos*, 200.

12. It is a public secret that the General Hospital is where the poor serve as guinea pigs to freshly graduated doctors and even to first-year medical students. While, as John Hess points out, it may well be an "incompetent [and] impoverished" establishment, it is by no means always "heartless," nor in the least "designed to serve only the rich." "Neo-realism and New Latin American Cinema: *Bicycle Thieves* and *Blood of the Condor*," in *Mediating Two Worlds: Cinematic Encounters in the Americas,* ed. John King, Ana M. López, and Manuel Alvarado (London: British Film Institute, 1993) 113. Financial support for most social institutions in this impoverished country is all but nonexistent. The hospital provides free medical attention and use of their premises, but prescriptions for medicines, dressings, plasma, or even anaesthesia, have to be paid for by the patients themselves. Those who can afford it see private doctors or travel to the United States for medical care.

13. *Oprimidos pero no vencidos*, 1. For insight into the lives of women in the mines, see Domitila Barrios de Chungara, *Si me permiten hablar* (México: Siglo XXI, 1977). Compiled by Moema Viezzer, and translated as *Let Me Speak! Testimony of Domitila, a Woman of the Bolivian Mines* (New York and London: Monthly Review of Books, 1978). For an oral history of the Bolivian Union of Peasant Women, recorded by Javier Medina, see the testimonial *Las hijas de Bartolina Sisa* (La Paz: Instituto de Historia Social Boliviana, HISBOL, 1984). In English, see Rosario León "Bartolina Sisa: The Peasant Women's Organization in Bolivia," in *Women and Social Change in Latin America.* Elizabeth Jelin, ed., J. Ann Zammit and Marilyn Thomson, trans. (London, New Jersey: United Nations Research Insitute for Social Development and Zed Books Ltd., 1990) 135–50.

14. "Las masas en noviembre," 17.

15. See note 4 above. Javier Sanjinés, ed., *Tendencias actuales en la literatura boliviana*. Institute for the Study of Ideologies and Literature/Instituto de cine y radio/televisión: Minneapolis/Valencia, 1985, 9.

16. *El Comercio de Bolivia*, 29 September 1905, quoted by Alfonso Gumucio Dragón in *Historia del cine boliviano* (México: Filmoteca UNAM, 1983) 29.

17. Gumucio Dragón speculates that *Corazón Aymara* may have been made to fulfill a commitment made in Germany by producer Raul Ernst Rivera "to make a film that would show that the life of Bolivian 'indians' was not nearly as wild as was believed in Europe" *Historia del cine boliviano*, 57.

18. Gumucio Dragón notes the silence about the film in the national press as well. He obtained the information about the plot and related incidents from two of the director's surviving collaborators. Although there is no extant copy, it is not clear whether the film was in fact incinerated. *Historia del cine boliviano*, 65–7.

19. *Historia del cine boliviano*, 115.

20. The best interpretive study of the silent period to date is Pedro Susz K. *"La Campaña del Chaco": El ocaso del cine silente Boliviano* (La Paz: Universidad Mayor de San Andrés, 1990), 57–65.

21. *Oprimidos pero no vencidos*, p. 4. René Zavaleta Mercado has called it "the most extensive moment of self-determination in the whole history of the country [and] the constitutive moment of the state of 1952." "Las masas en noviembre," *Bolivia Hoy*, p. 43.

22. "Over a million individuals, affiliated to about 20,000 agrarian unions, is the enduring legacy of the process of organization of the Indian peasantry, which was promoted from within the state." Silvia Rivera, "Luchas campesinas contemporáneas en Bolivia: El movimiento 'Katarista': 1970–1980," in *Bolivia Hoy*, ed. René Zavaleta Mercado (Mexico: Siglo veintiuno, 1983), 132.

23. Silvia Rivera, *Pachakuti: los aymara de Bolivia frente al medio milenio de colonialismo*. Serie: cuadernos de debate, no. 1. Chukiyawu: Taller de historia oral andina, 1991. The appropriation of the term *Indio* to signify an antiassimilationist policy soon spread beyond Bolivia's borders. By 1981, for example, after a continentwide encounter of Indian leaders in Tiahuanaku, the mythical founding site of the Inca Empire, the South American Indian Council was formed. One year later, a follow-up seminar, held in a small rural town in Peru in 1982, concluded: "We, the INDIGENOUS PEOPLES of this continent, call ourselves INDIAN, because with this name we have been subjected during five centuries, and with this name we will free ourselves once and for all. TO BE INDIAN IS OUR PRIDE.

INDIANISM proposes Indians to be the authors and protagonists of their own destiny, that is why our fighting banner and slogan [*consigna*] of struggle is continental." "Aportes del primer seminario sobre ideología, filosofía y política de la Indianidad," Cushiviani, Perú, 1982. In *Conclusiones y Documentos.* La Paz, Consejo Indio de Sud América (CISA), 1983. For an early history of the movement from the point of view of an insider, see Fausto Reinaga, *La revolución india* (La Paz: Ediciones PIB [Partido Indio de Bolivia], 1970).

24. *Manifiesto de Tiahuanacu,* 178–79.

25. Reprinted as an appendix in Rivera, *Oprimidos pero no vencidos,* 203.

26. Jacques Lacan describes the psychic circumlocutions of this process, which he defines under the term *aphanisis,* in *Four Fundamental Concepts of Psychoanalysis.*

27. Silvia Rivera Cusicanqui, *Oprimidos pero no vencidos,* 161.

28. *La aventura del cine boliviano, 1952–1985* (La Paz: Editorial Gisbert, 1985) 12.

29. Gumucio Dragón, *Historia del cine boliviano,* 177.

30. Gumucio Dragón, *Historia del cine boliviano,* 180.

31. According to Gumucio Dragón, *Historia del cine boliviano,* 170, the film ended up in the festival against the wishes of the Bolivian authorities who, four years after the popular uprisings of 1952, would have "refused to have this film represent Bolivia, because 'a film about Indians could by no means represent the country.'" It has received numerous awards, notably in Venice in 1958, and the San Francisco and Berlin festivals in 1963.

32. Interview conducted in La Paz on December 7, 1990. Ruiz also regretted the elimination of conscription, because the army was one of the few opportunities for white-identified middle- and upper-class men from the city to come into protracted contact with Indian-identified peasants and workers.

33. Gumucio Dragón, *Historia del cine boliviano,* 158.

34. Gumucio Dragón, *Historia del cine boliviano,* 159.

35. Quoted in Gumucio Dragón, *Historia del cine boliviano,* 167.

36. Such dramatization/documentation of Indian-identified subjectivity was also unprecedented in the Americas. Fernando Birri's *Tire Dié,* generally considered as the first film to use native subjects (albeit not indigenous peoples) to denounce their own oppression by reenacting its terms, did not come out until 1960.

37. In the words of Carlos Mesa, the film "narrates a peculiar story of ethnic and cultural identity, unveiling for us a curious relationship of dependency and oppression between different peoples in the Altiplano." Carlos D. Mesa Gisbert, "Cine boliviano 1953–1983: Aproximación a una experiencia," in Sanjinés, ed., *Tendencias,* 189.

38. Carlos Mesa Gisbert, *Tendencias,* 189. In a similar vein, in his otherwise insightful and important interpretive history of Bolivian film, Mesa Gisbert describes the film as "the first great aproximation to the world of the Chipaya community (everyday more culturally cornered and penetrated) living in the midst of the arid highlands of [the province of] Oruro. The Chipayas were *one of the few primitive peoples to survive without altering their characteristics,* independently from the more powerful Aymara whose culture has influenced Bolivian society the most." *La aventura del cine boliviano,* 61 (my italics).

39. Native (generally third-world) informants is Gayatry Spivak's ironic designation for those called upon to represent, in the sense of speak for, their people before an audience who has framed him/her as an Other beforehand. See, for example, "The Problem of Cultural Self-Representation," *The Post-Colonial Critic: Interviews, Strategies, Dialogues.* Ed. Sarah Harasym (New York: Routledge, 1990), 50–58.

40. For the anthropologist's take on the subject, somewhat betrayed by the title, see, Jehan Albert Vellard, *Dieux et parias des Andes: les Ourus, ceux que ne veulent pas être entre des hommes* (Paris: Editions Emile-Paul, 1954).

41. Gumucio Dragón, *Historia del cine boliviano,* 203.

42. The "Grupo Ukamau" was cofounded by Sanjinés, Antonio Eguino, Oscar Soria, Ricardo Rada, and Alberto Villalpando that same year. The group was subsequently divided into two, when, after the Banzer coup of 1971, Sanjinés and Rada were sent into exile and Eguino and Soria returned to Bolivia to make commercially viable films, theorized by Eguino as "cine posible." Sanjinés's production company retained the name of Grupo Ukamau and Eguino's that of Productora Ukamau.

43. Bolivia has one of the highest infant mortality rates in the world. According to a 1964 public health study, the rate for infants from birth to one year is 110/1000 in the cities and 168/1000 in the rural areas. Among the latter, only 68.2% of the surviving children reach the age of six and only 48.5% live to be fifteen years old. As the study concludes, "this means that, by the time the stage of active productivity begins, the country has already lost more than 50% of its human capital." *Bolivia: Desarrollo Rural* (La Paz: Ministerio de Salud Pública, 1964), 7.

44. Quoted in Julianne Burton, ed. and trans., *Cinema and Social Change in Latin America: Conversations with Filmmakers* (Austin: University of Texas Press, 1986), 37.

45. Joseph William Bastien looks critically into some of these issues in *Mountain of the Condor: Metaphor and Ritual in an Andean Ayllu* (St. Paul: West Publishing, Monographs of the American Ethnological Society, 64, 1978). For an edited version of Sanjinés's account of this experience, see Julianne Burton's *Cinema and Social Change.*

46. Zuzana M. Pick, *The New Latin American Cinema: A Continental Project* (Austin: University of Texas Press, 1993) 118.

47. Jorge Sanjinés y Grupo Ukamau, Teoría y práctica de un cine junto al pueblo (México: Siglo XXI Editores, 1979) 86–87 and 32, respectively.

48. *The New Latin American Cinema,* 120.

49. *Filmo- videografía boliviana básica (1904–1990)* (La Paz: Ed. Cinemateca Boliviana, 1991), 169.

50. Tupaj Katari and his wife, Bartolina Sisa, were sentenced to death by quartering after the fall of the legendary late eighteenth-century siege of the city of La Paz. According to Dunkerly, the alliance they formed with Tupaj Amaru, who led a similar uprising in Cuzco, "displaced imperial authority over a region that stretched as far south as Salta [today in northern Argentina] for a number of months." *Rebellion in the Veins,* 23–24. According to oral tradition, Tupaj Katari's last words before his death on 15 November 1781 were, in Aymara, *Nayawa jiwtxa nayjarusti waranqa waranqanakawa kutanipxa,* which means, "I die but will return tomorrow as thousand thousands."

51. Jorge Sanjinés, "We invent a New Language through Popular Culture," *Framework* 10 (1979): 31.

52. *Filmo- videografía boliviana básica (1904–1990),* 169.

53. As opposed to theology, "words about God," logology is defined by Kenneth Burke as "words about words. . . . Thus statements that great theologians have made about the nature of 'God' might be adapted *mutatis mutandis* for use as purely secular observations on the nature of words." *The Rhetoric of Religion: Studies in Logology* (Berkeley: University of California Press, 1970 [1961]), 1.

54. Jacques Derrida, "The Violence of the Letter: From Lévi-Strauss to Rousseau," and ". . . That Dangerous Supplement," in *Of Grammatology,* trans. Gayatri Chakravorty Spivak (Baltimore: Johns Hopkins University Press, 1976),

101–14. And Luce Irigaray, *That Sex Which Is Not One*, trans. Catherine Porter with Carolyn Burke (Ithaca, N.Y.: Cornell University Press, 1985 [1977]), especially chapter 3, "Psychoanalytic Theory: Another Look," 34–67.

55. For further insights into the concept of Andean complementarity, see Tristan Platt, *Espejos y maíz: temas de la estructura simbólica andina* (La Paz: Centro de Investigación y Promoción del Campesinado, 1976); Thérèsa Bouysse-Cassagne/Olivia Harris, Tristan Platt, and Verónica Cereceda, *Tres reflexiones sobre el pensamiento andino* (La Paz: HISBOL, 1987); and Jean Billye Isbell, "La otra mitad esencial. Un estudio de complementaridad sexual en los Andes," *Estudios Andinos*, 37–56. Semiotic readings performed in various regions by scholars from the French Annales School about the cultivation of corn, textile weavings design, or storytelling patterns, among other things, have revealed that Andean communities as a whole articulate experience and memory by means of unconscious spaciotemporal structural coordinates that bear little resemblance to those of the Socio-Symbolic Order and Imaginary Register of the Judeo-Christian West.

56. *Estado Boliviano y Ayllu Andino: tierra y tributo en el norte de Potosí* (Lima: Instituto de Estudios Peruanos, 1982), 20

57. See note 12.

58. It was Banzer's decision to arrange for the transfer and settlement in Bolivia of about 150,000 white Rhodesians, after Zimbabwe's independence. West Germany was also involved in similar negotiations at the time.

59. Zuzana Pick reports that "Three weeks after its première, the film was withdrawn from exhibition. The censor's office banned the film at the demand of the Bolvian army and, in particular, General Ramón Azero, named in the film as co-author of a massacre of miners." *The New Latin American Cinema*, 122.

60. Zuzana Pick, *The New Latin American Cinema* 121.

61. *Las hijas de Bartolina Sisa,* 10 and 12, see note 13.

62. *Si me permiten hablar,* 34–35.

63. A long-time resident of Latin America, Labrousse also documented the Tupamaros in Uruguay and Chile's democratic socialist experiment under Allende. See as well film and cultural critic Luis Espinal's Sorelian meditations on the mythical power of strikes, inspired by this hunger strike, which he joined from its inception, in the posthumous critical edition of his text, *El testamento político espiritual de Luis Espinal* (La Paz: HISBOL, 1991).

64. In the late eighties, after a short working visit to Bolivia, a French film crew associated with Jean Rouch donated their equipment to a small group of

young Indian-identified film apprentices from the Telemayu Miner's Union. An agreement was signed with the Bolivian Miners Federation, mediated by the La Paz Cinematheque through its director, Pedro Susz, which give rise to the *Taller de Cine Minero*. The intention was to constitute a permanent film production center fully in the hands of its members. Internal politics and lack of financial means to bring shot film footage to postproduction have led to few tangible results as yet. None of the footage was shot by women, nor were there any women in the group.

65. Response to written interview questions, La Paz, January, 1991.

66. Interview, La Paz, January, 1991.

67. Danielle, Caillet, "La importancia de un cine llamado "POTENCIAL MUJER,'" *Primer Plano* (La Paz:) 2–3.

68. Caillet, 3.

69. Fátima López Burgos, *Ultima Hora.* La Paz, 5 January 1991.

70. Sanjinés, ed., "Cine boliviano 1953–1983," *Tendencias,* 194.

71. The Bartolinas had been insisting on this alliance for a couple of years. As they recount in their testimonial, "Already during the 1977 Peasant Congress we tried desperately to integrate the peasants into the COB. We felt we were being marginalized since all other workers were already affiliated. . . . With our entry, the COB has also won, because it is now a nationwide organization. Now we can hit the State with both hands: with strikes as well as roadblocks; from within and from without. It will no longer be as it was during the time of Tupaj Katari. Now we have an ally in the city," *Las hijas de Bartolina Sisa,* 15. As Zavaleta Mercado pointed out, "There are no precedents in Latin America of this kind of rural support to a typically urban form such as the strike. More important still . . . , what is here produced is the incorporation of the political methods of classical peasant struggles to the patterns of insurrection of the working class." Mercado, ed., "Las masas en noviembre," *Bolivia Hoy,* 21. Through their ties with other grassroots women's organizations such as the Housewives of the Mines and the Housewives of the Popular Neighbourhoods (*barrios*), the Bartolinas have also been instrumental in the growing politicization of the private sphere.

72. Javier Medina, "La oenegización de la sociedad," unpublished article.

73. Personal interview, La Paz, June 18, 1988.

74. Besides actively working with several groups of underprivileged women, Tahipamu publishes books and educational "*cuadernos*" designed to

facilitate access to information by the combination of drawings, photographs, and simple language in large print. See, for example, its account of the syndicate of cooks/homemakers, *Historia del sindicato de culinarias (1935–1958)* (La Paz: Ediciones Tahipamu, 1988).

75. The title comes from a line in Manuel Monroy's fashionable salsa tune, "Balada para Maribel," which proclaims the "end of patriarchy." "*No sé porque te has casado Maribel, con ese sordo del alma. . . . El patriarcado se acaba Maribel, . . . con ese sordo del alma.*"

76. The polemic summarized here transpired in the pages of the daily *La Razón,* in the order quoted: Mauricio Souza, "Una ranchera feminista," 18 August 1990; Elizabeth Machicao, 21 August 1990; and letter to *TV Guide,* 25 August 1990.

77. From beatings, rape, and forced sterilization, as in Sanjinés's *Ukamau* and *Yawar Mallku,* to incest and rape in Paolo Agazzi's *Los Hermanos Cartagena,* to name some of the better known films.

78. Silvia Rivera C. and Zulema Lehm A., *Artesanos Libertarios* (La Paz: Ediciones del Taller de Historia Oral Andina, 1988).

79. "Adrián Patiño, la música, la memoria, la contradicción de ser boliviano," *Presencia,* 8 May 1995.

80. Public debate, La Paz, 30 November 1990.

81. Among his credits are the experimental video *Puraduraluvia,* 1990, winner of the same prize, and the musicals *Pantomima de TV* and *El Repatriado,* in the same year.

82. Pier Paolo Pasolini, "The Cinema of Poetry," *Movies and Methods.* Bill Nichols, ed., University of California Press, Berkeley, Los Angeles, London, 1976, pp. 542–58. Originally read in Italian by Pasolini in June 1965 at the first New Cinema Festival at Pesaro.

83. "Adrián Patiño, la música, la memoria, la contradicción de ser boliviano," *Presencia,* 8 May 1995.

84. José María Arguedas, *Los ríos profundos* (Madrid: Alianza Editorial, 1981), 164 and 152, respectively. Initially published in 1958. I have used and modified Frances Horning Barraclough's translation, *Deep Rivers* (Austin: University of Texas Press, 1989).

85. Paul Gilroy, *The Black Atlantic: Modernity and Double Consciousness* (Cambridge: Harvard University Press, 1993), 71 and 68, respectively, quoted by

Tommy Lott in "Slavery, Modernity and the Reclamation of Anterior Cultures," *Found Object* 4 (Fall 1994): 44.

86. Tommy Lott, "Slavery, Modernity and the Reclamation of Anterior Cultures," *Found Object* 4 (Fall 1994): 44.

87. Silvia Rivera Cusicanqui, *Oprimidos pero no vencidos,* 161.

88. *Nation and Narration,* 4.

89. Mercado, ed., "Las masas en noviembre," *Bolivia Hoy,* 18.

CHAPTER SIX

The Seen of the Crime

KAREN SCHWARTZMAN

AN INTRODUCTION: GENRE AND GENDER

Macu, the Policeman's Wife (1987), a Venezuelan film by Solveig Hoogesteijn, would appear to fall within the typical police/crime film genre where a wife's adultery leads predictably to her husband's murder of her lover. This is the crime—the mystery to be solved—yet almost immediately the solution is made evident, so that instead of asking Who did it? the film is asking, Who is responsible and why? The film takes a journey into the psyche of a woman who has been the victim of another crime, which is Macu's story. At the same time that the film interrogates the social, it also interrogates the Law, that which culturally defines gendered identities, with women as commodities and men as their armed custodians.

Police stories commonly try to solve a crime and reinforce cultural codes; this genre typically follows the codes of classic cinema, which are also reciprocally bound in gender.[1] I will attempt to show that in *Macu* cultural codes, specifically in relation to gender, are deconstructed. Macu's story, set against Ismael's story both thematically and formally, serves to demystify and demythologize the role of the policeman as an exaggerated instance of masculinity by revealing how he is, or came to be, culturally constructed. The elaboration of Macu's story reveals these cultural codes at work on him. These same constructs work to define and determine

Macu's experience. Their stories are interdependent, dialectical even (as structuring and destructuring narratives), indicating that both male and female share responsibility for the construction of gendered roles and identities and, by implication, larger socioeconomic problems. As the film represents Macu's and Ismael's stories, there are reflected various parallels, mirrorings, and doublings evidenced, for example, in the double adulteries, betrayals, castrations; multiple transgressions of the Law; and multiple replications of Oedipal triangulation. The film is not optimistic, and there is no clear victory. Rather than experiencing a sense of satisfaction at solving the mystery, we are left asking what will become of the characters in the future.

In the final shot of the film Macu defiantly confronts the camera/spectator in a position of direct address, suggesting that the "whodunnit" has found a guilty party for the crime—in us. This look, perhaps less defiant than accusing, takes the spectator as its object, pointing the finger—directing the gaze—at society itself. By engaging in this kind of social criticism, *Macu* joins ranks with the large majority of Venezuelan national cinema productions whose "common thread," according to Pedro Martinez in his article "Principales tendencias del largometraje narrativo venezolano en los ultimos años," is that of social denunciation.[2] This tradition can, in fact, be observed within most of the contemporary national cinemas of Latin America, whose politics have been shaped by the theorization of a political cinema in the late 1960s and early 1970s that gave rise to the New Latin American Cinema. This was not so much a unified, organized movement, but the linking together of multiple groups and individuals who exhibited a variety of approaches yet worked under similar conditions of economic underdevelopment and similar ideologies of resistance.[3] Venezuelan national cinema in this context became a cinema of opposition, marked by anti-imperialist sentiment (explicit in the films of the 1970s) and the struggle to define itself against the dominant cinema of Hollywood. In this sense there is a shared endeavor with feminist cinema, or, for that matter, with any other alternative cinema practice. However, it doesn't suffice to contextualize *Macu* merely within a general category of national cinema and a feminist cinema that does not derive from Venezuela per se. Since its release in 1987, *Macu* continues to maintain its status as the largest grossing domestic film, surpassing even imports like *E.T., Rambo,* and *Superman*.[4] Within Venezuelan cinema *Macu* belongs to a genre known as "common crime" films, which, together with the "picaresque/magical-realist" genre, forms one of the "two fundamental pillars of Venezuelan cinema."[5] Common crime films may very often derive from a story taken from the newspaper or testimonial literature, and such is the case of *Macu*.[6] Yet *Macu* functions to subvert the codes of this genre by seducing the spectator into participating in the creation and legitimization of an alternate history.

There is much at stake here, and this is where my investigation begins. By questioning gender, genre is inevitably deconstructed, which then makes possible a reconstruction from another place of vision. This is my project—to reveal how *Macu* actively and "processively" reconstructs itself as a feminist film, demonstrated through its enunciative strategies, its positions of desire and its social thematic, which together create another place of reception, an/other subject that ultimately challenges the dominant, masculine constructions.

The film depends upon a complex formal strategy that juxtaposes a chronological narrative with a second nonconventional narrative line. This construction serves to reveal more than just the assumed "primary" plot of the murder investigation. The style of cinematography supports this structure with elegant, carefully composed, constantly panning, long takes that always open out beyond the subject to reveal context. The supposed primary plot is related in the present time and follows the events of the investigation of Ismael's crime in sequential order. However, this chronological narration is diverted in two ways:

1. It is contained within Macu's nonchronological flashback for almost the entire film, a series of flashbacks that occur within what I call the "main frame." This device subsequently functions to throw the "primary" plot of the murder case into a secondary position so that the *main* investigation becomes a different one. The main frame is marked by a sequence of shots that leaves and returns to the same image, yet unlike a conventional frame where we would return to the same past moment where the flashback originated (in this case, September, six months after the crime was committed), we are instead "returned" to a moment in the future some four months later when Ismael is apprehended by the police. This structural twist throws the entire film into a kind of "present-continuous" mode of address.

2. The narration is often interrupted by Macu's memories of past events—precrime moments with Simón and the deep past of her childhood—redefining, as we will see, the terms of enunciation. One strategy that will continuously traverse the various theoretical models engaged in this work is the construction of the "look." The "look" in

film contributes to the construction of point of view within the film, positioning the spectator as a desiring subject in relation to the film and controlling the mechanisms of identification and enunciation.[7] *Macu* problematizes this "look," reversing the terms from masculine to feminine in all shared relationships—author, spectator, and text.[8]

This chapter covers a large stretch of theoretical ground as it returns its author, like Macu, to the "scene of the crime." The writer/theorist has only found her way back and *out* due to the trail marked by great detectives before her—Julia Kristeva (whose "semiotic/ *chora*" was the initial inspiration for this work), Teresa de Lauretis, and Kaja Silverman. But, as in *Macu,* what was the "main" investigation proved itself to be another one—the *seen* of the crime is itself only a clue to yet another investigation.

HIS STORY

The two parts of the main frame appear to be symmetrically structured, somewhat like a Rorschach test where each half of an image is a mirror-like reversal of the other, except that in this case the two halves, as it were, are not quite identical. The first half of the main frame—the precredit and opening sequences—is a building-up, a constructing of the narrative. Unanswered questions and unsolved events are posed, a classic means of initiating narratives. The opposite side, or other half, of the frame—the final and postcredit sequences—that surrounds Macu's flashback narrative is structured in reverse order, depicting the unraveling, the undoing, of both the story and the "man."

In the precredit sequence, there is an exchange of almost matching looks (interchanging subject and object positions) with a man who follows Macu (María Luisa Mosquera) as she enters one of the city's *barrios* (in Venezuela, a working-class neighborhood), lending an atmosphere of intrigue as would be expected at the start of a police thriller. The looks between the male and female characters (in this scene and throughout the film) are direct, assertive, constructive and constructing of each other in turn, demonstrating an evident power play: looks from above to below, from below to above, indicative of who holds or contains the point of view. After passing some way through the tight, narrow passageways of the *barrio,* Macu rounds a corner and turns back to give the man a very ambiguous look—suggestive, provocative, seductive, while at the same time challenging and even defiant. It is this kind of ambiguity that will accompany and characterize Macu throughout the film as the question of her complicity in the crime is put "on trial" in response to accusations that she provoked Ismael (Daniel Alvarado) to murder. The "tail" is later revealed to be Willy (Tito Aponte), Ismael's police partner who has functioned as spy and "stand-in" for Ismael since Macu was a child. (This belated identification allows me to suggest retroactively that Macu's initial look might also contain a kind of hatred.) Macu is accosted by reporters as she approaches her house.[9] [Figure 6.1] A male reporter speaks into a tape recorder as Macu enters the house; his voice continues to speak in voice-over, stating facts about the case as the camera's gaze moves inside the house. A panning shot attempts to contextualize the character by showing her world, intimating that this house defines her in some way.[10]

Ismael's role is defined by his diplomas, his uniform and his gun; he is the personification of power in the *barrio;* he acts as protector (virtually omnipresent through Willy's spying), in control of his house, his family, his woman and the lie, or so he thinks. [Figure 6.2] Thus, he is set up as the ideal image of masculinity: strong, in control, representative of the Law, head of the household, "breadwinner," and initiator of sexual activity. [Figure 6.3] He is also shown as a good husband and father, loving toward Macu (he insists that Willy follow her "for her own protection") and toward the children (we see him put Teresita to bed, helping her to say her prayers). [Figure 6.4] Macu, in turn, appears to be contained by Ismael, subordinate to him. Even the television news report of her earlier entrance into the house (which we have just witnessed and that she watches with Teresita), appears to echo her complete confinement and objectification by all gazes—his, the television's, and ours. [Figure 6.5]

Later, when Ismael prepares for bed, he only partly undresses, keeping his uniform pants and t-shirt on as he lies down. In front of Macu he continues to assert his innocence of the crime, which the audience as of yet does not know to be a lie. We could also (retroactively) read this as continuing to assert the lie of his "manhood" or "manliness." Yet, it is precisely in the act of lovemaking (where virility is supposedly determined) that he is displaced. The transitional sequence from the "present" into Macu's flashback and another level of the narrative begins with Ismael in darkness; a rhythmic squeaking sound is heard over the image. Macu, in an orange shirt, is rocking a cradle with her foot. His hand passes over her shoulder to caress her breast. The couple that seemed so close before is then shown under different circumstances, each with someone else. There

FIGURE 6.1. Macu flanked by reporters as she arrives at the house in the opening sequence. Courtesy of Solveig Hoogesteijn.

FIGURE 6.2. Ismael. Courtesty of Solveig Hoogesteijn.

FIGURE 6.3. Ismael and Macu after the dance. Courtesy of Solveig Hoogesteijn.

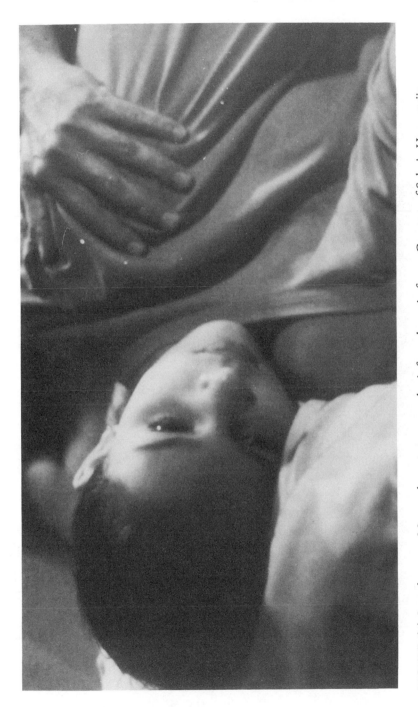

FIGURE 6.4. Ismael caresses Macu—the entrance to and exit from the main frame. Courtesy of Solveig Hoogesteijn.

214

FIGURE 6.5. Macu and Teresita watching on television Macu's earlier arrival at the house. Courtesy of Solveig Hoogesteijn.

215

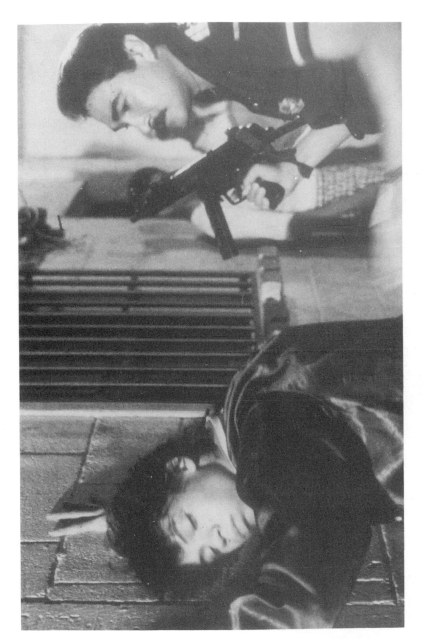

FIGURE 6.6. Ismael and Simón. Courtesy of Sclveig Hoogesteijn.

FIGURE 6.7. Macu and Ismael shortly before Ismael's surrender. Courtesy of Solveig Hoogesteijn.

FIGURE 6.8. Ismael's exit "live" on television. Courtesy of Solveig Hoogesteijn.

is an elliptical cut to a silent flashback image of Macu dancing with her lover, Simón (Frank Hernández), at a club; cut back to Ismael and Macu making love. Macu is shown "on top" (not that sexual positions are so clearly signifying, but in this case it works), as she fantasizes about her lover, Simón; cut back again to Macu and Simón dancing with full sound as Ismael watches from above on a balcony, joined by his mistress, Angela. (Later, the film will point out the double standard reserved for men, for whom adultery is something "natural" and expected, but for women so criminal as to inspire men to commit murder, murder often condoned by society.)[11]

The return back into the main frame at the end of the film (out of the flashback), at first appears to continue from where it left off, but in fact it takes place an undetermined number of months later after all the facts of the crime have been revealed to both the diegetic "public" and the film viewer. [Figure 6.6] This present-future "replay" of the earlier scene points out a double perspective, two versions of the same event. Macu wears the same orange shirt, and the image is accompanied by the same rhythmic sound of the rocking cradle. Ismael even leans over in the same manner as before and places his hand on her shoulder, only now he is very different. He is naked, stripped of the "lie," and acknowledges his crime.

This is the night before his surrender to the police. [Figure 6.7] There is the sound of thunder in the background. Macu and Ismael are placed in profile, facing each other with a deep black gap between them. The shot is one long take that pans very slowly back and forth from one to the other, emphasizing the space between them. He speaks about going down in the history of the country as the author of the perfect crime, for having the best alibi: killing three boys instead of one would mislead the investigation since his motive was "justified" for Simón alone. The moment is heavy; Ismael, the now fallen "hero," has become a tragic figure, pathetic even. They embrace, seeking mutual comfort. He lies back, but his look is not strong enough to hold hers and he turns his face away, tears in his eyes. Macu takes off her shirt, suggesting that she will give herself to him, a surrender less to him than to her fate (which they both appear to share) as she comforts him out of pity, not love. The movement of the main frame from "love" scene to "love" scene is a striking indictment of Ismael's macho pose, which effectively undermines his masculinized identity (and his power). What this says about Macu remains to be seen.

The next series of shots begin the process of unraveling. As the camera dollies back, it is revealed that Ismael is sitting alone in the kitchen looking down dejectedly and not, as it first appears, at the crowd below. The camera moves around his head; voices from outside seem to emanate from inside his head. A woman's voice predominates, crying, "Murderer!" and "They're going to take away your uniform!" The camera continues to move somewhat awkwardly back, framing Ismael so that he is contained by the doorway behind him. The camera continues back to form a composition that is now an over-the-shoulder shot of Macu with the baby, as if she is looking at Ismael. However, it becomes apparent that she is not looking at Ismael at all, but at the floor. We hear the television announcing the imminent "live" event and Macu goes to watch the television. The black and white wedding photograph, of the standing child bride and the sitting police-groom, on top of the television, now stands as a metaphor for Macu's story.

Macu sits in exactly the same position as in the opening sequence to watch television, only this time with the younger child in her lap. Where before she had watched the news report of her own entrance into the house (also a "replayed" scene), now she watches Ismael's surrender "live" on television as he exits the house, and we watch with her. Ismael is asked repeatedly by the same reporter who interviewed Macu in the beginning, Belkis Casales (Ana María Paredes), why he killed the three boys. [Figure 6.8] He replies that they soiled his honor and destroyed his home. He does not regret killing them and declares his innocence, believing that he has brought them to justice. His last remark is made directly to the woman reporter: "Why don't you take off your glasses? You have beautiful eyes." Ismael's remark is an indication of the only option left to him in the eyes of the public. He may be a criminal, he may be stripped of his position and authority, but he can still assert himself as a "man" by positioning a woman as the object of his assessment, and desire.

Television in general serves a dual function as both cultural product and producer. Ismael declares that he wants to enter the history of the country for committing the perfect crime; and, in fact, he does enter public history, hence our view of his story through the mediated television images. He enters the "image bank" of television, becoming an "insider" (literally confined to the television's image).[12] I would even go so far as to say that as such, he, or his "story," become(s) a commodity; an ironic twist in light of Macu's consciousness of herself as such, one of the main points of the film. It is his story that is documented by the television coverage, not Macu's. Moreover, his story *is* the "real-life" incident, as it was through the coverage of the case by the television news that the country did in fact come to know the real event upon which the film is based. Discussing "geographic specials" in her article, "Information, Crisis, Catastrophe," Mary Ann Doane writes that "the life of a particular animal or plant becomes most *televisual* when the species is threatened with extinction."[13] Perhaps this observation can be applied to the kind of machismo and power that Ismael represents, hence his privilege of "live" coverage at the end of the film when both these previous "assets" have been taken away.

We return to an unmediated image of the rioting crowd, the camera (hence, our view) now located outside the house, as in the opening sequence when Macu is seen walking toward the *barrio*. Now, in contrast, Macu is forced out of the house as a woman's voice from the crowd threatens to burn it down. (This voice works as the counterpart to those of some women who comment on Macu as she enters the *barrio*. Women's voices, then, also "frame" the film.) Macu wears the same blue dress for these two arrival/departure sequences that open and close the film. In the opening sequence, a dramatic crane shot from above pans across a bridge and lowers down the other side, emphasizing her crossing over from the "outside" world into the *barrio;* and in the final sequence, once again, a crane shot lifts the camera high to reveal Macu's passage with the baby through the crowd and out of the *barrio*. What has ultimately occurred in this quasi-reverse sequence is an undoing and an unbuilding of what came before, revealed in the backward moving shots where instead of the direct, forward gazes that we saw in the beginning, the gazes now miss each other. We are misled as the point-of-view shots are always revealed to be other than what we think they are.

There is an elliptical cut to Macu as she walks to the end of an extremely long line of women and children, visitors who are waiting to enter the prison. The final shot, almost a postscript after the credits have finished scrolling, is a closeup of Macu as she turns her face to confront the camera. I read this look as the match to the one in the opening sequence where she turns to look ambiguously back at Willy. In this last image of the film, Macu breaks out of the "objectified stance," by looking back.

Cinema's performative is the past tense and as such engages memory, whereas television, so caught up in its "nowness," its endless presentation of the immediate, banishes memory. Doane writes, "Meaning in story-telling has time to linger, to be subject to unraveling."[14] It is Macu's story, the cinematic representation of the not real-life story that remains, "lingers" in the memory, and that, in fact, we identify with, locate and experience as "real." The emphasis is on the telling of the untold, "forgotten" history of women's experience in order that it might also partake in History.

HER STORY

> The symbolic order—the order of verbal communication, the paternal order of genealogy—is a temporal order. For the speaking animal, it is the clock of objective time: it provides the reference point, and, consequently, all possibilities of measurement, by distinguishing between a before, a now and an after. If *I* don't exist except in the speech I address to another, *I* am only *present* in the moment of that communication. . . .
> I project not the moment of my fixed, governed work, ruled by a series of inhibitions and prohibitions . . . but rather the underlying causality that shapes it, which I repress in order that I may enter the socio-symbolic order, and which is capable of blowing up the whole construct.[15]

I have attempted to demonstrate in the previous section how *Macu* begins to posit a female subject (via discursive and, as we will see, symbolic positionings), writing a new episode, disrupting the boundaries of History. By applying to the film some of Julia Kristeva's modifications of Lacanian psychoanalysis and Kaja Silverman's concept of the female version of the negative Oedipus complex, I will attempt to show how the film deconstructs "his" story by reconstructing a new (female) subject. My project will be to (1) present Kristeva's concepts of "semanalysis" and the "semiotic/*chora*," (2) outline Silverman's critique and use of what she calls the "*choric* fantasy," and (3) present her (re)formulation of the female negative Oedipus complex. In the subsection, "Tailing the Narrative," I will attempt to apply these concepts by means of a close reading in order to show how the film suggests new terms, spaces, and possibilities as it follows the process by which the subject is constituted.

Semanalysis

According to Kristeva the semiotic disrupts the symbolic at random in what she names "semanalysis." Elizabeth Grosz summarizes Kristeva's proposition as follows: All texts and all cultural products are the results of a dialectical process: the interaction between two mutually modifying historical forces. One is the setting in place, the establishment of a regulated system, or "unity"—the symbolic. Underlying and subverting this "setting in place" is a movement [the semiotic] of "cutting through" or traversing, breaking down unities.[16]

Although Kristeva suggests that the semiotic will always be reincorporated and "reconstituted into a new symbolic system" that will absorb its subversive potential, nonetheless the symbolic system is ruptured and, hence, expanded.[17]

> The subject of the semiotic metalanguage must, however briefly, call himself in question, must emerge from the protective shell of a transcendental ego within a logical system, and so restore his connection with that negativity—drive-governed, but also social, political and historical—which rends and renews the social code.[18]

Kristeva sees the semiotic and the symbolic as "two modalities . . . of all signifying processes whose interaction is the essential even if unrecognized condition of sociality, textuality, and subjectivity."[19] These "modalities" then are as integral, inseparable, and as dialectical even as story from discourse (*histoire/discours*), as utterance from enunciation, or as signified from signifier, and I would add, utterly bound and entwined in gender *because* they presuppose a "subject of enunciation."[20] Kristeva recognizes these gender boundaries precisely in their relation to the symbolic—"the order of verbal communication, the paternal order of genealogy."[21] She specifies that as women we are still tied to language. "Reality," or lived experience, is such that women *must* enter the symbolic, and hence, language, as a necessary condition for speaking their subjectivity. Kristeva further defines these two aspects:

> We shall call *symbolic* the logical and syntactic functioning of language and everything which, in translinguistic practices is assimilable to the system of language proper. The term *semiotic*, on the other hand, will be used to mean: in the first place, what can be hypothetically posited as preceding the imposition of language, in other words, the already given arrangement of the drives in the form of facilitations or pathways, and secondly the return of these facilitations in the form of rhythms, intonations, and lexical, syntactic and rhetorical transformations. If the *symbolic* established the limits

and unity of a signifying practice, the *semiotic* registers in that practice the effect of that which cannot be pinned down as sign, whether signifier or signified.[22]

The semiotic then is that which is *outside* of the signification system (pre-Oedipal), that which is unassigned, unsigned, not named.

The Choric *Fantasy*

Kristeva also assigns a maternal or feminine connotation to the semiotic in the guise of the *chora,* a term that she uses interchangeably with semiotic.[23] Silverman's three main definitions of the Kristevan *chora* are both critically perceptive and necessary for an understanding of how the *chora* will be linked to her formulation of the female negative Oedipus complex. I quote the descriptions *in extenso.*

> [A] Kristeva associates [the *chora*] both with the mother and with the prehistory of the subject, referring it simultaneously to the primordial role played by the mother's voice, face, and breast, and to the psychic and libidinal conditions of early infantile life. . . . However, the *chora* is more an image of unity than one of archaic differentiation; prior to absence and an economy of the object, it figures the oneness of mother and child.
>
> According to the terms of this particular definition, the infant inhabits the interior of the *chora,* and . . . that interiority implies perceptual immaturity and discursive incapacity.
>
> . . . [B] According to the logic of *this* ["semiotic disposition"] definition, the *chora* is situated *inside* the subject, in the guise of a libidinal economy. However, because the mother's body "mediates the symbolic law organizing social relations," becoming "the ordering principle of the semiotic *chora,*" it would perhaps be more precise to speak of the latter as the subject's internalization of the mother in the guise of a "mobile receptacle" or provisional enclosure.
>
> . . . The *chora* is consequently the "place" where the subject is both generated and annihilated, the site where it both assumes a pulsional or rhythmic consistency and is dissolved as a psychic or social coherence.
>
> . . . Kristeva's theoretical model hinges upon a double temporality, affording a very different "take" on the *chora* depending upon

whether it is the pre-Oedipal child or the adult subject who is under discussion. In the first of these instances, the *chora* is itself the condition or regime under siege from the symbolic, the unity which must be ruptured if identity is to be found. In the second it is the force that assails language and meaning, the negativity that threatens to collapse both the *je* and the *moi*.[24]

Most useful in application to *Macu* is this latter definition (B), where the *chora* can be seen as an irruption within an already existing symbolic order and where the *choric* fantasy can be said to manifest at the level of articulation of the text (formal strategies). According to Silverman, Kristeva's *choric* fantasy ultimately excludes both mother and daughter from language, places women beyond representation and denies the possibility of a participation in new discourses, thus preventing the social disruption from being sufficiently meaningful. I believe, however, that the *choric* irruptions are significant and theoretically useful in both signaling and marking a new path toward a woman's entry into language and the negative Oedipus complex. In this way, the *chora* becomes the "'space' of feminism." However, according to Silverman, for this to occur, it is imperative for the *chora* to be finally ruptured, for the infant subject to emerge out of the maternal enclosure into a social space. Hence, this *semiotic chora* cannot be fully separated from Silverman's third definition, where now the *choric* fantasy can be seen to manifest at the level of the fiction (narrative strategies).

> [(C) Kristeva] . . . conceptualizes subjectivity as a spatial series. . . . That series begins with the *chora,* continues with the child's apprehension of space (presumably at the mirror stage), and his or her initial experiments with demonstrative and localizing utterances, and concludes with the accession to subject-predication. As the child proceeds through this series, s/he not only acquires a clearer and clearer understanding of spatial relations, but increases his or her psychic distance from the *chora.*
>   . . . the *chora* and the archaic mother continue to live on within the subject, no matter how linguistically proficient it becomes. The *chora* remains one of the permanent "scenes" of subjectivity.[25]

The "semiotic," or *chora,* manifests itself within texts as a group of reappearing sounds, rhythms, or images. Such manifestations can be seen to weave throughout *Macu* at both the level of articulation and the fiction in such representations as white window, passageways, sound effects, drumbeats, flute tones, colors, creaking doors, fluttering wings, rattles, metallic tinkling, silence, and in formal strategies such as the use of ellipses and multiple flashbacks. These irruptions function to remind us of "the desire that fuels [the *choric* fantasy] . . . [and] which is capable of assuming other forms." It is useful to retain the concept of a dialectical interaction between the *chora* and the symbolic, while keeping in mind that some of the maternal concepts provided by Kristeva may have inspired in part Silverman's reworking of the female version of the negative Oedipus complex. These various drives, or "pulsions," from the *chora* can be seen to cut a trail as they traverse the narrative, rupturing the "social," traditional (Oedipalized) subject and hinting (like clues) at the evolution and emerging constitution of a different subject (via the female version of the negative Oedipus complex). Likewise, the very *process* of Macu's growth is tracked by the *choric* representations, reflecting the developmental formation that compels her toward (a *new* position within) the symbolic.[26] It is important to note as well that Kristeva sees the two terms as constituting *processes,* not "static entities," so that the *chora* is read as "an endless flow of pulsions," itself containing the potential to become Silverman's previously mentioned "space of feminism."[27]

The Female Negative Oedipus Complex

Silverman's female version of the negative Oedipus complex derives from Freud's *The Ego and the Id.* Freud divides the Oedipus complex into two components, positive and negative, where a boy demonstrates ambivalence toward his father and affection toward his mother (positive Oedipus), but also "behaves like a girl and displays an affectionate feminine attitude to his father and a corresponding jealousy and hostility towards his mother" (negative Oedipus), due to the "bisexuality originally present in children."[28] Thus for the female version the poles are reversed. Silverman prefers Freud's "negative Oedipus complex" over his formulation of the "pre-Oedipal phase" for the female subject, and elaborates this structure within the context of Kristeva's work. I am going to take the liberty of considerably simplifying Silverman's work for the sake of its application to *Macu* and urge the reader to partake of her more complex reading directly.[29]

Silverman states that all subjects, male and female, assume identity by (1) separating from the mother, (2) losing access to the real, (3) entering into a field of preexisting meaning, that is, the symbolic order ("discursive interiority"), and (4) by sustaining identity within the gaze of the Other, subordinating to the gaze of the cultural Other. These are "the necessary terms of cultural identity." Silverman's formulation "does not give as much primacy to the paternal intervention as a properly Lacanian reading of the Oedipus complex would do." She sees for the female subject another dimension that has been repressed, or censored, and whose transformative potential is enormous, which is the girl's negative Oedipus complex, her desire for the mother and, by extension, her identification with her. It is by situating the daughter's desire for the mother within the Oedipus complex, making it an effect of language and loss, by contextualizing both it and the sexuality it implies within the symbolic, that it is brought within psychic "reality." Furthermore, it is now "possible to speak for the first time about a genuinely oppositional desire—to speak about a desire which challenges dominance from within representation and meaning, rather than from the place of a mutely resistant biology or sexual 'essence.'"[30] Silverman writes that this "paradigm closes off the pre-Oedipal domain both as an arena for resistance to the symbolic and as an erotic refuge," for, "to impute the daughter's erotic investment in the mother to the pre-Oedipal phase is to suggest that female sexuality precedes language and symbolic structuration," leaving women in a place of impotence.

However, this is, once again, not to lose the *chora* or pre-Oedipal as an important "space for feminism." Silverman asserts that it does represent "one of the governing fantasies of feminism, a powerful image both of women's unity and of their at times necessary separatism." From her reading of the film *Riddles of the Sphinx,* by Laura Mulvey and Peter Wollen, Silverman allows the image of the *chora* to "open out," an "emergence from what the film characterizes as an imaginary dyad into the world of the symbolic. It is a woman who "precipitates this rupture" in the place of the father. "The *chora*," she writes, "in effect becomes the subjective, economic, social, and political 'space' of feminism; the *enceinte* is transformed into an all-inclusive 'community of women.'" It is significant that the third term necessary to break the mother/child dyad and that has been traditionally figured as the father does not necessarily have to be male. Silverman even goes so far as to suggest another configuration for this critical third term: that the third term may be a woman *or* that it may be the *child* whom the daughter "both wishes to give to the mother and to receive from her."

The *choric* fantasy . . . projects a three-generational community of women.

This . . . narcissism may . . . [be read as] the female subject's . . . [refusal rather than] inability to cathect . . . with any object other than the one which was first in her history . . . female narcissism may represent a form of resistance to the positive Oedipus complex, with its inheritance of self-contempt and loathing.

This intersection of desire for and identification with the mother . . . should constitute the site of feminism's libidinal struggle against the phallus.[31]

Although Kristeva problematizes her formulation of the *chora* by not visualizing the mother within the symbolic or the daughter as able to maintain her relation to language while at the same time pursuing her unconscious desire for the mother, the "*choric* fantasy" maintains its desire in relation to other texts and is shown as "capable of assuming other forms."[32] In the spirit of reapplying and/or using Kristeva as a starting point, her concept of Mother as a disruptive role is intriguing, as that which "disturbs identity, system, order. What does not respect borders, position, rules. The in-between, the ambiguous, the composite."[33] The character of Macu fits this description: in light of her relationship with Simón and consequently Ismael's crime she has upset the existing order, defied the expectations of others and in turn set identity on its head by maintaining an ambiguous status throughout the film in regard to the question of her "guilt." Where Kristeva considers this "maternal" space the receptacle for the nonverbal, sensory experiences that overflow and intrude into the symbolic and as a "period is the precondition for and the object sacrificed by the child in establishing a position as a speaking subject within the symbolic";[34] for Silverman, it is precisely the reverse. The female negative Oedipus complex conceives of a female subject's entry into language without relinquishing desire for and identification with the mother. The incorporation of this "maternal image" (the *choric* fantasy at the heart of the female negative Oedipus complex) is in itself a subversive act, "a genuinely oppositional desire . . . which challenges dominance from within representation and meaning."[35] In *Macu* the presence of the elements from the *chora* (listed earlier) maintain the maternal voice as "a dialectic of union and division" throughout the narrative.[36] For Silverman, it is the recovery of the "lost" (archaic) maternal voice that is at stake.

TAILING THE NARRATIVE

Example 1: In the Beginning

Taking a clue from Kristeva, Macu's passage in the precredit sequence is, we learn, a return from her mother's house, which places Macu as a "daughter" as she begins to make her way through the narrative—as a daughter of a mother and a mother of a daughter—Kristeva's maternal trinity, or what is termed the "homosexual maternal facet."[37] (Although as Silverman points out, it is this desire for female fusion that is concealed, or even negated, within Kristeva.)[38] Moreover, this same passage toward and entrance into the house Macu shares with Ismael, viewed in conjunction with her similarly structured departure from the house at the end of the film, can also suggest the "psychic journey" Macu will take, into and out of the events of the film and the past, and which subsequently leads to her transformation. Not only the process of subjectivity, but the entire signification process, *significance,* is reflected in this opening sequence where Macu's long fast walk through the city streets, under the bridge and into the *barrio,* metaphorically characterizes the movement of language and the discursive process as she approaches the television camera crew that awaits her arrival and where the "fictional" television crew adumbrates the production (cinematic) apparatus.[39] Her status is in between places, in motion, on the way, coming from and going toward (and at the end of the film, her departure is again a "coming from," which can suggest a beginning), as she traverses the two distinct spaces marked by the bridge that divides the "outside" world of the crowded city from the "inside" world of the *barrio,* echoing the production of meaning within the symmetrically structured space of the narrative.

In this light the precredit and opening passages and the subsequent ambiguities surrounding her "guilt" can be seen to set up a transition from the traditional, Oedipalized female to the new, emerging female subject whose (continuously moving) path is traced, followed, intercepted, and recorded by both Hoogesteijn's camera and the news reporters' video camera and microphones that try to catch her voice. The film begins to foreground a series of interior spaces that Macu eventually appropriates for herself. However, at this point in the narrative Macu is seen as elusive, hard to catch, difficult to record (they try to "get a statement") and perhaps not so easy to "define" (identify) as she first appears.

The pivotal moment, the "threshold," whereby the spectator is drawn from the main frame of the present moment into the past comes shortly after Macu's entrance into the house and after Ismael's return home from work. The composition is formed by Macu lying on her side in bed rocking the baby's cradle with her foot. The rocking motion is accompanied by the rhythmic sound of the squeaking cradle as Macu's bare leg rocks the netted cradle; the sleeping baby can be seen through the netting. The motion is from Macu to her child. What is thus created is a motion and linkage between mother and child, a nonverbal (preverbal or pre-Oedipal) bond characterized by sound and rhythm, which also sets in motion the passage or crossing from one space to another. The transition to the next scene (and subsequently a different temporal and discursive space) does not occur in one cut but in a short sequence of intercuts that almost "shuffle" the two spaces or scenes into each other, just as sound effects and drum rhythms "impregnate" the image and the passage from one temporal space to another.

The linkage between mother and child relates the story from the Mother's perspective, positioning the child as the recipient of Macu's gaze and, hence, her story, and thus determines Macu as a speaking subject/author. The privileging of the Mother image/role in this scene suggests that it is Macu's own story, her memory, that she recounts to her child and to herself.[40] The story/memory enables her to revisit her past as a child herself, to relive her own relationship with her mother, thereby awakening her consciousness and empowering her to accuse Ismael of the crime.[41]

The physical act of sexual intercourse with Ismael undercuts the notion of Motherhood as asexual and transgresses the limitations and confinements of the classically constructed space of Motherhood. Furthermore, the so-called flashback contents of the frame are revealed to be both recollection and fantasy. Her own desire is in conflict with the roles of Mother/Wife that have just been constructed for her by the film. This is also the moment when we enter into Macu's subjectivity. She changes from an object to a subject. Likewise, the use of fantasy or memory can provide an "alternate mode of spectator involvement, offering multiple positions and interchangeable roles to the singularity suggested by the primacy of the male Oedipal scenario."[42]

Although Macu is placed in a speaking position, and would seem to relate the story from a fully constituted subjectivity, this moment is as of yet a "threshold" moment. This is the moment of the "birth" (suggested by the forward rocking motion from mother to child, linked by her stretched leg) of the idea, the possibility, the potential, of Macu's subjectivity. And, as we shall see, the image of the threshold as a window/doorway will be prominent among the "disruptive" elements from the *chora*. This sequence also provides the source for some of the other elements (such as music, sound effects, rhythms, etc.) that are representative of the *chora*, and that intrude upon the narrative to function as a kind of "commentary" (here, like a "chorus"—see note 26) on the progression of the forming subject, prompting it toward change.[43]

This "threshold" moment, from present into past, is the moment of separation from the mother and the loss of the real, but the subject does not yet make its full entrance to language and the gaze of the Other. What is effecting this separation, then, is the *act of telling* the story, which functions as the third term. The figure of the child, in this scene, can be seen as emblematic of the story as a product. The child is placed as Silverman's third term—the child the mother desires to both produce and give her mother, and the story (the journey into the past) and its telling are what enable Macu to speak about herself, to see herself for the first time.[44] The child as recipient of the story (established by the over-the-shoulder camera position that places the child as the object of Macu's speech), speaks more to Macu's own relation with her mother than of Macu as mother in relation to her child. It is the "telling" of the *choric* fantasy that subjects the central image to displacements.[45] Here, Macu begins to leave the space of the Mother to speak as a daughter of a mother and a mother of a daughter. Maybe, here she is the *first* in a new lineage. "The question of enunciation *in the feminine* recasts the very terms and relations of sexuality, vision, authorship, and text."[46]

Example 2: In the Abandoned House

Macu in her school uniform is crossing the street. As she crosses, drumbeats begin. Upon reaching the other side she looks back and sees Willy following her. More percussion instruments are added to the rhythm. The shot is from Willy's point of view (POV). A bus arrives obscuring his vision while Macu escapes through a broken fence eluding his "watchful eye." From the other side, Macu peeks through the fencing at Willy now seen through Macu's POV framed between the bits of wire. The camera moves back slightly as Macu retreats, suggesting a merging of camera view and character view, emphasizing her subjectivity, as, quite literally, we have entered a location only accessible to Macu at this moment.

An abandoned *quinta* (large house or estate) is seen as Macu approaches alongside from a distance. Macu climbs up a ladder into an upstairs window of the house. The cut is to the inside of the house, to a white, overexposed window, where she *should* be entering but isn't. This is another elliptical cut for now we are inside the house looking only at the window that Macu has already passed through. Sound effects begin, metallic tinkling and "exotic" sounds are heard as the camera starts to pull away, sweeping the interior, past an old wardrobe, down to the floor that displays a well-trod path through the debris. The atmosphere is light and airy. *This* is the house that "identifies" Macu. The camera flies through this labyrinth-like space (similar formally to the way in which the *barrio* is represented) of elusive depths, light and shadow, angular constructions depicted by concentric camera movements. As the camera, presumably looking for Macu, passes through a doorway, turning its view upon a corridor of doorways set in doorways, a pigeon's coo is heard distinctly. The camera hesitates between two doorways, but as soon as a woman's laughter is heard, the camera swings to the right to follow down another pathway of doorways framing doorways, this path bathed in a warm, orange light.

The theme music begins as the camera acknowledges it has discovered where she is. As we swoop down the hallway, passing through successive doorways (or "frames"), pigeons fly; the sound of wings flapping and bird noises are heard in conjunction with the music. Finding a crevice made by a door leaning over the doorway, we peek in at Simón and Macu making love, literally from a position of "looking through the keyhole." The saxophone enters the melodic line and suddenly we are in the midst of their passion, a closeup of Macu reaching up to kiss Simón. They exchange positions and pleasures, his to hers, no gaze privileging the other. She is on top, in ecstasy. [Figure 6.9]

A transitional sequence leads to Macu leaving her house at night. The theme music continues to play over this image but fades out as the sound of loud footsteps takes the place of the music and Ismael's silhouette and long, distorted shadow approach. She runs back through the streets, a fast drum rhythm accompanying her, back up the stairs to the house, entering before Ismael will see that she has tried to leave him. This short scene is the first in a series of scenes connected by elliptical cuts before returning to the "present" time frame.

This is a powerful sequence in its attempt to grapple with the terms of desire. Although the spectatorial configurations are different from the

FIGURE 6.9. Macu's pleasure. Courtesy of Solveig Hoogesteijn.

first example, the scene within the house is what I view to be the second primal scene within the film (the first primal scene occurring just after the dance scene in Example 1, where the daughter, Teresita, peeks out at her parents kissing).[47] Here the camera would seem to place the spectator in a direct, unmediated position vis-à-vis the naked couple, giving the impression of "pure" looking. Yet this is not so, as the scene is a flashback and as such contained within the larger frame of the film. So, although it is not explicit, this scene is seen through Macu's memory—or her fantasy—and the look is shared between Macu, the camera/filmmaker, and most pointedly, the spectator. I believe there are *three* subjects being produced here: (1) the spectator (identified as female), (2) Macu, as spectator to her own (fantasmatic) scene, and (3) the author (identified as female)—in other words, three subjects-in-process. Teresa de Lauretis writes, "Positions of identification, visual pleasure itself, then, are reached only *aprés coup*, as after-effects of an engagement of subjectivity in the relations of meaning; relations which involve and mutually bind image and narrative."[48] As this moment is narrated from a place of vision *aprés coup*, herein lies the crux where the terms of desire are changed. This image, produced by Macu (and, ultimately, by a woman filmmaker), plays out "the double or split identification which, film theory has argued, cinema offers the female spectator: identification with the look of the camera, apprehended as temporal, active or in movement, and identification with the image on the screen, perceived as spatially static, fixed, in frame."[49]

The contradiction set down in opposition to this "classically" configured posture is the emphasis placed on these operations of identification (and desire), exemplified by the pair of framed shots—(a) Macu looking through the fence at Willy, and (b) the camera looking through the doorway at Macu and Simón making love—and by the unabashed looking of the free-floating "eye," showing us our looking. This disembodied "eye" that traverses the interior, looking for its subject, finds its body in Macu, as the look breaks through from the place of the spectator into the midst of the spectacle.

There is an interesting association regarding instances of the maternal voice within the text in relation to what I have described as the labyrinthlike space of the house. Silverman, in her analysis of *Riddles of the Sphinx*, characterizes the Sphinx/mother's voice as an "imaginary narrator," or "overtly fantasmatic voice," which travels through a text and/or subject conceived "in terms of a maze or labyrinth."[50] The "Abandoned

House" scene could be suggested as literally depicting this same image as the camera/eye floats through this labyrinthine space looking for its body. If we make the equation of the disembodied "eye" with Silverman's disembodied voice, then the "all-seeing eye" that is usually attributed to masculine vision and authority, is revolutionized as a feminine "look-over"[51] (which does not pretend to a higher authority but finds its subject in a specific body). Where Silverman characterizes this disembodied voice as fantasmatic, the same could be said of this particular eye/look, confirming the connection of this female eye to the archaic maternal voice.[52]

The interior of the abandoned house is very suggestive of a *choric* space (where the *chora* is defined as an inhabitable space, and the place and condition of subjectivity). The juxtaposition of the *choric* space to the space of Macu and Simón's intercourse seen "through the keyhole" via Macu's memory (a now "symbolic" space by virtue of enacting the primal scene) reinforces the concern with entrance to the symbolic. It is the *traveling* look that functions to move the *chora* out of the pre-Oedipal scene and install it within the symbolic. Although, when Ismael's shadow looms across the street as Macu attempts to leave him, she is frightened and returns. So, for the time being, the symbolic entered in this example still respects the Law. Yet, what ultimately characterizes this scene is less an identification with the character of Macu, as with the *place* of the character, in this case as a subject-in-process. Perhaps the filmmaker/author, positioned in a similar relation, desires the same for her spectator: the desire to desire.

Example 3: In the Mothers' House

Macu, now certain of Ismael's guilt, has left Ismael and the children to go home to her grandmother, mother, and sister. Here, in the mothers' house, she revisits (remembers) her childhood; this is the place of a psychic journey into memory that ultimately leads to a new consciousness about her experience and to the ability to articulate these experiences. This series of scenes also attests to her entry into the symbolic and language. Within this sequence of past events, intercut with the "present" time of Macu's stay, I will detail two moments: the transitional scene from the "present" into the deep past of childhood, and the third primal scene, where Macu reexperiences this traumatic moment.

This sequence of past and "present" events is related in the same way to the main frame as the other textual examples I have detailed. However, these past events are not as explicitly tied to the main frame memory as the other scenes. Here, the past seems to be a product only of Macu's memory from the "present" of her mother's house. Nonetheless, it must be noted that these events, too, are contained within the main frame. The difference now is the change in our relationship to the present. The "present" of the main frame has by this point in the narrative moved to a "present" time located in the future from the moment of the initial entry into the past. This present could be described more aptly as a "present-continuous" tense highlighting a kind of narrative-in-process running parallel with the subject-in-process. Although this past flashback would seem only to be contained within the scene in the mothers' house, it, too, is located within the larger flashback of the film, that within the main frame. This sequence of past events then is a memory within a memory, what I term "deep-past," and what Silverman might describe as a moment "deep within the imaginary," indicative of the *chora* itself.

Macu's color image is seen reflected in the glass of a large (blown-up), black-and-white marriage photograph of herself as a child bride and Ismael in full police regalia. [Figure 6.10] Her reflection and her photographed image are set on either side of Ismael. His hand is positioned in such a way that it seems to be resting on the shoulder of her reflected, color image, serving to link the past and present images into one. The heavy gilt frame of the photograph frames the shot on each vertical border. Macu's theme music accompanies the scene in sporadic phrases, underscoring the visual action. As the melody is played in haunting flute tones, we see Macu seated viewing the photograph. We share her contemplation of what is revealed to the spectator as a shocking image. This photograph is the proof of another crime—Macu's marriage as a child to Ismael. This photographed image also serves to trigger Macu's memory back into the past, signifying an Oedipal trauma that will shortly be revealed in full.

The sound of a door opening beckons Macu out of the chair. The atmosphere is eerie and somewhat ominous. A siren is heard in the background.[53] Macu makes her way toward the tinkling sound of liquid. She follows the sound down a darkened hallway to an illuminated doorway. Shafts of light cross and illuminate her face as she looks into the bathroom at herself as a child sitting on the toilet. [Figure 6.11] This shot is seen as the POV of adult-Macu. Child-Macu looks up at her adult-self standing in the doorway. This pair of shots is repeated, but the second time, instead of Macu in the doorway, Ismael is now standing in for adult-

FIGURE 6.10. Adult-Macu's image reflected in her marriage photograph. Courtesy of Solveig Hoogesteijn.

FIGURE 6.11. Adult-Macu looks at child-Macu on the toilet. Courtesy of Solveig Hoogesteijn.

238

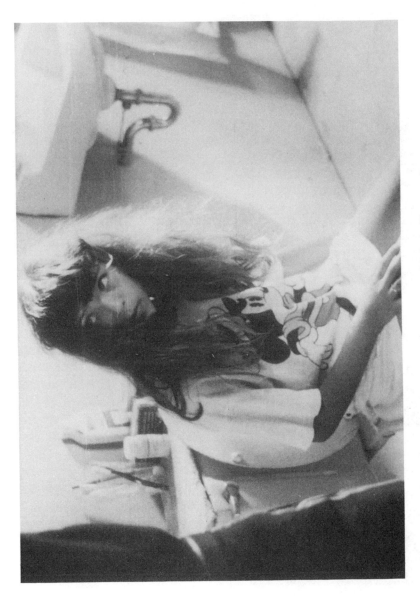

FIGURE 6.12. Child-Macu looks up at Ismael. Courtesy of Solveig Hoogesteijn.

Macu, her substitute. Child-Macu is still looking up at him. [Figure 6.12] She is seen from a lower camera angle, the shot including a bit of Ismael's waist indicating a POV *other* than Ismael's, as if another person (adult-Macu) were behind him looking onto the scene. Ismael hands child-Macu some toilet paper, which she refuses.

The transition from "present" to past occurs in a similar manner to the "threshold" sequence in the first textual example, where a shuffle-cut merges the two temporal spaces together. This kind of elliptical cut, in contrast to the straight elliptical cuts used throughout the film, functions to privilege the importance of these transitions as entry points. Whereas in the first example the transition was the triggering of the entire narration of events as a means of relating the events of the crime mentioned by the news reporters, now the shuffle-cut serves as entrance to the events of the other, hidden crime.

According to Lacanian psychoanalysis, this scene would appear to contain two important steps in the formation of the subject: (1) a kind of "mirror stage" takes place between child-Macu and adult-Macu, and (2) the necessary "castration" or separation (of the narcissistic self) occurs when the third term (father) enters as the substitution (of mother) requisite for the transference of identification in the case of the "positive" Oedipal complex for the girl.[54] However, I propose that the unexpected occurs here, inverting the terms of "classic" Oedipus. Rather than Ismael stepping in to replace adult-Macu, it is Macu who "places" Ismael—justified by the subjective POV shots that construct this scene whereby the gaze is "passed down" from POV adult-Macu to POV child-Macu. Macu "speaks" Ismael; she positions him. At this moment Ismael is divested of his power (and once back in the "present" will remain so for the rest of the film) as adult-Macu is empowered with the ability to "speak" within the symbolic. It is exactly at this moment—this double take—that adult-Macu, standing on the threshold, is able to visualize and consciously understand her childhood past with its "perverted" Oedipal scenario.[55] Lastly, child-Macu's refusal of the toilet paper Ismael hands to her could be read as a demand on the part of the Father/Phallus for recognition of (sexual) difference, for her acceptance of the status as cultural "other." Her refusal to accept castration on *his* terms, in a disempowered or subjugated position, is demonstrated by the rejection of the toilet paper (here functioning as a Lacanian *petit objet a*). Thus, a refusal to acknowledge the power of the Phallus or to desire it is suggested.

Ismael is teaching child-Macu to write her name. She tires of practicing and flirts with him to get out of the task. He starts to tickle her, but suddenly the playing becomes something else. Her grandmother closes the curtain to allow them their privacy. [Figure 6.13] Ismael caresses Macu's face. There is an elliptical cut to child-Macu, lying in bed at night; sounds of love-making are heard in the background. Moving shadows are cast on the wall from light coming through slatted blinds while the softly moving light over Macu's eyes gives an almost dreamlike character to the scene. Macu gets up and moves down the hallway. The noises grow more intense. As Macu peeks into her mother's bedroom, three gun shots are heard in place of the mother's sexual climax. The substitution of these three gunshot sounds for the *seen of the crime* functions to superimpose Ismael's two crimes in Macu's conscious (highlighting the very repressed and taboo nature of this scene). Macu quickly pulls her head back, squealing tires are heard, but it is clear to us that she has seen something. She runs back to bed, pretending to be asleep as sirens scream in the background. Ismael stands bare-chested in the crossed light next to the shadowed wall, then he leaves. Macu gets in bed with her grandmother, but the grandmother turns her back, rejecting Macu. The cut is back to the same shadow pattern on the wall except now the color is different, yellowish dawn. This image becomes the POV of adult-Macu's gaze and we are back in the "present."

There is a cut to Macu in the car with Ismael after leaving the mothers' apartment. She accuses Ismael of ruining her life, and also her grandmother and mother for "selling" her (to him). Yet, her ultimate realization is that she has only Ismael, presumably for support, family, comfort, love, etc. Shortly after this scene, she tells the police that she believes him to be guilty of the murders.

Ismael is now shown as the mother's live-in lover and supporter of the "family," which places Macu in the position of daughter. This stunning sequence of events has revealed the most illicit of all transgressions, that which establishes the boundaries of "culture" and society—incest. Moreover, this event from child-Macu's perspective is also seen as a betrayal, for at this point in the narrative she is already betrothed to him.

Structurally, this is the climactic moment of the narrative and is the transformative scene for the protagonist. It is a (future) memory of a memory of a childhood event, (re)witnessed/(re)experienced through the eyes of a young girl. For me, the key to a reading of this scene *à la* Silverman is that the transformative act of remembering takes place in the mothers' house, where Macu has gone to seek refuge from her relationship with Ismael. There "the *choric* fantasy is elaborated in . . . regressive

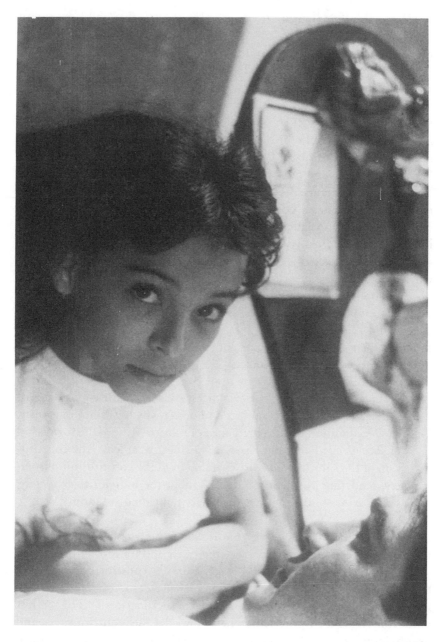

FIGURE 6.13. Child-Macu with Ismael as grandmother allows them privacy.
Courtesy of Solveig Hoogesteijn.

terms, as a threefold 'return': to the grandmother/mother/child *enceinte* of which Kristeva speaks, which is itself what might be called a 'double replay,' to the drives, and to an implied matriarchy."[56]

Again, within this scene Macu is the only subject of enunciation, and triply so. Here, the *choric* fantasy is told from an unestablished future-present moment, as part of the larger flashback: (1) POV adult-Macu from the main frame, (2) POV adult-Macu from the mothers' house, *and* (3) through the eyes of child-Macu within the scene. Adult-Macu as narrator has been so displaced within the narrative (an almost forgotten "voice-over"), that she now fits the bill as Silverman's "imaginary narrator," the "overtly fantasmatic voice."[57] Moreover, I suggest that by distancing these events so considerably from the larger flashback memory (their point of enunciation), *Macu*, in this way, exemplifies Silverman's linking of the maternal voice (Macu as narrator) to an archaic moment in the history of subjectivity that will later be retrieved (rediscovered maternal voice) during the return to the main frame.

The mothers' house also functions as "the point of crucial intersection between politics and subjectivity, economics and the family, personal history and collective future."[58] The maternal voice, having now arrived to the mothers' house in the course of relating the narrative, "lead(s) back into memory" and "out into society."[59]

> Not just murder, then, but also incest constitutes the coordinates of the separation between subject and object which is, simultaneously, the precondition of the emergence of subjectivity *and* the formation of society. . . . For, from Kristeva's perspective at least, the constitution of the subject is now inseparable from the constitution of society, rendering obsolete the debate about the individual *or* society, subjectivity *or* objectivity, structure *or* individual autonomy, etc.[60]

Overall, the film has been concerned with images and moments of transition, suggesting a focus on the emergence and transformation of the subject. In the same way that this scene finally constructs the psychic transition into the symbolic and world of language, so, too, is the subject moved "out of the home and into a series of social spaces."[61] For the rest of the film Macu is empowered by her knowledge, her consciousness, and her ability to "speak." Yet Macu is still impeded from taking full control of her destiny by the overwhelming social circumstances that remain beyond her individual capacity to change. This particular social vision

THE SEEN OF THE CRIME 243

and critique is established because of a *woman's* experience and *her* ability to articulate and analyze her experience.

Macu, like *Riddles,* is less concerned with the pre-Oedipal scene than with the "forgotten or censored details within the Oedipal narrative . . . which might permit that story to be told rather differently than it usually is."[62] In *Macu* it is the hidden, perverted Oedipal scene that *by its telling* changes the terms of the story—both Oedipus's and Ismael's. "If the crime of Oedipus is the destruction of differences, the combined work of myth and narrative is the production of Oedipus."[63] In *Macu,* difference is deconstructed in order to reconstruct it in different terms.

It is this primal scene that ruptures the *chora,* "the[se] memories which . . . dramatize the entry into the Oedipus complex,"[64] and here is the crucial point where the film veers away from Silverman's path of female negative Oedipus producing an experience of loss and betrayal by *both* parents that leaves Macu figuratively "orphaned." At this moment the film turns more toward a pathology of *both* sexes in their constructed roles than to the initiation of a desire for the mother. Here is where, perhaps, Hoogesteijn could be said to follow in Kristeva's footsteps, ultimately "negating" her desire by suppressing her desire for the mother. Yet I believe Hoogesteijn's film does create a place for a woman to speak; it does create a space for the mother in the ways I have attempted to show throughout this chapter. Silverman says the identification with the mother is only subversive if the negative Oedipus complex is activated, meaning desire for the mother. However, I am not yet willing to relinquish Macu to the path of "conventional female subjectivity," for the following reasons: (1) desire for *both* parents is "disinvested," (2) Macu's entry into language is at the expense of male potency (e.g., substitution/toilet scene), (3) the "overtly fantasmatic" character of the "voice-over," (4) the main frame that contains the narrative within Macu's voice, (5) the opening out of the *choric* fantasy whereby the character is transformed and, lastly, (6) the delegation of the voice to the child, who now "speaks" into the future-present moment, closing the frame, engaging the dialogue, acknowledging the Other who is mother.

The path of female negative Oedipus is followed and sustained because of the scene where we return to the main frame. Macu is on the street with Willy who wants her to run away with him. She calls him a "pig" and we are catapulted "back" (actually forward) into the main frame where the sequence of shots is replayed, only now, the cradle, instead of seen beyond Macu in the background as in the beginning when we entered the flashback, is positioned in the foreground of the image. The cradle (suggesting the newly emerged subject) is placed in the subject position of an over-the-shoulder shot as if to establish its POV. The child "speaks" the narrative, and we, with the child, rediscover the "lost maternal voice." There is an element of surprise when we return to this image, for we have quite forgotten the flashback status of the narration of events. This moment embodies the fourth of Silverman's prerequisites for the founding of subjectivity—"subordination to the gaze of the cultural Other"—given this exchange of perspectives. The frame is closed, the female subject engaged via the female negative Oedipus complex.

> The negative Oedipus complex thus constitutes not only a psychic "Philosopher's stone," able to effect the transformation of normative female subjectivity, but the model for a different kind of cinema as well—the path leading away from fixed and hierarchical schematizations to a transversality of spectacle and gaze, diegesis and enunciation, character and viewer, voice "in," "off," and "over."[65]

Above all, Macu's regressive fantasy into the *chora does* lead out and *is* confrontational because of the transformation that it inspires in the character.[66] The film speaks precisely to women being denied "cultural recognition," in Macu's case as a wife (cf. title of film) and mother. It is Macu's story in its entirety that "poses a serious challenge to the system that seeks to exclude and censor her—that what the symbolic order defines negatively is capable of returning as negativity."[67] Ultimately, it is conscious memory that has enabled the self-transforming discovery that Macu makes. As Silverman writes, it is "conscious 'recollection' or reconstruction" that can halt "the process of psychically devaluing the mother . . . at an unconscious level" (which eventually leads to the "normal" melancholic state of the woman).[68] That Macu is left "orphaned," creates the possibility for starting a new discourse. Macu's last look opens this discourse/dialogue from a feminine point of view.

THE AUTHOR RETURNS TO THE SCENE

The "newly" constituted female subject (now capable of assuming an authorial position) speaks and "performs" with her *different* voice as she "challenges dominance from within."[69] With the possibility of speaking in her own voice often denied, it is important to foreground female authorship (and authorial subjectivity) precisely because it has been historically relegated to an inferior position. Silverman's project, in other words, is "to grasp the author precisely as subject"—not just in her relation to subject processes inscribed within the text, nor as a "textual figuration," but as a desiring subject. Sandy Flitterman-Lewis writes that "to ignore sexuality in consideration of authorship is to, in essence, support the masculine status quo."[70] She further raises the questions, "How can we define a 'desiring look' when the position of looking is feminine? What are the parameters and articulations of a 'female discourse' as it traverses a particular text? And how can we conceptualize a 'woman's desire' from the triple standpoint of the author, text, and viewer?"[71]

Silverman sets out two ways in which authorial subjectivity can be inscribed: (1) via Emile Benveniste's linguistic model[72] supplemented with psychoanalysis (which appears close to Kristeva's "semanalysis"), and (2) through the "libidinal coherence" that a filmmaker's oeuvre may contain, "the desire that circulates there."[73] She proposes that the filmic author's subjectivity can be activated through the cinematic equivalents of linguistic markers (i.e., pronouns) such as sounds, images, motifs, narrative patterns, or formal configurations that are exibited within the work or works and that function as "utterances." In respect to the first means, the "semanalytical" model (1), "authorial citations"—what Silverman describes as the mirror that the author searches for—can be made three ways: (a) via direct appearance, (b) via "secondary" identification—fictional characters "stand in" for the author providing "authoritative vision, hearing and speech"—and (c) within the "body" of the text. In regard to category (c) Silverman provides a number of suggestions that are remarkably close to the way that Kristeva's *choric* elements may manifest within texts: choreography of movement; composition of objects within the frame; construction, disruption, multiplication of narrative; experimentation with sound; creation of "atmosphere"; articulation of light and shadow; identification; acting; use of color.

The second means of constituting authorial subjectivity elaborated by Silverman ("libidinal coherence") entwines both identification and desire, but she writes that this way is virtually inseparable from the three kinds of citations that determine the first model. "An author's identification with a fictional character will be determined by the subject-position the latter occupies not only within the narrative, but within the fantasmatic 'scene' which that narrative traces in some oblique and indirect way." This fantasmatic desire will manifest "around some such structuring 'scene' or group of 'scenes'" that derive from the Oedipus complex. In

Macu this is evidenced in the primal scene that is played out three times in the film. Silverman also suggests various "nodal points" that will give entry into this "libidinal economy," such as a sound, image, scene, place, or action to which the work repeatedly returns. "Identity is, after all, impossible not only outside the symbolic, but outside the imaginary."

Hoogesteijn situates herself within *Macu* through this structure, identification processes, and style. "Example 1: In the Beginning" sets up a crucial link between filmmaker, text, and spectator. The rocking cradle, the very means by which we enter the flashback, is an image repeated in Hoogesteijn's oeuvre, first depicted in her documentary *Puerto Colombia* (1975). This image, along with devices such as the frame and ellipses to break the linear narrative structure, which were also employed in her previous films, can be seen as "signature strokes" inscribed into the text.[74] Likewise, Hoogesteijn inscribes her authorial subjectivity through what Silverman calls "secondary identification" with her created character, Macu—by placing Macu as narrator. It is after all her story. The events of the film are related through her subjective flashback. An identification with the "body" of the text puts to use the entire list of filmic elements, their multiple effects working both within the logic of the narrative and within the complex structure of the film.

"Example 2: In the Abandoned House" firmly installs these recurring images and sounds (images and sounds that I have attributed to the *choric* fantasy: rhythms, sound effects, color, tone, doorways, passageways, and windows) that maintain and mark throughout the narrative the desire that Silverman writes about. For example, the twice-produced image of doorways set in doorways is another image repeated in Hoogesteijn's oeuvre, used for the opening and closing shots of *The Sea of Lost Time* (1977). The scene itself is one of the three primal scenes in *Macu,* yet the one in which the spectator and the author, by the camera's "stroke," are positioned at the place of loss and desire. The camera really has a life of its own in this scene, which can be attributed to Hoogesteijn's direct identification with her created character (*à la* Silverman) and, hence, functions to create this moment as that of the author's inscription onto and into the text. In this way, Macu and Hoogesteijn are both authors "outside" their texts who come into "being" through the production of their texts. The lack of any specific identification with (or mediation by) a character through which we view this scene privileges, in this case, a more direct linkage between the filmmaker and the spectator. We and the author "look through the keyhole" together, reexperiencing the first castration, the severing of the "pre-Oedipal umbilical cord."[75] Desire is triply inscribed (in the spectator, character, and author) as the desire for subjectivity on the part of all three viewers where the vision of Macu signifies the *process* of subjectivity (a subjectivity with all the complexity, heterogeneity, and multiplicity that this term will allow).

In "Example 3: In the Mothers' House," when Macu literally "takes the enunciating position with respect to herself through an identification with a man" during the "substitution" sequence,[76] the author identified with Macu brings the "outside" author into the text. Just as the present and the past collide within *Macu,* so does the "outside" author with her "inside" representative. Rather than being a mere reflection of the author "outside" the text, Silverman demonstrates that this type of moment constitutes her as a subject, "in the same way that the mirror reflection (retroactively) installs identity in the . . . child." Moreover, the "substitution" sequence functions as a kind of male castration. Silverman writes, "Male castration becomes the agency not merely whereby the masculine subject is forced to confront his own lack, and is remade in the image of woman, but whereby the female author constructs herself as a speaking subject, and emerges as a figure 'inside' the text."[77] This sequence then is the constitutive moment of the female authorial subject in *Macu.*

Silverman brings up the very intriguing notion that the female critic or theorist "reauthors" a (classic) work "from the site of its (feminist) reception." Following Silverman, we could make the following observation (I have reinserted general terms to form a paradigm):

> [The feminist theorist/critic/reader] enacts a discursive resistance to dominant cinema precisely through the resistance which she constitutes [the textual character] as having. [The character] thus functions not just as an enunciator within the diegesis, but as the subject of the speech whereby [the feminist theorist/critic/reader] rewrites [the text], and hence as a stand-in for the feminst theorist.[78]

I will leave the reader of *this* work to draw her own conclusions.

ELLIPSIS: NOW

In the film's final sequence, Macu walks with her children alongside the long line of women and children outside the prison as the film's credits begin to roll. She takes her place at the end of the line, sitting down against the building. The cut is to the last shot of the film—Macu, in closeup, looking directly at the audience through the final credits. The credits finish, revealing her challenging look directly into the camera (at us), at which point she juts her head up just a bit, even more defiantly, as the music concludes. End.

This last shot, Macu's "look back," lies in a very particular relation to the rest of the film. First of all, this is the only moment of the film whereby the "fourth wall," the invisible barrier separating the spectator from the spectacle, is bridged. Macu's challenging stare—now aligned with the filmmaker's—directly addresses to the audience of the film the question of her future, what will become of her. With this final, "direct-address" gaze, Macu breaks out of the confinement of virtual discourse, which functions both to constitute the film and to constitute Macu as a subject; for subjects are constituted in the act of discourse. A potential dialogue is opened by means of her direct gaze, a challenge from a woman to society, a society that sells (out) its children (and by implication, its future). This kind of lawlessness, menace to conventional boundaries, threatens the very nature/culture divide upon which societies define themselves. Hence, the challenge that comes from a woman against the system and against the society that has created her untenable situation evolves as a result of an experience, a story where sexual relationships are at stake.

Secondly, this scene makes explicit an analogy between the narrative and the social predicament of the country, where the final shot changes the narrative from a seemingly fictive, individual story to an almost testimonial experience with wider social implications. The narrative closes leaving the newly conscious subject still contained by the same social conditions— a subject without a future. The final credits roll up to leave Macu outside of the text, outside of the story and in the real. Insofar as she is condemned to wait day after day in the line of prison visitors until, one presumes, Ismael is released (a mutual imprisonment), this moment after the credits similarly positions her in an eternal "present tense," waiting for change with the question posed, What about now? What about my time and place in the apparatus, in the nexus of image, sound and narrative temporality?[79] Macu is, in fact, a subject in a new place, neither here nor there, but in between. Rather than offering a solution, the film asks us to step outside the fiction of the story space and into this discursive space of the "real" with Macu, engaging her look, her dialogue, by answering back from a new space "of a different temporality, another time of desire."[80]

NOTES

This chapter is a shortened version of my thesis presented for the M.A. in Film at San Francisco State University. I am grateful to Julianne Burton-Carvajal for her careful readings during the various stages of this text, and to Harel Calderón, Thyrza Goodeve, and Bill Nichols for comments on the original. I am also indebted to Julianne for the titles. Special thanks to Karen Davis for her edit of an earlier draft and to Daniel Gercke, who co-edited this version. A note of thanks to Robert Stam for looking over the final draft. I would also like to acknowledge Ira Jaffe and Diana Robin for their editorial suggestions, particularly Diana Robin, whose astute comments helped to polish the final version.

1. Teresa de Lauretis effectively argues this concept. See *Alice Doesn't: Feminism, Semiotics, Cinema* (Bloomington: Indiana University Press, 1980), 53, 113, 119.

2. "Amusing or serious, pornographic or violent, historical or police stories, the most dissimilar and heterogeneous films always have a touch of protest against inequality and abuse, as well as an uncovering of the evils of society" (translation mine). Pedro J. Martinez, "Principales tendencias del largometraje narrativo venezolano en los ultimos años," *Encuentros* 4 (Año 2): 13–14.

3. For more information on this subject see Julianne Burton, ed., *Cinema and Social Change in Latin America* (Austin: University of Texas Press, 1986); Michael Chanan, ed., *Twenty-Five Years of the New Latin American Cinema* (London: British Film Institute and Channel Four, 1983); Ana M. López, "An 'Other' History: The New Latin American Cinema," in *Resisting Images: Essays on Cinema and History,* ed. Robert Sklar and Charles Musser (Philadelphia: Temple University Press, 1990). See also Ana M. López, "Setting Up the Stage: A Decade of Latin American Film Scholarship," *Quarterly Review of Film and Video* 13:1–3 (1991) for further listings.

4. Solveig Hoogesteijn, interview by author, April 17, 1991, Caracas, Venezuela.

5. Martinez, "Principales tendencias," 9.

6. There was even a documentary film by Luis Correa, *Ledezma, el caso mamera* (1982), which the government censored at the time. John King documents that Correa obtained Ledezma's confession on camera, without remorse, and interviews with police officials who describe an inside cover-up of Ledzma's prosecution, as he knew too much about police corruption. Not only was the film banned, notes King, but Correa was imprisoned for forty-five days. John King, *Magical Reels: A History of Cinema in Latin America* (London and New York: Verso, 1990), 223.

7. Laura Mulvey's famous article, "Visual Pleasure and Narrative Cinema," *Screen* 16:3 (Autumn 1975), first brought attention to the gendered gaze.

8. Emile Benveniste's model from *Problems in General Linguistics* (translated by Mary Elizabeth Meek [Coral Gables: University of Miami Press, 1971]) proposes that "language is . . . the possibility of subjectivity because it always contains the linguistic forms appropriate to the expression of subjectivity, and discourse provokes the emergence of subjectivity because it consists of discrete instances. In some way language puts forth 'empty' forms which each speaker, in the exercise of discourse, appropriates to himself and which he relates to his 'person,' at the same time defining himself as *I* and a partner as *you*. The instance of discourse is thus constitutive of all the coordinates that define the subject" (227). Quoted in Kaja Silverman, *The Subject of Semiotics* (New York: Oxford University Press, 1983), 45.

9. The media is shown to be in the process of constructing a "story" as the television news crew tries to interview Macu entering the house. The film places importance on the relation of the media to the events of the film that are about to unfold, contrasting film and television as story- (or history-) telling apparatus. Mediated news images lend a sense of authenticity to the fictional narrative. The news is the means by which the "real" facts of the crime are revealed to the public within the fiction film. Likewise, this fictional news forces us to question the kinds of "truth" revealed via the news—that those isolated media interviews do not reveal the "whole story"; and that the "real story" is more complex, as the fiction film reveals to us. This in turn suggests a questioning of the construction of identity and its value: the public image versus the private one, and which is more truthful, real, and/or newsworthy.

10. Ironically, we learn that Macu's full name is *María Inmaculada* [Immaculate Mary], further underlining the ambiguity surrounding her complicity or noncomplicity in the events of the film. "Ismael," in turn, suggests an outcast according to both Webster's and the Oxford English dictionaries. Ishmael in the Bible was Abraham's son with Hagar, a sort of "illegitimate" child. "HE shall be a wild ass of a man, his hand against every man and every man's hand against him" (Gen. 16:12, *The Holy Bible*, Revised Standard Edition).

11. David Eugene Blank records the following astonishing information in *Venezuela: Politics in a Petroleum Republic*, Politics in Latin America: A Hoover Institution Series, gen. ed. Robert Wesson (New York: Praeger, 1984), 41: "Article 473 of the penal code, was only declared unconstitutional in 1980. This article permitted husbands, brothers, and fathers to kill (with impunity) female members of their families caught in the act of adultery."

12. Margaret Morse, "Mixed Formats and Low Resolution: The Textures of Electronic Culture" (unpublished article, 1991), 4. Quoted with permission of the author.

13. Mary Ann Doane, "Information, Crisis, Catastrophe," in *Logics of Television: Essays in Cultural Criticism,* ed. Patricia Mellencamp (Bloomington: Indiana University Press, 1990), 226.

14. Doane, "Information," 227.

15. Julia Kristeva, "About Chinese Women," in *The Kristeva Reader,* ed. Toril Moi (New York: Columbia University Press, 1986), 152–53.

16. Elizabeth Grosz, *Jacques Lacan: A Feminist Introduction* (New York: Routledge, 1990), 154.

17. Grosz, *Jacques Lacan,* 154.

18. Kristeva, "The System and the Speaking Subject," in *The Kristeva Reader,* 32–33.

19. Grosz, *Jacques Lacan,* 150.

20. Kristeva, "Revolution in Poetic Language," in *The Kristeva Reader,* 90–93.

21. Kristeva, "About Chinese Women," in *The Kristeva Reader,* 152.

22. Kristeva, "Signifying Practice and Mode of Production." *Edinburgh Review* 1 (1976): 68 (quoted in Grosz, *Jacques Lacan,* 152).

23. Kaja Silverman provides an excellent discussion of the multiple confusions surrounding Kristeva's various usages of her concepts that evolve and fluctuate through the progression of her oeuvre—writings that span from the late 1960s to the early 1980s. In addition, this subsection, "The *Choric* Fantasy," and the following, "The Female Negative Oedipus Complex," are based upon Silverman's theoretical proposal as elaborated in *The Acoustic Mirror: The Female Voice in Psychoanalysis and Cinema* (Bloomington and Indianapolis: Indiana University Press, 1988), 101–33 passim.

24. Silverman, *The Acoustic Mirror,* 102–104.

25. Silverman, *The Acoustic Mirror,* 104–105.

26. They function rather like a Greek chorus, commenting on and encouraging the progress of the narrative. By "working the signifier" (*The Kristeva Reader,* 16)—*choral/*chorus—fits beautifully with Kristeva's notion of a "maternal *chora*"—granted that her concept of *chora* (from the Greek, space, receptacle) is the space around, or containing, the impulses/drives that I am suggesting manifest as a "chorus." There can also be drawn a tenuous line to Hoogesteijn's first impression of the "real" crime story as a "Greek drama—as heavy and as round

and perfect . . . there is the story, you just have to scratch a bit more to get deeper into it, everything is there" (Hoogesteijn, interview).

27. Moi, *The Kristeva Reader,* 12.

28. Freud quoted in Silverman, *The Acoustic Mirror,* 120.

29. Silverman, *The Acoustic Mirror,* 101–53.

30. Silverman, *The Acoustic Mirror,* 124.

31. Silverman, *The Acoustic Mirror,* 153–54.

32. Silverman, *The Acoustic Mirror,* 124–25.

33. Kristeva, *Powers of Horror: An Essay on Abjection,* trans. Leon S. Roudiez (New York: Columbia University Press, 1982), 4. Quoted in E. Ann Kaplan, ed., *Psychoanalysis and Cinema,* AFI Film Readers, ed. Edward Branigan and Charles Wolfe (New York: Routledge, 1990), 133.

34. Grosz, *Jacques Lacan,* 151–52, 160.

35. Silverman, *The Acoustic Mirror,* 126, 124.

36. Silverman, *The Acoustic Mirror,* 88, 244.

37. Silverman, *The Acoustic Mirror,* 128–129.

38. Silverman, *The Acoustic Mirror,* 109–10.

39. "What we call *signifiance,* then, is precisely this unlimited and unbounded generating process, this unceasing operation of the drives toward, in, and through language; toward, in, and through the exchange system and its protagonists—the subject and his institutions. This heterogeneous process, neither anarchic, fragmented foundation nor schizophrenic blockage, is a structuring and de-structuring *practice,* a passage to the outer *boundaries* of the subject and society. Then—and only then—can it be jouissance and revolution." Kristeva, *Revolution in Poetic Language,* translated by Margaret Waller with an introduction by Leon S. Roudiez (New York: Columbia University Press, 1984), 17.

40. "She [the mother] is traditionally the first language teacher, commentator, and storyteller—the one who first organizes the world linguistically for the child, and first presents it to the Other. The maternal voice also plays a crucial part during the mirror stage, defining and interpreting the reflected image, and 'fitting' it to the child. Finally, it provides the acoustic mirror in which the child first hears 'itself.' The maternal voice is thus complexly bound up in that drama which 'decisively projects the formation of the individual into history'" (Silverman, *The Acoustic Mirror,* 100).

41. This "child who sees" is often suggested throughout the film in Teresita's mimetic relationship to Macu and who is placed as "witness" to Macu's various "past" events/memories.

42. Sandy Flitterman-Lewis, *To Desire Differently: Feminism and the French Cinema* (Urbana: University of Illinois Press, 1990), 36–37.

43. "Through a body, destined to insure reproduction of the species, the woman-subject, although under the sway of the paternal function (as symbolizing, speaking subject and like all others), [is] more of a *filter* than anyone else—a thoroughfare, a threshold where 'nature' confronts 'culture.' To imagine that there is *someone* in that filter—such is the source of religious mystifications" (Kristeva, *Desire in Language,* 238).

44. Silverman writes, "The French Marxist philosopher Louis Althusser helps us to understand that discourse may also consist of an exchange between a person and a cultural agent, i.e., a person or a textual construct which relays ideological information. (. . . the description which he offers would apply as well to a television program, a photograph, a novel, or a film.) The agent addresses the person, and in the process defines not so much its own as the other's identity. In 'Ideology and Ideological State Apparatuses,' Althusser refers to the address as 'hailing,' and its successful outcome as 'interpellation.' Interpellation occurs when the person to whom the agent speaks recogizes him or herself in that speech, and takes up subjective residence there" (*The Subject of Semiotics,* 48–49).

45. Silverman, *The Acoustic Mirror,* 130.

46. Flitterman-Lewis, *To Desire Differently,* 20.

47. Three "primal scenes," in the classic sense of peeking through a "keyhole" at a couple engaged in lovemaking, are set within the film. Freud's scenario—where the (male) child's traumatic vision of seeing his father engaged in sexual relations with his mother produces a "profound sense of loss, thereby inaugurating desire" and entrance to the symbolic—is symbolically "reenacted"or "played out" each time (Silverman, *The Acoustic Mirror,* 137). "The staging of the primal scene for the spectator is crucial to the apparatus, for it is one of the dominant modes of channelling spectatorial identification" (Flitterman-Lewis, *To Desire Differently,* 36). The second and third occurrences are described in Examples 2 and 3 respectively.

48. De Lauretis, *Alice Doesn't,* 79–80.

49. De Lauretis, *Alice Doesn't,* 123.

50. Silverman, *The Acoustic Mirror,* 130, 140.

51. I employ "look-over" as an analogue to "voice-over." "Because her [the mother's] voice is identified by the child long before her body is, it remains unlocalized during a number of the most formative moments of subjectivity. The maternal voice would thus seem to be the original prototype for the disembodied voice-over in cinema . . . [that has] become the exclusive prerogative of the male voice within Hollywood film" (Silverman, *The Acoustic Mirror*, 76).

52. Silverman, *The Acoustic Mirror*, 130–40 passim.

53. There are always many sirens heard in the background of the mothers' house, lending an overall disturbing character to the setting. Likewise, police sirens in such a quantity suggest the repressing of violent activity, and such is the nature of the "story" contained within the mothers' house, repressed—and/or denied—by everyone.

54. See Grosz, *Jacques Lacan*, 156.

55. Silverman, *The Acoustic Mirror*, 147.

56. Silverman, *The Acoustic Mirror*, 129.

57. Albeit that this "voice" has been designated as such through enunciative positioning within the narrative and not a "voice" that is literally heard within the diegesis. Macu creates the events of the film as much as she remembers them.

58. Silverman, *The Acoustic Mirror*, 132.

59. Silverman, *The Acoustic Mirror*, 132.

60. John Lechte, *Julia Kristeva* (London: Routledge, 1990), 162.

61. Silverman, *The Acoustic Mirror*, 133.

62. Silverman, *The Acoustic Mirror*, 134.

63. De Lauretis, *Alice Doesn't*, 120.

64. Silverman, *The Acoustic Mirror*, 137.

65. Silverman, *The Acoustic Mirror*, 183.

66. Silverman, The Acoustic Mirror, 125.

67. Silverman, *The Acoustic Mirror*, 134.

68. Silverman, *The Acoustic Mirror*, 155–59, 180.

69. Silverman, *The Acoustic Mirror*, 124. In "The Female Authorial Voice" Silverman outlines three paths that her chapter will take, one being "to carve out

a theoretical space from which it might be possible to hear the female voice speaking once again from the filmic 'interior,' but now as the point at which an authorial subject is constructed rather than as the site at which male lack is disavowed" (188). This section, "The Author Returns to the Scene," draws from the above cited chapter, 187–234 passim.

70. Flitterman-Lewis, *To Desire Differently*, 19.

71. Flitterman-Lewis, *To Desire Differently*, 19.

72. She uses Benveniste's model to "rethink authorship." "I have in mind an author who would be subordinate to all the discursive constraints emphasized by Benveniste, who would in fact *be nothing* outside cinema—an author 'outside' the text who would come into existence as a dreaming, desiring, self-affirming subject only through the inscription of an author 'inside' the text" (*The Acoustic Mirror*, 202). Succinctly put, the Benveniste model suggests that subjects are constituted in the *act* of discourse.

73. Silverman, *The Acoustic Mirror*, 212–18.

74. Hoogesteijn plays with narrative frames and ellipses in both of her two previous feature-length fiction films, *The Sea of Lost Time* (1977) and *Manoa* (1981).

75. Silverman, *The Acoustic Mirror*, 137.

76. Silverman, *The Acoustic Mirror*, 211.

77. Silverman, *The Acoustic Mirror*, 225.

78. Silverman, *The Acoustic Mirror*, 212.

79. De Lauretis, *Alice Doesn't*, 99.

80. De Lauretis, *Alice Doesn't*, 98.

CHAPTER SEVEN

Beyond the Glow of the Red Lantern; Or, What Does It Mean to Talk about Women's Cinema in China?

HU YING

To the question, Is there a women's cinema in China today? Dai Jinhua, a prominent feminist film critic in China, gives a definitive No. After conceding that China has perhaps one of the largest lineups of women directors in the world, Dai goes on to lament the absence of real women's films:

> What most directly reveals the plight of contemporary Chinese women's culture and its fight for survival is the fact that, in the first forty years of Chinese cinematic history, those films that could be called "women's films" are very few, if not non-existent. In the works of most women directors, it is extremely difficult to detect the gender of the filmmaker, whether in the subject matter, story, characterization, narrative mode, or use of cinematic language and structure. Unlike the literary works of contemporary women writers, films by women directors seldom exhibit any distinguishing gender markers of the creating subject or any indication of a female style.

This situation, Dai Jinhua concludes, is the work of a pervasive "ideology of everyday life," namely, women directors are considered and consider themselves as successful if and only if they "make themselves up as men." Thus, even the younger "female directors consider their own works part of the corpus of the Chinese New Cinema and . . . successfully erase their own gender."[1]

That a woman's success is judged by her performance as "the same" as men is a point well taken, a common enough occurrence in the history of China or the West. Simone de Beauvoir, for a famous example, opted for the rhetoric of equality because "difference" had so often signified inferiority and thus unequal treatment. Yet, this alone does not explain the situation in China. Two more questions arise from Dai Jinhua's provocative conclusion, questions that underlie my present inquiry: What is it about film, as opposed to fiction writing for example, that appears to elicit this erasure of a gendered or feminist perspective? And since I believe such erasure is at best incomplete and often over-written with layers of palimpsest, how then do we, as feminist scholars, phrase the question so that a different vision becomes readable, so that feminist inquiry itself may be challenged by difference, the difference of culture, of race, of the so-called Third World?

This chapter examines two Chinese films by the Fifth Generation, the group of Chinese filmmakers who were the first to graduate from Beijing Film Academy after the Cultural Revolution: the well-known *Raise the Red Lantern* (1991), directed by Zhang Yimou,[2] and the not-so-well-known *Bloody Morning* (1991) directed by Li Shaohong.[3] Both films are adaptations from fiction, *Raise the Red Lantern* from Su Tong's novella *Qiqie chengqun* (*Wives and Concubines*, 1988), and *Bloody Morning* from Gabriel García Márquez's *Crónica de una muerte anunciada* (*Chronicle of a Death Foretold*, 1981). As such, they provide ideal cases to investigate the otherwise invisible process of filmic representation, the gaps between versions offering us rare glimpses of the choices made and rejected. While the routes of adaptation are clearly different and the settings of the films quite dissimilar (one set in a 1920s traditional family, the other in rapidly changing contemporary China), both films are dramatic narratives that deal with tragedies resulting from traditional marriages. Thus in thematic terms, representation of gender system and cultural tradition are prominent in both. More important, in terms of narrative cinema, both films engage in the inscription of desire, and as such, they direct, sustain, or undercut identification by the spectator. In addition, both films exhibit an acute consciousness of the international scene, and as such, they are contemplations on the issue of cultural production in an international framework, each of the films working out issues of gender and culture in its own way. First, some necessary background on the debate about "culture film" of the Fifth Generation and its sexual politics.

THE USES OF "CULTURE"

Despite or perhaps because of the enthusiastic international reception of films such as *Raise the Red Lantern*, the phenomenon of the so-called Fifth Generation film remains a cipher. As a Chinese cultural critic vividly puts it, "In these films, the long arm of the camera is like the enormous hand of a westerner, slowly stroking the Chinese mountains and rivers, men and women. The effect is a stimulating pleasure, at once familiar and yet exotic."[4] While the commercial press hails the Fifth Generation films as showing the hidden face of real Chinese culture, China scholars attempt to read the films using traditional Chinese interpretive frameworks such as Taoism or Confucianism.[5] To different extents, both the commercial and the scholarly receptions of Fifth Generation films resort to the all-encompassing yet over-determined notion of Culture for an interpretation of the films and the phenomenon of their success. Indeed, this talk of Culture is echoed back and forth across the Pacific. In the past decade, one of the most heatedly debated issues in Chinese film circles has been the relationship between the production of "cultural film" and "international recognition."[6] Thus, a simplified formula much repeated in the 1980s goes: "the more national, the more international." The situation is inherently complicated since the very medium is, without a doubt, foreign—the film camera always already "a western hand."[7] By the late 1980s, there arose yet another prominent issue, that of the international market, as many of the films were banned in China but released abroad. Both in terms of funding and marketing, the Fifth Generation increasingly turned their gaze abroad. Their culture writing, then, is produced from a space that is not within, nor is it entirely without, but in a betwixt and between space, a space that is in part created by the global circulation of cultural products as well as the global circulation of resources and consumption. No longer is it possible for the directors or critics to imagine any self that is "self-sufficient," to use Mao's term, but a self that is always imagined in relation to another, produced vis-à-vis another, the seeing of the self intricately tied up with seeing the other seeing the self. A "cultural identity" produced through the film medium necessarily develops in a vis-à-vis fashion.

In this international cultural market, what then is the China presented? How is culture represented to achieve "authenticity"? Who will recognize it as authentic? Recognition (to identify as known) based on what past knowledge, or familiar fantasy? Formally, these self-conscious "cultural films" are marked with two distinctive features: (1) ritualization of culture, as a "culture"; and (2) "masculine" encoding through drastic gender polarization.

Central to the Fifth Generation's portrayal of culture is the abundance of rituals, the performance of rites that not only suggest tradition but are the very embodiment of it. Wedding scenes, for example, are particularly favored: we recall the ubiquitous red bridal sedan, red veil, and the bride clad in red; we recall the songs and banquet in *Yellow Earth* (1984), the boisterous sedan carriers in *Red Sorghum* (1988).[8] This ritualization is accompanied by a systemic process of dehistoricization. It betrays a complex kind of longing tinged with ambivalence, an ambivalence that is self-consciously devoid of sentimentality. This cool nostalgia, so to speak, goes hand in hand with the ethnographic gesture: for in the name of observation, it allows indulgence in detailed presentation of a cultural surface. While at the same time, in the name of nonevaluation, it refrains from, but also leaves room for, either exaltation or condemnation. The result of this ambivalence is that at times it can be conveniently construed as a critique of an undesirable traditional culture, such times as when the censorship bureau would be persuaded to accept its release, such times as when the audience, having consumed the visual splendor, would have the added pleasure of self-censorship, of critiquing the past. Once dehistoricized, rituals then provide an "authentic" cultural specimen, the eternal, unchanging ethnic, available for consumption both for the Self to whom this "cultural tradition" is no longer available, and to the Other, for whom the familiar Oriental characteristics are comfortably presented to be recognized through past fantasies, this time by the Orientals themselves.

Closely associated with this conscious refraining from sentimentality, the films of the Fifth Generation have often been described, by themselves as well as by film critics, as "masculine." One critic thus interprets the phenomenon as a "rejection of political emasculation of men . . . an important form of recuperating a male identity after the Cultural Revolution."[9] More than a recuperation of maleness, however, the masculine encoding in the films operates on the logic of "difference," and in that, it is part of a larger phenomenon of cultural production in contemporary

China. It is part of a revolt against the master narrative of the recent past, which is, among other things, a discourse of identity which operates on the logic of the Same. This discourse is bent on an elimination of all difference, hierarchical or otherwise: thus, each person is the same, defined through the lowest common denominator, exemplified by the famous image of the "nail," an interchangeable element in the socialist machine. Under this logic, the most deep-seated cultural binary opposition, namely, the difference between man and woman, is also under erasure, most powerfully represented by the much-quoted Mao saying, "Times are different; men and women are the same." For decades, desire itself became a discursive impossibility. Not surprisingly in the late 1980s, Desire writ large marks the new mode in cultural production. In the wake of the problematic "gender equality" sponsored by the state, avant-garde art arrives on the scene to reinscribe gender difference with a vengeance.[10]

The avant-garde filmic reinscription of gender difference in the late 1980s is, alas, often rather old garde. Where it departs from convention (whether Hollywood or prerevolutionary China) is in the justification of this gender encoding, for it is typically represented as warranted by the cultural system. This system is then visually represented through rituals that appear to signal difference as specifically Chinese. Zhang Yimou's *Raise the Red Lantern* is a prime example of such ritualization and masculine encoding of culture. Indeed, if not for the seductiveness of the "cultural" glow of the lanterns, the film could easily be seen as a textbook case of the male gaze, standard Hollywood issue.

SEDUCTION BY THE GLOW

As many critics have long pointed out, *Raise the Red Lantern* conforms to the classic Hollywood cinematic apparatus in its representation of the gender system.[11] In the conventional division of characters into "mobile" and "immobile," the film presents the male character as enjoying freedom and control of the plot space and the female characters whose function it is to represent this space.[12] Objectified by the classic controlling and curious gaze of the male character, of the camera, and of the spectator, the female characters are positioned in "a hermetically sealed world which unwinds magically, indifferent to the presence of the audience, producing for them a sense of separation and playing on their voyeuristic fantasy."[13] The protagonist Songlian is a classic example of the "heroine of a melodrama," who initially resists "the 'correct' feminine position" and whose resistance eventually fails, a failure to which the film bears witness.[14]

What then is it that draws Songlian into the "correct" feminine position? What is it that marks this film as different from the standard Hollywood fare long critiqued by feminist film critics? Or perhaps not so much *different* as better *legitimized?*

The answer lies in the lure of the red lanterns, the lure of a "different culture," or perhaps a culturized difference. For the glow of the lanterns in *Raise the Red Lantern* is powerful: against a background of drab colors (slate-gray tiles, lead-gray hallways, blue-gray sky), the luminous glow of the lanterns burnishes the beautiful but expressionless face of Gong Li, the lead actor. It colors the film from beginning to end and envelops the audience. This ubiquitous presence of the lanterns is, however, absent in the original novella "Wives and Concubines." This addition so significantly marks the product that it has retroactively altered the marketing of the novella: in the sleek production of the book in Taiwan and Hong Kong, the film title is given in big block letters while the original title appears in parenthesis; in its English version published by Penguin, not only is the title altered but Gong Li's face now graces the dust jacket.[15]

Structurally, the lanterns are crucial to the film. Together with the ritual of foot massage, they represent an unwritten code of ceremonies. Their sanctity, repeated again and again in the film, lies in their long history as "ancient rules of the house," supreme in their power, yet impersonal in their authority. The rituals signal the day-to-day power struggle between the four wives in the household, a power struggle engineered not so much by the husband and head of the household, but apparently by this abstract and impersonal "tradition." For in the film, the husband, omnipotent in his power as though he were an emperor, is nonetheless nearly invisible: at most, we see a shadow, a hand, we hear a voice. Sometimes, we see the world through his eyes, his power inflecting our very perception. But we do not *see* him; instead, we *feel* him, his presence, and its attending power, acutely sensed especially since he is visually absent. The lanterns act as the visual designation of his whim, powerful in its very capriciousness, a caricature of the famous Oriental despot.

Every day at dusk, when the four wives are lined up by the gates of their respective courtyards, when the master of the house perches somewhere on the central ceremonial archway, invisible to the wives as well as to the audience of the film, his perspective is precisely like that of the panopticon in a modern penitentiary, a structure that, as Michel Foucault cogently demonstrates, "assures the automatic functioning of power." As if illustrating Foucault's point, the evening ritual of the lanterns operates exactly as he describes the panopticon:

> So to arrange things that the surveillance is permanent in its effect, even if it is discontinuous in its action; that the perfection of power should tend to render its actual exercise unnecessary; that this architectural apparatus should be a machine for creating and sustaining a power relation independent of the person who exercises it; in short, that the inmates should be caught up in a power situation of which they are themselves the bearers.[16]

Initially, Songlian the young fourth wife does get caught up in this "automatized and disindividualized" power machine. Upon first entering the household, Songlian finds the rituals of lanterns and massage bizarre and ludicrous, as do the members of the audience who, not unlike Songlian, are from the outside world where the ceremonies must appear distinctly exotic (distant and unintelligible). Alarmingly, the audience then witnesses the process of Songlian's transformation: from questioning to resignation, she becomes quickly accustomed to the rituals (within ten days, to be exact). Barely a season passes before she goes on to enforce their arbitrary logic with a vengeance. When her ambitious maid dares to appropriate the lanterns for herself, thus attempting to cross the delicate divide between concubines and maids, Songlian punishes her precisely by invoking "ancient rules of the house," which eventually lead to the maid's death. The rapidity of Songlian's transformation appears to illustrate the efficiency of this power machine. Thus the film presents the power/gender structure in this microcosmic world as impersonal, overwhelmingly powerful in its ability to absorb alien elements, and most important, immutable.

More than the mere presence of rituals, it is the insistent process of ritualization that accomplishes this task, a process whereby apparently trivial details are given tremendous importance through repeated and public performances. Thus we see that the burly old servant meticulously lights each one of the large lanterns at dusk, and that she blows them out one by one every morning just as meticulously, with a deep and sonorous bassoonlike sound. Every evening, following on the heels of the lighted lanterns like clockwork, and with equal precision and skill, the old maid-servant taps the little massage hammers on the chosen concubine's feet, the delicate hammers with tiny bells attached to them making pleasant ringing noises. Even the lantern covers, oppressive black shrouds that they are, signaling punishment for an egregious offense by a concubine, provide yet a feast for the eye with their intricately embroidered patterns of dragons in silver thread. The richness of visual and auditory details is matched only by the slow pace of the performance of these rituals that gives them an increased density of meaning. As though underlining the performance quality of the rituals, the formal act of lantern raising is accompanied by highly stylized Peking opera music, while the old servant marches to its percussion rhythm as though on a stage.

This excess of visual and auditory detail, combined with an elaborate display of precision and masterly skill of the performers, functions to confer ritualistic importance upon these practices. What ritualization stresses in this film is the structure of a given "culture," in its functionalist, totalizing whole, thus preserving the status quo and resistant to change.[17] What is elided in the process is any sense of antistructure, anything that makes the structure not static, not totalizing in its power functioning, an antistructure that is always there if the structur*ing* rather than the static structure is the focus of attention. This is not unlike the famous problem that Foucault's critical theory is known to have: after a brilliant demonstration of the perfect functioning of the hegemonic, there is little room to account for any act or even the possibility of resistance. It is therefore theoretically impossible to imagine or to account for any change in the mode of hegemony. But the parallel with Foucault does not go very far: for in the film, the functioning of the patriarchal hegemony is not only presented as immutable, it is also represented as beautiful.

The luminous glow of the red lanterns makes for a visually resplendent film, as it enfolds everybody who comes within its dominion, the confines of the household or the aura of the cinema. When the rituals are interrupted, when the red lanterns are not lit, when the rhythmic tapping of the little massage hammers stops, then there is tension, the tension for the resuming of the rituals, the tension for the fulfillment of the spectator's desire. Incidentally, like the lanterns, the ritual of foot massage is a filmic addition, not present in the original novella. Yet the hyperrealistic effect of the ritual is so palpable and so obviously enticing that the author of the novella, Su Tong, has even received overseas phone inquiries for the purchase of such massage hammers as depicted in the film.[18]

Thus, the very physicality produced by the visual medium, the concrete and intense embodiment of the ritual, further reinforces the sense of cultural essence, and the resulting appearance of inevitability. What is being elided in the filmic process of ritualization is the sense of historical specifics that is present in the novella but suppressed by the sense of the inevitable and impersonal rituals. This becomes obvious if we compare the original novella and the film version. In the novella *Wives and Concubines*, the rules of the game are considerably less clear, the workings of desire somewhat murkier. Significantly, the young fourth wife, Songlian, is given a fuller premarital history. Before her marriage, Songlian has a life typical of a New Woman: she reads books and goes to college. Even her future husband's initial attraction to her has much to do with her difference from the other three wives: her "new"ness, her college education, her Western (read, modern) peculiarities, such as her insistence on ordering a birthday cake for herself on their first date. Then this carefree world suddenly closes its door on her when her father's business goes bankrupt and he commits suicide. Her stepmother presents her with the stark choice of work or a concubinage in a rich household. Not really knowing what it entails, Songlian chooses the latter. The conflict of the new and old life styles is repeatedly accentuated in the novella through the shadowy presence of the two older children of the household. The young mistress, like Songlian, also goes to college. In fact, when Songlian first comes to the household as the concubine bride without much fanfare, servants mistake her for the young mistress coming back from school, as they are both referred to as *nü xuesheng* (coeds). The young master is also a (weak) symbol of the new world, always in Western suit and so forth. These striking doublings between Songlian in her ultratraditional role in the household, and the young master and mistress in their modern roles are significant in that they represent the historical conflict that underlies the period of the 1920s, not long after the fall of the last dynasty. It was a time when Chinese society was in transition, when the "women's place" in particular was unstable, when traditional and new roles coexisted side by side. Songlian's tragedy in part results from her inexperience in the setting of the traditional household, her not knowing the rules of the game. Her tragedy then is not a timeless tragedy as represented in the film, but a tragedy *of* its time, of the collision between the entrenchment of the traditional family and an ever-threatened new life. In other words, in the novella, what is "cultural tradition" is seen in flux despite its appearance of permanence.

In contrast, the film version makes but one reference to history, and then obliquely. At the beginning of the film, we see Songlian come to her husband's family on foot, in her student outfit, the iconic white blouse and black skirt uniform of "coed" students since the May Fourth Movement of 1919. As she is progressively submerged by the "tradition" of the house, so is this historical reference. The potential time marker, her student's uniform, is replaced by one set after another of traditional gowns of silk brocade. Correspondingly, the young master in the film appears always clad in long gowns, traditional yet strikingly haute couture. Thus because of its isolation and the lack of a contextualized reference, Songlian's student uniform is rendered practically unreadable. The conflict that finally swallows up Songlian is then seen through a ritualized landscape; it becomes the eternal conflict between an uncontextualized "cultural tradition" and an unspecified archetypal tragic heroine. Once the historical reference is submerged, what then makes this "culture" recognizably Chinese are the popular images associated with that mystical Orient: images of lanterns, (auditory) images of massage.

Microscopically, the household depicted in *Raise the Red Lantern* thus produces a timeless and "recognizable" China. The resplendent ritualization, both visual and auditory, functions as the guarantee that this recognizable China will provide sensual pleasures. Because of the studied detachment of the "ethnographic" camera eye, the viewer, having enjoyed the glamorous display and having been gratified visually and auditorily, has the added satisfaction of a possible critique of the oppression of the traditional family structure. Simultaneously, the gender system of the East remains exotic, enticing, and above all, unchanging.

In her recent study of contemporary Chinese films, Rey Chow warns that "in criticizing Zhang's 'traditional' or 'patriarchal' treatment of women, feminist criticism may unwittingly put itself at the service of a kind of conservatism that values depth over surfaces, and nativism over universalism, in a manner that is, ultimately, antifeminist."[19] This is indeed a serious danger, given the inescapable historical link between feminism and colonialism/orientalism. The question is, to what extent is "autoethnography" and its attending "exhibitionism" in Zhang Yimou's film effective as parody of orientalism, as Rey Chow claims. What is disturbing to me is that, at best, Zhang's film seems to want things both ways: parodying conventions of depicting the Orient with its requisite despot and harem, while capitalizing on the very same orientalist fantasies. The effect of this exploitative mix on the audience appears to be an unmediated seriousness rather than irreverent laughter typical of parody. Only too quickly, the culture presented by this "autoethnography" becomes simultaneously symbolized (hence the scholarly search for its

Confucian roots) and literalized (hence the businessman's request for massage hammers).

Another important issue brought up by Rey Chow's critique of a simplistic feminist reading of Zhang Yimou's films is that of "universalism," or as I have put it in this chapter, the relationship between representation of local culture and international acceptance. I share the suspicion of "nativism" in all its varieties, from the conventional orientalist formulations to patronizing theories from the radical left that consign "Third World" literature to "national allegories."[20] Yet a questionable parody of orientalism such as that presented in *Raise the Red Lantern* at best offers a solution in a rather narrow definition of the universal, characterized by a one-on-one relationship between China and the West, locked in an endless hall of mirrors. The film *Bloody Morning*, directed by the Fifth Generation filmmaker Li Shaohong, offers us an alternative to this straightjacket model of universalism. While historically contextualized in its representation of China, this film is anything but parochial or "nativist" in its approach to culture writing. It presents a China, inauthentically, with all its messiness as well as richness, via García Márquez's *Chronicle of a Death Foretold.*

IMAGINING CHINESE CULTURE THROUGH GARCÍA MÁRQUEZ

Bloody Morning is a carefully contextualized tale presenting a complex web of issues that permeate the changing Chinese nation of the late 1980s. The "culture" portrayed here is a living one, seen as constantly molding and remolding itself, throbbing with dreams and frustrations. Rituals that mark the other Fifth Generation construction of culture also play an important role in this film, yet they are seen in their very moments of being constituted and reconstituted, constantly recontextualized in their economic and personal underpinnings.

Can a film such as *Bloody Morning*, which is "about" men, their marriage deals, their murders, their deaths, a film in which the women characters are not represented as particularly powerful, be a "women's film"? Dai Jinhua, for one, observes that in this film "women are not given any special attention or expression" (272). She then concludes that behind director Li Shaohong's success, there is "a certain camouflage of gender, a sort of nonverbal neglect of one's own gender, and an indiffer-

ence to the condition of existence and the artistic expression of the gender group to which one belongs." In the different context of women's
filmmaking in the West, the same question is raised by Gertrud Koch:
"the issue remains whether films by women actually succeed in subverting this basic model of the camera's construction of the gaze, whether the
female look through the camera at the world, at men, women and objects
will be an essentially different one."[21]

What, then, does it mean to talk about *Bloody Morning* as a women's
film? Rather than arguing that the film does pay attention to women, or
attempting to substantiate an "essentially different" female look, I will
shift the terms of the question and argue that it is precisely in the unpre-
dictability that director Li Shaohong offers us a theoretical and practical
alternative. In her rewriting of a murder mystery, narrative cinema resists
the standard plot, both of classic Hollywood and of some Fifth Generation directors. Instead of gender polarization in the service of conventional desire, the film questions the boundaries separating male and
female subjectivities, positing highly unstable formulations of gender
identity. Frequently, the camera solicits identification from a feminized
subject position, although this position is not always necessarily occupied
by a female. Thus, there is a concerted attempt to formulate the conditions of representability so that a different vision can be effected.

The basic line of narrative in the film remains the same as in García
Márquez's novella *Chronicle of a Death Foretold*. It is a murder story in
which the mystery is not "whodunit" but rather "how could it have happened." First a new bride is rejected by her husband on their wedding
night for not being a virgin. Her brothers then announce their intention,
practically to the whole village, to murder the man who "defiled" her. Several attempts at warning the victim somehow get botched and the murder draws to its apparently fated end, with the rest of the village watching, as though it were a public execution. In both the original novella and
the film, the story is narrated in a series of flashbacks as investigators question the villagers about the murder case. [22]

By far the most important change is that of setting: the film *Bloody
Morning* is set in a mountainous village in Shangxi, China, in the late
1980s, while the novella *Chronicle of a Death Foretold* is set in the small
town of Sucre, Colombia, between the 1950s and 1970s. In fact, so
strong is the emphasis on a society in flux that to call this adaptation
"Chinese" is already too simple. The murder victim Li Mingquang is the
teacher of the village school, himself first taught by the "Educated Youths"

who were ubiquitous in the countryside during the Cultural Revolution of the recent past. The groom Zhang Qiangguo is a carpenter who has recently become rich because of the "New Economic Policy" instituted in the early eighties. The same economic reform that enriches the carpenter is the cause of the poverty for the murderer Li Pingwa, who is himself too poor to have the requisite bride price to get married well into his late thirties. In short, the film *Bloody Morning* is meticulously located, both in terms of historical specificity and in terms of geographical environment. There is no apparent effort, in other words, of reproducing García Márquez's novella in its "authenticity."

What then is the function of the original text, or the function of adaptation from a foreign original, a practice not often seen in Chinese cinema and rarer still in Fifth Generation production? Given the hybridity of García Márquez's own art and the general recognition of "Magic Realism" as a successful offspring of multiple cultural heritages,[23] the choice of using *Chronicle of a Death Foretold* is itself a contemplation on the issue of cultural identity versus international acceptance. While earlier (North American) reception of García Márquez's work stresses the appeal of "magic" or mystery, increasingly critics have pointed to Latin America's historical specifics, especially its unique history of colonization in such a way that the "magical" functions as a cognitive mode within which the real is perceived.[24] For what García Márquez explores in this novella is precisely the blurring of two cultures, the elite, European culture with the oral tradition of the coastal region, the blurring of history and imagination. No total knowledge can ever be claimed in this world, yet no facile mystification is allowed to dominate either. The attempt to understand coexists with the admission of the lack of total knowledge. The culture portrayed cannot be known in any ready way because it is a complex, multifaceted, and changing world, not because it is, in some essential way, magical or mystical. Significantly, the film *Bloody Morning* is an adaptation of method rather than of "local color";[25] it is an adaptation of the same intense and sharply focused regional identity from a multiple, cosmopolitan source of languages.

In *Bloody Morning*, one prominent adaptation of method is the liberal use of apparently superfluous details, a feature often observed by critics of García Márquez. These superfluous details surface in the film when the villagers forget themselves and fail to tell a coherent story. On the morning before the murder, for example, several villagers gather in front of the breakfast café in the village. As one of them suggests notifying the militia leader upon learning of the impending murder, several voices chide him for his behind-the-times solution: "Come to your senses. There hasn't been a militia leader for quite some time." Another such superfluous detail appears when the woman who runs a breakfast café is questioned by the government authority investigating the case. Sitting in a student's seat in the semidark room of the village elementary school, facing the "cadre" who is seated behind the teacher's desk, the woman appeals to him to lower a hefty fine her daughter has to pay for having given birth to twins: "¥800, my dear sir! A farmer in his prime might not make that much in a whole year. . . . Besides, who'd have known there were two of them in there?" A misrecognition of authority (an official/DA investigating a specific case versus an omnipotent "cadre" from "above"), this woman's plea is at once checked by her husband with a non-too-subtle nudge, and then also cut short by the village chief, who commands her "to get to the point."

Yet the functioning (or the nonfunctioning) of authority is very much the point. For it is precisely in this vacuum of power, in the transition from the old model of the commune patrolled by Party-militia to the new model of village life organized by the law that such a murder should occur and not be checked in time. The official voice of the law that makes up much of the voice-over represents a new power structure that is not yet fully functional, an authority that is constantly misrecognized, sometimes questioned, even covertly contested. Indeed, every casual gesture, every unintentional negligence, may be complicit in the eventual murder so that in the end, nothing is superfluous. Like García Márquez's story, there is concurrently an inevitability about the murder as well as its mystery: inevitable because of economic, political, and personal interests, mysterious because of the highly coincidental confluence of all of these factors.

Yet another such apparently superfluous detail concerns the film medium itself. Several times villagers make references to film, an element not only clearly associated with a foreign life style, but one that also has the connotation of dreams, aspirations, and potential hints of danger and scandal. At one point in the film, when Hongxin, the would-be bride, and her best friend are engaging in "girl talk," the background is a vast gate of a temple carved into the cliffs, grand and dilapidated. Significantly, the young women talk not about anything associated with "cultural tradition," but about their immediate lives and aspirations, their dreams and fantasies, which are associated with a culture clearly designated as "modern": they talk about films, and what popular actor would serve as their ideal male partner. The young women are also known to frequent the school teacher's room, the ostensible reason for the eventual murder of the school teacher by Hongxin's brothers. When the women are in the school teacher's room, their favored activity is to read the new film magazines that he subscribes to, a rare thing in the village judging by the effect that one of the pictures has on the villagers. One day a young boy steals one issue from his teacher's stack of film magazines and mischievously pastes the picture of a bikini-clad foreign film star on the family front gate. When his mother sees it, her first reaction is to put her hand on the picture to cover the exposed body. She then tears it off while nervously condemning it to her fellow farm wives.

The scene is rife with overtones of taboo and potential sexual scandal, the danger of another life style significantly represented as "foreign" through the female body of a Western star. This apparently superfluous detail represents a highly self-conscious reference to film as a "dangerous" and "foreign" medium and, significantly, to its conventional link to pin-ups, its tradition of displaying women's bodies as erotic spectacle. Thus both sides of the cinematic apparatus are suggested here: as lure because of its powerful potential for inscribing desire, and as danger as a result of its conventional usage. A far-flung village in China is not an insulated picture of traditional practice but a complex world with ancient codes of conduct as well as rumors of different life styles, with taboos and inhibitions, but also dreams and aspirations.

Paradoxically yet appropriately, the very "inauthenticity" or hybrid origin of the film script is the ground on which to stage the improvisations of culture. Through the apparent gaps and incoherences, the film *Bloody Morning* endeavors to represent the complexity of the power system, complex because of its long history and deep-seated convention, as much as because things are changing, a good deal of power is as yet uncodified. In terms of representing local culture to an international market, what director Li Shaohong has done is to refuse to go the easy way, to adopt the conventional representation of the East, a totalized, coherent and immutable "Chinese culture."

RESISTING THE LURE OF RITUAL

In the film, there is one crucial plot change from the original novella by García Márquez: instead of one wedding, there are two in the film version. The wealthy groom Zhang Qiangguo has an older sister Xiuqin, who is handicapped from childhood polio and suffers from epilepsy. The pretty bride Li Hongxin has an older brother Pingwa in his late thirties, who is too poor to get married. Thus, the rich groom exchanges his handicapped sister for the beautiful sister of the poor groom, while the poor groom gets to have a wife with his sister as the bride price. When the marriage is annulled by the rich groom Zhang Qiangguo, the corresponding exchange marriage is simultaneously annulled as well. At this point, the poor groom Pingwa sets out to kill the offender of his sister's honor, the cause of his own annulled marriage. Compared with *Chronicle of a Death Foretold*, in *Bloody Morning*, the relationships between the murderer, the victim, and the bridegroom are far messier, although the murder motive is paradoxically clearer.

In the crucial scene of the double wedding procession, a scene rife with potential possibilities of ritualization, instead of visually resplendent representation that we have come to expect in Fifth Generation films, there is a modern remaking of an ancient tradition: the exchange of brides. Significantly, the procession is visually doubled: the two wedding parties pass each other on the way, one marching on the tortuous mountain road half a mile higher up than the other. The men in both processions salute each other, blow on their trumpets and seem to have a riotously good time. This spectacle of good fun, setting up the spectator for a display of lavish ritual like the dance of the sedan carriers in *Red Sorghum*, is yet sharply counterbalanced by brief medium closeups of the faces of the two brides on donkey backs, visible (rather than concealed by veils as dictated by tradition as well as by the convention of exoticism) and visibly glum, as only befits properties being exchanged without regard to their desires. The two women, despite their apparent difference in age and appearance, are rendered identical as a result of the mirroring effect of the two wedding processions: they are but abstract symbols in an equation of economic exchange. Paradoxically, once without the veil or the bridal sedan, once fully exposed to view, the brides lose much of the lure as objects of the curious gaze. Without the classic shot/reverse shot, the cinematic codes of their "to-be-looked-at-ness," after being evoked, are in the end broken. The representation of the wedding processions thus does not conform either to the cultural myth of beautiful brides and happy occasion, nor to the recent filmic conventions that capitalize on ritualized visual splendor.

In contrast to her characteristic use of medium and medium long shots that do not glamorize the women victims, director Li Shaohong reserves rare closeups for the exchange items in the wedding processions: item by item, carried by men or animals, the trunks of clothing, chests of drawers, beds, chairs, even a bicycle. One long shot follows the man who carries the bicycle, who, with the rest of the company, has to drag his feet through ankle-deep mud and momentarily loses one of his shoes. As he struggles to toe his shoe out of the mud while balancing the bicycle on his shoulder, the glamour and solemnity associated with such an occasion devolve into laughter. This comical detail effectively curtails the tendency to idealize the ritual procession, bringing it down to earth, so to speak. The explicit foregrounding of the economic factor in the ritual material parodies the plot of the hypersexualization of the bride. In effect, ritual is brought back to life, to lived experiences that put a damper on visual pleasure while providing clues for actual understanding.

Throughout the film, "Cultural Tradition" is thus problematized and seen in flux, as new "traditions" are constantly created and people's daily life evolves out of the old framework. Here rituals, rather than being signs of a static "culture," are markers of changes in social relations.[26] Not only do they hark back to the past, but they are constantly being re-invented, to suit the changing values of the society. Discontinuity is the key word here: Cultural Tradition necessitates improvisation, invention, and possible subversion.

One particularly striking reinvention of ritual is staged by Qiang-guo, who plans a lavish wedding with entertainment for people from surrounding villages. On the dirt stage in the village square, the wedding guests are being treated to a Peking opera performance. At the end of the performance, two men climb onto the stage and unfurl a large red banner with the traditional symbols of "double happiness" written across it. With a dramatic closeup shot, the audience of the film and the wedding guests realize simultaneously that the characters are entirely lettered with crisp bills pasted onto the banner. Like the bicycle in the mud scene, the wedding banner is again economically coded, in a peculiarly crass way that does not leave much room for romanticization or mystification. The money turns out to be his donation to the village community, a practice often seen in late 1980s China, a practice that particularly marks the late eighties as a transitional period when private wealth is viewed with considerable ambivalence. *Nouveaux riches* like the carpenter Qiangguo are known to donate large amounts of money so as to disperse some of the ambivalence. Like his banner with the conflation of the new and the old, despite his association with the new economic policy and the new tradition, this young carpenter's function in the film is to accentuate precisely the conflict between the new and the old. For he is the one who engineers the exchange marriage, a tradition that reaches back to ancient tradition and has been under attack ever since the early modern period.[27] Again, he is the one who returns his bride on the wedding night, thus adhering strictly to traditional practice. Yet neither the new nor the old tradition is mystified in the film. Underlying the old tradition as well as the new is the driving force of economics.

RESISTING THE PLOT OF DESIRE

At the center of García Márquez's story, the culture of machismo functions as the primary motivation for murder. The Vicario brothers, murderers in the original *Chronicle of a Death Foretold*, are brought up in a family with a strict code of honor. The murder victim, Santiago Nasar, on the other hand, is one who has little sense of honor, evident in his casual deflowering of many maidens in the town. In the context of the original story then, the bodies of women are always already saturated with sexuality, to be defiled, preserved, or defended. The bodies of men are in turn hypermasculinized—either through sexual acts or through murder. In Li Shaohong's film, instead, traditionally defined masculinity itself is under scrutiny. Furthermore, there is a glaring absence of the highly charged erotic female body, a prerequisite of the original story as well as the basic ground for traditional cinematic apparatus. It is this absence that signals a successful resistance of the plot of narrative cinema, as it hints at a differently inscribed desire.

Li Mingguang, the murder victim, is an odd model of masculinity and an unlikely Chinese incarnation of Santiago Nasar. A misfit in the largely illiterate village by his very occupation as a school teacher, Mingguang is set off as a marginal figure: he writes poetry, subscribes to film magazines, and his farming skills are not widely admired. Several times he is situated in a "feminine" position through his roles. In one flashback of the school scene, for example, he is seen teaching a roomful of children of drastically different ages. One girl has on her back her baby brother. When the infant starts to cry and the young surrogate mother fails in her attempt to calm him, it is the teacher Mingguang who takes over the task:

he puts the baby on his back in the baby sling and walks to and fro while reading aloud to the class. His familiarity with the posture and the effectiveness of his intervention highlights a performance of the gestures conventionally associated with motherhood. The transgression of his character then is not seen in terms of hypermasculinity, but in his very *difference* from it. With such a victim, the eventual murder, particularly the complicity of the whole village in the murder, is not so much the defense of masculine honor but a concerted effort at eliminating difference, eliminating any deviance from communal norm.

Perhaps more surprisingly, the body of one of the murderers is also repeatedly shown in a feminine position. Li Pingwa, the older brother of the rejected bride Hongxin, may be said to lose his masculinity three times during the film, a loss that is apparently compensated, or overcompensated, by the eventual murder. But it is only apparent compensation, for indeed, the "lost objects are the only ones one is afraid to lose."[28]

What first emasculates him is his poverty, his being too poor to be a man, as it were. A worn-out, close to middle-aged unmarried man is an object of pity as well as the laughing stock in the village, where he is derisively referred to as a "bare rod." Furthermore, his demasculinization is publicly and dramatically proclaimed by himself. During a pre-wedding banquet where the exchange deal of women is sealed between the men, the figure who plays the feminine/powerless role in the scene is Pingwa. He becomes considerably drunk during the course of the banquet and starts to cry uncontrollably. In his drunken and pathetic state, he elaborately addresses his would-be brother-in-law, the carpenter Qiangguo, as "elder brother." Considering that seniority is an important marker of status in the village culture, and considering that Pingwa is in fact more than ten years the senior of Qiangguo, this gesture is tantamount to self-emasculation. The symbolic inversion of seniority comes with another marker of demasculinization: profuse tears and loss of self-control. The third time he is robbed of his masculinity is on his wedding night, when he and his new wife are rudely awakened and his wife forcefully carried away, as both marriages are pronounced annulled. Through the whole scene of confused action, much tears and screaming, Pingwa stands by, unable to understand what is going on, unable to hold on to his wife and to his newlywed life that has begun to promise happiness. Thus, the motivation for the murder is carefully contextualized in the film. Behind the language of family honor and preservation of "face" is the overwhelming factor of economics; and behind the bloody story of masculine revenge is the final, blind struggle of desperation.

Perhaps the greatest temptation presented to the film is the representation of the bridal chambers, the standard arena for the inscription of male desire, the crucial plot link that frames women as eroticized narrative image. This is usually where, as Laura Mulvey argued years ago, "cinematic codes create a gaze, a world and an object, thereby producing an illusion cut to the measure of desire" (25). Even in apparent critiques of traditional marriage, such as another Fifth Generation film *The Yellow Earth*, the inscription of male desire is apparent and the cinematic solicitation of the spectator's identification unambiguous, as the camera follows the gaze of the old groom and focuses on the frightened but oh-so-beautiful face of the young bride.

These are the cinematic codes that Li Shaohong's film attempts to break, and in the process, to envision sexual difference differently. One such moment appears in the bedroom scene between Pingwa and Xiuqin, hardly the typical happy or beautiful newlyweds, in a moment of awkward tenderness and mutual identification. After the requisite banquet, Pingwa is found squatting under the eaves of his hut, refusing to go into the bridal chamber. In a brief conversation with his mother, Pingwa reveals his complete awareness of the "bad deal" he has made, an awareness that makes him identify with his sister to some extent. His sharpened realization of his own marginal status because of poverty does not endear his new wife to him, since her very presence symbolizes his emasculation at the hands of her brother. At this point, director Li Shaohong shows superb control in the handling of this painfully awkward moment, with her characteristic gritty yet humorous touch, unsentimentalized yet compassionate. The camera eschews the typical mastering vision of the bridal chamber, and instead, subtly produces an identification between the two marginal characters, an identification that, at least temporarily, achieves an erasure of the boundaries separating male and female subjectivity.

After an eternity of standoff, both grow weary and Xiuqin begins to yawn. Resignedly, she starts to prepare for bed. As she struggles to undress herself, her shriveled left hand gets caught up in a tangle of what seems to be half a dozen layers of red woolen sweaters. The camera follows her slow and painful movement in a medium closeup, her face hard and unsmiling. In the background, Pingwa looks on, apparently with little interest. Then he hesitates, stands up, walks over and helps her free of the tangle. His hands then go on to smooth out her shirt, which has ridden up underneath the sweaters. Unlike the typical bedroom scene of the male voyeuristic gaze, the undressing of the bride is presented in its most vulnerable state, a vulnerable state that resembles the one that Pingwa finds himself in. Divested of her bridal clothes, which are also the markers of economics, she smiles for the first time, a smile reciprocated by a rare smile from him. Identification with a female position, rather than objectification by a mastering vision, ultimately provides the connection between the man and woman, albeit for but a brief moment. Ultimately, that is what provides the points of identification between the spectators and filmic images, and further still, the potential point of identification of the spectator as female.

Toward the end of the film, when the investigation is complete, when the murderers are being taken away amid the shrill whistle of the police siren, the audience is once again invited to identify with a feminine perspective, this time that of mothers. They are the widowed mother of Li Pingwa, Gouwa, and Hongxin, and the widowed grandmother of Li Mingguang, women who in their widowed state are particularly identified as responsible for bringing up the young. All through the film, these women are at the margins of the story, the edges of the camera frame. In their black/gray peasant outfits, with dark towels covering their hair, these women have not captured our attention, although retrospectively, we may remember their presence, offering food to the investigators or the village chief, offers repeatedly turned down as bribery by the official investigator. The end of the film, however, reverses this trend and splits the identification of the camera and the voice-over. No longer represented by the distant and impersonal voice-over of the official investigator, the figure of authority is now embodied by the siren, while the camera eye, for once, adopts the perspective of the widowed mothers. A long shot follows the mother of Pingwa and Gouwa, whose grief is silently but powerfully expressed through her body, which is propped up by two other women dressed in identical black/gray outfits. The camera then cuts to another shot that follows Mingguang's grandmother as she shakily steps outside her threshold, her voice murmuring amidst the siren: "Where are they taking the children? They are all children." Apparently incongruous to the situation at hand, Grandma's words nonetheless challenge the logic of murder as well as the logic of law, the apparent ground for the whole film, which divides people into victims or perpetrators, the powerful or the powerless. Instead, her words reinforce the grief of the other mother and reframe the story, as we are invited to look at the tragic loss from a mother's perspective, which identifies everyone, victim or perpetrator, as (some) mother's children. The final perspective on the story, then, comes from the highly marginalized position of widowed mothers, a position with which the audience is asked to identify.

What then would be director Li Shaohong's answer to our initial question—what does it mean to talk about women's cinema in China? It is clearly not enough simply to give prominence to the representation of women, especially since there is no lack of such centrality of women in other Fifth Generation films like *Raise the Red Lantern*. Paradoxically, as demonstrated by *Bloody Morning*, one powerful way of inserting the "Real" into the film's texture while inscribing a gendered perspective is to depict women's marginalization forcefully, at the same time providing the means of filmic identification with that marginalized position for both the other characters and the audience. For it is precisely in resisting the plot of narrative cinema of Hollywood, it is precisely in "disappointing" the audience familiar with the typical Fifth Generation "cultural film," that a film such as *Bloody Morning* signals its difference—a different vision coming through at the very intersection of culture and gender, a historicized culture and problematized gender system. If this not-so-exotic China is "adapted" from a "foreign" text about another modern hybrid culture in flux, if as such it resists interpretation as "national allegory," then its very "inauthenticity" effectively stages the cross-cultural nature of Chinese, and more broadly, non-Western, filmmaking.

NOTES

Earlier versions of this chapter were presented at the 1994 Association for American Chinese Comparative Literature conference, and the 1995 Association for Asian Studies conference. I thank participants of both conferences, especially Wendy Larson and Tam King-fai in helping me to sharpen my argument. I would like to express my especial gratitude to Linda Williams, Ted Fowler, and Ira Jaffe, whose comments on drafts of this chapter are greatly appreciated.

1. More than thirty women directors in China have directed at least two films and continue to be active. By "women's films," Professor Dai means not only films made by women but "films from a female point of view." See Dai Jin-

hua, "Invisible Women: Contemporary Chinese Cinema and Women's Film," trans. Mayfair Young. *Positions: East Asia Cultures Critique* 3/1 (1995): 254–80.

2. *Dahong denglong gaogaogua* (Raise the Red Lantern), China Film Co-Production Corporation, 1991. It was reviewed at Venice Film Festival and received Academy Award Nominations.

3. *Xuese qingchen* (Bloody Morning), Beijing Film Studio. International sales: Era Intl., Hong Kong. The film finished lensing in mid 1990 and was released locally in the spring of 1991, its foreign release delayed until the fall of the same year because of problems with government censors. It was reviewed at London Film Festival, the Locarno Fest, Toronto Fest, and Nantes Fest.

4. Zha Xiduo, "Laorui Xige, dahong denglong, yiguo qingdiao jiqita" [Lore Segal, the Red Lanterns, Exoticism, etc.] *Dushu*, 8 (1992): 135–36. Translated excerpts of the paper can be found in Jane Ying Zha, *Public Culture* 5/2 (1993).

5. For a Taoist reading, see Mary Ann Farquhar, "The 'Hidden' Gender in *Yellow Earth*," *Screen*, 33/2 (1992): 154–64. For a more critical reading in the Confucian tradition, see W. A.Callahan, "Gender, Ideology, Nation: *Ju Dou* in the Cultural Politics of China," *East-West Film Journal* 7/1 (January 1993): 52–80.

6. Li Suyuan, "The Cultural Film: A Noticeable Change," in *Film in Contemporary China: Cultural Debates, 1979–1989*, ed. George S. Semsel, Chen Xihe, and Xia Hong (Westport, Conn.: Praeger, 1992), 51–53. Discussing his controversial film *Horse Thief* (1986), director Tian Zhuangzhuang speaks of "national and regional culture" and the importance of producing a "territorial identity." One of his interlocutors, Xia Hong, film critic trained in the United States, explicitly uses the model of "ethnography" in his analysis of Fifth Generation films. "The Debate over *Horse Thief,*" *Film in Contemporary China*, 43,46.

7. Paul Clark, for one, has argued that the Chinese have "particularly associated the film medium with non-Chinese, exotic art forms and subjects." "Ethnic Minorities in Chinese Films: Cinema and the Exotic," in *East-West Film Journal*, 1.2 (1987): 15. Compared to their forerunners, the Fifth Generation was particularly well trained in this respect, as one of their professors recalls his teaching method at the time: "There was really nothing I could teach them, so I just had them watch foreign films all the time."

8. Similarly, religious rituals are prominent. In *Horse Thief,* for example, Tian Zhuangzhuang "documented" the practice of Tibetan Buddhism. However, it is only the effect that appears to be documentary, as Tian readily admits that "the costumes" as well as the "customs" are "designed" in the film to fit the

protagonist's "psychological and emotional constitution." There has been a long history of the Chinese seeing the neighboring minorities, including the Tibetans, as its own exotic other, much as the West has seen China as its other. Not surprisingly, such filmic ethnography of "the Tibetan culture" would mirror similar ethnography of the Chinese culture. See "The Debate over *Horse Thief*," in *Film in Contemporary China*, 43–46.

9. Esther C. M. Yau, "Cultural and Economic Dislocations: Filmic Fantasies of Chinese Women in the 1980s," *Wide Angle*, 11:2 (1989): 18.

10. For discussion of this phenomenon in the larger context of avant-garde cultural production, see Hu Ying, "Writing Erratic Desire: Sexual Politics in Contemporary Chinese Fiction," *In Pursuit of Contemporary East Asian Culture*, ed. Xiaobing Tang and Stephen Snyder (Boulder, Colo.: Westview Press, 1996), 49–68.

11. See, for example, Wendy Larson, "International Aesthetics and Erotics," in *Cultural Encounters: China, Japan, and the West*, ed. Søren Clausen, Roy Starrs, and Anne Wedell-Wedellsborg (Aarhus, Denmark: Aarhus University Press, 1995): 215–26; and Peter Hitchcock, "The Aesthetics of Alienation, or China's 'Fifth Generation,'" *Cultural Studies*, 6:1 (1992): 116–41.

12. For a classic critique of such division, see Teresa de Lauretis, *Technologies of Gender: Essays on Theory, Film, and Fiction* (Bloomington: Indiana University Press, 1987), 31–50.

13. For the initial feminist critique of the "gaze," see Laura Mulvey, "Visual Pleasure and Narrative Cinema," originally published in *Screen* 16, no. 1 (Autumn 1975); reprinted in Laura Mulvey, *Visual and Other Pleasures* (Bloomington: Indiana University Press, 1989): 14–29.

14. Mulvey, "Afterthoughts on 'Visual Pleasure and Narrative Cinema' inspired by King Vidor's *Duel in the Sun* (1946)," *Visual and Other Pleasures*, 30.

15. *Raise the Red Lantern*, trans. Michael Duke (New York: William Morrow, 1993).

16. Michel Foucault, *Discipline and Punish: The Birth of the Prison*, trans. Alan Sheridan (New York: Vintage Books, 1977), 200–202.

17. Don Sutton, in his "Ritual, History, and the Films of Zhang Yimou," convincingly argues for the efficacy of using rituals in the representation of culture, especially Chinese culture. However, when the rituals are simplified so as to lose much of their complexity, or when they are invented according to a formula smacking of Orientalism, their very efficacy in culture writing becomes problematic. See Sutton, *East-West Film Journal* 8/2 (1994): 31–46.

18. Su Tong related this episode in his public presentation at University of California, Irvine. October, 1994.

19. Rey Chow, *Primitive Passions: Visuality, Sexuality, Ethnography, and Contemporary Chinese Cinema* (New York: Columbia Press, 1995), 152.

20. The term is used by Frederic Jameson, "Third-World Literature in the Era of Multinational Capital," *Social Text* 15 (Fall 1986). It has been widely cited and often criticized. See Aijiz Ahmad, "Jameson's Rhetoric of Otherness and the National Allegory," *Social Text* 17 (Fall 1987): 3–25; and Rey Chow, *Primitive Passions*, 55–65, 82.

21. "Exchanging the Gaze: Revisioning Feminist Film Theory," *New German Critique*, no. 2 (1977): 117.

22. Originally published in Colombia as *Crónica de una muerte anunciada* by Editorial La Oveja Negra Ltda., Bogotá, 1981. Trans. Gregory Rabassa (New York: Ballantine, 1982). For analyses of *Chronicle of a Death Foretold*, see Raymond L. Williams, "The Writer as Journalist," in his *Gabriel García Márquez* (Boston: Twayne, 1991), 134–51; and Carlos J. Alonso, "Writing and Ritual in *Chronicle of a Death Foretold*," *Modern Critical Views: Gabriel García Márquez*, ed. Harold Bloom (New York: Chelsea House, 1989): 257–71.

23. Critics point to the influence of Kafka and Faulkner in particular. See, for example, Harley Oberhelman, "The Development of Faulkner's Influence in the Work of García Márquez," *Critical Views: Gabriel García Márquez*, 65–80.

24. See, for example, Irlemar Chiampi Cortez, "In Search of a Latin American Writing," *Diacritics* 8, no. 4 (1978) and Kumkum Sangari, "The Politics of the Possible," *Journal of Arts and Ideas* 10–11 (1985).

25. For an effort at "authentically" representing García Márquez, see another version of the film (1985) by the Italian director Francesco Rosi, who shot his version in Cartagena-de-Indias, during seventeen weeks of tropical heat and rain, with the intention of going through the ordeal of a contact with reality to test the authenticity of people and places.

26. For two different definitions of ritual as conservative and as provocative of change, see Victor Turner, *The Forest of Symbols: Aspects of Ndembu Ritual* (Ithaca, N.Y.: Cornell University Press, 1967) and Catherine Bell, *Ritual Theory and Ritual Practice* (New York: Oxford University Press, 1992). For an argument that, in Turner's own writing, the two opposing senses of ritual are already present, see Ronald L. Grimes, "Victor Turner's Definition, Theory, and Sense of Ritual," *Victor Turner and the Construction of Cultural Criticism: Between Literature and Anthropology*, ed. Kathleen M. Ashley (Bloomington: Indiana University Press, 1990): 141–46.

27. The most famous critique is Lu Hsun's short story "New Year's Sacrifice," in *Selected Stories of Lu Hsun,* trans. Yang Hsien-yi and Gladys Yang (Beijing: Foreign Languages Press, 1960), 125–43. Originally published in 1924.

28. A psychoanalytical commonplace, it is succinctly phrased by Christian Metz, *The Imaginary Signifier: Psychoanalysis and the Cinema,* trans. Celia Britton, Annwyl Williams, Ben Brewster, and Alfred Guzzetti (Bloomington: Indiana University Press, 1982), 63.

CHAPTER EIGHT

"Can the Subaltern Weep?" Mourning as Metaphor in Rudaali (The Crier)

SUMITA S. CHAKRAVARTY

Physical pain does not simply resist language but actively destroys it, bringing about an immediate reversion to a state anterior to language, to the sounds and cries a human being makes before language is learned.

—Elaine Scarry, *The Body in Pain*

The title of this chapter is a play on Gayatri Spivak's famous query, "Can the Subaltern Speak?"[1] The controversy and ambiguity[2] that may have resulted from the rhetorical form in which her question was posed and the enormous ideological and philosophical charge involved in notions of speech, voice, and articulation are likely to evaporate when the act being considered is not speaking but weeping, not the prestige of *logos*, associated with man, but the banality of *pathos* or sentiment, generally considered the province of woman.[3] If the subaltern woman cannot speak (is spoken for) or speaks only under exceptional circumstances, weeping

284   SUMITA S. CHAKRAVARTY

would seem to be her allotted condition in life, and the conjunction of women's tears with third-world calamities has long been a staple of the mass media. Yet the image of the subaltern as woman and woman as the being-in-pain, while ubiquitous, is curiously undertheorized. Perhaps it is the oozing expressiveness of tears, their visual and emotive quality, that confers on them the taint of womanly body fluids and dissociates them from more acceptable and "legitimate" notions of language and voice. For the gap between voice and tears can be mapped onto a whole series of oppositions familiar to feminist criticism: male/female, mind/body, nature/culture, intellect/emotion, active/passive, subject/object. Yet my purpose in this chapter is not to provide one more demonstration of the operation of these dichotomies, this time on the terrain of Indian culture and society. Rather, my interest is in muddying these categories through an analysis of mourning as both a social and psychic phenomenon, as practice and symbol, art and artifice, body and voice. In particular, I focus on two texts that foreground mourning—a recent Indian film *Rudaali* and the antecedent short story on which it is based—in order to explore how commonly held notions of body and voice, the physical/material and the intellectual/expressive planes of human existence, are reworked in relation to gender.

Like mourning, the subject of women and filmmaking in India is at once an easy and a difficult one to tackle. Since women have only recently emerged as filmmakers in a country where the history of the cinema is almost a hundred years old, and their output has been intermittent and sparse, any straightforward account of their activity would be a brief one. Yet women's association with the cinema (on screen and off), and the cinema's imbrication in the social history and cultural politics of its place of origin and development, is not straightforward but complicated and multitextured. A discussion of any single text is an opening onto a larger terrain of meaning and signification. It is in this sense that the evocation of Spivak's formulation becomes crucial for my purposes, in both metonymic and metaphoric terms. On the associative level, I wish to point to Spivak's link with Mahasweta Devi, the author of "Rudaali," whose works she has translated and made known to American readers. On the metaphoric level, any investigation of subalternity, gender, and signification cannot but be informed by the whole corpus of Spivak's formidable theoretical contributions to the field of postcolonial feminist studies. As Caren Kaplan and Inderpal Grewal have noted,

"By bringing together Marxism, poststructuralism, and feminist perspectives within a comparative study of the first and third worlds, Spivak radically rewrites the paradigms of modernity and postmodernity."[4] In the context of the present chapter, Spivak's transdisciplinary methodology enables further exploration of the politics of gender in third cinema and the interlocked dynamics of the signifiers of "body" and "voice."

Rudaali is a film that wishes to evoke a subaltern ethos. Based on a story by Mahasweta Devi, a Bengali writer and activist who works tirelessly on behalf of India's tribal populations, it explores the many levels of oppression to which the lower-caste, impoverished female is subject. In recent years new trends in Indian historiography have also placed the subaltern at the center of India's political and nationalist struggles. My attempt in this chapter is to see *Rudaali* as part of this larger critical project and to assess the significance of its mode of reflexivity. An elaboration of mourning as metaphor is meant to throw light on this process.

Using the ritual of public mourning that the film foregrounds as a theoretical framework for the understanding of sexual difference and its concomitant range of subjugated positionalities, I would like to (a) present an archaeology of women's consciousness and subjectivity in terms of the symbolic functions of activities such as mourning, self-sacrifice, and archetypal suffering; (b) relate these phenomena to traditions of filmmaking in India and the ideologies accompanying them; and (c) examine the emancipatory possibilities of the kind of feminist depiction of the subaltern that the film undertakes. The questions I raise are as follows: In what ways does the film use mourning as an organizing principle and metaphor to encompass the totality of subaltern women's oppression in India? What are the specific links that the film tries to articulate between women's prescribed social roles (mourning) and their economic and spiritual devastation? Can the narrativization of "mourning" be seen as contributing to the production of a woman's genre? To what extent is the demystification and deromanticization of mourning tied to the film's feminist project? As a phenomenon with social, psychic/emotional, and performative dimensions pertaining primarily to women, the ritual of mourning in the film marks the intersection of notions of public and private, nature and culture, community and society.

DEATH AND MOURNING AS GENDERED CATEGORIES

> I saw her and him in the same instant of time—his death and
> her sorrow—I saw her sorrow in the very moment of his
> death.
>
> —Joseph Conrad, *Heart of Darkness*

In a recent interview, Derrida is quoted as saying, "All my writing is on death. If I don't reach the place where I can be reconciled with death, then I will have failed. If I have one goal, it is to accept death and dying."[5] The importance of death as a subject for philosophical rumination can hardly be overestimated. Indeed, there is scarcely a subject that has held interest for moderns and ancients alike, for philosophers, writers and performers as that of death. In all cultural traditions, elaborate social and intellectual systems have been devised to deal with death and human mortality. In his book *Eros and Mourning,* Henry Staten locates the anticipation of loss (of a loved one or object) and strategies to deal with it at the heart of the Western religious-philosophical tradition, saying that "a 'hidden and continual grief' (is) at the core of human experience as a consequence of the transitoriness of temporal things."[6] He calls it thanato-erotic anxiety and traces it in the Western tradition all the way from Homer to Lacan. Likewise Eric Santner points to a recurrence of the rhetoric of mourning in postmodern critical discourses, "of a metaphorics of loss and impoverishment."[7] He traces this tendency to the poststructuralist idea that to be a speaking subject is to be perpetually, constitutionally in mourning, for language opens up wounds that it cannot heal. Inflecting this linguistic formulation with the more socially informed notions of difference and alterity and how to come to terms with them, Santner argues that postmodernism's elegiac mode is a means to overcome the contemporary world's inability at times to mourn the suffering and death of victims. In the Hindu tradition, death is not accorded a finality but becomes the means of contemplating the futility of earthly attachments and strictures. In the highly acclaimed Kannada novel *Samskara: A Rite for a Dead Man* (1965), made into a controversial film in 1970, the author uses death to question the entire structure of orthodox Hindu belief systems. As the poet-translator A. K. Ramanujan comments:

> The opening event is a death, an anti-brahminical brahmin's
> death—and it brings in its wake a plague, many deaths, questions

without answers, old answers that do not fit the new questions, and the rebirth of one good brahmin, Praneshacharya. In trying to resolve the dilemma of who, if any, should perform the heretic's death-rite (a *samskara*), the Acharya begins a *samskara* (a transformation) for himself. A rite for a dead man becomes a rite of passage for the living.[8]

But if men have taken it upon themselves to try to fathom death (and hence the meaning of life), it is women who have been involved in the process of dealing with it as experience. Historically, the elaborate ritual of mourning for the dead has fallen to women. As Gail Holst-Warhaft writes, "Men and women may both weep for their dead, but it is women who tend to weep longer, louder, and it is they who are thought to communicate directly with the dead through their wailing songs."[9] She suggests that "we must consider lament not simply as a traditional female response to death, but as representative of the relationship of society to death, and so as fundamental to life."[10] Her metaphor of lamenting women as "dangerous voices" identifies male fears regarding women's access to death, a suggestion that Henry Staten exemplifies in what he calls the "thanatoerotophobic tradition."

However, there is another tradition of thinking associated with the mourning of loss, one that stresses the naturally therapeutic function and socially redemptive nature of crying and mourning. In "Mourning and Melancholia, " Freud states, "Mourning is regularly the reaction to the loss of a loved person, or to the loss of some abstraction which has taken the place of one, such as fatherland, liberty, an ideal, and so on." There is a naturalness about mourning, according to Freud, so that any interference with it is "inadvisable or even harmful."[11] The ability to mourn loss and bereavement is considered healthy and normal; an absence of mourning, as in the case of post-Holocaust Germany, a symptom of a collective denial of the past.[12] In a less psychoanalytic vein, Raymond Williams links the emotional charge associated with tears and mourning to the emergence of women's voices in nineteenth-century British fiction. His striking observation is worth quoting in full:

> I talked about the phenomenon of the women novelists of the English nineteenth century carrying so much of the most questioning consciousness in that culture and in that form. . . . I related this very specifically to the moment in English life and English fiction

when men stopped crying. I don't know whether men stopped crying before then; there are no statistics on how often men wept through our history or have wept since or weep today on the relevant occasions. But I know this was the moment in admitted social life and in fiction when men stopped weeping and it is exactly the same moment as the emergence of the remarkable generation of women novelists from Gaskell through the Brontes to George Eliot. . . . They admitted a kind of intense personal feeling which I analysed in different ways in that book, an intensity of feeling which was immediately categorized as women's fiction and is still, as a matter of fact, in some feminist history today described as important because it is specifically women's fiction. But I was saying that what they kept going was what a certain mutation in masculine self-perception and in certain norms of public life had excluded from permissible male behaviour.[13]

The relationship that Williams establishes between weeping and voice is indeed fascinating. With his usual sensitivity to the processes of history, Williams uses weeping as an organic metaphor of social transformation. As a result of the emergent regime of industrialism and bourgeois respectability, men no longer permit themselves the luxury of tears, but what they suppress now finds new avenues through women's voices expressed in fiction. In his own way, then, Williams reconciles the two traditions mentioned above, valorizing weeping as a necessary social activity at the same time that he articulates women's voices to a language of the body.

MOURNING THE NATION:
WOMEN'S VOICES AND SUBALTERN LIVES

The violence of history grows out of a refusal or an inability
on the part of the members of a society to assume the vocation
of mourner-survivor of what might be called the violence of
the signifier.

—Eric Santner, *Stranded Objects*

What is the relationship of the postcolonial nation-state to the processes of mourning and anamnesis? And how are women implicated in these processes? If, as Williams suggests, the social devaluation of tears has its own history, and poststructuralist criticism warns of the impending dangers of an inability to mourn, both at the level of the individual and the collectivity, what of the status of mourning in the aftermath of colonialism? It might be said that the identity of nations emerging out of colonialism is ontologically marked by both death and rebirth (they are at once old and new) and hence requires both mourning and forgetting. The heroic narrative of the nationalist struggle is kept alive by ritual acts of mourning, the death of the national father(s) providing the totemic source of renewal for the community; on the other hand, the tasks of building the new nation entail a degree of forgetting and a denial of difference that can feed into the interests of a hegemonic consolidation of power. What then happens as a nation goes about reconstructing its history in the light of contemporary realities and concerns is that the rhetoric of inclusion through which the past is mourned (all groups, dominant and marginal, helped in winning independence) exists alongside new regimes of exclusion and the institutionalization of hierarchies. For the nascent nation-state an accession to the symbolic order, akin to that experienced by the individual, may be said to occur, inherent in which are the dangers of what the postructuralists (Derrida in particular) have termed logo-, phono-, phallo-, and ethnocentric thinking. At the level of the national psyche begins the "work of denial and repression" of heterogeneity and difference whereby the presence of marginal groups in society is erased in the interests of mastery—political, economic, symbolic—by the dominant group. Perhaps this explains the inevitable rupture and decline that marks a preindependence from a postindependence phase in the history of decolonization. The unity of the National Imaginary is succeeded by the violence of entry into the postcolonial Symbolic order. Partha Chatterjee puts it another way when he writes that "the story of nationalist emancipation is necessarily a story of betrayal."[14]

India's postcolonial history may be taken as an example of this process at work. Prior to 1947, the British imperial powers had constituted an enemy against which all classes of people struggled and fought. Freedom from British rule and the emergence of a nation space in which age-old wrongs would be rectified, wealth redistributed, and hierarchies banished provided a sort of common dream for the privileged and the subaltern alike. Although recent historians have presented a considerably more complex picture of the actual dynamics of the national movement in India, particularly its class-stratified nature, the project itself was not in doubt. During the 1920s and 1930s, a genuine mass movement developed and was ultimately instrumental in driving the British out of India. After independence, however, as Susie Tharu and K. Lalita argue, "Frames of mind and structures of feeling that underwrote disobedience, resistance, and revolt were carefully dismantled and oppositional energies were consciously diffused as the national struggle was closed off and the nation state began to establish its dominance." They further point out, "It was in the forties and fifties that many of the myths, the institutions, the discursive and narrative regimes that have secured the popular understanding of our history, our tradition, our identity, and our problems today—in other words, the popular understanding of what India is, and what it means to live in this country and be an Indian—began to take on their current configurations."[15]

The role of women in this process of transition may be discussed in terms of the thematics of mourning and forgetting articulated above. The association of women with nationalist concerns goes back to the nineteenth century when Indian social and religious reformers foregrounded the subjugation and oppression of women as symptomatic of the larger malaise that has resulted in India's colonized state. While reiterating a line of argument advanced by the colonial powers, Indian social thinkers and activists nevertheless fought to eradicate oppressive practices such as *sati* (the burning of a widow on her husband's funeral pyre), child marriage, the prohibition against widow remarriage, women's domestic confinement and illiteracy, and the like. During the freedom struggle, women were actively recruited, and voluntarily participated in strikes, marches, and protests alongside men. They also wrote poems, songs, and stories foregrounding social problems and the tumultuous events of the time. After independence was won, women writers of the new nation took upon themselves the task of mourning the past and consolidating the nation-as-community. According to the editors of the anthology, *Women Writing in India,* an ideological conformity marked the output of most of the writers of the immediate postindependence period.

But if the fifties marked the transition between an imaginary nationhood and the real thing, between a state of mourning (the acceptance of difference and heterogeneity) and forgetting (the assertion of economic and cultural elites) within the Indian body politic, the following decades broke the fragile peace. "During the late sixties and through the seventies, for example, a variety of alternative visions challenged existing institutions and articulated the grievances and aspirations of the other

India whose people had suffered loss of power and agency as they were recast into the schemes of nationhood."[16] This was also the period that saw the rise of the new cinema in India with its stress on regionalism and the authenticity of local collectivities. Other critical projects, such as those in historiography, feminism, and postcolonial literary criticism, have emerged since the seventies. Yet critical accounts of these developments have remained curiously insular and isolationist. Literary critics have rarely looked at the role of the cinema while historians have ignored feminist concerns.[17] Commenting on the project of Subaltern Studies, a scholarly attempt to recast modern Indian historiography by writing a history-from-below, one contributor, Veena Das, remarks, "The question of gender in the constitution of the subaltern has been largely absent from the purview of the studies mentioned here."[18] Another contributor, Gyanendra Pandey, notes that the historical writing represented in Subaltern Studies has had no way of dealing with suffering, a subject that can only be found addressed in the popular cinema. Speaking of a particularly traumatic event in Indian history, the Partition, he writes that the "historian's craft has never been particularly comfortable with such matters, the horror of Partition, the anguish and sorrow, pain and brutality of the 'riots' of 1946–47 [being] left almost entirely to creative writers and filmmakers."[19] A similar bifurcation exists in critical accounts of the Bombay (all-India) and the art or alternative (postsixties, government-supported) cinema. While a tracing of the complex interrelationships between the institutions of literature, cinema, historiography, and feminism in postcolonial India must await another space and time, the historical convergence of these institutions *as* instruments of critique is surely noteworthy. Indeed, the new cinema may be taken as a privileged site of this convergence, its ideological playing ground and contradictory locus. Here the clash between (ideal) forms of self-definition and the contingent nature of infrastructural realities to which it was perforce subject made for a cinematic project often at odds with itself. The alternative cinema sought to dissociate itself from a homogenizing and market-governed popular cinema by turning to (regional) literary sources and social realist techniques, thereby feeding into an official ideology of an "authentic" text-based Indian tradition; its critical mission also foundered in terms of the very structures of economic support that only a nationally instituted or governmental structure could provide, even as it sought to expose the corruptions of the state and dominant society. Trying to stay clear of both the popular cinema's entertainment values and the state's compromised politics, the new cinema was nevertheless beholden to them in different ways.

Further, the new cinema's avowed commitment to women's issues is itself a complex renegotiation of the socially defined relationship between women and Indian popular cinema. Not only were women performers looked down upon in the early decades of filmmaking, but the popular film has never quite been able to shake off the taint of prostitution that has clung to it since those early years. (Thus Bombay cinema's hegemony in one area is undercut in another: it is both mainstream and marginal, an enemy and an ally.) What is interesting for our purposes is the intervention of nationalist concerns into this field of representational politics and the inflections it assumes in attitudes to cinema, with continued ramifications for the present. I shall appropriate Partha Chatterjee's arguments made in a slightly different context to consider these implications, as revealed in his poignant stories of two Bengali women: Binodini, a celebrated actress of the Calcutta stage at the end of the nineteenth century whose fame as an actress coexisted with her social marginality as a "woman of ill-repute," and a contemporary retired actress responding to a newspaper story about her liaison with a deceased actor whom she regarded as her husband of thirty years.[20] Chatterjee contends that bourgeois nationalism "could define a cultural identity for the nation only by excluding many from its fold; and it could grant the dignity of citizenship to some only because the others always needed to be represented and could not be allowed to speak for themselves."[21] A space for mourning the nation is thus opened up, in the writings of women and in the contestation over the popular cinema as weak, female, illegitimate, a contestation which the new cinema enters into for strategic purposes. Any consideration, then, of women's representation and self-representation must traverse the interlocking fields of social and political history, cinematic modes and institutions, and emergent state apparatuses. A reorientation, through a gendered understanding of cinema, of Partha Chatterjee's "radical suggestion that the cultural history of nationalism, shaped through its struggle with colonialism, contained many possibilities of authentic, creative, and plural development of social identities that were violently disrupted by the political history of the postcolonial state seeking to replicate the modular forms of the modern nation-state,"[22] has important, as yet unexplored ramifications for theories of postcolonialism and subalternity.

Mahasweta Devi's critical fiction advances some of these concerns and can be seen as a composite of the diverse cultural-critical movements of the late sixties onward. She confronts viscerally the most powerful forces of the Indian polity (including what she sees as the banal ubiquity of the Bombay cinema, its permeation into the fabric of the life of the underclass). As an author who came into maturity in the early sixties and from the left tradition, Mahasweta is less concerned with celebrating Indian independence and emergence as a nation-state and more with the failed promises of the new nation and its bourgeois leadership. Central to her fiction and activism are a number of themes and concerns: the discourses of nationalism and postcolonialism, modernization and development, capitalism, women's exploitation, and the rights of India's tribal populations. Mahasweta Devi's fiction sought to make the general reader aware of India's tribals, whose culture and livelihood are being negated by nationalist schemes of development. In an interview with Gayatri Spivak, she speaks on behalf of the tribals:

> They are Indians who belong to the rest of India. Mainstream India had better recognize that. Pay them the honor that they deserve. Pay them the respect that they deserve. There are no dowry deaths among the tribals. And when they are called criminal tribes, I say, there is crime all over the state of Bihar. All over India. All over the world. Do these tribes commit all these crimes? They are your easy victims, they are your prey, you hunt them. The system hunts them. And wants to brand them. The system which hunts them and uses them as a target is the criminal.[23]

In her various endeavors, she shows a keen awareness of subalterns (the rural poor, the tribals, the lower caste and untouchables of Indian society) as groups marked by difference and outside the pale of discursive rationality acceptable to the nation's elites. In a cruel twist to the dynamic of mourning and forgetting, they are mourned in the abstract and forgotten in the concrete. Mahasweta Devi follows the particular outrage that this process assumes on the bodies of subaltern women.

SPEAKING THE BODY: MAHASWETA DEVI'S "RUDAALI"

> We will not be able to speak to the women out there if we depend completely on conferences and anthologies by Western-trained informants. . . . In inextricably mingling historico-

political specificity with the sexual differential in a literary discourse, Mahasweta Devi invites us to begin effacing that image.

—Gayatri Spivak, *In Other Worlds*

Over and over in her fiction, Mahasweta Devi seeks to strip away the encrusted layers of convention in order to assert, on the one hand, what Elaine Scarry calls "the sheer material factualness of the human body,"[24] hence its vulnerability to pain and suffering, and on the other, the imbrication of the body in discourses and instrumentalities of power and subordination, where bodies are marked, signified, and read in particular ways, depending on their social sites. In a sense, Mahasweta reverses the direction that the critique of the mind/body or nature/culture division has taken in feminist discourse. Rather than fall in with the usual critique of representation of the female body, Mahasweta takes this critique to its logical conclusion, seeing the (concrete, not the metaphoric) body of woman as the brutal playing ground of patriarchal power and vengeful politics. As Spivak notes, "Mahasweta thematizes the postcolonial in a body model as opposed to the mind model (of the indigenous elite proclaiming their intellectual alienation and homelessness)."[25] Confronted by the wounds sustained by the physical body, the psychic effects of colonial "epistemic violence" tend to seem like narcissistic self-display.

The pain and horror of woman as body is therefore central to Mahasweta's fiction, as a concern with body fluids—tears ("Rudaali"), breast milk (Stanadayini or "Breastgiver"), vaginal blood ("Draupadi")—helps her to anchor the specificity of female victimization. Mahasweta uses these bodily secretions in ways that subvert their traditional or romanticized associations and become alienating devices. They are modes of exploitation and commodification of the female body. In her short story "Breast Giver," Jashoda the female protagonist's body is given over entirely to its womanly functions: "Jashoda doesn't remember at all when there was no child in her womb, when she didn't feel faint in the morning, when Kangali's body didn't *drill* her body like a geologist in a darkness lit only by an oil-lamp. She never had the time to calculate if she could or could not bear motherhood. Motherhood was always her way of living and keeping alive her world of countless beings. Jashoda was a mother by profession, *professional mother*."[26] Her breasts provide milk for all the offspring of her rich employer's household, but later grow cancerous and Jashoda dies a lonely, miserable death, abandoned by all whom she had served as a young woman. In "Draupadi," there is a searing description of the abuse to which a female body is subjected. The body is that of a captured tribal engaged in guerilla warfare against the authorities. Torture by multiple rape is a common method of eliciting information from female captives regarding their group's activities. "Opening her eyes after a million light years, Draupadi, strangely enough, sees sky and moon. Slowly the bloodied nailheads shift from her brain. Trying to move, she finds her arms and legs still tied to four posts. Something sticky under her ass and waist. Her own blood. Only the gag has been removed. Incredible thirst. In case she says 'water' she catches her lower lip in her teeth. She senses that her vagina is bleeding. How many came to make her?"[27] Parading her torn and naked body in front of her male captors as her only form of revenge, Draupadi rewrites the story of the mythical Draupadi in the *Mahabharata* by breaking the link between shame and its conventional association with woman's body. In "Children," the protagonist is a conscientious and well-intentioned government "relief officer" sent to a remote and impoverished area to distribute food to the local tribals. Finding that a group of children come to steal the bags of grain in the night, he gives chase, only to find that these are not children but stunted men and women whose bodies bear the marks of material deprivation. Naked and dancing around him in malicious glee, the men display their dry and shrunken penises and the women their dangling, withered breasts. "Standing still under the moon, listening to their deafening voices, shivering at the rubbing of their organs against his body, Singh knew that the ill-nourished and ridiculous body of an ordinary Indian was the worst possible crime in the history of civilization."[28] Stunned by this outrage and his own complicity in it, the protagonist loses his voice but finds tears streaming down his cheeks.

If death, torture, and rape as common scenarios in Mahasweta Devi's fiction signal the gravity of the issues at stake and the need to mourn the crash of an early promise and dream, "Rudaali" refuses to take even death seriously and may be the strongest indictment yet of the nation's corruption. Not only is the protagonist, Sanichari, not able to mourn the death of her own kith and kin (husband, son, mother-in-law), but she engages in the monetization of mourning, using the shedding of tears as her means of livelihood. Weeping is a performance rather than an affective response to loss, a means to scale the hierarchies of caste and class. The ritual act of mourning is, further, a means whereby the poor expose the vanity, competitiveness, and idle pastimes of the rich. The elaborateness of a mourner's lamentations is in direct proportion to the promise of monetary remuneration for the tears shed. In this starkly opposed social universe, the luxury of sentiment is denied to the subaltern. Sanichari cannot shed tears even when her friend and associate, Bhikni, dies; resolutely, she gathers together a band of prostitutes (the recurring emblem of the gendered outcast) as professional mourners needed for the final act of self-aggrandizement of the village chief. We have come a long way from Raymond Williams's women novelists protecting the realm of strong emotion as a safety valve for (male) society's inability to mourn. Mahasweta's women characters speak through bodies and body fluids reduced to their bare physiological stratum, at once humbled and humbling, a grim reminder to the nation of its moral degradation. In the very act of subverting mourning, "Rudaali," then, may be Mahasweta Devi's way of showing how far the act of forgetting has in fact gone in contemporary India, her own mournful critique of the status quo.

MOURNING AND MELODRAMA

> When one looks closely, film always has something to do with parting. Film concerns itself with things and people that disappear from our sensory perception, with this pain that every good frame reproduces and produces. . . . Parting is the great theme of every film.
>
> —Quoted in Eric Santner, *Stranded Objects*

At the heart of "Rudaali," then, lies a paradox. It aims to fulfill an end which it must critique as a means. Mourning as a socially prescribed role for women becomes a signifier of women's oppression, and its immanent critique signals the narrative's liberatory agenda. Yet if death itself loses its power to terrify and wound, all social relationships lose their meaning. A nation unmourned (and unmournful) is a nation lost.[29]

In the screen adaptation, therefore, an attempt is made to rework the paradox, to diversify the discourse and the sites of death and mourning. The first scene, for instance, presents a scenario of death in satiric terms, the impending death in question being that of the village overlord, whose body itself both parodies and invites death. (Ironically, the actor who plays the role, Amjad Khan, died in his prime before the film was released. The film is dedicated to him.) His bloated flesh emblematic of his worldly corruption, this upper-class character's mountainous carcass fills the screen as he is stretched out on a cot and dictates instructions to his hangers-on for mourning arrangements after he is gone. Death is mocked here, reduced to an empty form, shorn of its metaphysical implications. The last scene, on the other hand, contains the climax of the film, when Sanichari at last dissolves in great, convulsive sobs at the news of her friend (and long-lost mother) Bhikni's death. It signifies her release from a lifetime of social and psychic repression, her accession from a dehumanized state to humanization and a new existence as a professional mourner. Her life and livelihood are now linked with the death of the village landlord with which the film begins. The film's diegesis then takes place in the temporal gap between these two events that reveal the two faces of death and mourning, one artificial and orchestrated, the other genuine and deeply felt, the one social, the other personal.

Structurally, *Rudaali* seeks to reconcile these two dimensions by effecting narrative closure and resolution through the work of individual mourning which the original story intentionally leaves out. In doing so, it cocoons the harsh narrative of Sanichari's poverty-stricken life within the comforting (because familiar) conventions of the Indian film melodrama. Indeed the melodramatic mode provides the "consolations of form" (to borrow Robert Stam's phrase) in more ways than one in this film. Here one can also relate the trope of bereavement and lamentation to Santner's comment, quoted earlier, that film is about parting. Not only does Sanichari's act of weeping in the last scene provide the audience with the reassurance of her humanity despite the inhuman suffering she is subjected to in the narrative, but the recasting of that narrative itself as melodrama effects a series of shifts and reworkings that allows us to explore melodrama's own formal aspects and its complex relations to women's subjectivity and tears. What does it mean to cast Sanichari's life as melodramatic? Is there "literal" and "figurative/formal" melodrama? On the one hand it can be said that the ups and downs of the protagonist's existence, the buffettings of fortune that she is subjected to, are indeed the stuff of melodrama which is then further embellished through the use of specific formal strategies such as songs, a charged mise-en-scène, and the like. *Rudaali*'s putatively "melodramatic ending," then, added on in the film, logically builds on our associations and expectations of the form. Moreover, if this form signifies women's lives in the popular imagination and gives them meaning, *Rudaali* satisfies this expectation as well by giving Sanichari's tears in the final sequence of the film a larger significance.

Her ability to cry as she takes the place of the now-gone Bhikni as chief mourner, and the closing intertitle—"And so Sanichari became a great rudaali"—transform a life of an impoverished subaltern into that of an artist-performer. The "balance" between mourning as social ritual and private grief is reasserted, and the cinema itself projected as the means of restoring this balance in the minds of disaffected citizens. If Mahasweta Devi's story refuses the comforting scenario of such closure, Lajmi's film uses the conjunction of mourning and melodrama to reactivate the cinema as social imaginary. Through her tears, the subaltern earns her place in the social order and can be reintegrated into society.

Seen in this way, one can posit that although the critical literature on melodrama has little to say about mourning per se, the two modes have a deep affinity. The interesting question, however, is how Lajmi articulates this stance with what would appear as a lack of contestation with the dominant traditions of filmic melodrama in India. Arguably, in the present context, and for the discussion of Indian cinema generally, one could not get very far without engaging with its overpowering melodramatic tradition. This is not only because most Indian films assign a prominent place to songs and music in the articulation of the narrative, and hence fulfill the basic definition of the term *melodrama*, but also because the notion of melodrama has been central to debates around high culture and low culture, serious cinema and entertainment cinema, nation building and the "problem" of women. The challenge that *Rudaali* sets itself both formally and thematically is to combine the ethnographic impulse of social realist traditions in Indian writing and cinema with the more allegorical and symbolic propensities of film melodrama. Although it might be argued that *all* representation is ultimately allegorical, individual characters and situations being emblematic of social or universal phenomena, melodrama may be said to invert this process in that the foregrounding of the symbolic by means of mood and mis-en-scène predetermines characterological development and identifications. If social realism aims to create the impression of a precise space-time milieu, melodrama's distinctiveness lies in replaying conventional elements for the orchestration of its effects. What gives this tendency a negative aesthetic value (the "lack of realism" critique) is the association of melodrama with excessive emotion and tortuous plot development and, in the Indian context, with the use of songs (and dances) as expressive elements of narration. Both of these features have long been considered the hallmarks of the Bombay cinema, and willful detractions from the more serious concerns of art. Yet as a genre, melodrama promises a plenitude of affect, which Indian popular cinema has long seized upon as its "proper" communicative form. The failure of India's alternative cinema to capture the allegiance of mass audiences has, not without justification, been attributed to its shunning of the melodramatic elements of songs and emotionality, its gritty social realism.

As a film, *Rudaali* seeks to mediate these conventions by its ambivalent self-positioning, a fact that was reflected in its unexpected success at the box office. We can turn to these factors of production and reception for a moment. Made in 1992 by Kalpana Lajmi, young, female, and a relative newcomer to the film scene, *Rudaali* became a box-office hit and a musical sensation.[30] Produced under the auspices of government agencies (the National Film Development Corporation and the state-run television network, Doordarshan), both associated with India's "alternative cinema" traditions, it relied on established Bombay film talent in the persons of screenplay writer Gulzar and popular actress Dimple Kapadia. Based on Mahasweta Devi's short story in Bengali, it was made in an "ethnicized" Hindi (a variation of Hindi ostensibly spoken in the western state of Rajasthan), thus giving the film a broader appeal and address. And while keeping with the feminism of the original narrative by placing the subaltern, the marginal oppressed woman, at its visual and narrative center, it deflects its social radicalism by mobilizing cinematic structures of desire and romantic attachment. How and why does *Rudaali* traverse these seemingly incompatible cinematic traditions? If part of the answer lies in the filmmaker's desire to refurbish both tendencies by infusing each with its other, we must still consider the artistic and political implications of conjoining mourning and melodrama as a means to articulate subaltern consciousness.

As mentioned above, there is a perceived "natural" affinity between film melodrama and women's lives, an affinity that Mahasweta interrogates and that Lajmi explores strategically and builds upon structurally. Melodrama becomes a way of apprehending the social and psychic violence of Sanichari's life, and thus the grounds for viewer empathy and identification, while her inability to mourn a series of bereavements punctuating the diegesis moves the narrative forward. From Sanichari's own standpoint, her emotional and psychological development is deeply connected to the bitterness of a situation in which she, a bereaved woman, is unable to shed tears for her loved ones. Not only does Sanichari keep repeating this fact verbally in the flashbacks used to chronicle her life, but in one key incident early on in the film, she is driven to the verge of frenzy in trying to make herself weep. This episode follows her husband's death and involves a scene where Sanichari and her young son are working as wage laborers breaking stones on a construction site. Sanichari starts beating the stones harder and harder, as though she were trying to smash her heart turned to stone, as she repeats audibly, "Cry, Sanichari, cry, cry!" and yet the tears refuse to flow. Sanichari's obsessive need to cry becomes her link with the humanity that her lowly condition denies her, even as it signifies her inability to cut herself off emotionally from the nexus of social expectations that valorize mourning and tears as the mark of "true" womanliness.

Mourning and melodrama, then, become crucially linked in the narrative. Moreover, the demands of woman's melodrama also exert their influence on the place the domestic occupies in the film, since it is above all to notions of family and home that the melodrama as a genre points.[31] Sanichari's life unfolds through relationships with family members. First come the scenes with her mother-in-law, which serve the narrative function of situating Sanichari in her lowly lifestyle and end with the older woman's death and cremation. Then we see her as a young wife and mother, and she is briefly shown with her husband at a village fair when he contracts cholera and dies, along with half the village. The next episodes show Sanichari with her son, their loving and playful relationship, which continues into his youth but is stemmed when he brings home a prostitute as his wife. Sanichari's ideas of respectability are sorely shaken and scenes of dramatic conflict between the two women are plentiful here. This stage ends with the departure of Sanichari's son. Finally, there is Bhikni, her companion with whom Sanichari develops a tender relationship and who signifies her return to a maternal world of emotional support and comfort. Her death at last releases the floodgates of feeling without which Sanichari's subjectivity as a woman cannot be validated. Tears are portrayed as vital forces connecting a woman to a position in the social world.

If melodrama (particularly Indian melodrama) in some sense deals with a society's relationship to the ideal of suffering and to the suffering of its women, *Rudaali* draws upon a long tradition of such "idealism" in the cinema. This tradition, going back to the nineteenth-century Bengali novel, has provided the raw material for many a Bombay film and is responsible for a long history of female talent in a male-dominated industry. The dutiful wife, the suffering but unwaveringly virtuous widow, the sacrificing "other" woman, the struggling peasant woman: these roles constitute a typology within the melodramatic tradition that reaches its apotheosis in the courtesan film genre, which I have discussed elsewhere.[32] Through these roles, as much as through the tragic hero-centered melodramas that Ravi Vasudevan writes about, Indian cinema sought to explain the social impact of capitalist modernization.[33] Indeed, the classic nation-building melodrama of all time is *Mother India,* featuring the trials and tribulations of a poor, rural woman whose character becomes mythic in scope. The suffering woman, representing a continuum of values from mythology to modernity, becomes the repository of the culture's deepest hopes and fears regarding change. In deconstructing mourning in "Rudaali," Mahasweta Devi is critically examining Indian society's psychic investment in women as purveyors of suffering; and in shying away from the iconoclastic tendencies of the original, *Rudaali* is equally invested in the cinematic tradition of the idealized suffering woman. Where *Rudaali* departs from this tradition, however, is in investing its central female character with what feminists have regarded as the "true" sign of subjectivity, namely, a voice.[34]

Sanichari is as much a voice as she is a body and an image in *Rudaali.* Except for the first scene described earlier, she takes charge of her own life story and the film is structured as a series of flashbacks in which the aged Sanichari recalls different stages of her life as they are triggered off in memory. Her deep, husky voice seems to dredge up from the depth of her experiences a flow of words that give her the control over her fate, even if retrospectively, that is vital to her sense of self. She narrates her story to Bhikni, her friend whose role in the film is contrived to provide a greater sense of depth to the central character. She is Sanichari's interlocutor, her confidant and, as is later revealed, the mother who had abandoned her as a baby. Sanichari's voice takes on the plenitude that is usually reserved for tears; there is a relentlessness in her drive to narrativity that seems to compensate for her inability to weep. Unlike her screen predecessors, Sanichari can verbally counter the abuse that her social condition and her social superiors heap on her. Thus, in the first long flashback, which culminates in the death of her mother-in-law, Sanichari proves herself to be no longer the submissive daughter-in-law silently bearing the former's harangue. She preempts it by mimicking the village folk's common perception of her as "Sanichari, the ill-fated one, born on a Saturday, swallowed up her father the moment she arrived, the cursed one," all delivered in a sing-song voice. In her hut as she feeds her young son, and he asks her if the medicine for his grandmother will cure her of her illness, Sanichari responds, "God forbid!" In another sequence, when the village moneylender and the headman (who, along with the Brahmin priest, form the triumvirate of oppression in the world of Bombay films) accuse Sanichari of resorting to the world's oldest profession to support herself, she lashes out at them, calling them pimps and thieves who are social vampires fattening on the blood of others. Throughout the film, her quick verbal retorts signal the emancipation of her screen persona from the image of the silent suffering woman.

Yet if speech confers on the protagonist the mark of an enunciating subject and legitimizes the film as a feminist text, what of the body and its "spectacular" needs? How is female desire and pleasure invoked and represented? Here again melodrama (with its foregrounding of music and song) provides the means for the representation of women's emotional and psychic being. For if speech marks the paradigmatic dimension of the film, its social realist high points, then the syntagmatic or horizontal dimension, the structural base of melodrama, as it were, constitutive of emotion and bodily expressivity, is articulated through music and song. *Rudaali's* hauntingly beautiful musical score serves as a rhythmic under-current of emotional intensity throughout the film along with its moments of spectacle. At the beginning of the film, as the credits roll, the film's theme song plays on the soundtrack while the image track shows five women mourners in silhouette vigorously dancing in unison. The words of the song appeal to time's relentless flow to stop, and this refer-ence to fluidity is reinforced through the flow of music connecting the different episodes in Sanichari's life. Music, as Carol Flinn shows us, has been associated with femininity, emotions and the maternal body, an association that is denigrated by male critics and theorists.[35] Although the central role of music and song in Indian popular cinema means that it is not restricted to the subgenres of "women's films," the general tendency among Indian film critics and serious filmmakers to regard songs as redundant dressing up, does signal some similar patterns of response at work. *Rudaali's* use of songs, both diegetically motivated and as back-ground score, then, can be considered as stylistic markings on the body of the film text that accommodate both the desire of the narrative subject and the pleasure of the desiring spectator denied in the ideological con-ception of the art cinema. The first flashback contains a song in which Sanichari is closest to the traditional Hindi film heroine dancing and singing in an unexpected downpour of rain. As though pulling back from such indulgence, the filmmaker "closes off" these instances of libidinal desire by a repetitive scenario of death or calamity that visits Sanichari with fatalistic regularity. Perhaps the film's uncertainty about positioning women as caught between voice and body, belonging to herself or to society's image of her, is best reflected in Sanichari's brief liaison with the younger lord of the village. In this episode, included in the film as an obvious concession to the box office, Sanichari and Laxman Singh become each other's unattainable objects of desire. From his higher class and caste position, he can afford to invite her into his own social space, although it can only be as his concubine. Sanichari rejects such a role for herself, but is clearly torn by the vision of a protected and comfortable life that she cannot have on her own. Like the expansive desert landscape in which the film is shot (both suggesting and abolishing limits) and the meeting of gazes with which Laxman Singh seeks to bind Sanichari to himself in a utopic space, romance between these characters can only be possible in a general ambiance of nostalgia and longing.

CONCLUSION

Death and mourning have long been treated as gendered categories, the contemplation of the meaning of death the preoccupation of male philosophers and thinkers, the activity of mourning and weeping the domain mostly of women. Here is perhaps an instance when women are allowed to "speak" through their bodies, since mourning is linked to natural, affective responses to loss and bereavement, a society's inability to mourn the mark of a deep malaise. In her fiction, Mahasweta Devi both registers this malaise as characterizing life in postcolonial India, particularly for the gendered subaltern, and rejects any easy redemptive signifiers such as mourning. The bodies of women, she seems to be saying in "Rudaali," cannot mourn, they must *be* mourned. Only when this specific task is undertaken and women themselves put in charge of their bodies can the nation-state lay claim to any conception of unity or nationhood.

NOTES

1. Gayatri Chakravorty Spivak, "Can the Subaltern Speak?" In *The Post-Colonial Studies Reader*, ed. Bill Ashcroft, Gareth Griffiths, and Helen Tiffin (New York: Routledge, 1995), 24–28.

2. See Howard Winant, "Gayatri Spivak on the Politics of the Subaltern," *Socialist Review,* vol. 20 (1990), pp. 81–97.

3. See F. E. Peters, *Greek Philosophical Terms: A Historical Lexicon* (New York: New York University Press, 1967) for a more detailed account of the various associations connected with this term.

4. Caren Kaplan and Inderpal Grewal, "Transnational Feminist Cultural Studies: Beyond the Marxism/Poststructuralism/Feminism Divides," *Positions* 2:2 (1994): 437.

5. Mitchell Stephens, "Jacques Derrida." *The New York Times.* Jan 23, 1994.

6. Henry Staten, *Eros in Mourning: Homer to Lacan.* Baltimore, Md.: Johns Hopkins University Press, 1995.

7. Eric Santner, *Stranded Objects: Mourning, Memory and Film in Postwar Germany.* Ithaca, N.Y.: Cornell University Press, 1990.

8. A. K. Ramanujan, trans. *Samskara: A Rite for a Dead Man* (Delhi: Oxford University Press, 1978), 139.

9. Gail Holst-Warhaft, *Dangerous Voices: Women's Laments and Greek Literature.* New York: Routledge, 1992.

10. Ibid.

11. Sigmund Freud, "Mourning and Melancholia." *Collected Papers,* vol. 4. Trans. Joan Riviere. London: Hogarth Press, 1949.

12. See Santner, pp. 3–13.

13. Raymond Williams, *The Politics of Modernism.* (London: Verso, 1989), 195.

14. Partha Chatterjee, *The Nation and Its Fragments: Colonial and Postcolonial Histories* (Princeton, N.J.: Princeton University Press, 1993), 154.

15. Susie Tharu and K. Lalita, eds. *Women Writing in India,* vol. 2 (New York: Feminist Press, 1993), 43–44.

16. Ibid.

17. In the long introduction to their two-volume anthology devoted to women's writing, for instance, the editors mention the cinema only once in a footnote.

18. Veena Das, "Subaltern as Perspective," in Guha, Ranajit, ed. *Subaltern Studies* VI. Delhi: Oxford University Press, 1989.

19. Gyanendra Pandey, "The Prose of Otherness," in Guha, ed. *Subaltern Studies* VIII. Delhi: Oxford University Press, 1994.

20. Partha Chatterjee, *The Nation and Its Fragments*, 151–57.

21. Ibid, 154.

22. Ibid, 156.

23. Mahasweta Devi, *Imaginary Maps*. Translated and introduced by Gayatri Chakravorty Spivak. New York: Routledge, 1995.

24. Elaine Scarry, *The Body in Pain: The Making and Unmaking of the World* (New York: Oxford University Press), 14.

25. Judy Burns, ed. "An Interview with Gayatri Spivak." *Women and Performance* 5:1, no. 9 (1990).

26. Mahasweta Devi, "Breast Giver," in Gayatri Spivak, *In Other Worlds* (New York and London: Methuen, 1987), 222.

27. Mahasweta Devi, "Draupadi" in Spivak, *In Other Worlds*, 195.

28. Mahasweta Devi, "Children" in Tharu and Lalita, *Women Writing in India*, vol. 2, 250.

29. For a brief but suggestive comment linking mourning and the nation in terms of relieving "the burden of history," see Hayden White, "The Modernist Event" in Vivian Sobchack, ed., *The Persistence of History* (New York: Routledge, 1995).

30. The cost of production was rupees six million, profits were rupees twelve million. The film was released in ten theaters and on video from which it got 40 percent of its revenues. It was shown once on television and made $2 million. The soundtrack is very popular and over a million audio cassettes have been sold. Each cassette sold for Rs. 29, which is high for a cassette. (I am indebted to Radha Subramanium for these details.)

31. See Thomas Elsaesser, "Tales of Sound and Fury: Observations on the Family Melodrama" and other essays in Christine Gledhill, ed., *Home Is Where the Heart Is: Studies in Melodrama and the Woman's Film*. London: BFI, 1987.

32. See chapter 8 of my *National Identity in Indian Popular Cinema, 1947–1987* (Austin: University of Texas Press, 1993).

33. Ravi Vasudevan, "The Melodramatic Mode and the Commercial Hindi Cinema," *Screen* 30, 3 (summer 1989): 29–51.

34. For the idea of the female voice as articulated in cinema, see Kaja Silverman, *The Acoustic Mirror: The Female Voice in Psychoanalysis and Cinema* (Indianapolis: Indiana University Press, 1988).

35. Carol Flinn, "The 'Problem' of Femininity in Theories of Film Music," *Screen* 27, 6 (Nov.–Dec. 1986): 57–72.

CHAPTER NINE

Sacando los trapos al sol (airing dirty laundry) in Lourdes Portillo's Melodocumystery, The Devil Never Sleeps

ROSA LINDA FREGOSO

In narratives of migration, the return to the homeland is meant to soothe the psyche, re-member the broken strands of personal memory and history, and offer refuge to subjects of forced or voluntary exile and migration. In *The Devil Never Sleeps,* Portillo rethreads her ties to the homeland, severed by disruptions, fluctuations, and dispersals inherent in the process of migration. With this film, Portillo reenacts the desire common among transfrontera subjects to locate the "truth" of one's existence in a mythic or literal journey back to the homeland. The return is therapeutic, a return to the mirror image, the preoedipal of the psyche, to childhood dreams, broken visions—a return to the self, which for the Chicana is rooted in the extended family. *The Devil Never Sleeps* opens in a tone of self-reflexive irreverence, a shot of moving water, dissolving into a silver-framed portrait of Santa Rita, draped in nun's attire, flowers adorning the lower part of the frame, accompanied by the voice of the narrator/filmmaker.

"When I dream of home, something always slips away from me, just beneath the surface. Faces of my family, old stories, the land, mysteries about to be revealed. And sometimes I dream of Santa Rita, patron saint of Chihuahua, my hometown. She is also the patron saint of unhappy marriages, boils, and desperate causes." With this opening sequence, the film summons me to enter the universe of excess and familiarity it creates. The film abounds with spaces and gaps, resuscitating distant memories for me. Even the film's title, its linguistic play on words, is taken from a proverbial wisdom intimately familiar: the *dichos* (proverbs) spoken by my father and grandmother. Yet in the return to her homeland, Portillo treads in utterly fragile and uncertain terrain. By confronting the self through the extended family, this Chicana filmmaker awakens her familial demons and heterogeneous fragmentariness, discovering that there is no solace nor resolution in this narrative of return. For in the end, the return to the "primal scene" is elusive, unpredictable, and riddled with unintended effects.

Audience response to *The Devil Never Sleeps*:

> FEMALE VIEWER NUMBER ONE: I think it's an irony, how telenovelas are such a real part of our lives. I am Mexican. It's not what we watch, it's what we live. And I don't know if we are imitating the telenovela or if the telenovela is imitating our life. It gets to a point where there is really no answer to any mystery.
>
> MALE VIEWER: A hole, an absence at the center of the film. I think it's quite strong. Actually, it makes me very angry, this film. It never seeks to find the truth. It specifically avoids asking difficult questions . . . all these implications of political murder, possible homosexuality, ecology, nothing is stated, it's only implied. [The film] is creating a nexus of implications which the film refuses to deal with directly. Because to deal with [them] directly would undercut the primary premise of the film, which is the impossibility of creating history.
>
> FEMALE VIEWER NUMBER TWO: What she is doing cinematically is the revealing of things you are not supposed to see. She is revealing all these things that would be the illusions, very explicitly, out in the open. . . . She reveals all of that because of the rough edges. And she does that beautifully. . . . I don't even think that she is trying to say that she is looking for the truth.[1]

While uncertainty frames the narrative logic, death provides the plot with its point of departure. The next shot in the film is a closeup of a hand dialing an antiquated rotary telephone. The narrator continues: "It all started when I received a phone call that my favorite uncle, my Tio Oscar, had died. Immediately I called his widow, Ofelia." The unresolved death of Oscar Ruiz Almeida furnishes the plot for Portillo's border-crossing narrative. Tio Oscar dies under mysterious circumstances in Chihuahua, also the birthplace of the Mexican caudillo, Pancho Villa. An enigmatic figure who had risen from laborer to rancher, whose business ventures included large-scale construction, exporting vegetables, constructing a landing strip for the Hollywood film *Catch-22*, minting and selling gold coins (commemorating Pope John Paul's visit to Mexico), and whose ties to the ruling party's apparatus guaranteed him tenure as City Mayor, Tio Oscar is found dead one morning in a sports complex. Official accounts rule his death a suicide, whereas some family members and friends suspect murder; his mysterious death propels the filmmaker's exploration.

Starring as niece-detective-documentarist, Portillo leads an investigation into the death of her beloved uncle, utilizing his life to weave the strands of her inquiry. In searching for the truth behind his death, Portillo discovers that there is no singular truth or singular meaning, that the hierarchical organization of knowledge is neither plausible nor possible. [Figure 9.1] At the end of this film, Portillo provides no solution to the unresolved death, no certainty except for death. Instead, she constructs a field both heterogeneous and rich in plurality, which is thematically, and at the level of formal experimentation, metonymically linked to her own subjective narrative of return. And in so doing, the filmmaker goes against the grain of "official" documentary discourse, exposing the limits of its wisdom.

Long associated with "truth" and the "quest for knowledge," the documentary's authority derives from its privileged relation to social and historical "reality." The documentary's verisimilitude links it to the factual as opposed to the fictional and grounds it on actual or "real" historical events or problems. As an explanatory discourse on the real, the documentary is often organized in terms of well-established techniques for communicating truth: interviews, actuality footage, and the narrator's voice. While *The Devil Never Sleeps* is steeped in the documentary mode of representation, abiding by many of its techniques, the filmmaker rejects the pretense of objectivity, scientificity, or truth, but readily

FIGURE 9.1. Seance scene. Courtesy of Lourdes Portillo.

acknowledges her own partiality and perspectivity. One way the film accomplishes this is through the portrayal of Portillo as main protagonist in its narrative reality. The multiple screen roles occupied by Portillo, the persona of a novice detective, professional documentarist, and cathectic niece, subvert the documentary convention of objectivity and distance, insofar as the narrator's voice shifts from personal recollections (niece) to critical observation (filmmaker) to semiscientific inquiry (detective) to irreverent penitence (Catholic Chicana). Yet it is not just these multiple inflections in the narrator's voice but rather the on-screen presence of the filmmaker (and not simply as a character in the story) which renders problematic the status of documentary discourse, for the on-screen location of Portillo's visual range serves to further destabilize visual transparency.

In conventional documentary, the dominance of the visual hierarchically structures space in terms of a centralized, singularized point of view, namely the filmmaker's visual range aligned with that of the camera's. And it is, in part, the on-screen absence of the filmmaker's visual range (perspectivity) that gives film its veneer of transparency. *The Devil Never Sleeps* subverts the dominance of this hierarchical structure in several scenes where the filmmaker is portrayed wearing polarized sunglasses reflecting the object of her (the camera's) gaze for spectators. The reflections captured in the sunglasses transform "transparent" images into mirror images, specular reflections of interviewees, thereby making evident the reciprocity of sight—that is to say, how the filmmaker (camera) sees, as well as how she (it) is seen by an external witness. The doubling effect of the filmmaker's sunglasses functions like a split screen, producing split subjects, subject and object, suspended in the filmmaker's (camera's) gaze. Thus, the specular reflection of interviewees, filmed from the position of the interviewees' field of vision, deconstructs the dominance of a centralized or singularized point of view. While Portillo developed the "mirror" as a literal metaphor designed to capture her "own" mental reflections as she was making the film, more often these literal mirror reflections produce a virtual reality effect for spectators, suggesting culturally specific modes for representing social reality.

The filmmaker thus refuses to constitute a singular discourse on the basis of interpretation but instead formulates a plurality of versions. The strategic overlap of multiple modes of representation derived from distinct genres makes visible this refusal to privilege the documentary as the singular mode for interpreting and apprehending the social field. And

while the film reconstructs its plurality from a montage of modern techniques for gathering and classifying knowledge in documentary discourse
(the interview, footage from home movies, photo stills, actuality footage,
narration), the director complicates the status of "official" documentary
discourse within the film by drawing from other culturally specific forms
of knowledge more properly associated with the space of the "popular."
Specifically Portillo pursues clues and facts from popular forms of knowledge and experience, that is to say those "disqualified" or "inadequate"
sources of knowledge passed on in the form of legends, gossip, telenovelas, canciones rancheras, myth, proverbial wisdom, in sum, forms which
for Foucault represent "a particular, local, regional knowledge, a differential knowledge incapable of unanimity" (Foucault, p. 82). These sources
of knowledge are at odds with the modernist project of certainty, uniformity, and absolute truth, associated with "official" documentary discourse, for "popular" knowledges are often partial, contradictory, ambivalent, and in a conflictual relation with one dominant, singular
interpretation of social reality. Thus Portillo pursues the task of producing "truth" concerning Tio Oscar's death by juxtaposing "popular" with
"official" forms of knowledge, refusing to privilege one form over the
other.

This strategy is evident in the scene in which Portillo interviews Tia
Luz about Tio Oscar's conjugal relations. Pursuing a lead that implicates
Ofelia (Tio Oscar's widow) in the murder/suicide, the filmmaker begins
her inquiry with a question regarding the sexual affairs of the couple. The
scene opens with a shot of Tia Luz, expressing her visible reluctance to
entertain such an intimate question. Yet, upon further probing, Luz is
quick to confess the "truth" about the intimacies of the couple including
a conversation she had with Ofelia after her honeymoon with Tio Oscar
in which she revealed the proof of her virginity in "bloody panties." What
is striking about this scene is the manner in which Tia Luz's "official" testimony (interview) is structurally reconstructed by the filmmaker as thematically suspended and visually framed within two other "popular"
modes of representation: the telenovela and the legend. Tia Luz's off-
screen voice accompanies a sequence of shots depicting a mannequin
dressed in a wedding dress, shot through a bridal store's showcase while
public spectators look up adoringly at the mannequin, and culminates in
an over-the-shoulder pin-hole shot of Tia Luz watching the Brazilian
telenovela, "Roque Santeiro." From her confession about Ofelia's "indiscretions," Tia Luz turns with ease to a frivolous interpretation of plot

details from the telenovela, thus supplanting the narrative value of the former, since for Tia Luz one account has the same relevance as the other. As
the camera zooms in to the television set, the visual and narrative focus
shifts away from the interview to the telenovela, affecting a slippage
between two forms of discourse, the "official" interview and the more
properly "popular" discourse of the telenovela. In this instance as well as
in other places throughout the film, the strategic use of the telenovela
blurs the distinction between "reality" and "tele-reality." Yet, closure is not
anchored in the telenovela but rather slides to a distinct popular discourse, the legend, thereby further complicating the status of truth in this
film.

The narrative shifts once again by crosscutting to a closeup of the
bridal mannequin's face. Portillo's narrator-voice interjects: "There's a legend that the owner of a Chihuahua bridal shop had a daughter she dearly
loved. On the day of her wedding the daughter died in an accident. The
bereaved mother had her embalmed, dressed up as a bride and displayed
in her store window. A tribute to virginal love." Carefully crafted shots of
people looking up intently at the bridal mannequin suggest that the legend of the embalmed virgin captivates these spectators just as it secures
their alignment with those of us outside the screen who have been nurtured on Mexican fantastic stories of family ghosts and spirits, the
macabre flavor in legends of enchanted statues and embalmed saints, as
we too wonder about the legend's uncanny truth. The final shot of this
scene depicts store attendants raising the mannequin's (embalmed virgin's?) bridal gown, allowing us to glimpse beneath her dress as if to prove
the truth of the legend, and further cements my eerie bewilderment ("this
really must be the embalmed virgin; her face looks so real"). At this precise moment, the film resuscitates a distant glimmering from the past. I
travel to the "marvelous real" of my childhood memories—a visit to
Guadalajara's majestic cathedral where I stand before the statue of the
"child-saint," encased within a glass vitrine. My wide-eyed gaze rests on
the delicate, statuesque, feminine figure, with its long eyelashes and seemingly porous texture, as my Tia Fina whispers that we are witnessing a
miracle incarnate: "This is not really a statue, it's the actual body of a
young girl." I nod, fixated on those realistic features of the immobile girl
who refused decomposure and as a result was bestowed the gift of everlasting embodiment and canonization. Curiously, until this cinematic
moment of the "legend of the embalmed virgin," my childhood
encounter with the magical remained submerged in my psyche, unscruti-

nized by the laws of reason and rational discourse. Yet, it undoubtedly structures my beliefs and relation to the "real." Thus, depending on one's belief system the truth of the legend of the embalmed virgin seems just as plausible as the truth in Tia Luz's testimony of Ofelia's own account of her virginity.

In some respects, the legend's location in this scene has less to do with the process of gathering empirical evidence or "knowledge" for documentary truth and more to do with underscoring the veracity of popular forms of knowledge for making sense of one's reality. Reading the scene against the grain, the legend appears in conflictual relation to the interview, mapping the centrality of the cult of virginity in Mexican society. Insofar as Tia Luz's interpretation of Ofelia's virginity gains significance within the ideological framework of patriarchy, the scene highlights how we are all subjected and interpellated by familial and political apparatuses. The legend of the embalmed virgin gives meaning to this process, revealing how women in Mexico are both victims and agents, targets and vehicles of patriarchal discourse's sublimation of female sexuality in the figure of the Virgin.

If for the exacting viewer, family gossip, trivial talk about telenovelas, the hidden message behind legends, appear like tracks that lead nowhere, like clues that get one further away from solving Tio Oscar's mysterious death, perhaps it is because the force of the narrative directs viewers elsewhere, down a different path, further into the family's web. Like the legend, popular discourses of *telenovelas* and *rancheras* lead us into the Mexican family melodrama, with its themes of excess and repression, forbidden pleasure, seduction, suicide, illicit passion, sin, and repentance. In Mexico, the family melodrama is an entrée into the psychical life of the family and figures as the site of displacement, the domain in which the unspeakable may be framed and named. Portillo punctuates the documentary with the desires and interdictions typical of *telenovelas* and *rancheras*, exposing thus the intimate links between popular culture and the institution of the family.

Despite the priest's warning to Portillo about violating "another's personal intimacy," she crosses the imaginary divide between the public and the private, and divulges "la familia's" private affairs. Directing our attention to the toll that this transgression exacts on a Chicana, the scene at the acupuncture clinic portrays Portillo as the main protagonist, parodying the method she resorts to for absolving herself of pain and guilt. [Figure 9.2] The scene opens with a close up of Portillo's face under-

FIGURE 9.2. Acupuncture. Courtesy of Lourdes Portillo.

going treatment with puncturing needles, while her voice-over addresses us: "Sin, that's really bad news for a Catholic. Even a lapsed one gets shivers up her spine. Have I crossed the boundary of concern into manipulation? Is it a sin to look for the truth? I've gone too far to stop." But what is really bad news for this Chicana Catholic is the fact that she transgresses the artificial boundary between the public and the private; namely, that she makes available for public scrutiny the truths and falsities hidden behind the familial veil of secrecy and privacy. [Figure 9.3]

The filmmaker violates a cultural taboo forbidding the public disclosure of family matters—a taboo so sacred even Mexican políticos are bound by its strictures. It is a cultural taboo that circulates in the political arena in a form known as La Mordaza (the muzzle)—a gag order requiring former presidents to remain silent in political matters pertaining to the "familia" of the Institutional Revolutionary Party, even though they are no longer public servants. To the extent that the political apparatus of the PRI is based on the model of "la familia," Portillo's foray into the intimate realm of family affairs undermines the very foundation of Mexican patriarchy.

By transgressing the sacred covenant regarding public discussions of private family matters, The Devil Never Sleeps blurs the distinction between the private and the public, thus linking its project with feminist concerns about "la familia" as an element in power relations and as a form of domination in the microstructures of everyday life. Given its centrality in the sphere of domesticity, "la familia" plays a fundamental role in upholding the law of the father and the subjugation of women. As feminists of color note, the naturalization of male privilege and hegemony derives its force from a reluctance to contest the "idealized notion" of a monolithic community and, by extension, "the family romance on which this notion of community relies" (Smith, p. 381). Portillo breaks the silence around family unity and the family myth-making enterprise so central to Mexican and Chicana/o culture, and deconstructs attributes of Chicana/o (and Mexican) families, "including familism (beliefs and behavior associated with family solidarity), compadrazgo (extended family via godparents), confianza (a system of trust and intimacy)" (Segura and Pierce, p. 72).

Since the 1960s Chicana/o nationalists have invoked the "family . . . as the righteous causa" (Moraga, p. 131). Their investment in a single coherent representation of "la familia" can be traced to the "master narrative" of Mexican nationalism "with its appeal to rootedness, to place, and

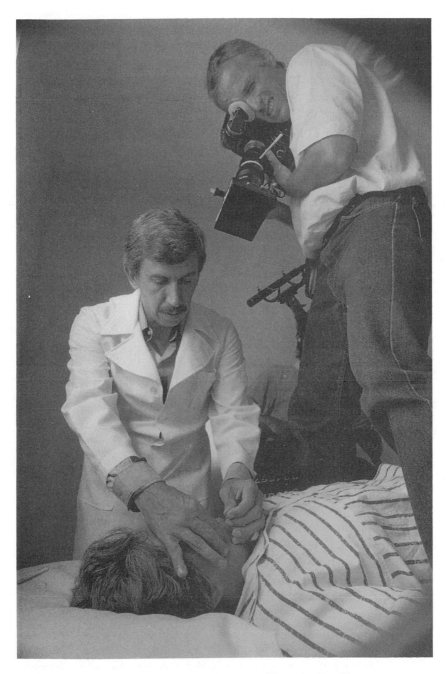

FIGURE 9.3. Filming acupuncture. Courtesy of Lourdes Portillo.

to community" (Franco, p. 135) Thus, the family is at the foundation of a protonationalist discourse on "community loyalty," and the mechanisms for its reproduction arise out of the strict division between the private and the public, the family/community as an internal sanctuary against external, outsider threats. Singlehandedly targeting the normativity of the attributes of "familism" and "*confianza,*" *The Devil Never Sleeps* serves as an instrument for criticizing Chicana/o and Mexican nationalism, for these very attributes also operate as twin pillars for endowing family mythologies, effacing its contradictions, and naturalizing male privilege. By taking her favorite uncle as subject matter, Portillo breaks Chicanas' investment in the "intertwined notions of family and community," in the artificial division between the public and private spheres, in "la familia" as a sacred institution. Positioned simultaneously as insider-outsider, Portillo liberates the family from its shroud of secrecy and publicly unveils its private face, exposing, not the blessed, untouchable, holy family, but the family as a site of conflict and contestation.

Combining the "official" voice-over of the external narrator with her personal view as a character, her role as outsider-insider, Portillo intrudes into her own family affairs, courageously exposing the hypocrisy, gossip, contradictory testimony of the widow, aunts and uncles, nieces and nephews. In this manner, Portillo directs viewers' attention to the mechanisms by which family members not only invest but also play a central role in reproducing the institution of "la familia." In an irreverent style that is also uniquely poignant, the filmmaker forsakes another uncle's admonition, rendered in Mexican proverbial wisdom ("if it is delicate to speak of the honor of a woman, it is much more delicate to speak of the honor of a man") and proceeds to dethrone her Tio Oscar. Through a montage of home movies, photo stills, and interviews, Portillo creates a composite of Tio Oscar that radically defies the sanitized image enshrined not simply in family members' recollections but also in her own childhood memories. The film exposes a man riddled with contradictions. Behind the happy smiles captured in idyllic home movies is an anguished man, tormented by the extravagance of his life, haunted by the choices he has made: Tio Oscar's vain quest for everlasting life through plastic surgery, acupuncture, injections of cattle hormones, his sexual indiscretions, closeted homosexuality, infidelities, bad business dealings, and direct contribution to environmental pollution. Insofar as *The Devil Never Sleeps* tracks a persistent path in the disintegration of a distressed man whose life choices undermined him, and a trail of family secrecy, deception, and machinations, the film positions spectators at the inter-section of the micro- and macrostructures of everyday life in Mexico. Por-tillo's family is a microcosm of Mexico's national melodrama.

As the political telenovela about the PRI autocratic family unfolded in 1995, Gabriel Garcia Marquez told Carlos Fuentes, "We are going to have to throw our books into the sea. We've been totally defeated by real-ity." For months the scandal of PRI machinations with their telenovela proportions has gripped the country—including the murder of a Catholic Cardinal in 1993, the assassination of the Secretary General of the PRI, José Francisco Ruíz Massieu the following year, the implication of his own brother, Mario, in the assassination along with Raul, brother of former president of Mexico, Carlos Salinas de Gortari, who in turn staged a hunger strike to rescue his honor, and later fled the country for exile in Cuba. Combined with Mexico's devastating economic crisis and state repression of dissenting voices, this spectacle of scandal and corruption has produced a general breakdown of the country's social psyche. But public disenchantment has not necessarily led to nihilism and self-efface-ment, for the PRI autocracy's corruption also forms the virtual backdrop for new expressions of oppositional cultural politics that examine and interrogate political institutions and social structures, including Mexico's sacred "family."

It is within this critical context that I situate the strategy of "telling secrets" in *The Devil Never Sleeps*. By telling family secrets of betrayal, intrigues, and excess, the filmmaker articulates the private with the pub-lic, the familial with the political, the specific with the general, revealing the seams of historical structures that repress genuine human equality, self-expression, and freedom. Indicative of a subtle yet potent movement in new Latin American cinema that for B. Ruby Rich expresses "collective subjectivity," the film creates "a new form for looking inward, that offers the possibility of a radical break with the past." Portillo does not provide us with a narrative closure, a solution to this mystery, nor with an abso-lute truth based on facts and confessions, but with "partial truths," with a path that offers this possibility of breaking with the past. Embracing the uncertainty and heterogeneous fragmentariness with which *The Devil Never Sleeps* begins, Portillo positions the self at the crossroads of incom-pleteness, the interstices between the local and the national, the public and the private, "official" facts and subjective memories, genres of repre-sentational discourse, cultural systems. By opening up a space for telling those repressed family secrets, Portillo sets a precedent for Chicana filmmaking. In so doing, the filmmaker provides a site through which a Chicana can speak from the position of a transfrontera subject engaged in a search for alternative political forms of struggle and collectivity. For by reenacting a continual crossing of frontiers, the transfrontera subject operates within and outside of traditions and communities.

AUTHOR'S INTERVIEW WITH LOURDES PORTILLO
(Summer 1994, San Francisco, California)

Q: How did the idea for the topic (investigating Tio Oscar's death) come about? or why did you decide to do a film about this subject matter?

A: I've been making heroic, celebratory films about Chicano culture. So at first, I didn't even think about making a film about Tio Oscar's death, actually I thought it was my personal life but I was really obsessed with everything that was happening after he died. And I kept telling Ruby, "Oh, this happened today, and guess what happened? and so and so called, and somebody found this out." And that's all I talked about for days and days. And she said, "Well, you should make a film about that." And it had never really sunk in that that's the kind of film that I would like to make. I had always wanted to make these other kinds of films, that were celebratory and heroic. So I thought, yes this is my chance to do this. This needs to be done. Do something very, very subjective. So that's how it came about, with my own obsession with everything that was happening. And also, which is funny to me because I think that there's a kind of distancing from the real subjective experience in terms of Chicano film that there is that wall that you have to break. And you have to come to terms with your own existence and who you are. And that is as valid as for example a film that celebrates the Chicano Moratorium or what have you.

Q: Tell me about the preproduction elements that went into the shooting. What kind of obstacles or paths did you have to clear?

A: The emotional obstacles were the biggest because I had to go back to Mexico, where I had not been in a long time, to my birthplace. I had not been to Chihuahua in the last fifteen years. And I had to be confronted with the past that I loved so much. And that was so much a part of everything that I ever aspired to. It was like heaven, going back to Mexico. But I also was very afraid because I knew that I had to be confronted with the fact that my grandmother didn't live anymore, some of my aunts and uncles were dead. So I knew that there were going to be a lot of painful things. More painful yet than finding out who my uncle was because, who my uncle was, was a known. But what was unknown to me at first was my emotional reaction to my birthplace.

Q: How did you prepare in order to be able to face these emotional aspects?

A: One of the things I did was I made phone calls to make contact with my cousins, especially one of them who I had never met. And it was exciting and it was distressing at the same time. Basically I spoke to my mother and father at length. They prepared me, they would go over many things for me that would enable me to cope with it once I got there. Other than that I didn't have any other preparations. I think, the thing with my parents was the most significant. They talked to me, they reminded me of places, they reminded me of my childhood.

Q: You are a central character in the film. And that used to be considered an avant-garde technique. Now it seems to be more common in film, especially in documentaries, to center the producer of the film; it's what Bill Nichols terms the "self-reflexive" style in the documentary form, a style that is more in use today. Could you talk about the function of the filmmaker's presence in the film?

A: Within the framework of my entire work and the importance of bringing forth Chicano filmmakers, I felt that it was important for me to be a part of the film at this point. I never felt that I would be one of the central characters of the film, so this was the first time. I was encouraged by the crew and by my friends who said, "just go ahead and do it, put yourself in the film." It's important to have that image for many reasons: a middle-aged woman, with gray hair, a Chicana. That's not what you see, that's unusual, it's not what you typically see in films.

Q: How did it come about, the decision to insert yourself in the film? Did you plan it? Or was it something that came about organically?

A: Before I shot, I went to Mexico. I went to see all my family and I did preinterviews to determine who I was going to interview on film. And I tried to reach my uncle's widow and she said "Okay, well, I'll think about it." She basically gave me a tenuous answer. And, my cousin who knows her quite well said, "Come on, Ofelia, its gonna look bad if you're not in the film. You should be a part of the film." And Ofelia responded, "Well, I'm going to think about it. And when she comes back, by then I'll have decided." So I knew at that moment that she wasn't going to be a part of the film. So when I came back and I proposed to her, "why don't you be a part of the film?" she said, "Absolutely not. I will not be in the film." So at that moment I realized that she was not going to be in the film, so I was going to put her in the film by hook or crook. And in fact, I would put myself in the film talking to her. So that's when the decision was made, very much at the beginning of the filming.

Q: When you talked to your family in Mexico, what did you tell them you were doing? What kind of a film? How did you present the subject matter?

A: I told them that I was going to make a film about my uncle. My uncle was a very much admired character in the whole familial scene. And they imagined that I would just make a film about all the great things that he did and all the wonderful things that he was. And they all agreed to do it. Some of them, the more intelligent ones, looked at me with a jaundiced eye and said, "hum" [Lourdes laughs].

Q: Did you find out things during the process about your uncle that you didn't know before? I mean he was your favorite uncle, and when we have favorite uncles, we tend to idealize them. And I'm just wondering if you found out some things, in the process of filming, that you didn't know about before?

A: I felt that I found out that my uncle, at the same time that he was very intelligent and able, was also very disabled, very ineffectual, as an emotional human being. That he really lacked a lot of things. And it enabled me to see a lot of the frailties of the upbringing that he had, and that generation had. So it was hard to see that. It was hard to see that a man who was so strong was at the same time so weak. That was one of the things that I discovered that made me feel, I guess you grow up and you find these things out. Aside from that, the whole thing about him being gay, I don't know if he was or wasn't, it's really kind of irrelevant. I think that men who have a lot of power are really polysexual. I mean they are avaricious in terms of the things they want to have, not just in terms of money but in terms of sexual things.

Q: My next question has to do with the overall structure of the film. Were there any major changes in terms of the way you perceived your subject matter, because we all have a general idea about what our finished product will look like, but in some cases, something happens to alter our perceptions drastically. Did you experience a similar situation?

A: No. What I set out to do, to make a film about family interactions, to make a film about gossip, about hearsay, a person's rise and demise, I pretty much expected that. The only thing that was a surprise was this whole thing about my uncle being "gay." That was totally unknown to me. And also the willingness of some of the members of my family to kind of sell him down the river, that was surprising.

Q: Were you ever frightened during the making of the film?

A: Oh yeah, I had a lot of fear. I felt like, I really believe that some people are innately bad and that there is evil in the world. And somehow I was always overshadowed by my own fear of his widow because she was so unwilling to cooperate and she had such a bad reputation within my family. So I had the notion that she was capable of doing anything. And I was actually afraid of her and her willingness to harm me, but she didn't know what I was doing really.

Q: Ofelia, to me, is a pitiful character, and I identify with her not because I'm that way, but because I feel like she is being set up, by you, the filmmaker, by some of the other family members. Because she's from a different class and she comes off as a person who is manipulative but at the same time there's a way that I kind of understand that person. I feel sorry for her. And I remember at the Pacific Film Archive's screening, talking to Jerry Garcia of the Grateful Dead, and he said to me that he liked Ofelia too. So I wonder if you ever foresaw that you would have people in the audience sympathetic to her? That some people would like her.

A: Oh when I met her she was immensely likeable. I have good memories of her. She was really exciting and lots of fun. I can't entirely dismiss the experiences that most of the members of the family had over the course of twenty years with her. Aside from being a family that has the natural prejudices of people of their class, they are also compassionate human beings. If this was a woman that came from a humble birth and was a good woman, and you knew it, there's nothing in the world that would stop them from liking her. The whole notion of class would be totally thrown out the window. My family never mentions that she is from a different class. I mention it and I don't think that that is their point. The bottom line is that she was not a good person to my uncle and she was not good to his children.

Q: Let's turn to style and form. You coined the term *melodocumystery* to describe the film.

A: Well, I didn't want the film to be a documentary in the traditional, North American documentarian tradition. But I wanted "melodrama" to be a part of my film, and I knew that in some way it would turn some people off because that's not what Americans like. Americans don't like this kind of melodrama. But I was bent on doing it. And it's a mystery because there's things that I don't know, that we try to discover. And it's docu, because it's documentary. One of my main objectives was really to make melodrama a part of a documentary which is really not done. It's kept separate. In traditional documentaries, there's a sense of objectivity in documentary where you're not supposed to feel strong feelings. And that's what melodrama is about, the exaggeration of drama.

Q: How do the storytelling techniques of *The Devil Never Sleeps* differ from others?

A: Deviating from the norm, from what I've seen and what my experience has been in the United States, is that the storytelling is always very logical, and one thing follows another so that ultimatelly you come to some conclusion. Well, I had the privilege of meeting a Mauri filmmaker in New Zealand, Maurita Mita. And she saw the film and she adored it, she really loved it. She told me that one of the things she loved about the film was that the storytelling is not linear or horizontal, it's a vertical story, the way we tell stories. That a story can go on for years, you can be telling a story by not only directly linking fact to fact but also by branching out and telling other stories, and then come back to the facts. And yes that's exactly the kind of story that this documentary tells. And I think that for that reason it breaks the pattern of storytelling in such a way that might be hard for some people.

Q: Hard? In what ways?

A: It's hard to follow. I've received this criticism from some people who think that some of the facts I have put in the film are not related and have nothing to do with the ultimate outcome of who killed my uncle and how did he die.

Q: What other techniques did you consciously break with?

A: The other one is a visual. Initially when I was thinking about the film I thought well what I want to do is a little re-creation or re-enactment and that never works. Re-creation is so unsatisfying in documentary, it's like, "what are you doing with this film?" You lose track and you think well is this really a dramatic film or is this a documentary? So I said, we need to develop a very, very specific visual technique. So my cinematographer and I decided that we were going to use different strategies for reenactment. For example, one of the subthemes of the film is reflection, how people are reflected. So we used mirrors. There are no re-creations, no reenactments. So that you could make a kind of mental-spiritual link between what you are hearing in the soundtrack and what you are looking at visually. And that's how we approached making this film. There's a kind of collage feeling to the film. And I also decided that my style would be one that incorporated a lot of different styles, and not simply a Eurocentric style of making a film.

Q: Yes, I just realized that there is a gap between what you hear and what you see in the film. You mentioned that the film is a collage, what are the other components of this collage?

A: Well, in the editing there was a great deal of freedom. A lot of intuitive freedom in the shooting. If we had a sense of the place and we wanted to give a feeling of dryness, then we would try to capture those images. It wasn't a literal kind of shooting. It wasn't like you see on PBS: and the lady took off her hat and then you see the image of a lady taking off her hat. It was a collage not only of images but also of images and sounds, impressions. And I hate to use the word, because it's overused, but also metaphorical kind of imagery.

Q: Can you mention any of your influences? Other filmmakers, other films that you saw that influenced this work?

A: I have been influenced by many, many filmmakers. There isn't any one filmmaker that I think is the end or be all, but I particularly like the young videomakers, and I think that they influence me. And more specifically, one film called the *Isle of Flowers*, made in Brazil. It's a short film that is fantastic in that way, in the way it uses its imagery and the way it tells its story in a nonlinear fashion, but tells a very poignant and wonderful story. It's by Jorge Furtado.

Q: You are certainly known for making films that are not straight-forward. For example, *La Ofrenda* at one level is about the "day of the dead" celebration, but at a deeper level, the film is about Chicana identity, and about how one negotiates that identity by crossing the border back and forth, and coming into contact with traditions that cross back and forth. By the same token, *The Devil Never Sleeps* is a film that is about something bigger than Tio Oscar's murder or suicide or people's perceptions of Tio Oscar.

A: Definitely. The film goes way beyond a specific incident in my family. And I intended the film to have an impact and meaning. What I feel the film tells is the story of Mexico. It tells the story of deception. It tells the story of pretense and of family ties, the strength of family ties, the strength of family love, the blindness of family love. It tells the folly of the filmmaker. It tells innumerable stories in my mind about what the film is really about besides what you see and what you hear. And I think when I showed the film in Mexico, the Mexicans agreed. They looked at the film and said, "I can't believe this film. This film is not about your uncle Oscar. This film is about Mexico right now, about the political situation, about deception, heroizing people."

Q: I just thought about something, Lourdes, your film is a "ranchera" because that's what rancheras are all about, about deception, betrayal, the family, about love, about the heroic, about men who die for the sake of honor—the songs of Vicente Fernandez, Jose Alfredo Jimenez, Lucha Villa.

A: And it ends with a ranchera.

Q: You are also presenting us with a culturally distinct notion of truth in the film. Could you elaborate on that?

A: It's very difficult to explain, the whole notion of what is truth. Like in this culture [U.S.], a truth is related to facts. Whereas in Mexico, truth is really a very subjective feeling. What is true is what you feel is true. So that's your truth, different from everyone agreeing on what the truth is. So there are partial truths and everyone has their own point of view and that point of view—their own genuine experience as the truth—you have to honor that. So there are partial truths in a way if you look at this from this cultural perspective. So I'm presenting the audience with this panorama of the Mexican truth: each person had their own genuine experience and they've experienced the truth. I'm sharing this in some way, which might be confusing to an American audience who might feel like, "Well they're all lying, and they're all negating what the other one is saying." And the American audience will get confused if they don't understand that each experience is just as much the truth.

Q: How is the *Devil* different from most Chicano documentaries?

A: First of all, it doesn't address the heroics of the Chicano people, like *Requiem 29* or *Agueda Martinez,* where Agueda is mostly a saint, or the heroic in films like *Yo Soy Chicano* or *Chicana.* This really pokes at the frailties in human character and human life. It dares to criticize where we come from—not to say that we all come from that kind of family. I'm sure that there are more honorable families. But, it is a part of our reality that that is Mexico. Mexico is that and more and even more sordid stories.

Q: It does treat the subject of *la familia,* and by extension, the community because, the Chicano community is based on the model of the family, and it's supposed to be a positive model.

A: Yeah, but the family of not only the Chicanos because we're like a remnant from Mexican culture. In Mexico, the family is sacred. You never say things outside the family. All the dirt stays in the family. Imagine the good stories people have. You don't tell about those things. And in turn, the political structure of Mexico in the past sixty or seventy years has been constructed the same way that a family functions. The PRI is a family and you don't know to this day what happens, what are the mechanisms at work in the PRI, the perversity of it, the corruption, the benevolence. You don't know any of it.

Q: You have thus broken a taboo. So how has your family responded to this film when they see it?

A: I have to say, that the first people to respond were my parents. And my parents are very loving people to me and in general. And my mother is a very appreciative mother. So, she loved the film, she loves it and she watches it every week. She used to watch every day, but now she's watching it every week and she even broke the cassette, so now I have to send her another one. She loves to watch her brother because she adores him. And my father loves the film so that my parents have been an incredible strength for me. They have validated my work and me and they have protected me a lot. A cousin of mine saw the film either in Chicago or San Antonio, I don't know where. One of my relatives saw the film before I showed it to them and they went crazy. My aunt and uncle, they just thought it was horrifying that I dared say the things that are not said outside of the family and put it in cinema and show it to strangers [laughter]. So they went wild. And just recently an aunt and a niece saw it and they loved it, they really, really loved it. So they called my mom and dad and told them that they loved it. I've had mixed responses. I have yet to take it to Chihuahua and show it to Ofelia [laughter].

Q: Tell me about the general audience and in particular, the critics' responses to your film.

A: Very few people have gotten it. I feel that it's very hard for people to get this film. I've made it in some way, maybe, that my approach to it was too complicated, maybe it was too much at one time. It's shown in really good places like "New Directors," "Sundance," "Toronto," and the critics, for example, an Israeli named Emmanuel Levy from *Variety*, and he absolutely did not get it. I don't know why he wanted to review it because he really just did not get it. *The New York Times,* they kind of got it. But I think that the driving force behind the critics' mind is always "who did it?" They miss the point that this film is not about "who did it." It's about this whole panorama of Mexican life. And maybe people don't find it as interesting as I found it. But, there's a critic, someone I admire, a French critic who really got it. So I think that it takes a sophisticated person. Maybe I made something too highbrow.

Q: But the Mexicans got it.

A: Exactly, the Mexicans get it. Maybe people are just not interested in Mexicans.

NOTES

I would like to thank Sarah Projansky and Herman Gray for their valuable comments.

1. I thank Lourdes Portillo for sharing the written transcript of this audience discussion of *The Devil Never Sleeps*. The discussion was conducted by Sylvie Thouard and Electa Arenal and taped on January 29, 1996 at City University of New York.

REFERENCES

Foucault, Michel. *Herculin Barbin: Being the Recently Discovered Memoirs of a Nineteenth Century French Hermaphrodite* (New York: Pantheon, 1980).

Franco, Jean. "The Incorporation of Women: A Comparison of North American and Mexican Popular Narrative," in *Studies in Entertainment: Critical Approaches to Mass Culture,* ed. Tania Modleski (Bloomington and Indianapolis: Indiana University Press, 1986), 119–38.

Moraga, Cherríe. *Loving in the War Years: Lo que nunca pasó por sus labios* (Boston: South End Press, 1983).

Rich, B. Ruby. "An/other View of New Latin American Cinema," in *Miradas de Mujer/Cineastas y videoastas Mexicanas y Chicanas,* ed. Norma Iglesias and Rosa Linda Fregoso (Berkeley: Third Woman Press, forthcoming).

Segura, Denise, and Jennifer L. Pierce. "The Chicana/o Family Structure and Gender Personality, Chodorow, Familism, and Psychoanalytic Sociology Revisited," *Signs* (Autumn 1993): 62–91.

Smith, Valerie. "Telling Family Secrets: Narrative and Ideology in *Suzanne, Suzanne* by Camille Billops and James V. Hatch," in *Multiple Voices in Feminist Film Criticism,* ed. Diane Carson, Linda Dittmar, and Janice R. Welsch (Minneapolis: University of Minnesota Press, 1994), 380–90.

CHAPTER TEN

María Luisa Bemberg's Miss Mary: *Fragments of a Life and Career History*

JULIANNE BURTON-CARVAJAL

INTRODUCTION

María Luisa Bemberg did not make her first, tentative foray into the film world until her children were grown and producing children of their own. Between her feature debut in 1981, on the eve of her sixtieth birthday, and her death in 1995, María Luisa's output of quality films was unrivaled in Latin America: two intimate dramas of contemporary (postmarital) life—*Momentos/Moments* (1981) and *Señora de nadie/Nobody's Wife* (1982)—followed by four period pieces markedly different in tone: the phenomenally popular love story *Camila* (1984), melodramatic catharsis for a nation emerging from the dark night of dictatorship; the elegantly detached *Miss Mary* (1986), a semiautobiographical tragedy of manners that inverts the postcolonial gaze; *Yo, la peor de todas/I, the Worst of All* (1990), an austerely stylized invocation of the personal struggles and eventual silencing of Latin America's most brilliant woman of letters; and *De eso no se habla/I Don't Want to Talk about It* (1993), a comic-satiric "fable" in defense of difference. Her seventh coauthored script (*Un extraño verano/A Strange Summer*) was ready to go into production when stomach cancer put a halt to her remarkable career.

331

The following extracts derive from "Opening Doors and Windows; Or, Destiny Defied: A Testimonial Mosaic," the concluding section of *Three Lives in Film: Illustrated Memoirs of Improbable Careers.* The first two life and career histories—of Mexico's Matilde Landeta and Venezuela's Margot Benacerraf—are the product of my own interviews. Acute illness interrupted my scheduled series of interviews with María Luisa, necessitating a different methodology in her case.

Composed of María Luisa Bemberg's own public declarations, but assembled after her death in a configuration she never saw, the life and career history from which these fragments are extracted was painstakingly amassed from nearly two hundred newspaper and magazine articles, the vast majority in Spanish, with additional material from publications in English, French, and Portuguese. Shaped by careful research and supplemented by notes from preliminary conversations with the filmmaker, the resulting "testimonial mosaic" is unique within the extensive genre of Latin American testimonial because it is both posthumous and a palimpsest of nearly two decades of otherwise ephemeral declarations to the press. Unlike conventional *testimonios*—the product of collaboration in synchronous time between a speaker of experience and a mediating figure who transcribes and transmutes her words into print—this life chronicle is simultaneously synchronic and diachronic, layering observations made to a host of individuals over a broad span of years.

This method could never have been contemplated without the technological advances of photocopying and word processing. In the fall of 1994, having prepared a chronology and series of questions for an extended series of interviews, I traveled to Buenos Aires. My arrival coincided with María Luisa's hospitalization in New York. In her absence, and with the assistance of her personal secretary, I spent several days scanning, selecting, and photocopying hundreds of potentially useful articles from the press clipping files that María Luisa had set aside for me in her home office.

María Luisa died in May, 1995, but she was a palpable presence during the summer months that followed as I combed through the photocopies I had made in Buenos Aires, marking all potentially significant passages, entering them into the computer. My tentative outline was continually transformed and expanded; as passages aggregated and reaggregated themselves, lacunae were filled and additional topics emerged. The resulting narrated life is the product of accretion and the ceaseless internal migration of selected fragments, of minute and repetitive acts of selection and recombination.

I call the final product a testimonial mosaic because each sentence or paragraph has been selectively chipped away from its original location and reinserted into a larger figure, whose contours and masses of color and contrast manifest the laboriousness of the process. The work could just as appropriately be described as a testimonial tapestry—since tapestry is much more notably a woman's art, given the meticulous and self-effacing dexterity required to blend myriad tiny threads into an intricate and expressive tableau. Both are combinatory art forms where authorship is submerged. Both assemble a whole from disconnected elements produced by or borrowed from others. Ironically, long after the process was complete and the manuscript sent out for review, I came across a precedent and a name for what I have undertaken here. Though the "precedent" is only eight pages long and fails to designate its sources, the name used by Beatriz González for her contribution to the memorial volume on Argentine art critic Marta Traba, published by Bogotá's Museum of Modern Art, is perfect: *entrevista atemporal*, atemporal interview.

In the narrative that follows, all sources are identified by date in parentheses—for example, (88-IV-17). The first two digits indicate the year (1988 in the foregoing example); the Roman numeral indicates the month of publication (April); the third number indicates the day, if available. Two articles published in the same month and year are designated "a," "b," and so on. The journalist's name is used when other identifying information is lacking. This parenthetical coding is designed to obstruct the flow of the text as little as possible while foregrounding the year of each declaration and allowing the reader to readily identify the source by consulting the chronological List of Sources. The initials JBC in parentheses identify material from our preliminary interviews.

In the laborious reweaving of this first-person narrative, numerous silent emendations have been necessary for the sake of clarity and consistency. The sequencing within quotations has occasionally been altered for greater coherence or impact. The English translation contains instances of inserted clarifications too numerous to mark. The number of instances in which a single press conference given by María Luisa resulted in notable variations of diction and emphasis in the various articles published as a result (within a larger, overall consistency of meaning) seems to validate the flexibility I have exercised in (re)ordering this material. Very rarely, I have taken the liberty of amending the original quote in order to achieve an integrated temporality, as, for example, in the last paragraph of the opening section, "A Career in Panorama." In 1987, Bemberg declared that she would like to have had "forty-four films rather than four" to her credit; I have updated the phrase to read "sixty-six rather than six."

In screening hundreds of pages covering seventeen years of conversations with the press, I discerned a subtle dialectic between María Luisa's propriety and sense of the personal as private on the one hand and, on the other, her feminist awareness that the personal is political and, for that reason, highly pertinent. She did not speak often about her personal and family life, but when she did, she made important connections between the destiny she felt she had inherited and the alternative destiny that she strove to create for herself. The following extracts from "Career Panorama" and "Itinerary of the Films," featuring her discussion of her most autobiographical film, emphasize these connections between her life and her work. I have underlined these connections still further by inserting fragments from another subsection, "Family Memories: The House of Bemberg," as footnotes to the account of *Miss Mary*.

"Opening Doors and Windows" was compiled first in Spanish, since the vast majority of sources are in that language. In my translation, I have made a special effort to achieve a flowing and idiomatic English that does full justice to the speaker's exemplary articulateness and deliberateness. María Luisa spoke English with impressive fluency, but of course her own rendering of her personal narrative into English would have been sprinkled with the traces of all those Irish nannies and the British education that they were hired to impart. I can only hope that she would have been tolerant of this more Americanized rendering.

FROM "A CAREER IN PANORAMA"

I opted for film because I've carried it within since I was a child. Because I seek to communicate with people. Because I wouldn't know how to do anything else. I didn't start earlier due to insecurity, subordination, and letting other voices rule over me (93-VI). I make movies because words are not enough for me, because seeing helps me think, and because—though, like all near-sighted people, I see rather poorly—I believe that I know how to look rather well (93-VI-27).

I wouldn't know how to live without making movies. It is a late-life passion that invaded my life, my thoughts, my dreams. It inhabits me, despite the enormous difficulties we must face in order to make movies in Latin America. But I believe that adversity sharpens the wits and that, despite our difficult economic situation, we manage to produce beautiful works. We Latin Americans need equal doses of passion, faith, and stubborn determination in order to keep on struggling to realize our dream (91-VI-8). Passion by itself is not enough, since it can be chaotic. The other pillar of our creativity must be rigor (93-VII).

When, as in my case, one discovers an expressive medium as passionately absorbing as filmmaking so late in life, it's almost like a drug. By comparison, everything else seems gray. To take on a film project is to go beyond the limits of reality and enter into a realm of magic, recreating that magic out of very concrete, tangible elements. It is so absorbing that I would not know how to live any other way (84-VII-8).

Having been born into a very closed social class has had great economic and cultural advantages, but it was a kind of suffocating ghetto (81-X-11). My formation is extremely uneven, due to an education that was very rigorous in some areas and very superficial in others. I've always had a passion for reading, and as a girl I had great opportunities for travel and the recreation of the spirit. But after I got married in my early twenties, my life became very conventional, subject to all the traditional prejudices, barriers, and dissatisfactions of the privileged social class to which I belonged (84–Spett).

I know that this is going to sound pretentious, but I was an engine idling at 60, ready to do 150 (84–Spett). I believe that I have finally succeeded in leaving behind that closed world of gilt and velvet, frivolousness, phoniness, and lack of culture. Women who belong to that class carry a desert within, and I did not want to be like them. I was destined to inherit a certain kind of life, but in the end I refused it. I wanted to invent another destiny for myself, and I succeeded in doing so, though it wasn't easy (81-X-11). I have listened to my inner voices and now I feel at peace. Having followed my own destiny helps me to reconcile myself with death, because I know I am fulfilling my reason for having existed on the planet (87-VIa).

Before getting my start in the film world by writing screenplays, I was just another housewife and mother who felt, like so many Latin American women, that I was the only one responsible for the well-being of my children. So I waited until they were grown before finding personal freedom for the first time in my life, before listening to my own inner voices (85-VII-19, 22). It was not a sudden change but, on the contrary, a very slow process. I think that the first step was my separation from my husband. I believe that matrimony is so absorbing and so limiting for women that it makes it extremely difficult for a married woman to express herself freely or integrate herself into a professional world (84–Spett).

I suppose that from childhood I've carried within a persistent vocation that I never allowed myself to acknowledge (87-VI-26). From the time I was quite young, I wrote, organized, and acted in household theater skits, directing my siblings and cousins. The realm of fantasy and spectacle always appealed to me (95-V-8).

I've felt a great love for the theater since I was very small, and I would have wanted to be an actress but when, as an adolescent, I proposed this career, I was told that I wouldn't be able to set foot in my parents' house again, and I lacked the courage to make a permanent break with my family. So I stayed within the mold and lived the life that was expected of me, the life I had been brought up to lead, until the moment came when I knew it was no longer working. I realized that all I had been taught was in violation of some inner truth, and I began to unlearn what had been so painstakingly ingrained (87-VI-26).

I began, finally, to think for myself in the early 1970s as part of a feminist consciousness-raising group, among women who shared the same frustrations, the same questions and concerns, the same anger. It was tremendously helpful to me to discover a solidarity that transcended age, social class, political ideology, and personal taste. We found common ground that enabled us to support one another and help each other to grow. Many of those women were active in different political parties, but no one intervened on behalf of a particular ideological position (87-VI-26).

That very intense and useful experience lasted three years, until the curfews and prohibitions of the military regime intervened. That was when I began to write with the purpose of developing female characters of flesh and blood, with all the conflicts and contradictions characteristic of any human being, women who do not surrender passively to their destiny but take risks, are audacious and brave and honest with themselves, women who dare to dare (87-VI-26).

For some time I had harbored the ambition of being able to write and even perhaps eventually to act, but I never thought I would be capable of putting myself behind that very "virile" machine, the camera. I was full of self-censorship until I finally succeeded in dismantling that ideological mechanism and emerging more or less unscathed (87-VI-29). Gestalt psychology and feminism have been the twin foundations of all I have accomplished. They enabled me to confront the possibility of failure. I underwent orthodox psychoanalysis as a girl; it was useless. When I decided I wanted to direct, I went back into analysis, because I was very, very afraid. This time a saw a Gestalt therapist who was enormously helpful to me (84-VII). I discovered that I was inhabited by two people, one paralyzed by fear and the other determined to direct at any cost (84–Spett).

I learned the technical aspects of filmmaking by watching others and by reading anything I could get my hands on. I also made two 16mm shorts [*El mundo de la mujer/Woman's World* (1972) and *Juguetes/Toys* (1978)], which is where I discovered the magic of editing. I guess you might say that I am self-taught (88-VI-19).

I felt that I couldn't pretend to direct professional actors without studying acting myself. So in 1980 I went to New York to take a course in acting from Lee Strasberg. That experience taught me that what an actor needs most is security. I want my actors to feel able to give themselves over to any excess, because that's how they achieve greatness. But if they go too far, I want them to know that I'm standing below them holding the net. I think that, more than giving direction, what's essential is the ability to convince. That's what the director is for. There is no art without ethics, and the way one treats actors involves a deeply ethical stance (88-VI-19).

I was able to make movies because I had the necessary economic backing. The production credits offered by the National Film Institute required collateral. Otherwise, it would have been extremely difficult, perhaps impossible, for me to find producers who believed in me (81-XI-29).

I am very conscious of the great privilege of which I am the beneficiary, and this is precisely what makes me feel indebted to society and makes me want to offer women a different image from the portrait that patriarchal society paints of them (86-XII-19a, b). In my personal development as a filmmaker, with the exception of the economic aspect, everything else was an uphill struggle. I did not feel supported by social or political or any other kind of contacts. It was a long, dark tunnel (94-VI-17).

My films reflect the virulence of a patriarchal system still in force (87-VI-29). I am committed to decolonizing women, to waking them from their culturally enforced chloroform sleep. I want to break the molds so that women enjoy the freedom to think for themselves that any human being should have (82-V-2). I am interested in speaking out in the name of women, in awakening in them the need of thinking autonomously about their lives rather than remaining subjected to cultural patterns dictated by everything from advertisements to women's magazines, soap operas, love songs, and advice columnists. Women are so much more varied and contradictory than the stereotypes conventionally used to represent us. I am anxious to open doors and windows for women who need them opened (82-I-24).

I believe that filming from a woman's point of view is like shifting the camera from one shoulder to the other. Because a woman's gaze is different, more inquisitive sometimes, it can contribute something new and interesting. We women are not going to repeat the errors of our male colleagues; we're not going to marginalize the male. Sexism, for me, is an absolutely reactionary way of looking at the world, the first expression of fascism (94-II-23).

All women share an alternative optics, though often, instead of using our own eyes, we prefer to accept the established codes. Yet it is clear that there are not two sides to the coin; until now, both sides express masculine culture. From the time the world began, we women have been told what we must do and how we must live. Now, all of a sudden, this marvelous end of the twentieth century comes along when women have begun to ask, Why? What if things were different? And so we began to redesign our roles, to get angry and kick open doors that had been closed to us (94-II-23).

From my little corner of the world, I have tried to propose autonomous, lucid, independent women and to create mechanisms of identification so that the women in the audience have an example for their own growth (94-II-23). I decided that all my stories would follow the thread of a woman who transgresses repressive rules, because I believe that transgression is the essence of liberty (90–Fonseca). I feel very pleased to have put my little grain of sand, to have helped prod women toward an awareness that we don't have to be heirs to our mother's and grandmother's destinies but have the opportunity to find our own personal destiny (94-II-23).

I believe that filmmaking is a path to self-knowledge (86-VI-11) and that all creative expression originates in the self. That is the only means to honest expression. You don't make movies by addressing issues from the outside; movies are made out of one's own life experiences. Every work is personal in multiple senses. I don't believe that it can be otherwise (87-VIb). I believe that I have grown as a filmmaker, trying out different modes of expression and taking more risks. I am satisfied to the degree that each of my films closely resembles what I aimed to achieve (91-VI-8).

I believe that it is absolutely idiotic to complain about what didn't happen. We always have to move forward. Surely some good things have accrued to me from the traditional lifestyle in which I was trapped for so many years. My circumstances are what they are, and one has to work with what one has. I would like to have directed sixty-six films instead of six, but regretting, which never solved anything, is a very negative way of being. I like to say that I got a late start because I hope that my example might help others of both sexes. I believe that it's never too late, because you're as young as your dreams (87-VI-26).

FROM "ITINERARY OF THE FILMS: *MISS MARY*" (1986)

Anyone who strives to be an artist has a responsibility to be critical, because artists must bear testimony to their era. I was in an almost unique situation regarding *Miss Mary* because the film deals with a class I know well and with a period I remember clearly. Other directors who might have wished to address this theme don't belong to that world, while the people who do belong to it are not filmmakers. This is the film I am fondest of. I believe that it is made with honesty, rigor, and sensitivity, without low blows (91-VIII-31).

Miss Mary is without doubt my most personal film (86-VIII). It is not the story of my own family, although my family also had a large country estate, a lot of children raised by governesses, and the custom of doing "Catholic mission work" among the local peons (87-I-18). Through *Miss Mary*, I've let go of a lot of personal baggage, untied knots, and dispelled ghosts. The film displays a certain desire to provoke, for which I take full responsibility (86-XII-19a).

The historical backdrop in this case is 1930s Argentina and in particular the political situation after the overthrow of constitutionally elected president Hipólito Yrigoyen, who was succeeded by several illegitimate regimes. Implicit in the film is a political critique of a chronically insensitive social class (86-XII-19a), one that completely isolated itself during a time of great political effervescence and change (86-VI-11).

In depicting a family that represents this social class, I am trying to show the need to become aware of past mistakes in order to avoid repeating them. This was the time of the New Deal in the United States, the Spanish Civil War, the Popular Front in France, the Bolshevik post-revolution in Russia. Yet in Argentina, the dominant class lived apart, either unaware of or refusing to acknowledge the different historical winds that were blowing, thus allowing the political void to be filled by Peronism, a movement that knew very well how to attract the more disadvantaged classes—people without voice or vote, faceless and completely ignored by the oligarchy. In the 1930s, Argentina was a prosperous country, the fifth most important worldwide in terms of its commercial potential, yet it was also scandalously unjust (88-XI-30). That ruling class treated its subordinates, the workers and peasants, in a paternalistic, almost feudal manner. Inevitably, this relationship would end on October 17, 1945 [with the enormous protest of workers and other disenfranchised masses which took over Buenos Aires that day demanding—and achieving—Juan Perón's release from prison] (86-VI-11).

Miss Mary, which ends on this date, is made up of flashbacks from the point of view of an English governess who came to Argentina in 1938 to educate the offspring of a very traditional family of landed gentry. I make a point of showing the enormous repression to which the daughters of such families were subjected and how Miss Mary, reactionary Victorian that she was, aligned herself with the designs of the landowner. The film's final shot is of Miss Mary in the port of Buenos Aires, about to board a ship bound for England, with the Peronist demonstrators and their chants in the background. World War II has ended, permitting Miss Mary to return to London, leaving behind a country in the throes of definitive change (86-VI-11).

I was interested in depicting an upper-class Argentine family during its apogee in order to show the influence such families exerted on the country and how the advent of Peronism split apart their members (86-II-2). *Miss Mary* is a fresco with multiple readings, each of them necessarily marked by the reactionary spirit of that era, its social insensivity and political blindness. These factors made it understandable that when Peronism arrived, it would completely take over Argentina. The film also reveals the hypocrisy beneath this apparently harmonious, beautifully elegant exterior, which turns out to be a sham—a vacuum in which both love and spirit are lacking. *Miss Mary* is a melancholy movie, mocking but balanced, I hope, by a sense of humor. We all have to know how to laugh at ourselves (87-VIa).

Making *Miss Mary* was not in any way a "betrayal" of my class because everything I say there is true: the educational system, the cult of appearances, the sexual degeneracy, the family's harsh treatment of the governess and the local peons, the manipulation of the electoral system.

All these anecdotes are based on actual events. The film is a way of taking cognizance of the many errors made by the ruling class. Those who enjoy special privileges must assume responsibility and contribute to their country by setting a good example, exercising leadership, and giving something back to society in return for all they have received (91-VIII-31).

I was always fascinated by the world of governesses, that curious species of mercenary surrogate mothers who pour out their affection toward the children of strangers (86-VI-11). I've known these women first-hand. They were eminently Victorian, often inclined to snobbery (86-VII-24). Their mere presence in a household was a symbol of class status (86-VI-11). Ironic as it may seem, they prided themselves on the wealth of their employers: the richer the family, the prouder they felt. They were victims of their education and of the puritanism of the British middle class (86-VII-24). Even their social location was hybridized: they boasted about other people's fortunes but couldn't feel at home in either the kitchen or the salon. Depending on the political and cultural affinities of the family in question, the governess might just as well be a *mademoiselle* or a *fraülein* (86-VI-11).

I have always felt a great tenderness toward these women because in fact they were such unprotected creatures. They wandered from one house to another, grew fond of each group of charges in turn, and then moved on or were dismissed. I remember the large trunk each one kept at the foot of her bed, her whole world locked up inside it: mementos, photographs of a long-lost sweetheart or distant family members, sometimes a bottle of whiskey for those difficult moments (86-VII-17).

Yet on the other hand, they were pretty sinister because they represented the tenets of Victorian education in all its dreadfulness, with all those clichés about what one must and must not do. They were the instrument through which the patriarchal system operated (86-VII-17). I have rendered them tribute through this film, and at the same time, the character of Miss Mary allows me to narrate the influence of the British on the Argentine upper class that always directed its gaze toward Europe rather than to its own shores (86-VI-11).

Governesses, like dinosaurs, no longer exist. In my childhood, each time one would depart, I would feel somehow orphaned. That scene in which the younger sister is locked in the bathroom screaming to be let out in order to bid farewell to Miss Mary is something I might have lived out as a little girl. I remember how moved I would be if, after a departure, I happened to come across something that had belonged to one of them. One time I cried for hours after finding a forgotten glove. Of course there were many moments when I detested my governesses because they were very repressive, strict, and severe, but in general I loved them a great deal and through my portrayal of Miss Mary I've tried to convey that mixture of adoration and rejection that so many of them provoked in me (86-VII-24).

I worked for more than a year on the script (86-VII-24). Since the story shares some points in common with my own life, perhaps I assumed a certain distance when filming it (90-III-4). The movie arose from images, situations, fragments of conversation that kept piling up over a long period of time (86-VII-24). I began writing the script on my own, and later called on Beda Docampo Feijóo and Juan Bautista Stagnaro, my cowriters on the *Camila* script, to help me restructure the plot line until it assumed the solidity of a story. Then I wrote the final script with Jorge Goldenberg. It was a bit like those Hollywood or Italian films where the credits list a number of screenwriters. Every person contributes something different, but since what matters is what's best for the film, the individual contributions fade into the whole (86-II-2).

Incidents from my childhood gave me my point of departure. Like something ghostly and a little unreal, I recalled those country estates, in the best English or French style, lost amid the pampas. I remembered the arrival and departure of guests, the long, leisurely afternoons of reading or horseback riding (86-II-2).

We all have our own interior landscape: the seashore, a forest, clouds. For me, the pampas are the metaphysical landscape of nothingness. From a more practical perspective, they are a point of interest for people outside of Argentina, and I'm pleased to show off the beauty of our countryside (86-VII-17). We also included various sequences in Buenos Aires—a cruise on a yacht, a wedding, a charity ball to raise funds to purchase ambulances for the British army, a Peronist demonstration (86-II-2).

I think the script turned out to be an intelligent, modern, subtle one, appropriate to an open film where no single figure has the lead. It's told from Miss Mary's point of view, but she is not the only protagonist. The film's gaze is broken up, like memory itself, which weaves in and out. This is not a film with a sharply defined storyline. It's evanescent, made of glances, hints, insinuations (86-VII-17).

Miss Mary begins in black and white with the parents bidding goodnight to their children, who are saying their prayers under the watchful eye of the governess of the moment.[1] Their elders are on their way out for the evening, to celebrate General José Félix Uriburu's successful coup d'etat (86-II-2). It is an historical fact that the Argentine upper class supported this first rupture of the republican order, establishing a precedent that we've paid dearly for in the succeeding decades (86-VII-27).

The movie ends on October 17, 1945, with actual footage of the events that produced another rupture of democracy: the (re)appearance of another military man, General Juan Perón, who managed to galvanize a previously submerged sector of the Argentine populace. We located some of this documentary footage in national archives and the rest in Washington, D.C. (86-II-2).

I wanted to recreate an epoch metaphorically, by means of a family invented to coalesce all the dominant traits of the traditional Argentine ruling families—of ruling families in any Western country, for that matter. Those families carry with them accumulated generations of money and travel, which explains how they have absorbed customs and fashions that they later put into circulation in their home countries. Theirs was a paternalistic society, with very little social conscience, in which fraud and deceit reigned. I believe that the film exudes the same asphyxiating melancholy that permeated my childhood (86-VII).

This family is made up of the father, the mother, three children, the mother's brother, and the two elderly grandparents. And of course the governess, who was originally named Miss Maggie. We changed to Miss Mary in order to avoid being construed as making any direct reference to then prime minister Margaret Thatcher (86-II-5). The other key character is the house, a huge Tudor mansion which we located in General Madariaga province (86-II-2).[2]

There is a bit of me in all of the characters—in the two young girls, in the mother, even in the father, a solitary, autocratic despot, the genuine *pater familias* with all the machismo this role implies.[3] We constructed the characters in such a way that just a few brush strokes would suggest the image of a complete human being, with all their loneliness, anguish, and dreams, but always conveyed through an impressionistic technique made up of nuances and half-tones. I like to let my characters live their lives freely. That's why I developed several sequences around each one that might or might not appear in the finished film but that were helpful in establishing their autonomy. Jorge Goldenberg and I got deeply involved with the most minor characters and the most major ones, and I grew to love them all, even those whom I like least or pity most (86-II-2).

In 1938, when the film opens, the young girls are free, inquiring, joyful, and mischievous. By 1945 it's clear how the family mold has constrained their enormous vitality (86-VII-17). This movie shows various stages of the process by which one of the daughters goes mad and the other is forced to marry a boy she doesn't love in order to protect the family honor (93–JBC). In response to the feelings of joy and pride that the older daughter expresses when discovering the proof of her entry into womanhood, the governess, with her rigidly Victorian attitude, inculcates feelings of bodily shame (86-VIIa). I believe this is one of the few instances in film history in which the topic of menstruation is addressed openly. That scene, which is absolutely autobiographical based on my experience with my older sister, is both amusing and horrifying (86-VIIc-17).[4]

I believe that all that sexual and physical repression is fundamental. I think it is extremely difficult for anybody—male or female—to be creatively free, to realize themselves in a work of art, in the grips of such repression (86-VIId-24). Perhaps men are not too interested in all the repression that we women have had to suffer in the flesh, but my understanding is that young men from the same social circle suffer similar repression and are similarly manipulated. The mother's brother, for example, is just as disconsolate and just as disconnected from his country's reality as she is; he will be one of those who participates in the Peronist coup d'etat (86-VIIa).

There's another scene in the film that shows the other side of the coin: when the son, Johnny (Donald McEntyre), is obliged to go to a brothel as part of his fifteenth birthday celebration, because that ritual experience is integral to the formation of his virility. In the same way as the females were conditioned to cultivate a perfect virginity, at least until they married, the mandate of masculinity obliged the males to prove their sexual potency (86-VIIc-17; 86-VIId-24), which seems every bit as reprehensible to me as the repression exerted upon the girls (86-VIId-24). Because of the way he has been educated and manipulated, Johnny has no idea who he is. He only knows how to shield himself behind his naval uniform. He follows in his father's footsteps and becomes a future supporter of military regimes that take power by force (87-I-18).

The mother is another element in this repressive schema. She is a victim of repression who in turn projects her frustation onto others in a cycle that goes from generation to generation like an endless chain (86-VIIa). Mecha (Nacha Guevara) is a neurotic, a woman who has never allowed herself to listen to her own inner voices. I have her play the piano obsessively, always the same piece, Eric Satie's "Les Gnosiennes." Why? As a girl, she had been a talented pianist. If she had been sent to a conservatory, she could have become a professional concert artist. But she remained locked in that suffocating world, and she forgot everything. The only thing she remembers is that melody (86–Sallas). Now she wanders among her family with her neurosis and her ancient, ancestral fears—all the subjection that has traditionally victimized women. She is a victim who at a certain point becomes a victimizer (86-VIIc-17).[5]

The neighbor woman, Perla (Luisina Brando), a widowed exmanicurist, is perhaps the only healthy, happy, vital being in the film. She expresses herself with complete spontaneity in the face of the astonished gaze of a family who consider her a vulgar social climber (86-VIIc-17).

This family undertakes a mission every year in order to arrange weddings, baptisms, and first communion ceremonies for the people who work on their estate. This sequence also shows the fraudulent political practices of the time: how the peons did not have possession of their voting books because these were always in the hands of the bosses. These elements are closely related to the terrible political situation of the period and contributed to the explosion of Peronism, an eruption made inevitable by a social class that remained blind and deaf to the rumblings of history, living like characters out of Chekhov—in a totally unreal world exempt of any sense of social justice except through "works of charity." Perón swept the country like wildfire (86-VIIc-17).

The film's style is conditioned by its theme and the narrative form we chose. I set out to film in a rather cold and distanced style, but with a slightly humorous tone—the polar opposite of *Camila* with its incandescent treatment (86–Figueras). With *Miss Mary* I felt the need to develop a cool palate, huge empty sets, leisurely gestures, and hushed voices—all with a touch of elegance and an edge of melancholy (86-VIId-24). *Miss Mary* is a movie made of nuances. It's also a movie made of silences. It's an impressionistic film based on subtle elements that surround each of the characters and accrue importance by separate routes (86-II-13). I talked a lot with my cinematographer, Miguel Rodríguez, about achieving a transparently chilly light and then being able to shift to the golden light of the long summer evenings (86-II-2).

Only an English actress could play the part of Miss Mary (86-VIIb). Julie Christie was always my first choice because what I had in mind was an attractive woman with a certain sensuality (86-VIId-24). With her charm and talent, I thought that she would be able to embody to perfection one of those desolate old maids, as confused as her charges (86-VIIb). After she had read the script, we spoke on the telephone and she told me that she had liked it a lot but that she still felt some hesitation (86-VIId-24).

I made a quick trip to London to speak with her in person. We met in my hotel room and began rehearsing right then and there, despite my jet lag from a sixteen-hour trip (86-VIId-24). She enthusiastically agreed to leave her glamour behind and immediately assumed an awkward and graceless way of walking (86-VIIb), enabling me to confirm at once that she was right for the part (86-VIId-24).

Working with Julie was an exceptional experience. She is the most generous, uncomplicated, disciplined person you can imagine (86-VIId-24). Living on location with thirty people on a remote *estancia*, she set a real example through her professionalism and naturalness. She always appeared on time, never complaining or disputing anything, and this contributed a great deal to the harmony that prevailed among the cast and crew (86-VIIe-27). She came to Argentina for seven weeks and ended up staying twice as long and traveling around half the country. A situation that could have been tense, given the deplorable Malvinas/Falklands war, turned out to be a pleasant surprise because we found ourselves in the presence of a pacifist, an anti-imperialist, someone who was in complete disagreement with British Prime Minister Margaret Thatcher's policies toward our islands (86-VIIb).

How did I come to cast someone as arresting as the popular singer Nacha Guevara in the role of the timorous mother? Simple. She is a very forceful person, but she looks fragile because she is very pale and slender, so that was the point of correspondence with the character of Mecha. But I also made this choice because I like actors to escape from their habitual type casting; to me it seems like a great waste for them to be always working in the same register because I abhor clichés (86-Figueras).[6] I talked this over with my producer, Lita Stantic, whose opinion I value highly, and we agreed that it would be intriguing to transform a woman as extravagant, free, and extroverted as Nacha Guevara into a conventional matron in pearls (86-VIIb). The mixture of her personal style and evanescent air and this conventional and slightly neurotic character seemed perfect to us (86-II-5). It was Lita's idea, equally apt, to cast Tato Pavlovsky in the role of the father; he radiates great authority and convincingly projects the arrogance of this *pater familias* (86-VIId-24).

I shot this film simultaneously in Spanish and English because an American distributor was interested in buying it, and North American audiences are so spoiled that they are reluctant to read subtitles, and won't accept dubbing either. I would never do it again. It was exhausting to have to shoot each take twice, once in each language. It was like making two movies (86-VI-11).

In the version we shot for the Spanish-speaking world, there are also some subtitled dialogues in English. The characters interact in Spanish except when Miss Mary intervenes, when everyone switches to English. The intention here was to focus on language as an issue. There's a very significant exchange related to this theme in the dining room, when the butler asks the governess, in Spanish, how many cubes of sugar she would like in her tea. "Two, please," she replies. The brother-in-law remonstrates, "By now, you might have learned to say '*Dos, por favor*.'" "Nonsense," Miss Mary replies. "That's the strength of the British empire. Even the butler is learning English." (87-I-2).

I didn't want *Miss Mary* to seem either self-satisfied or pamphleteering. Nothing is too explicit; everything is implicit for those viewers who know how to see it (86-Figueras). I don't want to set myself up as a judge of Peronism. I recognize that October 17, 1945[7] was an historical date because it changed many things in Argentina, maybe everything, but I just tell the story, nothing more. This is all I can do, since I cannot forget the ferocious persecution that my family was subjected to under Perón, and I think that those memories rob me of my objectivity (87-I-18).

If my mother hadn't passed away, I doubt I would ever have made this film. If she were still alive, she would not be able to understand it. She was too tight-laced ever to manage to take a distanced view. Papá was more open in his attitudes. He would have been interested in *Miss Mary*, and it would have amused him, though of course this does not mean that he would not have been irritated by it as well—as he was or would have been with all my films. (93-JBC)

NOTES

This chapter was compiled and translated by Julianne Burton-Carvajal.

1. The scene is patterned on one of María Luisa's childhood memories: "My mother was a very apprehensive person. When she would come into the nursery to kiss us goodnight, she always told us to look under our beds to be sure no man was hiding there. A child like me, with a head full of fantasies, had a hard time separating the reality from the projection. My mother would go away and

I would beg the governess to leave the door open or a light on, but she would staunchly refuse. I remember lying awake many nights listening anxiously for the milk wagon that arrived at dawn" (82-II-14).

2. This *estancia* belonged to one of María Luisa's cousins.

3. "My father, Otto Eduardo Bemberg, was a very vital, capable, intelligent, and powerful man whom I saw very little, only five or ten minutes per day as a child (82-II-14). I detested him. To me he seemed a sinister being, the incarnation of everything I hated. Much later, I understood that he was a noble man who had been obliged by birth to live an existence that he would not have chosen. The Bemberg family fortune made a prisoner of him" (90-III-4,9).

4. "I remember how one night my older sister Josefina let out a shout: 'I'm dying! I'm dying!' I went running for our nanny, an older woman who had never been married. She sat down at the foot of Josefina's bed, smiled, and said, 'Don't be frightened. Now you're a woman.' And she began to explain. My sister listened proudly to the news that, from now on, her body would give monthly testimony to its capacity to bear achildren. She grew radiant and exclaimed, 'How wonderful! Let's have a party! This is better than a super-birthday!' The old governess gave a horrified look and admonished, 'Never! One doesn't speak of these things.' This is how I discovered that female modesty means concealing what happens to us" (84-IX).

5. "My mother, Sofía Elena Begolea de Bemberg, famed beauty in her era, was a typical upper-class Argentine *señora*. She was a victim who busied herself shaping future victims. I never got on well with her. She was too dependent, too submissive. I would look at her and say to myself, 'What I want most is not to be like her; that would be the worst thing that could happen to me.' Yet somewhere deep down, I felt sorry for her. In some obscure way, I wanted to avenge her. She could have encouraged me to break with my surroundings, but instead she transformed herself into the custodian of the very values that had curtailed her own existence" (90-III-4).

6. Actress Nacha Guevara's striking physical resemblance to Sofía Elena Bengolea de Bemberg is accentuated in *Miss Mary* by hairstyle and jewelry identical to those worn by the director's mother in the portrait photograph that accompanied her 1984 obituary.

7. Coincidentally, this was also María Luisa's wedding day. The marriage ceremony was scheduled for La Iglesia del Socorro, the very same church where Camila O'Gorman fell in love with her confessor Padre Ladislao Gutiérrez more than a century before. The oligarchs perceived such a threat in the throngs of Peronist demonstrators that María Luisa's union with the young student of

architecture Carlos Miquens took place at the family mansion on Talcahuano Street, in front of a makeshift altar. For a fuller account, see Hugo Beccacece (90-III-4).

LIST OF SOURCES

Sources are listed in parenthesis in the text by the last two digits of the year of publication, followed by the month of publication (in Roman numerals) and the day (if available). Correspondingly, the following list is organized chronologically by year, and within each year, by month and then date, followed by the full citation. (In several cases, citations are incomplete due to missing information on the the originals, which in most cases were photocopied from Bemberg's personal archives.) In instances where more than one article was published on the same date, one is marked "a" and the other "b" (e.g., 81-XI-29a = November 29, 1981, the first of two or more articles published on that date). JBC designates the compiler's conversations with Bemberg, which took place in 1993.

1981

X-11   Pérez Siudreu de García, Pilar. "María Luisa Bemberg: Momentos en la vida de una señora." Rio Negro, Argentina.

XI-29   "María Luisa Bemberg y su segunda película." *Gaceta,* La Plata, Argentina.

1982

I-24   "María L. Bemberg filma *Señora de Nadie:* La mujer y la búsqueda de una nueva identidad." *La Nación.*, Buenos Aires.

II-14   Barriero, Néstor. "La vida de María Luisa Bemberg." *La Semana,* Buenos Aires.

V-2   Down, Albert. "Cronica de una obsesión: María Luisa Bemberg y *Señora de Nadie.*" *La Nueva Provincia,* Bahía Blanca, Argentina.

1984

VII   Sánchez, Matilde. "Una feminista cacarea su verdad: La Bemberg ¿Es la que lleva los pantalones en el cine nacional?" *Satiricón* , Buenos Aires.

VII-8   Morelli, Alejandrina. "Mas allá del éxito y del fracaso." [source not identified]

IX   Ventura, Any. "Crónica de la señora de nadie." *Superhumor,* Buenos Aires.

84-Spett Spett, Liz. "María Luisa Bemberg." [source not identified]

1985

VII-19   M.R.I. "*Camila*: Un sueño hecho realidad." *Vanidades Continental.*

1986

86-Figueras   Figueras, Marcelo. "*Miss Mary*, el último film de María Luisa
               Bemberg: Fantasmas de un tiempo que pasó." [source not identi-
               fied]

86-Sallas   Sallas, Renée. "'No cambio mis 64 de hoy por mis 35 de ayer."
               [source not identified]

II-2   "María Luisa Bemberg promete un filme impresionista y hecho de
               matices." *La Nación*, Buenos Aires.

II-5   Pacitti, Teresa y Liliana Castamo. *La Semana*, Buenos Aires.

II-13   Torres, Vicente. "Silencio: Mujeres Trabajando." *Siete Días.*

VI-11   García Luna, Raúl. "Miss Bemberg." *Somos* , Buenos Aires.

VIIa   Asqueta, Cristina. "[María Luisa Bemberg]: enfoca temática
               femenina." Montevideo, Uruguay. [source not identified]

VIIb   Torralba, María Amelia. "Una película ambiciosa." *Vanidades
               Continental.*

VIIc-17   Soto, Moira. "*Miss Mary*: madres mercenarias y 17 de octubre."
               Tiempo Argentino.

VIId-24   Tabbia, Alberto. "El opus cuarto de la directora de *Camila*: María
               Luisa Bemberg y una historia sobre el no amor." *Clarín*, Buenos
               Aires.

VIIe-27   López, Fernando. "Crónica de una señora cineasta, 'La Bem-
               berg.'" *La Nación*, Buenos Aires.

VIII   Absatz, Cecilia. "Yo, Bemberg." *Claudia.*, Buenos Aires.

XII-19a   "'Mi cine está comprometido con la ideología feminista' Afirmó
               la cineasta María Luisa Bemberg en los EE. UU." *La Gaceta*,
               Tucumán, Argentina.

XII-19b   "Declaraciones de María L. Bemberg sobre el feminismo y el
               machismo." *La Nación*, Buenos Aires.

1987

I-2   Hachem, Samir. "A late start didn't hurt *Mary* maker." *Los Ange-
               les Herald Examiner,* p. 67

I-18   Quebleen, Rodolfo C. "María Luisa Bemberg habla sobre *Miss
               Mary* y *Camila*." *El Diario-La Prensa* , New York.

VIa   Sáez, María Inés. "María Luisa Bemberg: '*Miss Mary* es algo de mi
               vida.'" *Somos,* Chile.

VIb   "María Luisa Bemberg, cineasta argentina: 'Creo que las mujeres
               tenemos muchas cosas que contar en el quehacer de un país y su
               cultura.'" Chile. [source not identified]

| VI-26 | "María Luisa Bemberg: 'Me gustaría tener 44 películas detrás mío en vez de cuatro." *El Mercurio,* Chile. |
| VI-29 | Foxley, Ana María. "Una mujer 'desatada': María Luisa Bemberg cuenta de su vida y su próxima obra." *Hoy,* Chile. |

1988

| VI-19 | Bosch Esteves, Rosa. "Maria Luisa Bemberg o el arte de lo posible." *La Opinión,* Los Angeles. |
| XI-30 | Montero Otondo, Tereza. "Maria Luisa Bemberg, por um cinema feminino." *Caderno 2: Video* , São Paulo, Brazil. |

1990

| 90? | Fonseca, Elena. "*Yo, la peor de todas.*" [source and country of origin not identified] |
| III-4 | Beccacece, Hugo. "La conquista de una identidad." *La Nación,* Buenos Aires. |

1991

| VI-8 | Pasará, Luis. "Define su objetivo la cineasta María Luisa Bemberg: 'Mostrar mujeres libres'," *Caretas,* Lima, Peru. |
| VIII-31 | Daneri, Graciela. "María Luisa Bemberg: ¿La mejor de todas?" *El Litoral,* Santa Fe, Argentina. |

1993

III-V?-27	Lladós, Gustavo. "María Luisa Bemberg: Una mujer con nombre propio." *Caras,* Buenos Aires.
VI	Battelli, Miriam. "María Luisa Bemberg: En la búsqueda de la libertad del ser humano." *Imagen,* Bahía Blanca, Argentina.
VII	López-Chavez, Celia. "Imaginación y pasión del cine latinoamericano." *El Nuevo Mexicano* , New Mexico.

1994

| II-23 | Holst, Jens. "María Luisa Bemberg, con la cámara en el otro hombro: Fue la primera directora latinoamericana en el jurado de Berlín." *La Epoca,* Chile. |
| VI-17 | Godoy Divin, Marcela. "María Luisa Bemberg, cineasta: Un larguísimo túnel . . ." *La Nación,* Santiago de Chile. [date not specified, but before June 17] |

1995

| V-8 | "Murió María Luisa Bemberg." *Clarín,* Buenos Aires. |

SELECTED
BIBLIOGRAPHY

Ahmad, Aijaz. "Jameson's Rhetoric of Otherness and the 'National Allegory.'" In *Social Text* 17 (Fall 1987): 3–25.

Aidou, Ama Ata. "The African Woman Today." *Dissent* 39 (Summer 1992).

Alea, Tomás Gutiérrez. "Tribute to Sara Gómez." In *Cuba: A View from Inside: Short Films by and about Cuban Women*. New York: Center for Cuban Studies, 1992.

Armes, Roy. *Third World Film Making and the West*. Berkeley: University of California Press, 1987.

Attile, Martina, and Maureen Blackwood. "Black Women and Representation." In *Films for Women*, ed. Charlotte Brunsdon. London: British Film Institute, 1986.

Bambara, Toni Cade. "Reading the Signs, Empowering the Eye: *Daughters of the Dust* and the Black Independent Cinema Movement." In *Black American Cinema*, ed. Manthia Diawara. New York: Routledge, 1993.

Barrios de Chungara, Domitila. *Let Me Speak! Testimony of Domitila, A Woman of the Bolivian Mines*. New York and London: Monthly Review of Books, 1978.

Benamou, Catherine. "Women's Interventions in Cuban Documentary Film." In *Cuba: A View from Inside by and about Cuban Women*. New York: Center for Cuban Studies, 1992.

Benjamin, Walter. *Illuminations*, ed. Hannah Arendt. New York: Schocken Books, 1969.

Burton, Julianne, ed. *Cinema and Social Change in Latin America: Conversations with Filmmakers.* Austin: University of Texas Press, 1986.

————, ed. *The Social Documentary in Latin America.* Pittsburgh, Pa.: University of Pittsburgh Press, 1990.

————, ed. *Latin American Cinema: Gender Perspectives.* In *Journal of Film and Video* 44:3&4 (Fall 1992 and Winter 1993).

Burton-Carvajal, J. See Julianne Burton.

Carson, Diane, Linda Dittmar, and Janice R. Welsch, eds. *Multiple Voices in Feminist Film Criticism.* Minneapolis: University of Minnesota Press, 1994.

Chakravarty, Sumita. *National Identity in Indian Popular Cinema, 1947–1987.* Austin: University of Texas Press, 1993.

Chanan, Michael. *The Cuban Image.* Bloomington: Indiana University Press, 1985.

————, ed. *Twenty-Five Years of the New Latin American Cinema.* London: British Film Institute and Channel Four, 1983.

Chatterjee, Partha. *The Nation and Its Fragments: Colonial and Postcolonial Histories.* Princeton, N.J.: Princeton University Press, 1993.

Chow, Rey. *Primitive Passions: Visuality, Sexuality, Ethnography, and Contemporary Chinese Cinema.* New York: Columbia University Press, 1995.

Cook, David A. *A History of Narrative Film.* New York: W. W. Norton, 2d ed. 1990; 3d ed. 1996.

Cusicanqui, Silvia Rivera. *Oprimidos pero no vecidos.* Geneva: United Nations Research Institute for Social Development, 1982.

————, ed. "Indigenous Women and Community Resistance: History and Memory." In *Women and Social Change in Latin America,* ed. Elizabeth Jelin. Trans. J. Ann Zammit and Marilyn Thomson. London and New Jersey: Zed Books, Ltd. and UNRISD, 1990, 51–181.

Dash, Julie. *Daughters of the Dust.* New York: New Press, 1992.

Davis, Zeinabu Irene. "Woman with a Mission: Zeinabu Irene Davis, on Filmmaking." In *Voices of the African Diaspora* (University of Michigan Center for Afroamerican and African Studies Research Review) 7:3 (Fall 1991).

Demelas, Danielle. *Nationalisme sans nation? La Bolivie aux XIXème et XXème siecles.* Paris: Éditions du Centre National de Recherche Scientifique, 1980.

Devi, Mahasweta. *Imaginary Maps.* Trans. and intro. Gayatri Chakravorty Spivak. New York: Routledge, 1995.

Diawara, Manthia. "The Nature of Mother in *Dreaming River*," *Black American Literature Forum* 25:2 (Summer 1991): 283–98.

———. *African Cinema: Politics and Culture.* Bloomington: Indiana University Press, 1992.

———, ed. *Black American Cinema.* New York: Routledge, 1993.

Doane, Mary Ann, Patricia Mellencamp, and Linda Williams, eds. *RE-VISION: Essays in Feminist Film Criticism.* Los Angeles: American Film Institute, 1984.

Downing, John D. H., ed. *Film and Politics in the Third World.* New York: Automedia, 1986.

Ebert, Teresa L. "Ludic Feminism, the Body, Performance, and Labor: Bringing *Materialism* Back into Feminist Cultural Studies." *Cultural Critique* 23 (Winter 1992–93): 5–50.

Flitterman-Lewis, Sandy. *To Desire Differently: Feminism and the French Cinema.* Urbana: University of Illinois Press, 1990.

Franco, Jean. "The Incorporation of Women: A Comparison of North American and Mexican Popular Narrative." In *Studies in Entertainment: Critical Approaches to Mass Culture,* ed. Tania Modleski. Bloomington: Indiana University Press, 1986.

Fregoso, Rosa Linda. *The Bronze Screen: Chicana and Chicano Film Culture.* Minneapolis: University of Minnesota Press, 1993

Fusco, Coco, ed., *Reviewing Histories: Selections from New Latin American Cinema.* Buffalo: Hallwalls Contemporary Arts Center, 1987.

Gabriel, Teshome H. *Third Cinema in the Third World.* Ann Arbor: University of Michigan Research Press, 1982.

Gisbert, Carlos D. Mesa. "Cine boliviano 1953–1983: Aproximacion a una experiencia." In *Tendencias actuales en la literatura boliviana,* ed. Javier Sanjinés. Minneapolis/Valencia: Institute for the Study of Ideologies and Literature, 1985.

Gledhill, Christine, ed. *Home Is Where the Heart Is: Studies in Melodrama and the Woman's Film.* London: British Film Institute, 1987.

Goldman, Karen. "A Third Feminism." In *Iris* 13 (1991): 82–95.

Grossberg, Lawrence, Cary Nelson, and Paula Treichler. *Cultural Studies.* New York: Routledge, 1992.

Guattari, Felix, and Suely Rolnik. *Micropolitica: Cartografias do Desejo.* Petrópolis, Brazil: Editora Vozes, 1986.

Heath, Stephen. *Questions of Cinema.* Bloomington: Indiana University Press, 1981.

Hebdige, Dick. *Subculture: The Meaning of Style.* New York: Methuen, 1987.

hooks, bell. *Black Looks: Race and Representation.* Boston: South End Press, 1992.

Jameson, Fredric. "Third World Literature in the Era of Multinational Capital." In *Social Text* 15 (Fall 1986).

Jinhua, Dai. "Invisible Women: Contemporary Chinese Cinema and Women's Film." In *Positions: East Asia cultures critique* 3/1 (1995): 254–80.

Johnson, Randal. *Cinema Novo X5: Masters of Contemporary Brazilian Film.* Austin: University of Texas Press, 1984.

Kaplan, E. Ann, ed. *Psychoanalysis and Cinema.* New York: AFI Film Readers, Routledge, 1990.

————, ed. *Postmodernism and Its Discontents: Theories, Practices.* New York: Verso, 1988.

King, John, Ana M. López, and Manuel Alvarado, eds. *Mediating Two Worlds: Cinematic Encounters in the Americas.* London: British Film Institute, 1993.

King, John. *Magical Reels: A History of Cinema in Latin America.* London and New York: Verso, 1990.

Kotz, Liz. "Unofficial Stories: Documentaries by Latinas and Latin American Women." *The Independent* (May 1989): 21–27.

Kristeva, Julia. *Desire in Language: A Semiotic Approach to Literature and Art.* Ed. Leon S. Roudiez. Trans. Thomas Gora et al. New York: Columbia Univerisity Press, 1980.

————. *Revolution in Poetic Language.* Trans. Margaret Waller with an introduction by Leon S. Roudiez. New York: Columbia University Press, 1984.

Lesage, Julia. "The Political Aesthetics of the Feminist Documentary Film." . *Quarterly Review of Film Studies* 4 (Fall 1978).

López, Ana M. "An 'Other' History: The New Latin American Cinema." In *Resisting Images: Essays on Cinema and History.* Ed. Robert Sklar and Charles Musser. Philadelphia: Temple University Press, 1990.

————. "Setting Up the Stage: A Decade of Latin American Film Scholarship." *Quarterly Review of Film and Video* 13:1–3 (1991).

Martinez, Pedro J. "Principales tendencias del largometraje narrativo venezolano en los últimos veinte años." *Encuentros* 4:2 (1988).

Matellart, Michele. "Women and the Cultural Industries. *Media, Culture, and Society* 4 (1982).

Mellencamp, Patricia, ed. *Logics of Television: Essays in Cultural Criticism.* Bloomington: Indiana University Press, 1990.

Mercado, René Zavaleta, ed. *Bolivia Hoy.* Mexico: Siglo veintiuno, 1983.

Mercer, Kobena, ed. *Black Film/British Cinema.* London: British Film Institute, ICA Document 7, 1988.

————. "Diaspora culture and the dialogic imagination." In *Blackframes: Critical Perspectives on Black Independent Cinema,* ed. M. Cham and C. Andrade-Watkins. Cambridge, Mass.: MIT Press, 1988.

Minh-ha, Trinh T. *When the Moon Waxes Red: Representation, Gender and Cultural Politics.* New York: Routledge, 1991.

————. *Woman, Native, Other: Writing Post-Coloniality and Feminism.* Bloomington: University of Indiana, 1989.

Moi, Toril, ed. *The Kristevan Reader.* New York: Columbia University, 1986.

Moray, Mercedes Santos. "Aparte con Rebeca Chávez." *Cine Cubano* 122 (1988): 25–26.

Mulvey, Laura. "Visual Pleasure and Narrative Cinema." *Screen* 16:3 (Autumn 1975).

Naficy, Hamid, and Teshome H. Gabriel, eds. *Discourse of the Other: Postcoloniality, Positionality, and Subjectivity. Quarterly Review of Film and Video.* Philadelphia: Harwood Academic Publishers, 1991.

Noriega, Chon A. *Chicanos and Film: Representation and Resistance.* Minneapolis: University of Minnesota Press, 1992.

Paranagua, Paulo Antonio. "Pioneers: Women Filmmakers in Latin America." *Framework* 37 (1989).

Pick, Zuzana. *The New Latin American Cinema: A Continental Project.* Austin: University of Texas Press, 1993.

———, ed. *Latin American Filmmakers and Third Cinema.* Ottawa: Carleton University, 1978.

Pines, Jim, and Paul Willemen, eds. *Questions of Third Cinema.* London: British Film Institute, 1989.

Pfaff, Francois. *The Cinema of Ousmane Sembene.* Westport, Conn.: Greenwood Press, 1984.

———. *Twenty-Five Black African Filmmakers.* Westport, Conn.: Greenwood Press, 1988.

Randall, Margaret. *Women in Cuba: Twenty Years Later.* New York: Smyrna Press, 1981.

Reid, Mark. *Redefining Black Film.* Berkeley: University of California Press, 1993.

Rich, B. Ruby. "An/Other View of New Latin American Cinema." In *Iris* 13 (1991): 5–28.

Rivera, Silva. See Cusicanqui.

Rocha, Glauber. "An Aesthetic of Hunger." In *Brazilian Cinema,* ed. Randal Johnson and Robert Stam. Austin: University of Texas Press, 1988.

Sanjinés, Javier, ed. *Tendencias actuales en la literatura boliviana.* Minneapolis/Valencia: Institute for the Study of Ideologies and Literature [Instituto de cine y radio/television], 1985.

Sanjinés, Jorge. *Teoria y practica de un cine junto al pueblo.* Mexico: Siglo XXI Editores, 1979.

Santner, Eric L. *Stranded Objects: Mourning, Memory and Film in Postwar Germany.* Ithaca, N.Y.: Cornell University Press, 1990.

Scarry, Elaine. *The Body in Pain: The Making and Unmaking of the World.* New York: Oxford University Press, 1987

Silverman, Kaja. *The Subject of Semiotics.* New York: Oxford University Press, 1983.

———. *The Acoustic Mirror: The Female Voice in Psychoanalysis and Cinema.* Bloomington: Indiana University Press, 1988.

Solanas, Fernando E., and Octavio Getino. *Cine: Cultura Descolonizacion.* Buenos Aires: Siglo XXI Argentino Editores, 1973.

———. "Towards a Third Cinema." In *Movies and Methods,* ed. Bill Nichols. Berkeley: University of California Press, 1976.

Spivak, Gayatri Chakravorty. *In Other Worlds.* New York and London: Methuen, 1987.

———. "Subaltern Studies: Deconstructing Historiography." In *The Spivak Reader: Selected Works by Gayatri Chakravorty Spivak,* ed. Donna Landry and Gerald Maclean. New York: Routledge, 1996.

———. "Can the Subaltern Speak?" In *Colonial Discourse and Post-Colonial Theory: A Reader,* ed. Patrick Williams and Laura Chrisman. New York: Harvester/Wheatsheaf, 1994, 66–111.

Stam, Robert. *Subversive Pleasures: Bakhtin, Cultural Criticism, and Film.* Baltimore and London: Johns Hopkins University Press, 1989.

Taussig, Michael. *The Devil and Commodity Fetishism in South America.* Chapel Hill: University of North Carolina Press, 1980.

Ukadike, N. Frank. *Black African Cinema.* Berkeley: University of California Press, 1994.

Vilásis, Mayra. "La mujer y el cine: apuntes para algunas reflexiones latinoamericanas." In *La mujer en los medios audiovisuales.* Mexico, D.F.: Universidad Nacional Autonoma de Mexico, 1987.

Williams, Raymond. *The Politics of Modernism.* London: Verso, 1989.

Worsley, Peter. *The Three Worlds: Culture and World Development.* Chicago: University of Chicago Press, 1984.

Yau, Esther C. M. "Cultural and Economic Dislocations: Filmic Fantasies of Chinese Women in the 1980s." *Wide Angle* 11:2 (1989).

Yearwood, Gladstone L., ed. *Black Cinema Aesthetics: Issues in Independent Black Filmmaking.* Athens: Ohio University Center for Black Studies, 1991.

Zayas, Josefina, and Isabel Larguia. "La Mujer: Realidad e Imagen." In *La Mujer en los Medios Audiovisuales.* Mexico, D.F.: Universidad Nacional Autonoma de Mexico, 1987.

Zhen, Ni. *Raise the Red Lantern,* trans. Michael Duke. New York: William Morrow, 1993.

CONTRIBUTORS

Catherine Benamou is a Ph.D. candidate in cinema studies at New York University. A specialist in Latin American and indigenous film and video, she has curated a number of exhibitions in the New York City area, and was co-founder of "Punto de Vista: Latina," a distribution project for works directed by Latin American women at Women Make Movies, Inc. Her articles and reviews have appeared in *Afterimage, Cineaste, Discourse, Motion Picture,* and *Persistence of Vision.* Also active in film production, she recently acted as associate producer and senior research executive on *It's All True,* based on an unfinished film by Orson Welles and released through Paramount Pictures.

Julianne Burton-Carvajal, a leading figure in Latin American film studies, is founding director of the CineMedia Project at the University of California, Santa Cruz. Author of more than one hundred critical essays and interviews, she is the editor of *Cinema and Social Change in Latin America: Conversations with Filmmakers* (Austin: University of Texas Press, 1986; expanded edition in preparation) and *The Social Documentary in Latin America* (Pittsburgh: University of Pittsburgh Press, 1990), and author-compiler of the forthcoming *Three Lives in Film: Illustrated Memoirs of Latin America's Foremost Women Filmmakers* (Austin: University of Texas Press, 1999).

Sumita S. Chakravarty teaches in the Department of Communication at the New School for Social Research in New York City, and holds Ph.D. degrees from both Lucknow University in India and the University of Illinois at Urbana-Champaign. She is the author of *National Identity in*

Indian Popular Cinema, 1947–1987 (Austin: University of Texas Press, 1993) and *Mrinal Sen: The Cinema of Politics, The Politics of Cinema* (London: Flicks Books, 1998), and is at work on a new book, *The Erotic Imagination: Intersections of Gender and Visual Technologies in non-Western Cultures.*

Elena Feder holds a Ph.D. in Comparative Literature from Stanford Univerity, and is founding co-editor of *Stanford Humanities Review.* Her research centers on film theory and Latin American film. Feder's dissertation examines the influence of European avant-garde aesthetics on Mexican film melodrama of the 1940s. Her more general interest has been the construction of postrevolutionary Mexican subjectivity. Feder is a native of Bolivia.

Rosa Linda Fregoso is Associate Professor of Women's Studies at the University of California at Davis, where she also teaches Chicana/o culture and film studies. Fregoso is the co-editor of Cruzando Fronteras and of a special issue of *Cultural Studies.* More recently, she is the author of *The Bronze Screen: Chicana and Chicano Film Studies* (Minneapolis: University of Minnesota Press, 1993).

Ira Jaffe is head of the Media Arts Program and Professor of Film Studies at the University of New Mexico. His articles and reviews have appeared in *ARTSPACE: A Magazine of Contemporary Art, East-West Film Journal, Film Quarterly, Journal of Film and Video, Literature/Film Quarterly,* and in the anthologies *Hollywood as Historian: American Film in a Cultural Context,* ed. Peter C. Rollins (Lexington: University Press of Kentucky, 1983), and *Perspectives on Citizen Kane,* ed. Ronald Gottesman (New York: G. K. Hall, 1996). Jaffe organizes the International Cinema Lecture Series at UNM.

Patricia Mellencamp is Professor of Art History at the University of Wisconsin, Milwaukee, where she teaches film and television. She is the author of *Indiscretions: Avant-Garde Film, Video, and Feminism* (Bloomington: Indiana University Press, 1990) and *High Anxiety: Catastrophe, Scandal, Age, and Comedy* (Bloomington: Indiana University Press, 1992). She is the co-editor of three books on film, including *Re-vision: Essays in Feminist Film Criticism* (Frederick, Md.: University Publications of America, 1984), which she co-edited with Mary Ann Doane and Linda

Williams. Mellencamp is the editor of *Logics of Television: Essays in Cultural Criticism* (Bloomington: Indiana University Press, 1990). She has written numerous articles in major journals of film, media, and culture.

Diana Robin is director of Comparative Literature and Cultural Studies and Professor of Classics at the University of New Mexico. She is the author of *Filelfo in Milan: Writings, 1451–1477* (Princeton, N.J.: Princeton University Press, 1991), *Collected Letters of a Renaissance Feminist* (Chicago: University of Chicago Press, The Other Voice in Early Modern Europe Series, 1997), and *Cassandra Fedele: Autobiographical Letters and Orations* (Chicago, University of Chicago Press, The Other Voice in Early Modern Europe Series, forthcoming). Robin's recent articles in edited books include "Woman, Space, and Renaissance Discourse," in *Sex and Gender in Medieval and Renaissance Texts: The Latin Tradition,* ed. Barbara K. Gold, Paul Allen Miller, Charles Platter (Albany: State University of New York Press, 1997), and "Cassandra Fedele's Epistolate (1488–1477): Biography as Ef-facement," in *The Rhetorics of Life-Writing in Early Modern Europe: Forms of Biography from Cassandra Fedele to Louis XIV,* ed. Thomas Mayer and Daniel Woolf (Ann Arbor: University of Michigan Press, 1995).

Karen Schwartzman is a doctoral candidate in the Cinema Studies Department at New York University and the curator of a contemporary retrospective of Venezuelan cinema held at the Museum of Modern Art in New York City in the fall of 1994.

Diane Sippl has an interdisciplinary Ph.D from the University of California, Irvine, in Comparative Culture, with an emphasis on visual, verbal, and performance arts. She has taught cinema, literature, writing, women's studies, and Latin American studies at UCLA and Occidental College. She writes on Third World cinema, Hollywood film, and independent filmmaking in the United States and abroad. Her articles have appeared in numerous journals, including *CineAction!* and *Discourse.*

N. Frank Ukadike teaches in the Department of Communication and the Program of African and Diaspora Studies, Tulane University, New Orleans. He is the author of *Black African Cinema* (Berkeley: University of California Press, 1994) and the forthcoming book, *A Questioning Cinema: Conversations with Black African Filmmakers.*

Hu Ying is an assistant professor of Chinese literature at the University of California at Irvine who received her training at Beijing University and Princeton University. The focus of her research is cross-cultural interpretation. Her articles have appeared in *Positions: East Asia cultures critique*, *In Pursuit of Contemporary East Asian Culture*, and *CLEAR (Chinese Literature: Essays, Articles and Reviews)*. She is working on a book entitled *Tales of Translation: Imaging the Chinese Woman in the Late Qing*, to be published by Stanford University Press.

INDEX